In praise of *Documenting Software Architectures*

For many years, box and line diagrams have decorated the text that describes system implementations. These diagrams can be evocative, sometimes inspirational, occasionally informative, but are rarely precise and never complete. Recent years have brought appreciation for the importance of a deliberate structural design, or architecture, for a system. Now, in *Documenting Software Architectures,* we have guidance for capturing that knowledge, both to aid design and—perhaps more significantly—to inform subsequent maintainers, who hold over half the total cost of a system's software in their hands. Half of this cost goes into figuring out how the system is organized and where to make the change. A documented architecture is the essential roadmap for the system, leading the maintainer through the implementation jungle.

   —*Mary Shaw, Alan J. Perlis Professor of Computer Science, Carnegie Mellon University*
   Coauthor of Software Architecture: Perspectives on an Emerging Discipline

Multiple software architecture views are essential because of the diverse set of stakeholders (users, acquirers, developers, testers, maintainers, inter-operators, and others) needing to understand and use the architecture from their viewpoint. Achieving consistency among such views is one of the most challenging and difficult problems in the software architecture field. This book is a tremendously valuable first step in defining analyzable software architecture views and frameworks for integrating them.

   —*Barry Boehm, TRW Professor of Software Engineering*
   Director, USC Center for Software Engineering

There is probably no better set of authors to write this book. The material is readable. It uses humor effectively. It is nicely introspective when appropriate, and yet in the end it is forthright and decisive. The philosophical elements of the book are fascinating. The authors consider concepts that few others even are aware of, present the issues related to those concepts, and then resolve them! This is a tour de force on the subject of architectural documentation.

   —*Robert Glass, Editor-in-Chief,* Journal of Systems and Software
   Editor/Publisher, The Software Practitioner

We found this book highly valuable for our work with our business units and would recommend it to anyone who wants to understand the needs for and improve their skills in describing software architectures for complex systems.

   —*Steffen Thiel, Robert Bosch Corporation*

Since our projects involve numerous stakeholders, documenting the architecture from various views is of particular importance. For this task, this book provides pragmatic and well-structured guidance and will be an important reference for industrial practice.
—*Martin Simons, Daimler Chrysler Research and Technology*

Software architecture is an abstract representation of the most essential design decisions. It is expressed using concepts that are not directly visible in software implementation. How to identify these decisions? How to represent them? How to find the concepts that make complex software understandable? This excellent book is written by a group of expert architects sharing their experience and understanding of useful architectural concepts, essential design decisions, and practical ways to represent architectural views of complex software.
—*Alexander Ran, Principal Scientist of Software Architecture, Nokia*

I particularly appreciate the major theme of the book: that a software architecture consists of a variety of different structures, each defined by a set of elements and a relationship among those elements. I further appreciate the authors pointing out why the diagrams that seem so beloved by today's software designers are often deceptive and of little value. (I frequently say that in software engineering every diagram takes a thousand words to explain it.) It was also refreshing to see an explanation of why 'levels of abstraction,' a favorite term of many software designers, is an empty phrase. These are just a few of the elements that made me impatient to see this book published.
—*David Weiss, Director of Software Technology Research, Avaya Laboratories*

The authors have written a solid book that discusses many of the most important issues facing software designers. They point out many decisions that can be considered, discussed, and made before coding begins to provide guidance for the programmers. These issues are far more important than most of the decisions that programmers focus on. Properly made and documented, the decisions discussed in this book will guide programmers throughout the remainder of the software development process.
—*David Parnas, Director of the Software Engineering Programme, McMaster University*

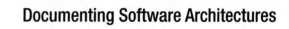

Documenting Software Architectures

Documenting Software Architectures
Views and Beyond

Paul Clements
Felix Bachmann
Len Bass
David Garlan
James Ivers
Reed Little
Robert Nord
Judith Stafford

✦ Addison-Wesley

Boston • San Francisco • New York • Toronto • Montreal
London • Munich • Paris • Madrid
Capetown • Sydney • Tokyo • Singapore • Mexico City

Carnegie Mellon
Software Engineering Institute

Library of Congress Cataloging-in-Publication Data

Documenting software architecture : views and beyond / Paul Clements . . . [et al.]
    p. cm.—(The SEI series in software engineering)
  Includes bibliographical references and index.
  ISBN 0-201-70372-6
1. Computer architecture. 2. Software documentation. I. Clements, Paul, 1955–
II. Series.
QA76.9.A73 D63 2002
004.2'2—dc21   2002024940

Text printed on recycled and acid-free paper.

ISBN 0201703726

9 101112 DOC   08 07

9th Printing   February 2007

These pictures are meant to entertain you. There is no significant meaning to the arrows between the boxes.

—A speaker at a recent software architecture conference, coming to a complex but ultimately inadequate boxes-and-lines-everywhere view-graph of her system's architecture and deciding that trying to explain it in front of a crowd would not be a good idea

At the end of the day, I want my artifacts to be enduring. My goal is to create a prescriptive, semi-formal architectural description that can be used as a basis for setting department priorities, parallelizing development, [managing] legacy migration, etc.

—A software architect for a major financial services firm

Contents

Part II Software Architecture Documentation in Practice

About the Cover

The cover shows a drawing of a bird's wing, a motif chosen because it has much in common with software architecture. Rather than appeal to the tired analogy of house architectures, we find physiological systems to be a new and rich metaphor for software and system architectures. Among such systems, a bird's wing is one of the most compelling examples.

How would you "document" a bird's wing for someone who did not know what it was? A bird's wing, like a software system, can be shown by emphasizing any of a number of structures—feathers, skeleton, circulatory system, musculature; each structure must be compatible with the others and work toward fulfilling a common purpose. The feathers, for example, are elements that, at a glance, are replicated countless times across the wing; on closer inspection, however, the feathers reveal a rich substructure of their own and small but systematic variations such that all feathers are almost alike, but no two are identical.

The wing exhibits strong quality attributes: lightness in weight, aerodynamic sophistication, outstanding thermal protection. The wing's reliability, cycling through millions of beats, is unparalleled. Unlike a house, which mostly just sits there, the essence of a wing is in its dynamic behavior. In coarse terms, the wing extends, flaps, and retracts; in finer terms, the bird commands movements almost too subtle to see, controlling pitch, roll, and yaw with exquisite finesse. For millennia, humans have tried to comprehend the wing by examining its parts and from different points of view. But the whole wing is much more than the sum of its elements and structures: It is in the whole that beauty and grace emerge. Mankind's technology still cannot replicate the wing's exquisite abilities. The common starling, a merely average flier, can slip through the air at 21 body lengths per second. That's about what the world's fastest aircraft—at 2,000 miles per hour—is able to manage.

Structure, substructure, replication with variation, behavior, quality attributes, and emergent properties of the entire system: All these aspects are important to capture when documenting a software architecture. We haven't learned how to document beauty and grace yet, but for that we substitute the documentation of rationale, or what the designer had in mind. For software, we can do this. For the wing of a bird, we can only admire the result.

Foreword

Ten years ago, I was brought in to lead the architecture team of a new and rather ambitious command-and-control system. After some rocky beginnings, the architectural design work started to proceed full speed, and the architects were finally forging ahead, inventing and resolving and designing and trying, almost in a euphoric state. We had many brainstorming sessions, filling whiteboards with design fragments and notebooks with scribblings; various prototypes validated or invalidated our reasoning. As the development team grew in size, the architects had to explain the principles of the nascent architecture to a wider and wider audience, consisting of not only new developers but also many parties external to the development group. Some were intrigued by this new concept of a software architecture. Some wanted to know how this architecture would impact them: for planning, for organizing the teams and the contractors, for delivery of the system, for acquisition of some of the system parts. Some parties wanted to influence the design of this architecture. Further removed from development, customers and prospects wanted a peek, too. So the architects had to spend hours and days describing the architecture in various forms and levels and tones to varied audiences, so that each party could better understand it.

Becoming this center of communication slowly stretched our capacity. On the one hand, we were busy designing the architecture and validating it; on the other hand, and at the same time, we were communicating to a large audience what it was and why it was that way and why we did not choose some other solution. A few months into the project, overwhelmed, we even began having a difficult time agreeing among ourselves about what it was we had actually decided.

This led me to the conclusion that "if it is not written down, it does not exist." This became sort of a leitmotiv in the architecture team for the following two years. As the ancient Chinese poet Lao-Tsu says in the *Tao Te Ching:*

> Let your workings remain a mystery.
> Just show people the results.
> (Tablet #36)

The architecture *could be* whatever we had talked about, argued, imagined, or even drafted on a board, and so on. But the architecture of this system *was* only what was described in one major document: the *Software Architecture Document (SAD)*. Architectural elements and architectural decisions not captured in this document simply did not exist. This one rule— *"If it is not in the SAD, it does not exist."*—became our incentive to evolve and to keep the document up-to-date, almost to the week; there was also an incentive to not include anything and everything and untried ideas, as this was the project's definite arbiter.

The SAD rapidly became a central element in the life of the project. It became our best display window for showing off our stuff, our comfort when we were down, and our shield when attacked.

The key problem we faced at the time was: What do we document for a software architecture? How do we document it? What outline do we use? What notation? How much or how little? There were few exemplars of architectural description for systems as ambitious as ours. Driven by necessity, we improvised. We made some mistakes and corrected some. We discovered rapidly that architecture is not flat but rather a multidimensional reality, with several intertwined facets, and some facets—or views—of interest to only a few parties. We found out that many readers would not even open a document that weighed more than a pound, and we would have a difficult time updating it anyhow. We realized that without capturing the reasons for our choices, we were doomed to reconstruct them again and again, every time a new stakeholder with a sharp mind came around. We picked a visual notation, not too vague and fuzzy but not too esoteric and convoluted, either, in order to not discourage most parties.

Today, software architects have a great starting point for deciding how to document their software architectures. You have it in your hands. The authors went through many experiences similar to mine and extracted the important lessons learned. They read many software architecture documents. They reviewed the academic literature, studied all the published books, checked the standards, and synthesized all this wisdom in this handbook: the essential things you need to know to define your own software architecture document. You will find guidance for the scope of software architecture; its organization; the techniques, tools, and notation to use or not to use; and comparisons, advice, and rules of thumb. In here, you'll find the templates to get you started and the continuing guidance for when you get lost or despairing on the way.

This book is of immense value. The description and communication of software architecture is quite crucial to its many stakeholders, and this handbook should save you months of trials and errors, lots of undeserved hassle, and many costly mistakes that could potentially jeopardize the whole endeavor. It will become an important reference on the shelf of the software architect.

—Philippe Kruchten
Director of Process Development
Rational Software Canada, Vancouver

Preface

For all but the most trivial software system, success will be elusive if you fail to pay careful attention to its architecture: the way the system is decomposed into constituent parts and the ways those parts interact. Without an architecture that is appropriate for the problem being solved, the project will fail. Even with a superb architecture, if it is not well understood and well communicated—in other words, well documented—the project is likely to flounder.

Accordingly, software architecture is at the center of a frenzy of attention these days. A new book about it seems to pop out monthly. In response to industrial need, universities are adding software architecture to their software engineering curricula. It's now common for "software architect" to be a defined position in organizations, and professional practice groups for software architects are emerging. Software architecture has been the subject of major international conferences and workshops. The purveyors of the Unified Modeling Language (UML) promote their product by calling it "the standard notation for software architecture," a claim that may say at least as much about the pervasiveness of architecture as about UML. The Software Engineering Institute of Carnegie Mellon University (SEI) maintains a bibliography of about 1,000 journal and conference papers on software architecture.

Rather surprisingly, practical guidance that is independent of language or notation for how to capture an architecture is lacking. To be sure, piles of books exist about how to use a particular language—again, UML comes to mind—but what an architect really needs is guidance in which architecture is a first-class citizen, with language relegated more appropriately to a supporting role.

First, let's agree on some basic context. The field has not anointed a single definition of **software architecture**, and so there are many, but we can specify the one we'll use, which is

> **DEFINITION**
>
> A **software architecture** for a system is the structure or structures of the system, which consist of elements, their externally visible properties, and the relationships among them.

adapted from Bass, Clements, and Kazman (1998). Although much of this book is about the meaning of elements and relationships, we use this definition now to emphasize the plurality of structures that exist in architectures. Each structure is characterized by various kinds of elements and relationships, and each structure provides a view that imparts a particular kind of understanding of the architecture.

"Externally visible properties" are those assumptions other components can make of a component, such as its provided services, quality attribute properties, shared resource usage, and so on.

The architecture serves as the blueprint for both the system and the project developing it, defining the work assignments that must be carried out by design and implementation teams. The architecture is the primary carrier of system qualities, such as performance, modifiability, and security, none of which can be achieved without a unifying architectural vision. Architecture is an artifact for early analysis to make sure that the design approach will yield an acceptable system. Architecture holds the key to postdeployment system understanding, maintenance, and mining efforts. In short, architecture is the conceptual glue that holds every phase of the project together for all its many stakeholders.

Documenting the architecture is the crowning step to crafting it. The perfect architecture is useless if it has not been expressed understandably. If you go to the trouble of creating a strong architecture, you *must* go to the trouble of describing it in enough detail, without ambiguity, and organized so that others can quickly find needed information. Otherwise, your effort will have been wasted, because the architecture will be unusable.

The audience for this book includes the people involved in the production and consumption of architectural documentation: the community of software developers. The goal of this book is to help you decide what information about an architecture is important to capture and to provide guidelines, notations, and examples for capturing it. We intend this book to be a practitioner-oriented guide to the various kinds of information that constitute an architecture. We give practical guidance for choosing what information should be documented and show—with examples in various notations, including but not limited to UML—how to describe that information in writing so that others can use it to carry out their architecture-based work: implementation, analysis, recovery, and so on. Therefore, we cover

- *Uses of software architecture documentation.* How one documents depends on how one wishes to use the documentation. We lay out possible end goals for architecture documentation and provide documentation strategies for each.

- *Architectural views.* We hold that documenting software architecture is primarily about documenting the relevant views and then augmenting this information with relevant information that applies beyond views. The heart of the book is an introduction to the most relevant architectural views, grouped into three major families, which we call *viewtypes,* along with practical guidance about how to write them down. Examples are included for each.

- *Packaging the information.* Once the views have been understood, the problem remains of choosing the relevant views, including information not contained in a view, and packaging all the information as a coherent whole. We give practical advice for all these facets.

We believe strongly in the importance of architecture in building successful systems. But no architecture can achieve this if it is not effectively communicated, and documentation is the key to successful communication. We hope that we have provided a useful handbook for practitioners in the field.

—P.C.C.,
Austin, Texas
—F.B., L.B., D.G., J.I., R.L., R.N., J.S.,
Pittsburgh, Pennsylvania

Acknowledgments

We would like to thank a large number of people for making this book a reality. The management of the SEI, especially Linda Northrop, provided unstinting support for this effort. We also thank Thomas Murphy and Dan Paulish of Siemens for their support.

Jeromy Carrière and Steve Woods were early members of our team whose profound influence lasted far beyond their active participation. We consider this book their work as well as our own.

Mark Klein, Liam O'Brien, and Rich Hilliard provided thorough reviews of a very early draft. Their work helped put us on the right track in a number of areas. Special thanks to Cheryl Mackewich for her many helpful comments on various drafts of this book. Other reviewers who provided helpful comments include Joe Batman, Siobhán Clarke, Stefan Ferber, Robert Glass, Mike Grier, Rich Hilliard, Duane Hybertson, Philippe Kruchten, Steffen Kowalewski, John McGregor, Jeff Melanson, A. J. Mims, Alexander Ran, Paul Seljak, Neil Siegel, Martin Simons, Elizabeth Sisley, Steffen Thiel, Peter Trimmel, Rob van Ommering, Kurt Wallnau, David Weiss, and Jacco Wesselius.

We are grateful to the people who attended our workshop on software architecture documentation: Rich Hilliard, Christopher Dabrowski, Stephen B. Ornburn, Tony Thompson, and Jeffrey Tyree. They all provided invaluable insights from the practitioner's point of view.

At the SEI, Barbara Tomchik, Carolyn Kernan, and Laura Novacic provided superb support. Bob Fantazier contributed greatly to the artistic vision for the book, and he and his colleagues Jeannine Caracciolo, Maria Manautou, and Stacy Mitchell did an outstanding job producing the figures. Sheila Rosenthal amazed us with her ability to track down elusive references and esoteric quotations, often in a matter of minutes.

At Addison-Wesley we are grateful to Patrick Cash-Peterson for seeing the book through production. And of course, Peter Gordon was once again the taskmaster with the velvet whip.

David Garlan's research on software architecture has been supported by the Defense Advanced Research Projects Agency (DARPA) under Grant Nos. F30602-97-2-0031, F33615-93-1-1330, and F30602-00-2-0616, and by the National Science Foundation under Grant No. CCR-9357792. Special thanks are due to John Salasin, the DARPA program manager for the DARPA research.

Thanks to Michael Jackson for letting us borrow his delightful parable about dataflow diagrams which first appeared in *Software Requirements and Specifications* (Jackson, 1995). Thanks to Kathryn Heninger Britton for letting us use her writing about active design reviews and to Dan Hoffman and Lucent Technologies, holders of its copyright, for their permission to reproduce it. Thanks to Preston Mullen of the U.S. Naval Research Laboratory for not only authoring the SCR-style interface example in Chapter 7, but also unearthing it from its archival resting place and sending it to us. Thanks to Dave Weiss for writing the sidebar about active design reviews. Thanks to Bill Wood for helping with the sidebar "A Glossary Would Have Helped." Thanks to Paul Seljak for practical insight on the use of documentation in real projects. Thanks to Philippe Kruchten for writing our foreword.

Special thanks to Mike Moore of NASA's Goddard Space Flight Center for help and encouragement and for making ECS available to us as a running example of a documented architecture. We gratefully acknowledge the people who created and maintained the original ECS documentation that we adopted and adapted.

One inspiration for the layout style, especially cross-references and definitions, was Connie Smith and Lloyd Williams's book, *Performance Solutions: A Practical Guide to Creating Responsive, Scalable Software*. For some of the material about notations for component-and-connector styles, we are indebted to Andrew J. Kompanek, Pedro Pinto, and Owen Cheng, who, along with David Garlan, worked on the paper "Reconciling the Needs of Architectural Description with Object-Modeling Notations."

The rules for sound documentation cited in the Prologue are based on those in "A Rational Design Process: How and Why to Fake It" (Parnas and Clements, 1986).

Finally, we would like to thank our friends and families, who suffered while we were working on this book. You know who you are.

Reader's Guide

Audience

This book was written primarily for software architects and technical writers who are charged with producing architectural documentation for software projects. However, it was also written keeping in mind those who digest and use that documentation. A software architect can provide this book as a companion to his or her documentation, pointing consumers to specific sections that explain documentation organizing principles, notations, concepts, or conventions.

We assume basic familiarity with the concepts of software architecture but also provide pointers to sources of information to fill in the background. In many cases, we will sharpen and solidify basic concepts that you already may be familiar with, such as *architectural views, architectural styles,* and *interfaces.*

Contents and Organization

The book consists of a prologue and two parts. The prologue establishes the necessary concepts and vocabulary for the remainder of the book. It discusses how software architecture documentation is used and why it is important. It defines architectural viewtypes, styles, and views, three concepts that provide the foundation of the book's approach to documentation. It also contains seven basic rules for sound documentation.

Part I, Software Architecture Viewtypes and Styles, introduces the basic tools for software architecture documentation: the viewtypes. A viewtype is a specification of the kind of information to be provided in a view. The three basic viewtypes are modules, component-and-connectors, and allocation. Within each viewtype reside a number of architectural styles, or specializations of the viewtype. The introduction to Part I includes a brief catalog of the styles that are described in Chapters 1–5.

- *Chapter 1, The Module Viewtype:* A module is an implementation unit of software that provides a coherent unit of functionality. Modules form the basis of many standard architectural views. This chapter defines modules and outlines the information required for documenting views whose elements are modules.

- *Chapter 2, Styles of the Module Viewtype:* This chapter introduces the prevalent styles in the module viewtype: decomposition, uses, generalization—the style that includes object-based inheritance—and layered. Each style is presented in terms of how it specializes the overall module viewtype's elements and relations.

- *Chapter 3, The Component-and-Connector Viewtype:* Components and connectors, used to describe the runtime structure(s) of a software system, can exist in many forms: processes, objects, clients, servers, and data stores. Component-and-connector models include as elements the pathways of interaction, such as communication links and protocols, information flows, and access to shared storage. Often, these interactions will be carried out using complex infrastructure, such as middleware frameworks, distributed communication channels, and process schedulers. This chapter introduces components and connectors and rules for documenting them.

- *Chapter 4, Styles of the Component-and-Connector Viewtype:* This chapter introduces some prominent styles of the component-and-connector viewtype, including communicating-processes, pipe-and-filter, client-server, peer to peer, shared data, and publish-subscribe. The chapter describes how each style is a specialization of the generic elements and relations of the viewtype, discusses what the style is useful for, and explains how it is documented.

- *Chapter 5, The Allocation Viewtype and Styles:* Software architects are often obliged to document nonarchitectural structures and show how their software designs are mapped to them: the computing environment in which their software will run, the organizational environment in which it will be developed, and so on. This chapter introduces the allocation viewtype, which is used to express the allocation of software elements to nonsoftware structures, and the three major styles of the allocation viewtype: the deployment style, which allocates software to hardware processing and communication units; the implementation style, which allocates software units to a configuration structure; and the work assignment style, which allocates software units to development teams in an organizational structure.

Part II, Software Architecture Documentation in Practice, concentrates on the complete package of architecture documentation that is incumbent on a good architect to produce. Part II completes the picture painted by Part I.

- *Chapter 6, Advanced Concepts:* This chapter discusses concepts that cut across viewtypes and more advanced concepts:
  - Information chunking and refinement
  - Context diagrams
  - Combining views
  - Expressing variability of the architecture
  - Expressing the architecture of dynamic systems
  - Creating and documenting new styles
- *Chapter 7, Documenting Software Interfaces:* The interfaces of the elements are a critical part of any architecture, and documenting them is an important part of the architect's overall documentation obligation. This chapter establishes the information needed to adequately specify an interface and explores the issues associated with doing so.
- *Chapter 8, Documenting Behavior:* This chapter covers the techniques and notations available for expressing the behavior of elements and the emergent system as it runs.
- *Chapter 9, Choosing the Views:* This chapter provides guidance for selecting views, given the intended use of an architecture: analysis, reconstruction, achieving common understanding, basis for deriving code, and so on. Two case studies in view selection are presented.
- *Chapter 10, Building the Documentation Package:* This chapter explains how the documentation is organized to serve a stakeholder. The chapter shows how the various elements discussed in the prior chapters fit together in order to produce usable documentation. It includes templates for architecture documentation.
- *Chapter 11, Other Views and Beyond:* This chapter ties related work to the prescriptions given in this book. The 4+1 view model of architecture is mapped to the views and documentation conventions prescribed in this book. The chapter does the same for UML diagrams, the Siemens Four Views model, the U.S. Department of Defense's C4ISR model of architecture, the recently approved ANSI IEEE standard for architecture documentation, and RM-ODP.
- *Appendix A, Excerpts from a Software Architecture Documentation Package.* This appendix provides an extended example of a software architecture documentation package, which demonstrates many of the concepts discussed in this book.

Stylistic Conventions

The book's main message is contained in the main flow of the text. But we have also provided extra information in the margin, including definitions, nuggets of practical advice, pointers to sources of additional information, and illuminating quotations. Advice is sometimes also called out in the body of the text. A bold term (for example **view**) is sometimes defined in the margin for a quick reference. These terms are also listed in the glossary. Longer diversions occur as sidebars, which are visually distinguished passages that appear at the end of a section. "Coming to Terms" sidebars tackle issues of terminology, while "Perspectives" sidebars are observations or background information written and signed by one of the authors.

At the end of each chapter, you can find

- A summary checklist that highlights the main points and prescriptive guidance of the chapter
- A set of discussion questions that can serve as the basis for classroom or brown-bag-lunch-group conversation
- For Further Reading, a section that offers references for more in-depth treatment of related topics

A glossary appears at the end of the book.

DEFINITION

A **view** is a representation of a set of system elements and relationships among them.

ADVICE

Every graphical presentation should include a key that explains the notation used.

FOR MORE INFORMATION

Section 6.4 discusses dynamic architectures.

A good notation should embody characteristics familiar to any user of mathematical notation: Ease of expressing constructs arising in problems, suggestivity, ability to subordinate detail, economy, amenability to formal proofs.

(Iverson 1987, p. 341)

How to Read and Use This Book

We distinguish between a first-time reader of this book and someone who has already read it but now wishes to use it as a companion for documenting an architecture. We also identify a "lightweight" path for those documenting small systems.

A first-time reader should concentrate on

- The Prologue, to gain an appreciation for the necessity and uses of sound architecture documentation
- The introduction to Part I, to gain an understanding of viewtypes, styles, and views and to get a glimpse of the three viewtypes and the collection of styles discussed in this book
- Sections 6.1, 6.2, and 6.3, to become familiar with the foundational concepts of view packets, refinement, context diagrams, and combining views
- Chapter 9, to learn how to choose the important views for a particular system
- Chapter 10, to learn the organizational scheme for a documentation package

In addition, the first-time reader should

- Browse through Chapters 1–5 to gain an overview of the views that can be included in a documentation package
- Read Sections 6.4 and 6.5 to gain understanding about documenting variability and dynamism, and creating new styles
- Read Chapter 7 to learn about documenting software interfaces
- Skim Chapter 8 to learn about documenting the behavior—as opposed to the structure—of a software system and its architectural elements
- Browse through Chapter 11 to see how other people have approached the problem of architecture documentation and to compare their ideas

A reader wishing to use the book as a companion in a documentation effort should consider the following strategy.

- To refresh your memory about the organization and structure of an architecture documentation package, revisit the Prologue and Chapter 10.
- Use those two selections and Chapter 9 as the basis for planning your documentation package. Let it help you match the stakeholders you have and the uses your documentation will support with the kind of information you need to provide.
- For each view you have elected to document, use the Part I chapter in which that view is discussed.
- To make sure that your documentation complies with other prescriptive methods, such as Rational's 4+1 approach, consult Chapter 11.

A reader seeking a lightweight approach to documentation should consider the strategy of reading those chapters that contain templates for documentation and then looking up those concepts that are unfamiliar. Section I.2: Style Guides: A Standard Organization for Documenting a Style, Chapter 7: Documenting Software Interfaces, and Chapter 10: Building the Documentation Package contain templates.

Commercial Tools and Notations

Heavily marketed tool suites are available for capturing design information, especially in the realm of object-oriented systems. Some of these tools are bound up with associated design methods and notations. Some tools are aimed at points in the design space other than architecture. If you have decided to adopt one of these tools and/or notations, you may wonder how the information in this book relates to you.

The answer is that we have explicitly tried to be language and tool independent. Rather than concentrate on the constraints imposed by a particular tool or notation, we have concentrated on the information you should capture about an architecture. We believe that is the approach you should take, too: Concentrate on the information you need to capture, and then figure out how to capture it using the tool you've chosen. Almost all tools provide ways to add free-form annotations to the building blocks they provide; these annotations will let you capture and record information in ways you see fit. Remember that not all the people for whom architecture documentation is prepared will be able to use the tool environment you've chosen or understand the commercial notation you've adopted.

Having said that, however, we note that the Unified Modeling Language (UML) is a fact of life and in many cases is the right choice for conveying architectural information. And so this book uses UML 1.4 in many, but not all, its examples. We also show how to use UML to represent each concept we discuss. We assume that you are familiar with the basic UML diagrams and symbology; our purpose is not to teach UML but to show how to use it in documenting architectures. On the other hand, we also recognize that in some situations, UML may not be the best notational choice, and we do not hesitate to show alternatives.

Prologue: Software Architectures and Documentation

P.1 The Role of Architecture

Software architecture has emerged as an important subdiscipline of software engineering, particularly in the realm of large-system development. Architecture, which is the prudent partitioning of a whole into parts, with specific relations among the parts, is what allows groups of people—often groups of groups of people separated by organizational, geographical, and even temporal boundaries—to work cooperatively and productively together to solve a much larger problem than any of them would be capable of individually. Architecting is "divide and conquer" followed by "now mind your own business" followed by "so how do these things work together?" That is, each part can be built fairly independently of the other parts; in the end, however, these parts must be put together to solve the larger problem. A single system is almost inevitably partitioned simultaneously in a number of different ways: different sets of parts and different relations among the parts.

Architecture is what makes the sets of parts work together as a successful whole. Architecture documentation is what tells developers how to make it so.

For nearly all systems, quality attributes or engineering goals—such as performance, reliability, security, or modifiability—are every bit as important as making sure that the software computes the correct answer. Architecture is where these engineering goals are met. Architecture documentation communicates the achievement of those goals.

- If you require high performance, you need to
  - Be concerned with the decomposition of the work into cooperating processes

1

- Manage the interprocess communication volume and data access frequencies
- Be able to estimate expected latencies and throughputs
- Identify potential performance bottlenecks
- Understand the ramifications of a network or processor fault

- If your system needs high accuracy, you must pay attention to how the data elements are defined and used
- If security is important, you need to
  - Legislate usage relationships and communication restrictions among the parts
  - Pinpoint parts of the system that are vulnerable to external intrusions
  - Possibly introduce special, trusted components
- If you need to support modifiability and portability, you must carefully separate concerns among the parts of the system.
- If you want to field the system incrementally, by releasing successively larger subsets, you have to keep the dependency relationships among the pieces untangled in order to avoid the "nothing works until everything works" syndrome.

All these engineering goals and their solutions are purely architectural in nature. Given these uses of architecture, a fundamental question emerges: *How do you document an architecture so that others can successfully use it, maintain it, and build a system from it?* This book exists to answer that question.

COMING TO TERMS

Software Architecture

If we are to agree on what it means to document a software architecture, we should establish a common basis for what it is we're documenting. Although the term *software architecture* has multiple definitions, no universal definition exists. The Software Engineering Institute's Web site collects definitions from the literature and from practitioners; so far, more than 90 definitions have been collected. Following are a few of the most-cited definitions from published literature.

By analogy to building architecture, we propose the following model of software architecture: Software Architecture = {Elements, Form, Rationale}. That is, a software architecture is a set of architectural (or, if you will, design) elements that have a particular form. We distinguish three different classes of architectural elements: processing elements; data elements; and connecting elements. The processing elements are those components that supply the transformation on the data elements; the data elements are those that contain the information that is used and transformed; the connecting elements (which at times may be either processing or data elements, or both) are the glue that holds the different pieces of the architecture together. For example, procedure calls, shared data, and messages are different examples of connecting elements that serve to "glue" architectural elements together. (Perry and Wolf, 1992, p. 44)

...beyond the algorithms and data structures of the computation; designing and specifying the overall system structure emerges as a new kind of problem. Structural issues include gross organization and global control structure; protocols for communication, synchronization, and data access; assignment of functionality to design elements; physical distribution; composition of design elements; scaling and performance; and selection among design alternatives. (Garlan and Shaw 1993, p. 1)

The structure of the components of a program/system, their interrelationships, and principles and guidelines governing their design and evolution over time. (Garlan and Perry 1995, p. 269)

The software architecture of a program or computing system is the structure or structures of the system, which comprise software components, the externally visible properties of those components, and the relationships among them. By "externally visible properties," we are referring to those assumptions other components can make of a component, such as its provided services, performance characteristics, fault handling, shared resource usage, and so on. (Bass, Clements, and Kazman 1998, p. 27)

An architecture is the set of significant decisions about the organization of a software system, the selection of the structural elements and their interfaces by which the system is composed, together with their behavior as specified in the collaborations among those elements, the composition of these structural and behavioral elements into progressively larger subsystems, and the architectural style that guides this

FOR MORE INFORMATION

Additional definitions may be found at www.sei.cmu.edu/ata.

organization—these elements and their interfaces, their collaborations, and their composition. (Booch, Rumbaugh, and Jacobson 1999, p. 31)

The fundamental organization of a system embodied in its components, their relationships to each other, and to the environment, and the principles guiding its design and evolution. (IEEE 2000a, p. 9)

These and other similar definitions take a largely structural perspective on software architecture. They hold that software architecture is composed of elements, connections among them, and, usually, some other aspect or aspects, such as configuration or style, constraints or semantics, analyses or properties, or rationale, requirements, or stakeholders' needs. Mary Shaw has observed that there seem to be three additional main perspectives on architecture beyond the structural:

- Framework models are similar to the structural perspective, but their primary emphasis is on the usually singular coherent structure of the whole system as opposed to concentrating on its composition. The framework perspective concentrates on domain-specific software architectures or domain-specific repositories and often elevates middleware or communication infrastructures to a distinguished role.

- Dynamic models emphasize the behavioral quality of systems. "Dynamic" might refer to changes in the overall system configuration, setting up or disabling preenabled communication or interaction pathways, or the dynamics involved in the progress of the computation, such as changing data values.

- Process models focus on construction of the architecture and the steps or process involved in that construction. From this perspective, architecture is the result of following a process script.

These perspectives do not preclude one another; nor do they represent a fundamental conflict about what software architecture is. Instead, they represent a spectrum in the software architecture community about the emphasis that should be placed on architecture: its constituent parts, the whole entity, the way it behaves once built, or the building of it. Taken together, they form a consensus view of software architecture and help us make sense of the concept.

What's the Difference Between Architecture and Design?

The question of how architecture is different from design has nipped at the heels of the architecture community for years.

Fortunately, the answer is easy. Architecture *is* design, but not all design is architecture. That is, many design decisions are left unbound by the architecture and are happily left to the discretion and good judgment of downstream designers and implementers. The architecture establishes constraints on downstream activities, and those activities must produce artifacts—finer-grained designs and code—that are compliant with the architecture, but architecture does not *define* an implementation.

You may ask, "What decisions are nonarchitectural? That is, what decisions does the architecture leave unbound and at the discretion of others?" To answer this question, we return to our definition of software architecture, cited in the preface: "…the structure or structures of the system, each of which comprises elements, the externally visible properties of those elements, and the relationships among them."

Thus, if a property of an architectural element is not visible, or discernible, to any other architectural element, that element is not architectural. The selection of a data structure, along with the algorithms to manage and access that data structure, is a typical example. Suppose that the architectural prescription for the data structure is that it provides programs, invoked from other architectural elements, that store and retrieve data; whether we choose a linked list, an array, a stack, or any other solution is therefore immaterial to those other elements, as long as our choice lets us meet the developmental, behavioral, and quality requirements levied on us.

"But wait," you protest. "You used the term *architectural element*: What's that? Are there nonarchitectural elements? If so, what's the difference?"

There may be nonarchitectural elements; their existence is unknown except to those who are outside an architectural context. For instance, a module may correspond to a work assignment for a development team; a module created under the doctrine of information hiding encapsulates a changeable aspect about the system. Modules are hierarchical entities; that is, a complex module, such as a work assignment, can be decomposed into smaller modules: smaller work assignments. Each module has an interface and an implementation. The interface to the parent is a sub-set of the union of the interfaces of the children.

Suppose that you're in charge of implementing module M and that, as far as the architect has stipulated, M has no submodules. Perhaps you discover that M's interface routines could all be implemented quite straightforwardly if you also designed and implemented a common set of services that they could all use. You assign a small subteam to design and implement this—this—this what? Well, it's a work assignment, and it encapsulates a changeable secret—namely, the algorithms and data structures used by the common services—so that makes it a module, a sub-module of M. Let's call it M2:

"I get it," you say. "Because its existence is not known out-side of M, M2 is not an architectural module."

It's tempting to agree at this point and be done with this, but that's not quite the right way to look at things. In some lay-ered architectures, the layers at the top are not allowed to use the layers at the bottom; in essence, the bottom layers' services are not known to the top layers. But we would never say that the bottom layers of an architecture are nonarchitectural. The argument about "unknown outside of" appeals to a relation different from the one present in a module structure. Modules are related to one another by the *contains* relation, or *shares a secret with* relation. Whether a module's services are known or unknown by another module is a property of the *uses* relation, which is a different kind of animal.

"OK," you say. "So is module M2 an architectural element or not?"

I would say not, but *not* because it's "invisible" to the other modules outside its parent. I'm afraid you're not going to like the reason. It's a nonarchitectural element because the architect said so—that is, he or she didn't make it part of the architecture.

"You're joking," you say. "That's a completely arbitrary defi-nition!"

Not really. The reason the architect didn't make it part of the architecture is that its existence or nonexistence was not material to the overall goals of the architecture. The architect gave you the freedom to structure your team—implementing M—as you saw fit.

The fact is, no scale or scope or measure or line divides what is architectural and what is not. One person's architecture may be another person's implementation and vice versa. Suppose that M2 turns out to be very complicated and that the subteam you assign to it begins by giving M2 an internal structure. To the coders of M2, that structure is an architecture. But to the architecture of the system that includes M, the very existence of M2, let alone its internal structure, is an implementation detail.

Modules and other hierarchical elements[1] are subject to confusion about where to draw the line between architecture and nonarchitectural design. If you want to be tediously precise about the matter, the coding of each subroutine—or even the coding of a single line of code—could be considered a separate work assignment. Of course, we would not want to consider such minutiae to be architectural: The whole point of architecture is to let us reason about larger issues. So when should an architect stop decomposing modules into smaller and smaller work assignments? One heuristic comes from David Parnas [Parnas, 86, p. 363]. He says that a module is "small enough" when, in the face of a change, it would be just as easy to recode it as it would be to alter it. Technically speaking, you can't know a module's code size at design time, but if you can't make a good guess, you're probably not the right person to be the architect for the system you're working on.

Processes and other nonhierarchical elements can also be nonarchitectural. Suppose that the architect gave you a budget and the freedom to create up to 12 tasks and that these tasks do not synchronize or interact with any other tasks outside your work assignment. In that case, we could make the same argument: that these tasks, or elements, are nonarchitectural.

"All right," you sigh. "Once more, with clarity?"

Sure. Architecture is design, but not all design is architectural. The architect draws the boundary between architectural and nonarchitectural design by making those decisions that need to be bound in order for the system to meet its development, behavioral, and quality goals.

---

1. By "hierarchical element," we mean any kind of element that can consist of like-kind elements. A module is a hierarchical element because modules consist of submodules, which are themselves modules. A task or a process is not a hierarchical element.

(Decreeing what the modules are achieves modifiability, for example.) All other decisions can be left to downstream designers and implementers. Decisions are architectural or not, according to context. If structure is important to achieve your system's goals, that structure is architectural. But designers of elements, or subsystems, that you assign may have to introduce structure of their own to meet their goals, in which case such structures are architectural: *to them* but not to you.

Architecture is truly in the eye of the beholder. And what does all this have to do with documentation? If your goals are met by an architecture, document it as such, but expect the possibility that subsequent, finer-grained design may produce architectural documentation—about a small piece of your system—on its own.

—P.C.C.

COMING TO TERMS

Documentation, Description, Representation, Specification

What shall we call the activity of writing down a software architecture for the benefit of others or for our own benefit at a later time? Leading contenders are *documentation, representation, description,* and *specification*. For the most part, we use *documentation* throughout this book, and we want to explain our reasoning.

Specification tends to connote an architecture rendered in a formal language. Now, we are all for formal specs. (We have to be. One of us—Ivers—counts himself as a formalist, and he intimidates the rest of us. In an early draft one of us called data flow diagrams a formal notation, and he just about gave himself an aneurysm. We recanted.) But formal specs are not always practical; nor are they always necessary. Sometimes, they aren't even useful: How, for example, do you capture in a formal language the rationale behind your architectural decisions?

Representation connotes a model, an abstraction, a rendition of a thing that is separate or different from the thing itself. Is architecture something more than what someone writes down about it? Arguably yes, but it's certainly pretty intangible in any case. We felt that raising the issue of a model versus the thing being modeled would only raise needlessly diverting questions best left to those whose hobby, or calling, is philosophy: Does an abstraction of a tree falling in a model of a forest make a representation of a sound? Don't ask me; I haven't a clue. (Better yet, ask Ivers.)

Description has been staked out by the architecture description language (ADL) community. It's mildly curious that the formalists snagged the least rigorous-sounding term of the bunch. (If you don't believe this, the next time you board a jet ask yourself if you hope its flight control software has been specified to the implementers, or merely described.) One would think that the ADL purveyors' ambitions for their languages are not very great, but that is not the case. In any event, we did not want anyone to think that writing down an architecture is tantamount to choosing and using an ADL, so we eschewed *description*.

FOR MORE INFORMATION

ADLs are discussed in Section 4.7, the For Further Reading section of Chapter 8, and in Section 11.9.1. For an overview of ADLs, see Stafford and Wolf 2001.

That leaves *documentation*. Documentation connotes the creation of an artifact: namely, a document, which may, of course, be electronic files, Web pages, or paper. Thus, documenting a software architecture becomes a concrete task: producing a software architecture document. Viewing the activity as creating a tangible product has advantages. We can describe good architecture documents and bad ones. We can use completeness criteria to judge how much work is left in producing this artifact and determining when the task is done. Planning or tracking a project's progress around the creation of artifacts, or documents, is an excellent way to manage. Making the architecture information available to its consumers and keeping it up-to-date reduces to a solved problem of configuration control. Documentation can be formal or not, as appropriate, and may contain models or not, as appropriate. Documents may describe, or they may specify. Hence, the term is appropriately general.

Finally, documentation is a longstanding software engineering tradition. Documentation is the task that you are supposed to do because it's good for you. It's what your software engineering teachers taught you to do, your customers contracted you to do, your managers nagged you to do, and what you always found a way not to do. So if documentation brings up too many pangs of professional guilt, use any term you like that's more palatable. The essence of the activity is writing down—and keeping current—the results of architectural decisions so that the stakeholders of the architecture—people who need to know what it is to do their job—have the information they need in an accessible, nonambiguous form.

P.2 Uses of Architecture Documentation

FOR MORE INFORMATION

In Chapter 9, the documentation's expected uses, along with the documentation obligations each use imparts, become the basis for helping an architect plan the documentation package.

Architecture documentation must serve varied purposes. It should be sufficiently abstract to be quickly understood by new employees. It should be sufficiently detailed to serve as a blueprint for construction. It should have enough information to serve as a basis for analysis.

Architecture documentation is both prescriptive and descriptive. For some audiences, it prescribes what *should* be true, placing constraints on decisions to be made. For other audiences, it describes what *is* true, recounting decisions already made about a system's design.

The best architecture documentation for, say, performance analysis may well be different from the best architecture documentation we would wish to hand to an implementer. And both of these will be different from what we put in a new hire's "welcome aboard" package. The process of documentation planning and review needs to ensure support for all the relevant needs.

Understanding the uses of architecture documentation is essential, as the uses determine the important forms. Fundamentally, architecture documentation has three uses.

1. *Architecture serves as a means of education.* The educational use consists of introducing people to the system. The people may be new members of the team, external analysts, or even a new architect.

DEFINITION

A **stakeholder** of an architecture is someone who has a vested interest in it.

2. *Architecture serves as a primary vehicle for communication among stakeholders.* An architecture's precise use as a communication vehicle depends on which stakeholders are doing the communicating. Some examples are described in Table P.1.

Table P.1: Architecture documentation and stakeholder communication needs

Stakeholder	Communication
Architect and requirements engineers who represent the customer(s)	A forum for negotiating and making trade-offs among competing requirements
Architect and designers of the constituent parts	To resolve resource contention and to establish performance and other kinds of runtime resource consumption budgets
Implementers	To provide inviolable constraints and exploitable freedoms on downstream development activities

Table P.1: Architecture documentation and stakeholder communication needs (continued)

Stakeholder	Communication
Testers and integraters	To specify the correct black-box behavior of the pieces that must fit together
Maintainers	A starting point for maintenance activities, revealing the areas a prospective change will affect
Designers of other systems with which this one must interoperate	To define the set of operations provided and required and the protocols for their operation
Managers	Basis for forming development teams corresponding to the work assignments identified, work breakdown structure, planning, allocation of project resources, and tracking of progress by the various teams
Product line managers	To determine whether a potential new member of a product family is in or out of scope and, if out, by how much
Quality assurance team	Basis for conformance checking, for assurance that implementations have in fact been faithful to the architectural prescriptions

Perhaps one of the most avid consumers of architecture documentation, however, is none other than the architect in the project's future. The future architect may be the same person or may be a replacement, but in either case is guaranteed to have an enormous stake in the documentation. New architects are interested in learning how their predecessors tackled the difficult issues of the system and why particular decisions were made. Even if the future architect is the same person, he or she will use the documentation as a repository of thought, a storehouse of detailed design decisions too numerous and hopelessly intertwined to ever be reproducible from memory alone.

`QUOTATION`

In our organization, a development group writes design documents to communicate with other developers, external test organizations, performance analysts, the technical writers of manuals and product helps, the separate installation package developers, the usability team, and the people who manage translation testing for internationalization. Each of these groups has specific questions in mind that are very different from the ones that other groups ask:

- What test cases will be needed to flush out functional errors?
- Where is this design likely to break down?

- Can the design be made easier to test?
- How will this design affect the response of the system to heavy loads?
- Are there aspects of this design that will affect its performance or ability to scale to many users?
- What information will users or administrators need to use this system, and can I imagine writing it from the information in this design?
- Does this design require users to answer configuration questions that they won't know how to answer?
- Does it create restrictions that users will find onerous?
- How much translatable text will this design require?
- Does the design account for the problems of dealing with double-byte character sets or bi-directional presentation?

—Kathryn Heninger Britton (Hoffman, Weiss 2001, pp. 337–338)

FOR MORE INFORMATION

Perspectives: Architecture Trade-off Analysis Method (ATAM) on page 302 contains more information about one particular architecture evaluation method.

3. *Architecture serves as the basis for system analysis.* To support analysis, the architecture documentation must contain the information necessary for the particular analyses being performed.

- For performance engineers, architecture documentation provides the formal model that drives analytical tools, such as rate-monotonic real-time schedulability analysis, simulations and simulation generators, and even theorem provers and model-checking verifiers. These tools require information about resource consumption, scheduling policies, dependencies, and so forth.

- For those interested in the ability of the design to meet the system's other quality objectives, the architecture documentation serves as the fodder for evaluation methods. The architecture documentation must contain the information necessary to evaluate a variety of attributes, such as security, performance, usability, availability, and modifiability. Analyses for each one of these attributes have their own information needs, and all this information must be in the architecture documentation.

P.3   Interfaces

DEFINITION

An **interface** is a boundary across which two independent entities meet and interact or communicate with each other.

If you've been reading the sidebars, you've already encountered the term **interface** several times. This term is widely used when describing software elements and can mean many different things to different people. The term is so important when documenting software architecture that we have devoted Chapter 7 to the subject.

It is both possible and likely that an entity will have more than one interface through which it interacts or communicates. An interface is more than a list of its available services. Ideally, an interface specification should provide enough information to avoid unexpected interactions that can occur because of assumptions an entity makes about either the environment in which it is to be placed or the entities with which it interacts.

FOR MORE INFORMATION

Chapter 7 ("Documenting Software Interfaces") prescribes the contents of an element's interface documentation.

P.4 Views

Perhaps the most important concept associated with software architecture documentation is that of the *view*. A software architecture is a complex entity that cannot be described in a simple one-dimensional fashion. Our analogy with the bird wing proves illuminating. There is no single rendition of a bird wing. Instead, there are many: feathers, skeleton, circulation, muscular views, and many others. Which of these views *is* the "architecture" of the wing? None of them. Which views *convey* the architecture? All of them.

In this book, we use the concept of **views** to give us the most fundamental principle of architecture documentation, illustrated in Figure P.1:

> Documenting an architecture is a matter of documenting the relevant views and then adding documentation that applies to more than one view.

DEFINITION

A **view** is a representation of a set of system elements and the relationships associated with them.

What are the relevant views? It depends on your goals. As we saw previously, architecture documentation can serve many purposes: a mission statement for implementers, a basis for analysis, the specification for automatic code generation, the starting point for system understanding and asset recovery, or the blueprint for project planning.

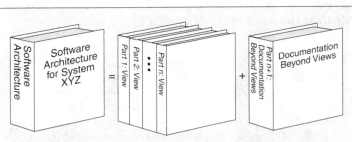

Documenting an architecture is a matter of documenting the relevant views, and then adding documentation that applies to more than one view.

Figure P.1
A documentation package for a software architecture is composed of one or more view documents and documentation that explains how the views relate to one another, introduces the package to its readers, and guides them through it.

FOR MORE INFORMATION

Layered views are covered in Section 2.4, and the deployment view is covered in Section 5.3.

FOR MORE INFORMATION

Chapter 9 explains how to select the set of relevant architectural views for a particular system.

Different views also expose different quality attributes to different degrees. Therefore, the quality attributes that are of most concern to you and the other stakeholders in the system's development will affect the choice of what views to document. For instance, a *layered view* will tell you about your system's portability, a *deployment view* will let you reason about your system's performance and reliability, and so forth.

Different views support different goals and uses. This is fundamentally why we do not advocate a particular view or collection of views. The views you should document depend on the uses you expect to make of the documentation. Different views will highlight different system elements and/or relationships. According to Jazayeri, Ran, and van der Linden (2000, pp. 16–17):

> Many projects make the mistake of trying to impose a single partition in multiple component domains, such as equating threads with objects, which are equated with modules, which in turn are equated with files. Such an approach never succeeds fully, and adjustments eventually must be made, but the damage of the initial intent is often hard to repair. This invariably leads to problems in development and occasionally in final products.

It may be disconcerting that no single view can fully represent an architecture. Additionally, it feels somehow inadequate to see the system only through discrete, multiple views that may or may not relate to one another in any straightforward way. The essence of architecture is the suppression of information not necessary to the task at hand, and so it is somehow fitting that the very nature of architecture is such that it never presents its whole self to us but only a facet or two at a time. This is its strength: Each view emphasizes certain aspects of the system while deemphasizing or ignoring other aspects, all in the interest of making the problem at hand tractable. Nevertheless, no one of these individual views adequately documents the software architecture for the system. That is accomplished by the complete set of views along with information that transcends them. As Gamma et al. (1995, p. 22) say:

> An object-oriented program's runtime structure often bears little resemblance to its code structure. The code structure is frozen at compile-time; it consists of classes in fixed inheritance relationships. A program's runtime structure consists of rapidly changing networks of communicating objects. In fact, the two structures are largely independent. Trying to understand one from the other is like trying to understand the dynamism of living ecosystems from the static taxonomy of plants and animals, and vice versa.

The documentation for a view contains

- A primary presentation, usually graphical, that depicts the primary elements and relationships of the view
- An element catalog that explains and defines the elements shown in the view and lists their properties
- A specification of the elements' interfaces and behavior
- A variability guide explaining any built-in mechanisms available for tailoring the architecture
- Rationale and design information

The documentation that applies to all of the views contains

- An introduction to the entire package, including a reader's guide that helps a stakeholder find a desired piece of information quickly
- Information describing how the views relate to one another, and to the system as a whole
- Constraints and rationale for the overall architecture
- Such management information as may be required to effectively maintain the whole package

FOR MORE INFORMATION

Chapters 1–5 introduce specific views and the uses for each. Section 10.2 prescribes the contents of a view document in detail. Section 10.3 prescribes the contents of the beyond views documentation in detail.

COMING TO TERMS

Architectural Views

Nearly three decades ago, Parnas (1974) observed that software consists of many structures, which he defined as partial descriptions showing a system as a collection of parts and showing some relations among the parts. This definition largely survives in architecture papers today. Parnas identified several structures prevalent in software. A few were fairly specific to operating systems, such as the structure that defines what process owns what memory segment, but others are more generic and broadly applicable. These include the *module structure*—the units are work assignments, the relation *is-a-part-of* or *shares-part-of-the-same-secret-as*—the *uses structure*—the units are programs, and the relation is *depends on the correctness of*—and the *process structure*—the units are processes, and the relation is *gives computational work to*.

More recently, Perry and Wolf (1992) recognized that, similar to building architecture, a variety of views of a system are required. Each view emphasizes certain architectural aspects that are useful to different stakeholders or for different purposes.

FOR MORE INFORMATION

To see how the 4+1 views correspond to views described in this book, see Section 11.2.

Later, Kruchten (1995) of the Rational Software Corporation wrote an influential paper describing four main views of software architecture that can be used to great advantage in system building, along with a distinguished fifth view that ties the other four together: the "4+1" approach to architecture.

1. The *logical view* primarily supports behavioral requirements: the services the system should provide to its end users. Designers decompose the system into a set of key abstractions, taken mainly from the problem domain. These abstractions are objects or object classes that exploit the principles of abstraction, encapsulation, and inheritance. In addition to aiding functional analysis, decomposition identifies mechanisms and design elements that are common across the system.

2. The *process view* addresses concurrency and distribution, system integrity, and fault tolerance. The process view also specifies which thread of control executes each operation of each class identified in the logical view. The process view can be seen as a set of independently executing logical networks of communicating programs—processes—that are distributed across a set of hardware resources, which in turn are connected by a bus or a local area network or a wide area network.

3. The *development view* focuses on the organization of the software modules in the software development environment. The units of this view are small chunks of software—program libraries or subsystems—that can be developed by one or more developers. The development view supports the allocation of requirements and work to teams and supports cost evaluation, planning, monitoring of project progress, and reasoning about software reuse, portability, and security.

4. The *physical view* takes into account the system's requirements, such as system availability; reliability; performance; and scalability. This view maps the various elements identified in the logical, process, and development views—networks, processes, tasks, and objects—onto the processing nodes.

Finally, Kruchten prescribes using a small subset of important scenarios—instances of use cases—to show that the elements of the four views work together seamlessly. This is the "+1" view, redundant with the others but serving a distinct purpose. The 4+1 approach has since been embraced as a foundation piece of the Rational Unified Process.

At about the same time, Soni, Nord, and Hofmeister of Siemens Corporate Research made a similar observation about views of architecture they observed in use in industrial practice. They wrote (1995):

- The *conceptual view* describes the system in terms of its major design elements and the relationships among them.

- The *module interconnection view* encompasses two orthogonal structures: functional decomposition and layers.

- The *execution view* describes the dynamic structure of a system.

- The *code view* describes how the source code, binaries, and libraries are organized in the development environment.

These views have become known as the Siemens Four View model for architecture.

Other "view sets" are emerging. In their book *Business Component Factory,* Herzum and Sims (1999) prescribe these four as the most important:

- The *technical architecture,* concerned with the component execution environment, the set of tools, the user interface framework, and any other technical services/facilities required to develop and to run a component-based system

- The *application architecture,* concerned with the set of architectural decisions, patterns, guidelines, and standards required to build a component-based system

- The *project management architecture,* consisting of those elements—the concepts, guidelines, principles, and management tools—needed to build a scalable large system with a large team

- The *functional architecture,* where the specification and implementation of the system reside.

Each view of a software architecture is used for a different purpose, often by different stakeholders. As such, the various views form the basic unit for documenting a software architecture.

FOR MORE INFORMATION

To see how the Siemens Four View model corresponds to the views described in this book, see Section 11.4.

P.5 Viewtypes and Styles

P.5.1 Viewtypes

Although no fixed set of views is appropriate for every system, broad guidelines can help us gain a footing. Architects need to think about their software in three ways simultaneously:

1. How it is structured as a set of implementation units
2. How it is structured as a set of elements that have runtime behavior and interactions
3. How it relates to nonsoftware structures in its environment

DEFINITION

A **viewtype** defines the element types and relationship types used to describe the architecture of a software system from a particular perspective.

Each view we present in Part I falls into one of these three categories, which we call **viewtypes**. The three viewtypes are

1. The *module* viewtype
2. The *component-and-connector (C&C)* viewtype
3. The *allocation* viewtype

Views in the module viewtype—module views for short—document a system's principal units of implementation. Views in the C&C viewtype—C&C views—document the system's units of execution. And views in the allocation viewtype—allocation views—document the relationships between a system's software and its development and execution environments. A viewtype constrains the set of elements and relations that exist in its views.

P.5.2 Styles

Within the confines of a viewtype, recurring forms have been widely observed, even if written for completely different systems. These forms occur often enough that they are worth writing and learning about in their own right. Perhaps they have interesting properties not shared by others. Perhaps they represent a significant and oft-used variation of the viewtype. Our description of each viewtype includes a section on commonly occurring forms and variations. We call these

DEFINITION

An **architectural style** is a specialization of element and relation types, together with a set of constraints on how they can be used.

architectural styles, or **styles**. Styles have implications for architectural documentation and deserve definition and discussion in their own right.

A **style** defines a family of architectures that satisfy the constraints. Styles allow one to apply specialized design knowledge to a particular class of systems and to support that class of system design with style-specific tools, analysis, and implementations. The literature is replete with a number of styles, and most architects have a wide selection in their repertoires.

For example, we'll see that modules can be arranged into a useful configuration by restricting what each one is allowed to use. The result is a layered style—a member of the module viewtype—that imparts to systems that use it qualities of modifiability, portability, and the ability to quickly extract a useful subset. Different systems will have a different number of layers, different contents in each layer, and different rules for what each layer is allowed to use. However, the layered style is abstract with respect to these options and can be studied and analyzed without binding them.

For another example, we'll see that client-server is a common architectural style, a member of the component-and-connector viewtype. The elements in this style are clients, servers, and the protocol connectors that depict their interaction. When used in a system, the client-server style imparts desirable properties to the system, such as the ability to add clients with little effort. Different systems will have different protocols, different numbers of servers, and different numbers of clients each can support. However, the client-server style is abstract with respect to these options and can be studied and analyzed without binding them.

Some styles are applicable in every software system: decomposition, uses, deployment, and work assignment, for example. Other styles occur only in systems in which they were explicitly chosen and designed in by the architect: layered, communicating-processes, and client-server, for example.

Choosing a system style, whether covered in this book or somewhere else, imparts a documentation obligation to record the specializations and constraints that the style imposes and the properties that the style imparts to the system. We call this piece of documentation a **style guide**. The obligation to document a style can usually be discharged by citing a description of the style in the literature: this book, for example. If you invent your own style, however, you will need to write a style guide for it.

No system is built exclusively from a single style. On the contrary, every system can be seen to be an amalgamation of many different styles. Some occur in every system, but systems also exhibit a combination of "chosen" styles as well. This amalgamation can occur in several ways.

- Different "areas" of the system might exhibit different styles. For example, a system might use a pipe-and-filter style to process input data but route the result to a database that is accessed by many elements. This system would be a blend of a pipe-and-filter and shared-data styles. Documentation for this system would include (1) a pipe-and-filter view that showed one part of the system and (2) a shared-data view that showed the other part. In a case like this, one or more elements must occur in both views and have properties of both kinds of elements. (Otherwise, the two parts of the system could not communicate with each other.) These *bridging elements* provide the continuity of understanding from one view to the next. They likely have multiple interfaces, each providing the mechanisms for letting the element work with other elements in each of the views to which it belongs.

- An element playing a part in one style may itself be composed of elements arranged in another style. For example, a server in a client-server system might, unknown to the other servers or its own clients, be implemented using a pipe-and-filter style. Documentation for this system would include a client-server view showing the overall system, as well as a pipe-and-filter view documenting that server.

- Finally, the same system might simply be seen in different lights, as though you were looking at it through filtered glasses. A system featuring a database repository may be seen as embodying either a shared-data style or a client-server style. If the clients are independent processes, the system may be seen as embodying a communicating-processes style. The glasses you choose will determine the style that you "see."

In the last case, your choice of style-filtered glasses depends, once again, on the uses to which you and your stakeholders intend to put the documentation. For instance, if the shared-data style gives you all the analysis tools you need, you might choose it rather than the other two options. If you need the perspective afforded by more than one style, however, you have a choice. You can document the corresponding views separately, or you can combine them into a single view that is, roughly speaking, the union of what the separate views would be.

All three cases make clear the need to be able to document different parts of a system by using different views. That is, a view need not show the entire system.

FOR MORE INFORMATION

Combining views is an important concept covered in Section 6.3.

P.5.3 Summary: Viewtypes, Styles, and Views

The three viewtypes—module, C&C, and allocation—represent the three perspectives that an architect must consider when designing a system: the system as units of implementation, the system as units of runtime execution, and the mapping from software elements to environmental structures. A viewtype restricts the element types—modules in the module

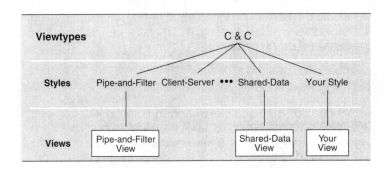

Figure P.2
For each viewtype, we describe several styles. You can add to the set by creating your own style or adapting one from another source. And within the confines of a style, choices need to be made: how the element and relation types in a style are bound to elements and relations in a system. These are the views of your architecture.

viewtype, for instance—and the corresponding relationship types.

But even within the confines of a viewtype, choices must be made: how the elements are restricted, how they relate to one another, and constraints on their use or configuration. A style is a specialization of a viewtype and reflects recurring patterns of interaction, independent of any particular system (Figure P.2).

Even within the confines of a style, choices need to be made: how the element and relation types in a style are bound to elements and relations in a system. In the context of viewtypes and styles, then, a view can now be seen as a style that is bound to a particular system. For example, Chapter 4 describes the publish-subscribe style in terms of loosely coupled components whose interfaces allow the reporting of events and subscription to events, but the description of the style in Chapter 4 is independent of any system. If you choose the publish-subscribe style as a design strategy for your system, you will produce a publish-subscribe view by naming the components and the events they report and to which they subscribe.

COMING TO TERMS

Module, Component

In this book, we divide the universe of software architectures into three categories: a module viewtype, a component-and-connector viewtype, and an allocation viewtype. This three-way distinction allows us to structure the information we're presenting in an orderly way and, we hope, allows you to recall it and to access it in an orderly way. But for this strategy to succeed, the distinctions have to be meaningful. Two of the categories rely on words that, it must be admitted, are not historically well differentiated: *module* and *component*.

Like many words in computing, these two have meanings outside our field. Furthermore, both terms have come to be associated with movements in software engineering that have overlapping goals.

During the 1960s and 1970s, software systems increased in size and were no longer able to be produced by one person. It became clear that new techniques were needed to manage software complexity and to partition work among programmers. To address such issues of "programming in the large," various criteria were introduced to help programmers decide how to partition their software. Encapsulation, information hiding, and abstract data types became the dominant design paradigms of the day, using *module* as the carrier of their meaning. The 1970s and 1980s saw the advent of "module interconnection languages" and features of new programming languages such as Modula modules, Smalltalk classes, and Ada packages. Today's dominant design paradigm—object-oriented programming—has these module concepts at its heart. Components, by contrast, are in the limelight with component-based software engineering and the component-and-connector perspective in the software architecture field.

Both movements aspire to achieve rapid system construction and evolution through the selection, assembly, and wholesale replacement of independent subpieces. Both modules and components are about the decomposition of a whole software system into constituent parts. But beyond that, the two terms take on different shades of meaning.

- A module *tends* to refer first and foremost to a design-time entity. Parnas's foundational work in module design (1972) used information hiding as the criterion for allocating responsibility to a module. Information that was likely to change over the lifetime of a system, such as the choice of data structures or algorithms, was assigned to a module, which had an interface through which its facilities were accessed.

- A component *tends* to refer to a runtime entity. Shaw and Garlan (1996), for example, speak of an architecture of a system as a collection of "computational components—or simply components" along with a description of their interactions. Szyperski (1998, p. 30) says that a component "can be deployed independently and is subject to composition by third parties." Herzum and Sims (2000, p. 6) say that a component is "a self-contained piece of software with a well-defined interface or set of interfaces. We imply a clear runtime and deployment connotation; that is, the component has interfaces that are accessible at runtime, and at some point in its development life cycle, the component can be independently delivered and installed." The emphasis is clearly on the finished product and not on the design considerations that went into it. Indeed, the operative model is that a component is delivered in the form of an executable binary only: Nothing upstream from that is available to the system builder.

In short, a module suggests encapsulation properties, with less emphasis on the delivery medium and what goes on at runtime. Not so with components. A delivered binary maintains its "separateness" throughout execution. A component suggests independently deployed units of software with no visibility into the development process.

Of course, there's overlap. How can something be independently deployable and replaceable without involving encapsulation? That is, how can components not be modular? But, in fact, you could imagine a well-designed module that isn't independently deployable, because it requires all sorts of services from other modules. You could also imagine a component that didn't encapsulate very much or encapsulated the wrong things. This is why plug-and-play, the current mantra of component-based systems engineering, is more accurately rendered as plug-and-pray. In their *IEEE Software* article, Garlan, Allen, and Ockerbloom (1995) describe the frustrations of trying to assemble a system from components that were built with subtly conflicting assumptions about their environments.

Our use of the terms in this book reflects their pedigrees. The module viewtype contains styles that reflect primarily design-time considerations: decompositions that assign parts of the problem to units of design and implementation, layers that reflect what uses are allowed when software is being written, and classes that factor out commonality from a set of instances. Of course, all these styles have runtime implications; that's the end game of software design, after all. Similarly, the component-and-connector viewtype contains styles that focus on how processes interact and data travels around the system during execution. Of course, all these runtime effects are the result of careful design-time activities.

This conceptual overlap is one thing, but a given architecture will usually also exhibit a concrete overlap. An element that you document in a module view may well show up in a component-and-connector view as the runtime manifestation of its design-time self. As a component, the element might be replicated many times—across different processors, for example. As a module, however, it would be very unlikely to be duplicated: Why would you ask someone to produce the same piece of code twice? As a rule, an element shows up once in a module view; a corresponding

FOR MORE INFORMATION

Section 10.3 describes how to document the mapping between a system's modules and its components.

component might occur many times in a component-and-connector view.

Modules and components represent the current bedrock of the software engineering approach to rapidly constructed, easily changeable software systems. As such, modules and components serve as fundamental building blocks for creating and documenting software architectures.

P.6 Seven Rules for Sound Documentation

ADVICE

These rules for any software documentation, including software architecture documentation, follow:

1. Write documentation from the reader's point of view.
2. Avoid unnecessary repetition.
3. Avoid ambiguity.
4. Use a standard organization.
5. Record rationale.
6. Keep documentation current but not too current.
7. Review documentation for fitness of purpose.

Architecture documentation is much like the documentation we write in other facets of our software development projects. As such, it obeys the same fundamental rules for what distinguishes good, usable documentation from poor, ignored documentation.

P.6.1 Rule 1: Write Documentation from the Reader's Point of View

Seemingly obvious but surprisingly seldom considered, this rule offers the following advantages.

* A document is written approximately once—a little more often if you count the time for revisions—but if useful will be read many scores of times. Therefore, the document's "efficiency" is optimized if we make things easier for the reader. Edsger Dijkstra, the inventor of many of the software engineering principles we now take for granted, once said that he would happily spend two hours pondering how to make a single sentence clearer. He reasoned that if the paper were read by a couple of hundred people—a decidedly modest estimate for someone of Dijkstra's caliber—and he could save each reader a minute or two of confusion, it was well worth the effort. Professor Dijkstra's consideration for the reader reflects his classic manners, which brings us to the second advantage.

* Writing for the reader is polite. A reader who feels that the document was written with him or her in mind appreciates the effort but, more to the point, will come back to the document again and again in the future, which brings us to the third advantage.

* Documents written for the reader will be read; documents written for the convenience of the writer will not. Similarly, we like to shop at stores that seem to want our business and to avoid stores that do not.

- Avoid unnecessary insider jargon. The documentation may be read by someone new to the field or from a company that does not share the same jargon.

In the realm of software documentation, documents written for the writer often take one of two forms: stream of consciousness or stream of execution. Stream-of-consciousness writing captures thoughts in the order in which they occurred to the writer and lacks an organization that is helpful to a reader. Avoid stream-of-consciousness writing by making sure that you know what question(s) are being answered by each section of a document; that is, architect your documentation.

Stream-of-execution writing captures thoughts in the order in which they occur during the execution of a software program. For certain kinds of software documentation, this is entirely appropriate, but it should never be given as the whole story.

P.6.2   Rule 2: Avoid Unnecessary Repetition

Each kind of information should be recorded in exactly one place. This makes documentation easier to use and *much* easier to change as it evolves. It also avoids confusion; information that is repeated is likely to be in a slightly different form, and now the reader must wonder: Was the difference intentional? If so, what is the meaning of the difference?

> I have made this letter rather long only because I have not had time to make it shorter.
>
> —Blaise Pascal, French mathematician, physicist, and moralist, 1623–1662

Now, expressing the same idea in different forms is often useful for achieving a thorough understanding. However, it should be a goal that information never, or almost never, be repeated verbatim unless the cost to the reader of keeping related information separate is high. Locality of information reference is important; unnecessary page flipping leads to reader dissatisfaction. Also, two different views might have repetitive information for clarity or to make different points. If keeping the information separate proves too high a cost to the reader, repeat the information.

P.6.3   Rule 3: Avoid Ambiguity

A primary reason architecture is useful is that it suppresses or defers the plethora of details that are necessary to resolve before bringing a system to the field. The architecture is therefore ambiguous, one might argue, with respect to these suppressed details. Even though an architecture may be brought to fruition by any number of elaborations/implementations, as long as those implementations comply with the architecture, they are all correct. Unplanned ambiguity occurs when documentation can be interpreted in more than one way and at

> Clarity is our only defense against the embarrassment felt on completion of a large project when it is discovered that the wrong problem has been solved.
>
> —C. A. R. Hoare (1987, p. 85)

least one of those ways is incorrect. The documentation should be sufficient to avoid multiple interpretations.

A well-defined notation with precise semantics goes a long way toward eliminating whole classes of linguistic ambiguity from a document. This is one area where architecture description languages help a great deal, but using a formal language isn't always necessary. Simply adopting a set of notational conventions and then avoiding unplanned repetition, especially the "almost-alike" repetition mentioned previously, will help eliminate whole classes of ambiguity. But if you do adopt a notation, then the following corollary applies:

3a. Explain Your Notation

ADVICE

We have several things to say about box-and-line diagrams masquerading as architecture documentation.

- Don't be guilty of drawing one and claiming that it's anything more than a start at an architectural description.
- If you draw one yourself, make sure that you explain precisely what the boxes and lines mean.
- If you see one, ask its author what the boxes mean and what, *precisely,* the arrows connote. The result is usually illuminating, even if the only thing illuminated is the author's confusion.

The ubiquitous box-and-line diagrams that people always draw on whiteboards are one of the greatest sources of ambiguity in architecture documentation. Although not a bad starting point, these diagrams are certainly not good architecture documentation. For one thing, the behavior of the elements, a crucial part of the architecture, is not defined. Furthermore, most such diagrams suffer from ambiguity. Are the boxes supposed to be modules, objects, classes, processes, functions, procedures, processors, or something else? Do the arrows mean submodule, inheritance, synchronization, exclusion, calls, uses, data flow, processor migration, or something else?

Make it as easy as possible for your reader to determine the meaning of the notation. If you're using a standard visual language defined elsewhere, refer readers to the source of the language's semantics. (Even if the language is standard or widely used, different versions often exist. Let your reader know, by citation, which one you're using.) For a home-grown notation, include a key to the symbology. This is good practice because it compels you to understand what the pieces of your system are and how they relate to one another and it is also courteous to your readers.

P.6.4   Rule 4: Use a Standard Organization

Establish a standard, planned organization scheme; make your documents adhere to it; and ensure that readers know about it. A standard organization offers many benefits.

- It helps the reader navigate the document and find specific information quickly. Thus, this benefit is also related to the write-for-the-reader rule.

- It also helps the document writer plan and organize the contents and reveals what work remains to be done by the number of sections labeled TBD (to be determined).

- It embodies completeness rules for the information; the sections of the document constitute the set of important aspects that need to be conveyed. Hence, the standard organization can form the basis for a first-order validation check of the document at review time.

Corollaries are

1. *Organize documentation for ease of reference.* Software documentation may be read from cover to cover at most once, probably never. But a document is likely to be referenced hundreds or thousands of times.

2. *Mark as TBD what you don't yet know rather than leaving it blank.* Many times, we can't fill in a document completely because we don't yet know the information or because decisions have not been made. In that case, mark the document accordingly rather than leave the section blank. If the section is blank, the reader will wonder whether the information is coming or whether a mistake was made.

> **FOR MORE INFORMATION**
> Section I.2 contains a standard organization for a style guide. Chapter 10 contains a standard organization that we recommend for documenting views and information beyond views. Chapter 7 contains a standard organization for the documentation of a software interface.

P.6.5   Rule 5: Record Rationale

When you document the results of decisions, record the alternatives you rejected and state why. Later, when those decisions come under scrutiny or pressure to change, you will find yourself revisiting the same arguments and wondering why you didn't take another path. Recording your rationale will save you enormous time in the long run, although it requires discipline to record your rationale in the heat of the moment.

> **FOR MORE INFORMATION**
> Section 10.3 discusses the documentation of rationale.

P.6.6   Rule 6: Keep Documentation Current But Not Too Current

Documentation that is incomplete or out-of-date does not reflect truth, does not obey its own rules for form and internal consistency, and is not used. Documentation that is kept current and accurate is used. Why? Because questions about the software can be most easily and most efficiently answered by referring to the appropriate document. Documentation that is somehow inadequate to answer the question needs to be fixed. Updating it and *then* referring the questioner to it will deliver a strong message that the documentation is the final, authoritative source for information.

During the design process, on the other hand, decisions are made and reconsidered with great frequency. Revising documentation to reflect decisions that will not persist is an unnecessary expense.

Your development plan should specify particular points at which the documentation is brought up-to-date or the process for keeping the documentation current. Every design decision should not be recorded the instant it is made; rather, the document should be subject to version control and have a release strategy, just as every other artifact being produced does.

P.6.7 Rule 7: Review Documentation for Fitness of Purpose

Only the intended users of a document will be able to tell you whether it contains the right information presented in the right way. Enlist their aid. Before a document is released, have it reviewed by representatives of the community or communities for which it was written.

FOR MORE INFORMATION

Section 10.4 discusses how to review software architecture documentation to make sure that it is of high quality and utility and that it conforms to these rules, among other things.

PERSPECTIVES

Quivering at Arrows

Many architectural diagrams with an informal notation use arrows to indicate a directional relationship among architectural elements. Although this might seem like a good and innocuous way to clarify a design by adding visual semantic detail, it creates a great source of confusion in many cases. What do the arrows mean? Do they indicate direction of data flow? Visibility of services or data? Control flow? Invocation? Any of these might make sense, and people use arrows to mean all these things and more, often using multiple interpretations in the same diagram.

Consider the following architectural snippet:

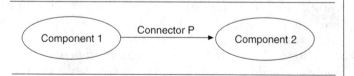

Suppose that Component 1 (C_1) invokes Component 2 (C_2) via a simple procedure call. What might the arrow mean? It might mean that C_1 calls C_2. It might mean that C_1 passes data to C_2 via its parameters. It might mean that C_1 obtains a return result from C_2. It might mean that C_1 causes C_2 to come into existence or be loaded into a memory space. It might mean that C_2 cannot execute until C_1 does. It might mean that C_1 cannot execute until C_2 terminates. All these interpretations are valid under the assumption that C_1 invokes C_2.

Alternatively, suppose that we know that C_1 invokes C_2 and we want to show a data flow between the two. We could use the preceding figure, but if C_2 returns a value to C_1, shouldn't an arrow go both ways? Or should a single arrow have two arrowheads? These two options are not interchangeable. A double-headed arrow typically denotes a symmetric relationship between two elements, whereas two single-headed arrows suggest two asymmetric relationships at work. In either case, the diagram will lose the information that C_1 initiated the interaction. Suppose that C_2 also invokes C_1. Would we need to put *two* double-headed arrows between C_1 and C_2?

The same questions would apply if we wanted to show control flow. How should we depict the fact that C_2 returns control to C_1 after its execution has completed?

Of course, the situation is even worse if the relationship is a more complex form of interaction, possibly involving multiple procedure calls, complex protocols, rules for handling exceptions and timeouts, and callbacks. To avoid confusion, follow this advice.

When arrows represent nontrivial interactions, document the *behavior,* using some form of behavior or protocol specification. For example, a dotted line might be used to indicate a control relationship; a solid line, a data transfer relationship. Similarly, different arrowhead shapes can help make distinctions. But by the same token, a procedure call-based interaction, for example, should use the same kind of connecting line throughout the architectural documentation.

Although arrows are often used to indicate interactions, often one can avoid confusion by not using them where they are likely to be misinterpreted. For example, one can use lines without arrowheads. Sometimes, physical placement, as in a layered diagram, can convey the same information.

—D.G.

FOR MORE INFORMATION

Chapter 8 provides guidance on documenting behavior.

ADVICE

Explain what semantic and notational conventions you are using.

ADVICE

Use different visual conventions to distinguish between semantically distinct types of interaction within a diagram.

ADVICE

Use the same visual conventions for like interactions throughout.

ADVICE

Don't feel compelled to use arrows.

P.7   Summary Checklist

- The goal of documenting an architecture is to write it down so that others can successfully use it, maintain it, and build a system from it.

- Documentation exists to further architecture's uses as a means of education, as a vehicle for communication among stakeholders, and as the basis for analysis.

- Documenting an architecture is a matter of documenting the relevant views and then adding documentation that applies to more than one view.

- The module viewtype helps architects think about their software as a set of implementation units. The component-and-connector viewtype helps architects think about their software as a set of elements that have runtime behavior and interactions. The allocation viewtype helps architects think about how their software relates to the nonsoftware structures in its environment.

- A viewtype constrains the set of elements and relations that exist in its views. An *architectural style* is a specialization of a viewtype's elements and relationships, together with a set of constraints on how they can be used. A style defines a family of architectures that satisfy the constraints.

- Some styles are applicable in every software system: decomposition, uses, deployment, and work assignment, for example. Other styles occur only in systems in which they were explicitly chosen and designed in by the architect: layered, communicating-processes, and client-server, for example.

- Follow the seven rules for sound documentation. Some styles are applicable to every system; others apply only to those for which they were chosen and architected in. And even styles that apply to every system will not always be documented.

  - Write documentation from the point of view of the reader, not the writer.
  - Avoid unnecessary repetition.
  - Avoid ambiguity. Always explain your notation.
  - Use a standard organization.
  - Record rationale.
  - Keep documentation current but not too current.
  - Review documentation for fitness of purpose.

- There are many views on views. See Chapter 11 for a discussion of how the views described in this book relate to the others.
- Use arrows carefully. Always say what they mean.

P.8 Discussion Questions

1. Think of a technical document that you remember as being exceptionally useful. What made it so?

2. Think of a technical document that you remember as being dreadful. What made it so?

3. List several architectural aspects of a system you're familiar with, and state why they are architectural. List several aspects that are not architectural, and state why they are not. List several aspects that are "on the cusp," and make a compelling argument for putting each into "architectural" or "nonarchitectural" categories.

4. If you visit Seoul, Korea, you might see the following sign presiding over one of the busy downtown thoroughfares:

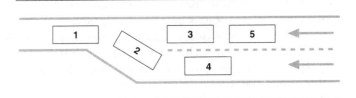

   What does it mean? Is the information this sign conveys structural, behavioral, or both? What are the elements in this system? Are they more like modules or like components? What qualities about the notation make this sign understandable or not understandable? Does the sign convey a dynamic architecture, or dynamic behavior within a static architecture? Who are the stakeholders for this sign? What quality attributes is it attempting to achieve? How would you validate it, to assure yourself that it was satisfying its requirements?

5. List the stakeholders for a software architecture. How do project managers, chief technical officers, chief information officers, analysts, customers, and end users fit into your list?

6. How much of a project's budget would you devote to software architecture documentation? Why? How would you measure the cost and the benefit?

P.9 For Further Reading

The full treatment of software architecture—how to build one, how to evaluate one to make sure it's a good one, how to recover one from a jumble of legacy code, and how to drive a development effort once you have one—is beyond the scope of this book. However, general books on software architecture are becoming plentiful. Bass, Clements, and Kazman [Bass+ 98], Hofmeister, Nord, and Soni [Hofmeister+ 00], Shaw and Garlan [ShawGarlan 96], Bosch [Bosch 00], and Malveau and Mowbray [MalveauMowbray 01] provide good coverage.

The Software Engineering Institute's software architecture Web page [SEIATA] provides a wide variety of software architecture resources and links, including a broad collection of definitions of the term.

David Parnas first made the observation that software can be described by many structures, not just one [Parnas 74]. This insight led directly to the concept of views that we use today. Architectural views in general, and the so-called "4+1 views" in particular, are a fundamental aspect of the Rational Unified Process for object-oriented software [Kruchten 98]. An overview of views is given in [Bass 98] and [Jazayeri 00]; a comprehensive treatment appears in [Hofmeister 00].

One of the goals of documentation is to provide sufficient information so that an architecture can be analyzed for fitness of purpose. For more about analysis and evaluation of software architectures, see [Clements 01].

The seven rules of sound documentation are adapted from [ParnasClements 86], which also espouses a philosophy directly relevant to this book. That paper holds that although system design is often subject to errors, false starts, and resource-constrained compromises, systems should be documented as though they were the product of an idealized, step-by-step, smoothly executed design process. That is the documentation, it says, that will be the most helpful in the long run. This book is consistent with that philosophy, in that it lays out what the end state of your documentation should be. We understand (and sympathize with), but do not emphasize, that the intermediate states may fall considerably short of that goal. It's the final product that is the object of our efforts.

Architectural styles that one chooses (as opposed to the ones that are present in every system) are thoroughly treated in [ShawGarlan 96]. Chapter 3 consists of a number of example problems. For each one, several architectural solutions are presented, each based on the choice of a different style. These side-by-side comparisons not only reveal qualities of the styles themselves, but richly illustrate the overall concept. A tour de force in style comparison is found in [Shaw 95], in which the author examines 11 different previously published solutions to the automobile cruise-control problem and compares each solution through the lens of architectural style.

For encyclopedic catalogs of architectural styles, see [Buschmann+ 96] and [Schmidt+ 00].

Design patterns, the object-oriented and finer-grained analog of architectural styles, are covered in [Gamma+ 95], [Alur+ 01], as well as a host of online resources and conferences. Jacobson et al. devote an entire section to architectural styles for object-oriented systems designed with strategic reuse in mind [Jacobson+ 97]. Smith and Williams include three chapters of principles and guidance for architecting systems in which performance is a concern [SmithWilliams 01].

Software Architecture Viewtypes and Styles

Chapters 1–5 present the three viewtypes—module, component-and-connector, and allocation—in detail with several common styles of each. Here we introduce those styles and the organization we use to describe them.

I.1 Viewtypes and Style Catalog

I.1.1 Module Viewtype

We begin by discussing the module viewtype. A module is a code unit that implements a set of responsibilities. A module can be a class, a collection of classes, a layer, or any decomposition of the code unit. Every module has a collection of properties assigned to it. These properties are intended to express the important information associated with the module, as well as constraints on the module. Sample properties are responsibilities, visibility information, and author. Modules have relations to one another. Example relations are *is part of* or *inherits from*.

The module viewtype contains several styles.

- The *decomposition style* represents the decomposition of the code into systems, subsystems, subsubsystems, and so on. This style represents a top-down view of the system. (The term *system* or *subsystem* also has a runtime interpretation, and so its use needs to be clarified in a particular context.) This style, used to give an overall view of the system and its pieces to stakeholders, is particularly useful for education and manager-level communication. This style helps new members of the development team understand what their roles are in terms of code development and is often the basis of work assignments and completion measures.

- The *uses style* depends on the *uses* relation, which is a special form of the *depends-on* relation. A unit of software P_1 is said to *use* another unit, P_2, if the correctness of P_1 depends on P_2 being correct as well. This style tells developers which other modules must exist for their portion of the system to correctly execute. This style supports incremental development, as it enables the identification of useful system subsets that can be fielded early.

- The *generalization style* shows how different code units are related to one another, as in a class hierarchy: Which classes inherit from which other classes can be determined by looking at the generalization style. This style is commonly used to express object-oriented designs, as well as to support a variety of forms of maintenance. Reuse is frequently based on classes, new functions are often added by modifying old functions, and the portion of the code to be repaired in the case of an error is usually specified in terms of classes.

DEFINITION

A **layer** is a collection of code that forms a virtual machine and that interacts with other layers only according to predefined rules.

- The *layered style* organizes the code into disjoint **layers** where code in higher layers is allowed to use code in lower layers according to predefined rules. For example, rules may stipulate that only code in the next lower layer may be used, that code in any lower layer may be used, or that code in the lower layers or in a utility layer may be used. This style is used to show how code is decomposed in virtual machines. Typically, the lower levels involve those portions of the system close to the hardware, including the operating system, whereas the higher layers contain more application-dependent software. The layered style is used for education and to support reuse. This style is also used to support portability. Having hardware-dependent code localized, for example, supports changing the hardware.

I.1.2 Component-and-Connector Viewtype

Styles in the component-and-connector viewtype express runtime behavior. They are described in terms of components and connectors. A component is one of the principal processing units of the executing system; a connector is an interaction mechanism for the components. Objects, processes, or collections of objects may all be components. Connectors include pipes, repositories, and sockets. Middleware can be viewed as a connector between the components that use the middleware. Components and connectors can be decomposed into other components and connectors. The decomposition of a component may include connectors and vice versa. Decomposing middleware—a connector, for example—will yield various components and additional connectors. Components and connectors also have properties that can be used to assist with the analysis. We discuss six component-and-connector styles.

- The *pipe-and-filter style* is one in which the pattern of interaction is characterized by successive transformations of data. Data arrives at a filter, is transformed, and is passed through the pipe to the next filter in the pipeline. Examples of such systems are signal-processing systems and UNIX pipes.

- The *shared-data style* centers on the retention of persistent data. Multiple elements access the persistent data, which is retained in at least one repository. Database systems and knowledge-based systems are examples of shared-data styles. One characteristic of a shared-data style is how the consumer of data can discover that data of interest is available.

- The *publish-subscribe style* is characterized by components that interact by announcing events. Components may subscribe to a set of events. This style is commonly used to decouple message producers and consumers. This decoupling allows deferring the binding of producers and consumers of messages until runtime, and hence supports the modification of these producers and consumers.

- The *client-server style* shows components interacting by requesting services of other components. The essence of this style is that communication is typically paired. A request for service from a client is paired with the provision of that service. Servers in this style provide a set of services through one or more interfaces, and clients use zero or more services provided by other servers in the system. There may be one central server or several distributed ones. Examples of client-server systems include: (1) window systems that partition the system according to client application and screen server, (2) name directory services that partition according to name resolver and name server, (3) two-tier database systems that partition the system according to clients and data, and (4) distributed Web-based systems that partition the system according to such concerns as client applications, business logic, and data management services.

- The *peer-to-peer style* is characterized by direct component interaction of peers exchanging services. Peer-to-peer communication is a kind of request/reply interaction without the asymmetry found in the client-server style. That is, any component can, in principle, interact with any other component by requesting its services. Thus, connectors in this style may involve complex bidirectional protocols of interaction reflecting the two-way communication that may exist between two or more peer-to-peer components. Examples of peer-to-peer systems include architectures that are based on distributed object infrastructure, such as CORBA, COM+, and Java RMI (remote method invocation). More generally, runtime architectural views of object systems, such as shown in collaboration diagrams, are often examples of this C&C style.

- The *communicating-processes style* is distinguished by the interaction of concurrently executing components through various connector mechanisms. Examples of the connector mechanisms are synchronization, message passing, data exchange, start, stop, and so forth. Communicating processes are common in most large systems and necessary in all distributed systems. Thus, for most systems, the communicating-processes style is appropriate for understanding any behavior associated with concurrency.

I.1.3 Allocation Viewtype

The allocation viewtype includes the following styles. Each allocation style describes the mapping of software units to elements of the environment (the hardware, the file systems, or the development team).

- The *deployment style* maps processes to hardware elements: processing nodes, communication channels, memory stores, and data stores. The software elements in this style are usually processes. This style, used to describe how processes are allocated to hardware and the resulting message traffic, is used for analysis of performance, security, and reliability and provides a basis for estimating the cost of deployment of a single node.

- The *implementation style* maps modules of a module viewtype to a development infrastructure. Elements of the implementation style are modules and configuration entities. This style is used to describe how modules are mapped to entities within the configuration management system, as well as to manage versions and branches and to coordinate multi-team development.

- The *work assignment style* maps modules of a module viewtype to human development teams. Elements of the work assignment style are modules and development teams. The style is used to describe which teams are responsible for which elements of the work-breakdown structure, as well as to inform schedule and budget estimates.

I.2   Style Guides: A Standard Organization for Documenting a Style

All of the viewtype and style descriptions in Chapters 1–5 follow the same outline that constitutes the standard organization of a style guide.

1. *Overview.* The overview explains why this viewtype/style is useful for documenting a software architecture. It discusses what it is about a system that the viewtype/style addresses and how it supports reasoning about and analysis of systems.

2. *Elements, relations, and properties*
   a. **Elements** are the architectural building blocks native to the viewtype/style. The description of elements tells what role elements play in an architecture and furnishes guidelines for effective documentation of the elements in views.

   > **DEFINITION**
   >
   > An **element** is the architectural building block that is native to a viewtype/style.

   b. **Relations** determine how the elements work together to accomplish the work of the system. The discussion names the relations among elements and provides rules on how elements can and cannot be related.

   > **DEFINITION**
   >
   > A **relation** determines how elements cooperate to accomplish the work of a system.

   c. **Properties** are additional information about the elements and their associated relations. When an architect documents a view, the properties will be given values. For example, properties of a layer—an element of the layered style, which is in the module viewtype—include the layer's name, the units of software the layer contains, and the nature of the virtual machine that the layer provides. A layered view will, for each layer, specify its name, the unit of software it contains, and the virtual machine it provides. Thus, the existence of a property in a viewtype/style imparts an obligation to the architect, when documenting a corresponding view, to fill in that property. The viewtypes and styles of Chapters 1–5 are described with a set of properties likely to be useful for each. But the architect should compile his or her own list of properties when adopting a style, and include that list in the documentation.

   > **DEFINITION**
   >
   > A **property** is additional information about elements and relations.

3. *What it's for and not for.* This section describes the kind of reasoning supported and, just as important, the kind of reasoning not supported by views in the viewtype or the

style. This section describes typical users and their use of the resulting views in order to help the architect understand to what purpose(s) a view in this viewtype or style may be put.

4. *Notations.* Descriptions are given of graphical and/or textual representations that are available to document views in the viewtype/style. Different notations will also support the conveyance of different kinds of information in the primary presentation.

5. *Relation to other views.* This section describes how views in the viewtype/style might be related to those in different viewtypes or even in different styles in the same viewtype. For example, views in two styles might convey slightly different but related information about a system, and the architect will need a way to choose which one to use. This section might also include warnings about other views with which a particular view is often confused, to the detriment of the system and its stakeholders. Finally, this section might include a suggestion about useful mappings that can be built by combining a view in this viewtype with another.

6. *Examples.* This section provides or points to an example of a system documented in the given style.

The Module Viewtype

1.1 Overview

In this chapter and the next, we look at ways to document the modular structures of a system's software. Such documentation enumerates the principal implementation units, or modules, of a system, together with the relationships among these units. We refer to these descriptions as *module views*. As we will see, these views can be used for each of the purposes outlined in the Prologue: education, communication among stakeholders, and the basis for analysis.

The concept of modules emerged in the 1960s and 1970s, based on the notion of software units with well-defined interfaces providing a set of services—typically, procedures and functions—together with implementations that either fully or partially hide their internal data structures and algorithms. More recently, these concepts have found widespread use in object-oriented programming languages and modeling notations, such as UML.

Today, the way in which a system's software is decomposed into manageable units remains one of the important forms of system structure. At a minimum, it determines how a system's source code is partitioned into separable parts, what kinds of assumptions each part can make about services provided by other parts, and how those parts are aggregated into larger ensembles. Choice of modularization often determines how changes to one part of a system might affect other parts and hence the ability of a system to support modifiability, portability, and reuse.

It is unlikely that the documentation of any software architecture can be complete without at least one view in the module viewtype.

ADVICE

Plan for your documentation package to include at least one view in the module viewtype.

We begin by considering the module viewtype in its most general form. In the next chapter, we identify four common styles:

- The *decomposition* style, used to focus on containment relationships among modules
- The *uses* style, to indicate functional dependency relationships among modules
- The *generalization* style, to indicate specialization relationships among modules
- The *layered* style, to indicate the *allowed-to-use* relation in a restricted fashion between modules

1.2 Elements, Relations, and Properties of the Module Viewtype

Table 1.1 summarizes the discussion in this section of the elements, relations, and properties of the module viewtype.

Table 1.1: Summary of the module viewtype

Elements	The element of a module view is a module, which is an implementation unit of software that provides a coherent unit of functionality.
Relations	Relations shown in a module view are a form of *is part of, depends on*, or *is a*. • The *is-part-of* relation defines a part/whole relationship between the submodule A—the part, or child—and the aggregate module B—the whole, or parent. • The *depends-on* relation defines a dependency relationship between A and B. Specific module styles elaborate what dependency is meant. • The *is-a* relation defines a generalization relationship between a more specific module—the child A—and a more general module—the parent B.
Properties of elements	Properties of a module include the following: • *Name,* which may have to comply with namespace rules • *Responsibilities* of the module • *Implementation information,* such as the set of code units that implement the module

Table 1.1: Summary of the module viewtype (continued)

Properties of relations	• The *is-part-of* relation may have an associated visibility property that defines whether a sub-module is visible outside the aggregate module. • The *depends-on* relation can have constraints assigned to specify in more detail what the dependency between two modules is. • The *is-a* relation may have an implementation property, denoting that a more specific module—the child A—inherits the implementation of the more general module—the parent B—but does not guarantee to support the parent's interface and thereby does not provide substitutability for the parent.
Topology	The module viewtype has no inherent topological constraints.

> **FOR MORE INFORMATION**
> See Coming to Terms: Substitutability on page 46.

1.2.1 Elements

System designers use the term **module** to refer a variety of software structures, including programming language units, such as Ada packages, Modula modules, Smalltalk or C++ classes, or simply general groupings of source code units. In this book, we adopt a broad definition.

> **DEFINITION**
> A **module** is an implementation unit of software that provides a coherent unit of functionality.

We characterize a module by enumerating a set of responsibilities, which are foremost among a module's properties. This broad notion of "responsibilities" is meant to encompass the kinds of features that a unit of software might provide.

Modules can both be aggregated and decomposed. Different module views may identify a different set of modules and aggregate or decompose them based on different style criteria. For example, the layered style identifies modules and aggregates them based on an *allowed-to-use* relation, whereas the generalization view identifies and aggregates modules based on what they have in common.

1.2.2 Relations

The module viewtype has the following relations:

• *Is part of.* The *is-part-of* relation defines a part/whole relationship between the submodule A—the part—and the aggregate module B—the whole. In its most general form, the *is-part-of* relation simply indicates aggregation, with little implied semantics. In general, for instance, one module might be included in many aggregates. This relation, however, has stronger forms. In Chapter 2, for example, this relation is refined to a decomposition relation in the module decomposition style.

- *Depends on.* A *depends-on* B defines a dependency relation between A and B. The *depends-on* relation is typically used early in the design process when the precise form of the dependency has yet to be decided. Once the decision is made, *depends-on* usually is replaced by a more specific form of the relation. Later, we look at two in particular: *uses* and *allowed-to-use*, in the module uses and layered styles, respectively. Other, more specific examples of the *depends-on* relation include *shares-data-with* and *calls*. A call dependency may be refined to *sends-data-to, transfers-control-to, imposes-ordering-on,* and so forth.

FOR MORE INFORMATION
See Coming to Terms: Substitutability on page 46.

- *Is a.* The *is-a* relation defines a generalization relationship between a more specific module—the child A—and a more general module—the parent B. The child is able to be used in contexts in which the parent is used. Later, we look at its use in more detail in the module generalization style. Object-oriented inheritance is a special case of the *is-a* relation.

1.2.3 Properties

As we will see in Section 10.2, properties are documented as part of the supporting documentation for a view. The list of properties pertinent to a set of modules will depend on many things but is likely to include the following:

- *Name.* A module's name is, of course, the primary means to refer to it. A module's name often suggests something about its role in the system: a module called "account_mgr," for instance, probably has little to do with numeric simulations of chemical reactions. In addition, a module's name may reflect its position in a decomposition hierarchy; the name A.B.C.D, for example, refers to a module D that is a submodule of a module C, itself a submodule of B, and so on.

FOR MORE INFORMATION
Section 2.1.6 provides an extended example of documenting a set of modules' responsibilities.

- *Responsibilities.* The responsibility property for a module is a way to identify its role in the overall system and establishes an identity for it beyond the name. Whereas a module's name may suggest its role, a statement of responsibility establishes it with much more certainty. Responsibilities should be described in sufficient detail to make clear to the reader what each module does.

- *Visibility of interface(s).* An interface document for the module establishes with precision its role in the system by specifying exactly what it may be called on to do. A module may have zero, one, or several interfaces.

In a view documenting an *is-part-of* relation, some of the interfaces of the submodules exist for internal purposes only; that is, the interfaces are used only by the submodules within the enclosing parent module. These interfaces are never visible outside that context and therefore do not have a direct relationship to the parent interfaces.

Different strategies can be used for those interfaces that have a direct relationship to the parent interfaces. The strategy shown in Figure 1.1(a) is encapsulation in order to hide the interfaces of the submodules. The parent module provides its own interfaces and maps all requests, using the capabilities provided by the submodules. However, the facilities of the enclosed modules are not available outside the parent.

Alternatively, the interfaces of an aggregate module can be a subset of the interfaces of the aggregate. That is, an enclosing module simply aggregates a set of modules and selectively exposes some of their responsibilities. Layers and subsystems are often defined in this way. For example, if module C is an aggregate of modules A and B, C's implicit interface will be a subset of the interfaces of modules A and B (see Figure 1.1(b)).

- *Implementation information.* Because modules are units of implementation, recording information related to their implementation from the point of view of managing their development and building the system that contains them is useful. Although this information is not, strictly speaking, architectural, it is convenient to record it in the architecture

FOR MORE INFORMATION

Documenting software interfaces is discussed in Chapter 7.

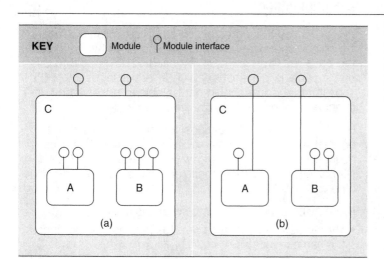

KEY ☐ Module ♀ Module interface

(a)

(b)

Figure 1.1
(a) Module C provides its own interface, hiding the interfaces of modules A and B; (b) Module C exposes a subset of the interfaces of modules A and B as its interface.

FOR MORE INFORMATION

In addition to identifying the code units, one also needs to identify where they reside in a project's filing scheme: a directory or folder in a file system, a URL in an intranet, a storage location in a software engineering environment or toolset, or a branch, node, and version in a configuration management system's tree space. This information is in the purview of the implementation view, defined in Section 5.4.

documentation where the module is defined. Implementation information might include

- *Mapping to code units.* This identifies the files that constitute the implementation of a module. For example, a module ALPHA, if implemented in C, might have several files that constitute its implementation: ALPHA.c, ALPHA.h, ALPHA.o—if precompiled versions are maintained—and perhaps ALPHA_t.h to define any data types provided by ALPHA.

- *Test information.* The module's test plan, test cases, test scaffolding, test data, and test history are important to store.

- *Management information.* A manager may need the location of a module's predicted completion schedule and budget.

- *Implementation constraints.* In many cases, the architect will have a certain implementation strategy in mind for a module or may know of constraints that the implementation must follow. This information is private to the module and hence will not appear, for example, in the module's interface.

Styles in the module viewtype may have properties of their own in addition to these. Also, you may find other properties useful that are not listed.

COMING TO TERMS

Substitutability

We have used the term *substitutability* to explain the meaning of the generalization relationship between two modules. We have relied on an intuitive notion of being able to use one module in place of another: In principle, users of the substituted module should not be able to observe any differences in behavior from the original module.

But this informal notion of substitutability begs the question of what we mean by "differences in behavior." This phrase might be interpreted in many ways. For example, if B is substitutable for A, we might mean any of the following, among others.

- B may be used in the same situations as A.
- B may be used in the same situations as and produces the same results as A.

- B may be used in the same situations as, produces the same results as, and has the same performance charac-   · teristics as A.

In the preceding progression, the definition of substitutability becomes stronger at each step, moving from syntactic properties to semantic properties to quality attributes.

Which definition is the "right" one? Any of these might be reasonable, but you need to be clear which you mean. The implications for documentation are that when you use a style in which generalization is one of the relations, you should state what kind of substitutability is intended.

1.3   What the Module Viewtype Is For and What It's Not For

Expect to use the module viewtype for

- *Construction.* A module view can provide a blueprint for the source code. In this case, the modules and physical structures, such as source code files and directories, often have a close mapping.
- *Analysis.* Two important analysis techniques are requirements traceability and impact analysis. Because modules partition the system, it should be possible to determine how the functional requirements of a system are supported by module responsibilities. Often, a high-level requirement will be met by a sequence of invocations. Documenting such sequences shows how the system is meeting its requirements and identifies any missing requirements. Impact analysis, by contrast, helps to predict the effect of modifying the system. Context diagrams that describe the module's relationships to other modules or to the outside world build a good basis for impact analysis (see Section 6.2). Modules are affected by a problem report or a change request. Impact analysis requires a certain degree of design completeness and integrity of the module description. In particular, dependency information has to be available and correct in order to create good results.
- *Communication.* A module view can be used to explain the system's functionality to someone not familiar with the system. The various levels of granularity of the module decomposition provide a top-down presentation of the system's responsibilities and therefore can guide the learning process.

On the other hand, it is difficult to use the module viewtype to make inferences about runtime behavior, because this viewtype is a partition of the functions of the software. Thus, a module view is not typically used for analysis of performance, reliability, or many other runtime qualities. For those, we typically rely on component-and-connector and allocation views.

1.4 Notations for the Module Viewtype

1.4.1 Informal Notations

A number of notations can be used in a module view's primary presentation. One common informal notation uses bubbles or boxes to represent the modules, with different kinds of lines between them representing the relations. Nesting is used to depict aggregation, and arrows typically represent a *depends-on* relation. In Figure 1.1, for example, nesting is used to describe aggregation, and dots are used to indicate interfaces, similar to the UML "lollipop" notation introduced in Section 7.5.

A second common form of informal notation is a simple textual listing of the modules with description of the responsibilities. Various textual schemes can be used to represent the *is-part-of* relation, such as indentation, outline numbering, and parenthetical nesting. Other relations may be indicated by keywords. For example, the description of module A might include the line "Imports modules B, C," indicating a dependency between module A and modules B and C.

1.4.2 UML

Object-modeling notations, such as UML, provide a variety of constructs that can be used to represent various kinds of modules. Figure 1.2 shows some examples for modules using UML notation. Figure 1.3 shows how the relations native to the module viewtype are denoted using UML.

UML has a class construct, which is the object-oriented specialization of a module as described here. UML packages can be used when grouping of functionality is important, such as to represent layers and collections of classes. The UML subsystem construct can be used to support specification of interface and behavior.

1.5 Relation to Other Viewtypes

Module views are commonly mapped to views in the component-and-connector viewtype. The implementation units shown in

FOR MORE INFORMATION

Figure 2.2 on page 58 is an example of a textual notation for modules, using indentation to indicate *is-part-of.*

FOR MORE INFORMATION

See Coming to Terms: Subsystem on page 62.

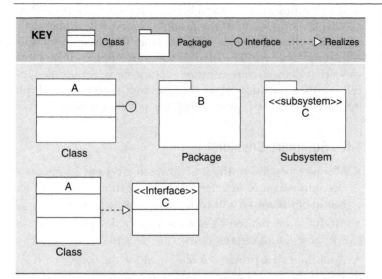

Figure 1.2
Examples of module notation in UML. A module may be represented as a class, a package, or a subsystem. The graphic on the bottom says that Class A realizes the interface defined by Interface C.

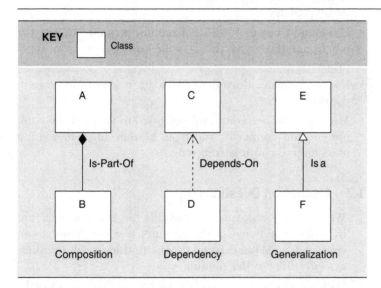

Figure 1.3
From left to right, these examples of relation notations in UML read as follows: module B *is part of* module A, module D *depends on* module C, and module F *is a* type of module E.

module views have a mapping to components that executes at runtime. Sometimes, the mapping is quite straightforward, even one-to-one. Often, a single module will be replicated as many components; this one-to-many mapping is also straightforward. However, the mapping can be quite complex, with fragments of modules corresponding to fragments of components.

A common problem is the overloading of the module viewtype with information pertaining to other viewtypes. This can be quite useful when done in a disciplined fashion but can also lead to confusion. For example, showing a remote procedure call (RPC) connection in the module viewtype is implicitly introducing the "connector" concept from the component-and-connector viewtype. The module views are often confused with views that demonstrate runtime relationships. A module view represents a partitioning of the software; therefore, multiple instances of objects, for example, are not shown in this view.

1.6 Summary Checklist

- Modules pertain to the way in which a system's software is decomposed into manageable units of functionality, which is one of the important forms of system structure.
- Modules are related to one another by forms of *is-part-of*, *depends-on*, and *is-a* relations.
- A module view provides a blueprint for the source code.
- Expect to have at least one module view in your documentation package.
- You should not depend on a module name to define the functional duties of the module: use the responsibility property.
- Use an interface document to establish a module's role in the system.
- Module views are commonly mapped to views of the component and connector viewtype. Module implementation units map to runtime components.

1.7 Discussion Questions

1. What is it possible and not possible to say about data flow by looking at a view in the module viewtype? What about control flow? What can you say about which modules interact with which other modules?

2. Which properties of a module might you think of as worthy of having special notational conventions to express them, and why? For example, you might want to color a commercial-off-the-shelf (COTS) module differently from modules developed in-house.

3. The *depends-on* relation among modules is very general. What specific types of dependencies might be reflected in a style in the module viewtype?

4. A primary property of a module is its set of responsibilities. How do a module's responsibilities differ from the requirements that it must satisfy?

5. When documenting a particular system, you might wish to combine modules into an aggregate, to market them as a combined package, for example. Would this package itself be a module? That is, are all aggregates of modules themselves modules?

1.8   For Further Reading

DeRemer and Kron describe programming-in-the-small languages for writing modules and a "module interconnection language" for knitting those modules together [DeRemer-Kron 76]. Prieto-Diaz and Neighbors present a survey of module interconnection languages that are specifically designed to support module interconnection and includes brief descriptions of some software development systems that support module interconnection [PrietoNeighbors 86].

The chapter on the Module Architecture View in [Hofmeister 00] describes a view of a system in terms of modules and layers and how to represent them in UML.

Styles of the Module Viewtype

In this chapter, we look at four styles of the module viewtype:

- Decomposition
- Uses
- Generalization
- Layered

Each of these styles constrains the basic module viewtype, perhaps adding specialized versions of some of the element and relation types.

2.1 Decomposition Style

2.1.1 Overview

By taking the elements and the properties of the module viewtype and focusing on the *is-part-of* relation, we get the module decomposition style. You can use this style to show how system responsibilities are partitioned across modules and how those modules are decomposed into submodules. Unlike other styles of the module viewtype, decomposition features fairly weak restrictions on the viewtype itself but is usefully distinguished as a separate style, for several reasons.

First, almost all architectures begin with the module decomposition style. Architects tend to attack a problem with divide-and-conquer techniques, and a view rendered in this style records their campaign. Second, a view in this style is a favorite tool with which to communicate the broad picture of the architecture to newcomers. Third, this style begins to address the modifiability that will be built into the architecture by allocating functionality to specific places in the architecture.

The criteria used for decomposing a module into smaller modules depend on the purpose of the decomposition:

- *Achievement of certain quality attributes.* For example, to support modifiability, the information-hiding design principle calls for encapsulating changeable aspects of a system in separate modules, so that the impact of any one change is localized. Another example is performance. Separating functionality that has higher performance requirements from other functionality enables application of different strategies, such as scheduling policies or judicious assignment to processors, to achieve required performance throughout the various parts of the system.

- *Build-versus-buy decisions.* Some modules may be bought in the commercial marketplace or reused intact from a previous project and therefore already have a set of functionality implemented. The remaining functionality then must be decomposed around those established modules.

- *Product line implementation.* To support the efficient implementation of products of a product family, it is essential to distinguish between common modules, used in every or most products, and variable modules, which differ across products.

A decomposition view may represent the first pass at a detailed architectural design; the architect may subsequently introduce other style-based specializations and evolve the view resulting from decomposition into a more detailed use, layered, or other module-based view in some other style.

2.1.2 Elements, Relations, and Properties

FOR MORE
INFORMATION

See Coming to Terms: Subsystem on page 62.

Table 2.1 summarizes the discussion of the characteristics of the decomposition style. Elements of the decomposition style are modules, as described in Section 1.2. Certain aggregations can be called *subsystems*. The principal relation, the *decomposition* relation, is a specialized form of the *is-part-of* relation and has as its primary constraint the guarantee that an element can be a part of at most one aggregate.

The *decomposition* relation may have a *visibility* property, which defines whether the submodules are visible to only the aggregate module—the parent—or also to other modules. A module is said to be visible if it can be used by other modules. With this property, an architect has some control over the visibility of modules, as illustrated in Figure 1.1. A decomposition relation in which no contained module is visible outside its parent is sometimes called a *containment* relation. In a decomposition relation, loops are not allowed; that is, a module cannot

Table 2.1: Summary of the module decomposition style

Elements	*Module,* as defined by the module viewtype. A module that aggregates other modules is sometimes called a *subsystem.*
Relations	The *decomposition* relation, which is a refined form of the *is-part-of* relation. A documentation obligation includes specifying the criteria used to define the decomposition.
Properties of elements	As defined by the module viewtype.
Properties of relations	*Visibility,* the extent to which the existence of a module is known, and its facilities are available, to those modules outside its parent.
Topology	• No loops are allowed in the *decomposition* graph. • A module cannot be part of more than one module in a view.

contain any of its ancestors. No module in a decomposition view can have more than one parent.

2.1.3   What the Decomposition Style Is For and What It's Not For

A decomposition style view presents the functionality of a system in intellectually manageable pieces that are recursively refined to convey more and more details. Therefore, this style is well suited to support the learning process about a system. Besides the obvious benefit for the architect to support the design work, this style is an excellent learning and navigation tool for newcomers in the project or other people who do not necessarily have the whole functional structure of the system memorized. The grouping of functionality shown in this style also builds a useful basis for defining configuration items within a configuration management framework.

The decomposition style most often serves as the input for the work assignment view of a system, which maps parts of a software system onto the organizational units, or teams, that will be given the responsibility for implementing and testing them. A decomposition view also provides some support for analyzing effects of changes at the software implementation level, but because this view does not show all the dependencies among modules, you cannot expect to do a complete impact analysis. Here, views that elaborate the dependency relationships more thoroughly, such as the module uses style described later, are required.

FOR MORE INFORMATION

The work assignment style is presented in Section 5.5.

2.1.4 Notations for the Decomposition Style

Informal Notations

In informal notations, modules in the decomposition style are usually depicted as named boxes that contain other named boxes. Containment can also be shown using indentation, as in Figure 2.2.

The nesting notation can use a thick border suggesting opaqueness—and explained in the key—indicating that children are not visible outside the parent. Similarly, various kinds of arcs can be used to indicate containment, or nonvisibility, as opposed to an ordinary *is-part-of* relation. If a visual notation is not available for indicating visibility, it can be defined textually, as is done for other properties, especially the modules' responsibilities.

UML

FOR MORE INFORMATION

See Coming to Terms: Subsystem on page 62.

In UML, the subsystem construct can be used to represent modules that contain other modules; the class box is normally used for the leaves of the decomposition. Subsystems are both a package and a classifier. As a package, they can be decomposed and hence are suitable for the aggregation of modules. As a classifier, they encapsulate their contents and can provide an explicit interface.

In UML, aggregation is depicted in one of three ways:

1. Modules may be nested, as in Figure 2.1(a).

2. A succession of two diagrams, possibly linked, can be shown, with the second a depiction of the contents of a module shown in the first.

FOR MORE INFORMATION

This blurring of implementation-time and runtime concerns is discussed in Perspectives: UML Class Diagrams: Too Much, Too Little on page 97.

3. An arc denoting composition may be drawn between the parent and the children, as in Figure 2.1(b). In UML, composition is a form of aggregation with implied strong ownership. That is, parts live and die with the whole. If module A is composed of modules B and C, for example, B or C cannot exist without the presence of A. If A is destroyed at runtime, so are B and C. Thus, UML's *composition* relation has implications beyond the structuring of the implementation units; the relation also endows the elements with a runtime property. As an architect, you should make sure that you are comfortable with this property before using UML's *composition* relation.

Other properties, such as the modules' responsibilities, are given textually, perhaps using an annotation.

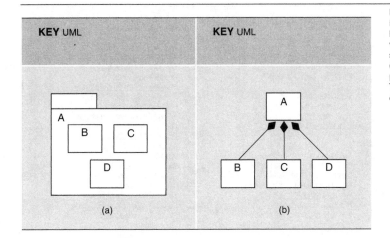

Figure 2.1
In UML, aggregation may be shown by (a) nesting, with the aggregate module shown as a package, or by (b) using arcs between the parent and the children. The solid diamond indicates the parent module.

2.1.5 Relation to Other Styles

It is possible, and often desirable, to map between a module decomposition view and a component-and-connector view. We discuss this in greater detail later. For now, it is sufficient to say that the point of providing such a mapping is to indicate how the software implementation structures map onto runtime structures: generally, a many-to-many relationship. The same module might implement several components or connectors. Conversely, one component might require several modules for its implementation. The mapping may be fairly straightforward or quite complex.

The decomposition style is closely related to the work assignment style, a member of the allocation viewtype. The work assignment style maps modules resulting from a decomposition to a set of teams responsible for implementing and testing those modules.

2.1.6 Examples of the Decomposition Style

ECS

Appendix A contains an example of a module decomposition view for NASA's ECS system.

A-7E Avionics System

An example of the decomposition style comes from the A-7E avionics software system described in Bass, Clements, and Kazman 1998, Chapter 3. Figure 2.2 shows the graphical part of the view. The figure names the elements and shows the *is-part-of* relation among them for the A-7E system.

Figure 2.2
The decomposition of the
A-7E software architecture
results in three modules
and *is-part-of* relations
(Bass, Clements, Kazman,
2001, p. 61).

Hardware-Hiding Module
Extended Computer Module
  Data Module
  Input/Output Module
  Computer State Module
  Parallelism Control Module
  Program Module
  Virtual Memory Module
  Interrupt Handler Module
  Timer Module
Device Interface Module
  Air Data Computer Module
  Angle of Attack Sensor Module
  Audible Signal Device Module
  Computer Fail Device Module
  Doppler Radar Set Module
  Flight Information Displays Module
  Forward Looking Radar Module
  Head-Up Display Module
  Inertial Measurement Set Module
  Input-Output Representation Module
  Master Function Switch Module
  Panel Module
  Projected Map Display Set Module
  Radar Altimeter Module
  Shipboard Inertial Navigation System Module
  Slew Control Module
  Switch Bank Module
  TACAN Module
  Visual Indicators Module
  Waypoint Info. System Module
  Weapon Characteristics Module
  Weapon Release System Module
  Weight on Gear Module

Behavior-Hiding Module
Function Driver Module
  Air Data Computer Module
  Audible Signal Module
  Computer Fail Signal Module
  Doppler Radar Module
  Flight Information Display Module
  Forward Looking Radar Module
  Head-Up Display Module
  Inertial Measurement Set Module
  Panel Module
  Projected Map Display Set Module
  Shipboard Inertial Navigation System Module
  Visual Indicator Module
  Weapon Release Module
  Ground Test Module
Shared Services Module
  Mode Determination Module
  Panel I/O Support Module
  Shared Subroutine Module
  Stage Director Module
  System Value Module

Software Decision Module
Application Data Type Module
  Numeric Data Type Module
  State Transition Event Module
Data Banker Module
  Singular Values Module
  Complex Event Module
Filter Behavior Module
Physical Models Module
  Aircraft Motion Module
  Earth Characteristics Module
  Human Factors Module
  Target Behavior Module
  Weapon Behavior Module
Software Utility Module
  Power-Up Initialization Module
  Numerical Algorithms Module
System Generation Module
  System Generation Parameter Module
  Support Software Module

Except for the modules' names, however, the figure shows none of the properties associated with this style. Supporting the figure is textual documentation that explains the decomposition criteria and for each module lists

- Its responsibilities
- Its visibility to other modules outside its parent
- Implementation information

In this example, the criterion for decomposition is the information-hiding principle, which holds that there should be a module to encapsulate the effects each kind of change considered likely. A module's responsibilities, then, are described in terms of the information-hiding secrets it encapsulates.

In A-7E, the first-order decomposition produced three modules: hardware hiding, behavior hiding, and software decision hiding. Each of these modules is decomposed into two to six submodules, which are in turn decomposed, and so forth, until the granularity is fine enough to be manageable. A useful design heuristic holds that a module is small enough if it could be discarded and begun again if the programmer(s) assigned to implement it left the project.

The A-7E module view documentation describes the responsibilities of the three highest-level modules as follows:

- *Hardware-Hiding Module:* The Hardware-Hiding Module includes the procedures that need to be changed if any part of the hardware is replaced by a new unit with a different hardware/software interface but with the same general capabilities. This module implements "virtual hardware" or an abstract device that is used by the rest of the software. The primary secrets of this module are the hardware/software interfaces. The secondary secrets of this module are the data structures and algorithms used to implement the virtual hardware.

- *Behavior-Hiding Module:* The Behavior-Hiding Module includes procedures that need to be changed if there are changes in requirements affecting the required behavior. Those requirements are the primary secret of this module. These procedures determine the values to be sent to the virtual output devices provided by the Hardware-Hiding Module.

- *Software Decision Module:* The Software Decision Module hides software design decisions that are based upon mathematical theorems, physical facts, and programming considerations such as algorithmic efficiency and accuracy. The secrets of this module are not described in the requirements document. This module differs from the other modules in that both the secrets and the interfaces are determined by software designers. Changes in these modules are more likely to be motivated by a desire to improve performance or accuracy than by externally imposed changes.

Following is how the documentation describes the decomposition of the Software Decision Module into second-level modules. Unless otherwise indicated, a module is visible outside its parent:

- *Application Data Type Module:* The Application Data Type Module supplements the data types provided by the Extended Computer Module with data types that are useful for avionics applications and do not require a computer dependent implementation. Examples of types include distance (useful for altitude), time intervals, and angles (useful for latitude and longitude). These data types are implemented using the basic numeric data types provided by the Extended

Computer; variables of those types are used just as if the types were built into the Extended Computer. The secrets of the Application Data Type Module are the data representation used in the variables and the procedures used to implement operations on those variables. Units of measurements (such as feet, seconds, or radians) are part of the representation and are hidden. Where necessary, the modules provide conversion operators, which deliver or accept real values in specified units.

- *Data Banker Module:* Most data are produced by one module and consumed by another. In most cases, the consumers should receive a value as up-to-date as practical. The time at which a datum should be recalculated is determined both by properties of its consumer (e.g., accuracy requirements) and by properties of its producer (e.g., cost of calculation, rate of change of value). The Data Banker Module acts as a "middleman" and determines when new values for these data are computed. The Data Banker obtains values from producer procedures; consumer procedures obtain data from Data Banker access procedures. The producer and consumers of a particular datum can be written without knowing when a stored value is updated. In most cases, neither the producer nor the consumer need be modified if the updating policy changes.

  The Data Banker provides values for all data that report on the internal state of a module or on the state of the aircraft. The Data Banker also signals events involving changes in the values that it supplies. The Data Banker is used as long as consumer and producer are separate modules, even when they are both submodules of a larger module. The Data Banker is not used if consumers require specific members of the sequence of values to be computed by the producer, or if a produced value is solely a function of the values of input parameters given to the producing procedure (such as $\sin(x)$). The Data Banker is an example of the use of the blackboard architectural style. The choice among updating policies should be based on consumers' accuracy requirements, how often consumers require the value, the maximum wait that consumers can accept, how rapidly the value changes, and the cost of producing a new value. This information is part of the specification given to the implementor of the Data Banker.

FOR MORE INFORMATION

Blackboards are described in Section 4.2.

- *Filter Behavior Module:* The Filter Behavior Module contains digital models of physical filters. They can be used by other procedures to filter potentially noisy data. The primary secrets of this module are the models used for the estimation of values based on sample values and error estimates. The secondary secrets are the computer algorithms and data structures used to implement those models.

- *Physical Models Module:* The software requires estimates of quantities that cannot be measured directly but can be computed from observables using mathematical models. An example is the time that a ballistic weapon will take to strike the ground. The primary secrets of the Physical Models Module are the models; the secondary secrets are the computer implementations of those models.

- *Software Utility Module:* The Software Utility Module contains those utility routines that would otherwise have to be written by more than one other programmer. The routines include mathematical functions, resource monitors, and procedures that signal when all modules have completed their power-up initialization. The secrets of the module are the data structures and algorithms used to implement the procedures.

- *System Generation Module:* The primary secrets of the System Generation Module are decisions that are postponed until system-generation time. These include the values of system generation parameters and the choice among alternative implementations of a module. The secondary secrets of the System Generation Module are the method used to generate a machine-executable form of the code and the representation of the postponed decisions. The procedures in this module do not run on the on-board computer; they run on the computer used to generate the code for the on-board system.

In the case of the A-7E architecture, this second-level module structure was enshrined in many ways: Design documentation, online configuration-controlled files, test plans, programming teams, review procedures, and project schedule and milestones all were pegged to this second-level module structure as their unit of reference. If you use a module decomposition structure to organize your project, you need to pick a level of the hierarchy as was done here, based on a granularity of modules that is manageable. The module guide describes a third—and in some cases a fourth—level of decomposition, but that has been omitted here.

Mil-Std 498 CSCIs and CSCs

Readers familiar with U.S. military software standards, such as MIL-STD-498 and MIL-STD-2167A, will recognize that CSCIs (Computer Software Configuration Items), and CSCs (Computer Software Components) constitute a decomposition view of a system and nothing more. A CSCI is an aggregation of software that satisfies an end use function and is designated for separate configuration management by the acquirer. CSCIs are selected based on trade-offs among software function, size, host or target computers, developer, support concept, plans for reuse, criticality, interface considerations, the need to be separately documented and controlled, and other factors. A CSC is a distinct part of a CSCI and may be further decomposed into other CSCs and CSUs (Computer Software Units).

COMING TO TERMS

Subsystem

When documenting a module view of a system, you may choose to identify certain aggregated modules as subsystems. A subsystem can be pretty much anything you want it to be, but it often describes a part of a system that (1) carries out a functionally cohesive subset of the overall system's mission, (2) can be executed independently, and (3) can be developed and deployed incrementally. An air traffic control system, for example, may be divided into the following areas of capability:

- Interpreting radar data to display aircraft positions on screens
- Detecting aircraft that are about to violate separation constraints
- Running simulations for training
- Recording and playback for after-situation analysis and training
- Monitoring its own health and status

Each of these areas might reasonably be called a subsystem. Informally, a *subsystem* refers to a system portion that can be usefully considered separately from the other portions.

But not just any portion of a system will do. At a minimum, a subsystem must exhibit some coherent, useful functionality. More than that, however, the term also suggests a portion of the system that can execute more or less independently and that directly supports the system's overall purpose. In our air traffic control application, for example, a math utilities library is certainly a portion of a system and an aggregation of modules and even has coherent functionality. But the library is unlikely to be called a subsystem, because it lacks the ability to operate independently to do work that's recognizably part of the overall system's purpose.

Subsystems do not partition a system into completely separate parts, because some parts are used in more than one subsystem. For example, suppose that the air traffic control system looks like this:

Position Display	Collision Avoidance	Simulation	Recording & Playback	Monitoring
Display Generation			Workstation Scheduler	
Network Communications				
Operating System				

In this case, a subsystem consists of one segment from the top layer, as well as any segments of any lower layers that it needs in order to carry out its functionality. A subset of the system formed in this way is often called a *slice,* or a *vertical slice*.

The "more or less independent" nature of a subsystem makes it ideal for dividing up a project's work. You may, for example, ask an analyst to examine the performance of a subsystem. If a user's interaction with a system can be confined to a subsystem, its security properties become important. A subsystem can often be fielded and accomplish useful work before the whole system is complete. A subsystem makes a convenient package to hand off to a team or a subcontractor to implement. The fact that it executes more or less independently allows that team to work more or less independently even through testing. An arbitrary module, by contrast, can certainly be assigned to a team for implementation, but it probably requires the presence of other modules to see it through testing.

The UML world has co-opted the term *subsystem* to mean something quite specific: an aggregation of elements that exhibits behavior—the collective behavior of the aggregated elements—and possibly offering one or more interfaces—realized by the interfaces of the aggregated elements. According to the UML specification:

> A subsystem is a grouping of model elements, that represents a behavioral unit in a physical system. . . . The contents of a Subsystem are divided into two subsets: specification elements and realization elements. The former provides, together with the Operations of the Subsystem, a specification of the behavior contained in the Subsystem, while the ModelElements in the latter subset jointly provide a realization of the specification. . . . The purpose of the subsystem construct is to provide a grouping mechanism for specifying a behavioral unit

of a physical system. . . . The contents of a subsystem are defined in the same way as for a package. . . . A subsystem has no behavior of its own. All behavior defined in the specification of the subsystem is jointly offered by the elements in the realization subset of the contents. . . . A subsystem may offer a set of interfaces. This implies that for each operation defined in an interface, the subsystem offering the interface must have a matching operation, either as a feature of the subsystem itself or of a specification element. The relationship between interface and subsystem is not necessarily one-to-one.

The observation that a subsystem has no behavior or interface of its own except for that of its aggregated parts corresponds to Figure 1.1(b). In UML, the notation for subsystems is based on the package construct. Any of the following are correct:

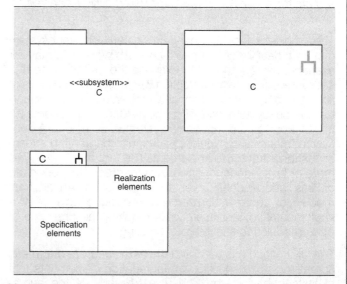

You may decide to identify subsystems in your design. If you do, make sure that your rationale explains why you chose the ones you did and what you plan to do with them.

2.2 Uses Style

2.2.1 Overview

The uses style of the module viewtype comes about when the *depends-on* relation is specialized to uses. An architect may employ this style to constrain the implementation of the architecture. This style tells developers what other modules must exist in order for their portion of the system to work correctly. This powerful style enables incremental development and the deployment of useful subsets of full systems.

2.2.2 Elements, Relations, and Properties

Table 2.2 summarizes the discussion of the characteristics of the uses style. The elements of this style are the modules as in the module viewtype. We define a specialization of the *depends-on* relation to be the *uses* relation, whereby one module requires the correct implementation of another module for its own correct functioning. This view makes explicit how the functionality is mapped to an implementation by showing relationships among the code-based elements: which elements use which other elements to achieve their functions.

FOR MORE INFORMATION

See Coming to Terms: Uses on page 68.

2.2.3 What the Uses Style Is For and What It's Not For

This style is useful for planning incremental development, system extensions and subsets, debugging and testing, and gauging the effects of specific changes.

2.2.4 Notations for the Uses Style

Informal Notations

Informally, the *uses* relation is conveniently documented as a matrix, with the modules listed as rows and columns. A mark in element (x,y) indicates that module x uses module y. The finest-grained modules in the decomposition hierarchy should be the ones listed, as fine-grained information is needed to produce incremental subsets.

Table 2.2: Summary of the module uses style

Elements	Module as defined by the module viewtype.
Relations	The *uses* relation, which is a refined form of the *depends-on* relation. Module A *uses* module B if A *depends on* the presence of a correctly functioning B in order to satisfy its own requirements.
Properties of elements	As defined by the module viewtype.
Properties of relations	The *uses* relation may have a property that describes in more detail what kind of uses one module makes of another.
Topology	The uses style has no topological constraints. However, if loops in the relation contain many elements, the ability of the architecture to be delivered in incremental subsets will be impaired.

FOR MORE INFORMATION

See Coming to Terms: Uses on page 68 for more about loops in the uses relation.

The *uses* relation can also be documented as a two-column table, with using elements on the left and the elements they use listed on the right. Alternatively, informal graphical notations can show the relation by using the usual box-and-arrow diagram with a key. For defining subsets, a tabular—that is, nongraphical—notation is preferred. It is easier to look up the detailed relations in a table than to find them in a diagram, which will rapidly grow too cluttered to be useful except in trivial cases.

UML

The uses style is easily represented in UML. The UML subsystem construct (see the graphic on page 64) can be used to represent modules; the *uses* relation is depicted as a dependency with the stereotype <<uses>>. In Figure 2.3(a), the User Interface module is an aggregate module with a uses dependency on the DataBase module. When a module is an aggregate, the decomposition requires that any *uses* relation involving the aggregate module be mapped to a submodule using that relation. In Figure 2.3(b), the User Interface module is decomposed into modules A, B, and C. At least one of

---

Figure 2.3
(a) The User Interface module is an aggregate module with a *uses* dependency on the DataBase module. We use UML Package notation to represent modules and the specialized form of *depends-on* arrow to indicate a *uses* relation.

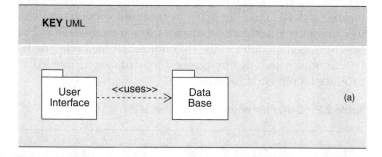

(b) Here is a variation of Figure 2.3(a) in which the User Interface module has been decomposed into modules A, B, and C.
At least one of the modules must depend on the DataBase module or the decomposition would not be consistent.

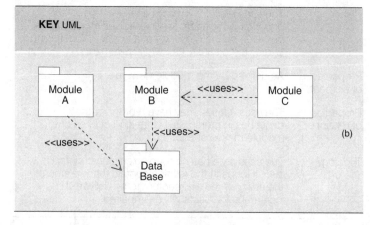

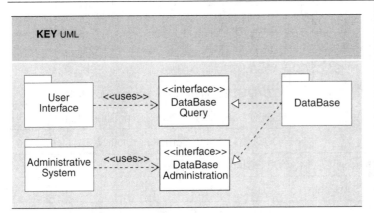

Figure 2.4
UML can be used to represent the uses view and show interfaces explicitly. Here, the DataBase module has two interfaces, which are used by the User Interface and the Administrative System modules, respectively. The lollipop notation for interfaces would also work well here.

the modules must depend on the DataBase module; otherwise, the decomposition is not consistent.

The convention for showing interfaces explicitly and separate from elements that realize them can also be shown in a uses view. In Figure 2.4, the DataBase module has two interfaces, which are used by the User Interface and the Administrative System modules, respectively.

2.2.5   Relation to Other Styles

The uses style also goes hand in hand with the layered style, with the *allowed-to-use* relation governing. An *allowed-to-use* relation usually comes first and contains coarse-grained directives defining the degrees of freedom for implementers. Once implementation choices have been made, the uses view emerges and governs the production of incremental subsets.

2.2.6   Example of the Uses Style

The following, taken from Appendix A, is a small excerpt of a uses view's primary presentation. The notation is textual, using the two-column format described earlier. Like most primary presentations, this one names only the elements; they are defined in the view's supporting documentation (not shown here).

SDPS Element			Uses This Element
Science Data Processing Segment			
	Ingest Subsystem		
		INGST CSCI	ADSRV CSCI in the Interoperability Subsystem
			STMGT CSCI in the Data Server Subsystem
			SDSRV CSCI in the Data Server Subsystem
			DCCI CSCI in the Communications Subsystem
	[etc.]		other CSCIs within the Ingest Subsystem
	Data Server Subsystem		
		DDIST CSCI	MCI CSCI in the System Management Subsystem
			DCCI CSCI in the Communications Subsystem
			STMGT CSCI in the Data Server Subsystem
			INGST CSCI in the Ingest Subsystem
	[etc.]		other CSCIs within the Data Server Subsystem
[etc.]			other subsystems within the Science Data Processing Segment

COMING TO TERMS

Uses

Two of the module viewtype styles that we present in this book—the uses style and the layered style—are based on one of the most underutilized relations in software engineering: *uses*. The *uses* relation is a special form of the *depends-on* relation. A unit of software P_1 is said to *use* another unit P_2 if P_1's correctness depends on a correct implementation of P_2 being present.

The *uses* relation resembles, but is decidedly not, the simple *calls* relation provided by most programming languages. Here's why.

- A program P_1 can use program P_2 without calling it. P_1 may assume, for example, that P_2 has left a shared device in a usable state when it finished with it. Or P_1 may expect P_2 to leave a computed result that it needs in a shared variable. Or P_1 may be a process that sleeps until P_2 signals an event to awaken it.

- A program P_1 might call program P_2 but not use it. If P_2 is an exception handler that P_1 calls when it detects an error, P_1 will usually not care what P_2 does. The following figure shows an example: P_0 calls P_1 to accomplish some work and depends on its result. (P_0 thus uses P_1.) Suppose that P_0 calls P_1 incorrectly. Part of P_1's specification is that in case of error, it calls a program whose name is passed to it by its caller.[1] Once it calls that program, P_1 has satisfied its specification. In this case, P_1 calls but does not use P_2. P_0 and P_2 may well reside in the same module, for P_2 is likely privy to the same knowledge about what was intended as P_0.

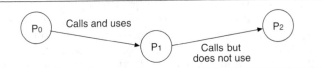

So "uses" is not "calls" or "invokes." Likewise, "uses" is different from other *depends-on* relations, such as *includes* or *inherits from*. The *includes* relation deals with compilation dependencies but need not influence runtime correctness. The *inherits-from* relation is also usually a preruntime dependency not necessarily related to uses.

The *uses* relation imparts a powerful capability to a development team: It enables the building of small subsets of a total system. Early in the project, this allows incremental development, a development paradigm that allows early prototyping, early integration, and early testing. At every step along the way, the system carries out part of its total functionality, even if far from everything, and does it correctly. Fred Brooks (1995) writes about the "electrifying effect" on team morale that is caused by seeing the system first succeed at doing something. Absent incremental development, nothing works until everything works, and we are reduced to the somewhat eschewed waterfall model of development. Subsets of the total system are also useful beyond development. They provide a safe fallback in the event of slipped schedules: It is much better for the project manager to offer the customer a working subset of the system at delivery time rather than apologies and promises. And a subset of the total system can often be sold and marketed as a downscaled product in its own right.

Here's how it works. Choose a program that is to be in a subset; call it P_1. In order for P_1 to work correctly in this subset, correct implementations of the programs it uses must also be present. So include them in the subset. For them to work correctly, their used programs must also be present, and so forth. The subset consists of the transitive closure of

1. Or perhaps it calls a program whose name was bound by a parameter at system-generation time or a program whose name it looks up via a name server. Many schemes are possible.

P_1's uses.[2] Conceptually, you pluck P_1 out from the uses graph and then see what programs come dangling beneath it. There's your subset.

The most well-behaved *uses* relation forms a hierarchy: a tree structure. Subsets are then defined by snipping off sub-trees. But architecture is seldom that simple, and the *uses* relation most often forms a nontree graph. Loops in the relation—that is, for example, where P_1 uses P_2, P_2 uses P_3, and P_3 uses P_1—are the enemy of simple subsets. A large *uses* loop necessitates bringing in a large number of programs—every member of the loop—into any subset joined by any member. "Bringing in a program" means, of course, that it must be implemented, debugged, integrated, and tested. But the point of incremental development is that you'd like to bring in a small number of programs to each new increment, and you'd like to be able to choose which ones you bring in and not have them choose themselves.

A technique for breaking loops in the *uses* relation is called sandwiching. It works by finding a program in the loop whose functionality is a good candidate for splitting in half. Say that program P_4 is in a *uses* loop. We break program P_4 into two new programs, P_{4A} and P_{4B}. We implement them in such a way so that

- They do not use each other directly.
- The programs that used to use P_4 now use only P_{4A}.
- P_{4A} does not use any of the programs that the former P_4 used, but P_{4B} does.

This breaks the loop:

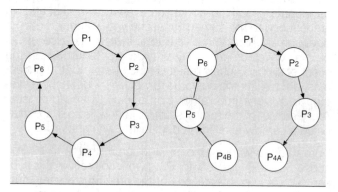

2. Of course, *calls* and other *depends-on* relations must be given their due. If a program in the subset calls, includes, or inherits from another program but doesn't use it, the compiler is still going to expect that program to be present. But if it isn't *used,* there need not be a correct implementation of it: a simple stub, possibly returning a pro forma result, will do just fine.

In the figure on the left, if any element is a member of a subset, they all must be. In the figure on the right, P_4 has been divided into two parts that do not use each other directly. Now, including, say, P_2 in a subset necessitates inclusion of only a small number of additional elements. If P_{4B} is desired in a subset, the situation is as before. But we could use sandwiching again on, say, P_6 to shorten the uses chain.

Besides managing subsets, the *uses* relation is also a useful tool for debugging and integration testing. If you discover a program that's producing incorrect results, the problem is going to be either in the program itself or in the programs that it uses. The *uses* relation lets you instantly narrow the list of suspects. In a similar way, you can employ the relation to help you gauge the effects of proposed changes. If a program's external behavior changes as the result of a planned modification, you can backtrack through the *uses* relation to see what other programs may be affected by that modification.

As originally defined by Parnas (1979), the *uses* relation was a relation among "programs" or other relatively fine-grained units of functionality. The modern analog would be methods of an object. Parnas wrote that the *uses* relation was "conveniently documented as a binary matrix," where element (i,j) is *true* if and only if program i uses program j.

As with many relations, there are shorthand forms for documenting uses; a complete enumeration of the ordered pairs is not necessary. For example, if a group of programs made up of module A use another group of programs made up of module B, we can say that module A uses module B. We can also say A uses B if *some* programs in A use *some* programs in B, as long as you don't mind bringing in all of module B to any subset joined by any program of module A. This makes sense if module B is already implemented and ready to go, is indivisible—maybe it's a COTS product—or if its functionality is so intertwined that B cannot be teased apart. The main point about size is that the more finely grained your *uses* relation, the more control you have over the subsets you can field and the debugging information you can infer.

2.3 Generalization Style

2.3.1 Overview

The generalization style of the module viewtype comes about when the *is-a* relation is specialized to generalization. This style comes in handy when an architect wants to support extension and evolution of architectures and individual elements.

FOR MORE INFORMATION

See Coming to Terms: Generalization on page 76.

Modules in this style are defined in such a way that they capture commonalities and variations. When modules have a generalization relationship, the parent module is a more general version of the children modules. (Even though this style shares the terms *parent* and *child* with the decomposition style, they are used differently. In decomposition, a parent consists of its children. In generalization, parents and children have things in common.) The parent module owns the commonalities, and the variations are manifested in the children. Extensions can be made by adding, removing, or changing children; a change to the parent will automatically change all the children that inherit from it, which would support evolution.

Generalization implies inheritance of both interface and implementation. The child inherits structure, behavior, and constraints from its parent. Within an architectural description, the emphasis is on sharing and reusing interfaces and not so much on implementations.

2.3.2 Elements, Relations, and Properties

Table 2.3 summarizes the discussion of the characteristics of the generalization style. The element of the module generalization style is the module as defined by the module viewtype. We define a specialization of the *is-a* relation to be the *generalization* relation, whereby one module is a specialization of another module, and the second is a generalization of the first.

Table 2.3: Summary of the module generalization style

Elements	*Module,* as defined by the module viewtype.
Relations	*Generalization,* which is the *is-a* relation as in the module viewtype.
Properties of elements	Besides the properties defined for a module in the module viewtype, a module can have the "abstract" property, which defines a module with interfaces but no implementation.
Properties of relations	The *generalization* relation can have a property that distinguishes between interface and implementation inheritance. If a module is defined as an abstract module—the abstract property—restricting the *generalization* relation to implementation inheritance is not meaningful.
Topology	• A module can have multiple parents, although multiple inheritance is often considered a dangerous design approach.

Table 2.3: Summary of the module generalization style (continued)

Topology (cont.)	• Cycles in the *generalization* relation are not allowed; that is, a child module cannot be a generalization of one or more of its parent modules in a view.

A module can be an abstract module. Such a module defines its interfaces but does not have an implementation, at least not an implementation that is executable on its own. Child modules that comply with the parent's interface provide the necessary implementations.

In the transitive closure of the generalization relation, a module that inherits information is referred to as a descendant; the module providing the information is an ancestor. Cycles are not allowed. That is, a module can not be an ancestor or a descendant of itself.

The generalization relation can be used in several ways to implement various strategies. The fact that module A inherits from module B using **interface inheritance** is a promise that module A complies to at least the public interface from B. Module A may also inherit and use behavior implemented by module B, but this is not defined by this type of inheritance. This strategy is useful when variants of a module with different implementations are needed and one implementation of the module can substitute for another implementation with little or no effect on other modules.

With **implementation inheritance**, a module inherits behavior from its ancestors and modifies it to achieve its specialized behavior. The use of the generalization relation for implementation inheritance does not guarantee that the child module complies with the interfaces of the parent module; therefore, substitutability may be violated.

> **DEFINITION**
>
> **Interface inheritance**—the definition of a new interface based on one or more previously defined interfaces. The new interface is usually a subset of the ancestors' interface(s).

> **DEFINITION**
>
> **Implementation inheritance**—the definition of a new implementation based on one or more previously defined implementations. The new implementation is usually a modification of the ancestors' behavior.

2.3.3 What the Generalization Style Is For and What It's Not For

The generalization style can be used to support

- *Object-oriented designs.* The generalization style is the predominant means for expressing an inheritance-based object-oriented design for a system.
- *Extension and evolution.* It is often easier to understand how one module differs from another, well-known module rather than to try to understand a new module from scratch. Thus, generalization is a mechanism for producing incremental descriptions to form a full description of a module.

- *Local change or variation.* One purpose of architecture is to provide a stable global structure that accommodates local change or variation. Generalization is one approach to define commonalities on a higher level and to define variations as children of a module.

- *Reuse.* Finding reusable modules is a by-product of the other purposes. Suitable abstractions can be reused at the interface level alone, or the implementation can be included as well. The definition of abstract modules creates an opportunity for reuse.

2.3.4   Notations for the Generalization Style

UML

Expressing generalization lies at the heart of UML. Modules are shown as classes, although they may also be shown as subsystems, as discussed in the decomposition style. Figure 2.5 shows the basic notation available in UML. Figure 2.6 shows how UML expresses interface and implementation inheritance. Figure 2.7 shows how UML represents multiple inheritance.

2.3.5   Relation to Other Styles

Inheritance relationships complement the other module viewtype relations. For complex designs, it is useful to show inheritance relationships in a diagram separate from other types of relationships, such as decomposition.

Figure 2.5
UML provides two line styles to show generalization. These two diagrams are semantically identical. UML allows an ellipsis (…) in place of a submodule, indicating that a module can have more children than shown and that additional ones are likely. Module Shape is the parent of modules Polygon, Circle, and Spline, each of which is in turn a subclass, child, or descendant of Shape. Shape is more general; its children are specialized versions. Therefore, the arrow points toward the more general entity.

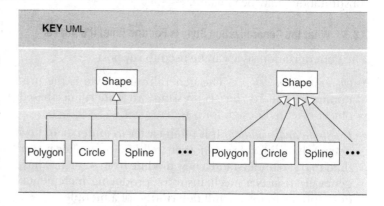

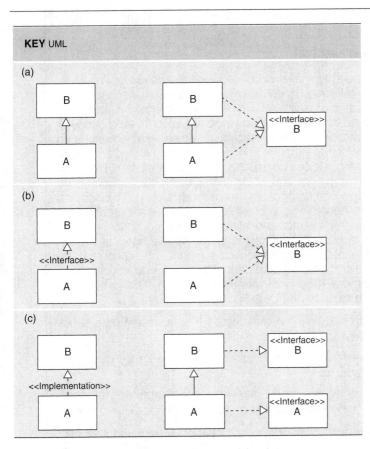

Figure 2.6
UML shows interface and implementation inheritance in different ways. As this figure shows, the graphics must be enhanced with textual annotations to indicate whether it is the interface or implementation that is inherited. The graphical expression of UML is not powerful enough to differentiate. For example, in diagram (a) the generalization relation with properties shown on the left side usually means what is indicated on the right side; module A inherits the implementation of module B and realizes the same interface as module B. Whereas in diagram (b), generalization using interface inheritance indicated by the «interface» textual annotation usually means what is indicated on the right side: module A realizes the same interface as module B. Finally, in diagram (c), generalization using implementation inheritance indicated by the «implementation» textual annotation usually means module A inherits the implementation of module B but realizes its own interface.

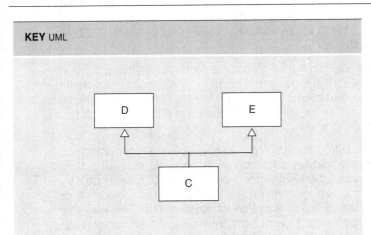

Figure 2.7
Showing multiple inheritance graphically in UML is cumbersome. As with single interface and implementation inheritance, UML's graphical notation lacks expressive power to adequately describe what is inherited. So without additional textual annotations the graphic may be ambiguous. In this figure, module C is supposed to be a subclass/child/descendant of modules D and E, which means modules D and E are parents of module C.

COMING TO TERMS

Generalization

Although typically associated with the generalization style, the notion of inheritance is also a useful technique for imposing organizational structure on other architectural elements. Inheritance relationships are used in descriptions of metamodels, styles, patterns, frameworks, or reference models more than in the description of a single system. Metamodels can be used to describe the element hierarchy in viewtypes or styles, for example. An element can be a module or a component, and a module can be a class or a layer. Accordingly, a class *is-a* module *is-a* element. Patterns, frameworks, and reference models describe a collection of elements and relations that appear again and again in the descriptions of various systems. Inheritance can be used in the architecture pattern itself. For example, examine the model-view-controller (MVC) pattern. This pattern has three pieces:

1. model, which is the classes that represent data structure and behavior;
2. view, which is the classes that represent the user interface; and,
3. controller, which is the classes that represent the communication mechanism between the model and view.

There are observer elements, between view and controller classes, that keep the user views up-to-date with changes in the model. View and controller elements may inherit from observer elements so they (view and controller) are notified of events of interest. The user of the MVC pattern may also use inheritance to specialize the elements of the particular application.

Viewed in this way, inheritance introduces the notions of architectural types and subtyping. The subtype relationship is used to evolve a given type to satisfy new requirements. This promotes off-the-shelf reuse and analysis through type checking and conformance.

UML refers to this organizing principle as *generalization,* making the distinction between generalization as a taxonomic relationship among elements and inheritance as a mechanism for combining shared incremental descriptions to form a full description of an element. Generalization implies inheritance of both interface and implementation. The child inherits structure, behavior, and constraints from its parent.

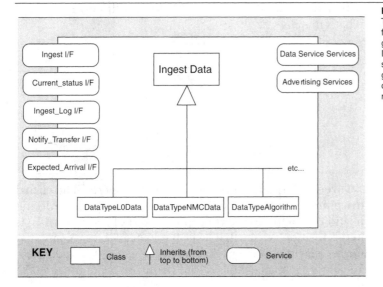

Figure 2.8
The primary presentation for part of an ECS module generalization view. The Ingest Data subsystem is shown as a class that is a generalization of a number of classes and provides a number of services.

2.3.6 Examples of the Generalization Style

Figure 2.8 shows part of the module generalization view from the ECS system of Appendix A.

2.4 Layered Style

2.4.1 Overview

Layering, like all module styles, reflects a division of the software into units. In this case, the units are layers; each layer represents a **virtual machine**. Furthermore, there are constraints on the relationship among the virtual machines. The layered view of architecture, shown with a layer diagram, is one of the most commonly used views in software architecture, is poorly defined, and is often misunderstood. Because true layered systems have good properties of modifiability and portability, architects have an incentive to show their systems as layered, even if they are not.

Layers completely partition a set of software, and each partition constitutes a virtual machine—with a public interface—that provides a cohesive set of services. But that's not all. The following figure, which is intentionally vague about what the units are and how they interact, shows three divisions of software—and you'll have to take our word that each division is a

DEFINITION

A **virtual machine** is an abstract computing device; typically, it is a program that acts as an interface between other software and actual hardware (or another virtual machine).

virtual machine—but none of them constitutes a layering. What's missing?

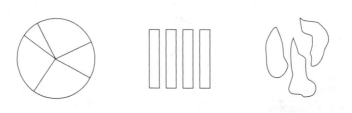

Layering has one more fundamental property: The virtual machines are created to interact according to a strict ordering relation. Herein lies the conceptual heart of layers. If (A,B) is in this relation, we say that layer B is beneath layer A, and that means that the implementation of layer A is allowed to use any of the public facilities of the virtual machine provided by layer B.

By **use** and **used**, we mean something very specific, but the definition has some loopholes. If A is implemented using the facilities in B, is it implemented using *only* B? Maybe or maybe not. Some layering schemes allow a layer to use the public facilities of *any* lower layer, not just the nearest lower layer. Other layering schemes have so-called layers that are collections of utilities and can be used by any layer. *But no architecture that can be validly called layered allows a layer to use, without restriction, the facilities of a higher layer.* Allowing unrestricted upward usage destroys the desirable properties that layering brings to an architecture; this will be discussed shortly. Usage in layers generally flows downward. A small number of well-defined special cases may be permitted, but these should be few and regarded as exceptions to the rule. Hence, the following architectural view *resembles* a layering *but is not*:

> **DEFINITION**
>
> Element A is said to **use** element B if A's correctness depends on a correct implementation of B being present.

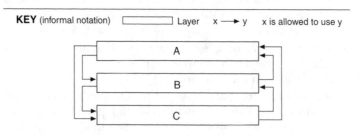

Figures like the preceding show why layers have been a source of ambiguity for so long, for architects have been calling such diagrams layered when they are not. There is more to layers than the ability to draw separate parts on top of each other.

In many layered systems, modules of a lower layer will sometimes have to use—and therefore must be *allowed to use*—modules in a higher layer, and these usages will have to be accommodated by the architecture. In other cases, modules in a very high layer might be required to directly use modules in a very low layer where normally only next-lower-layer uses are allowed. The layer diagram or an accompanying document will have to show these exceptions. The case of software in a higher layer using modules in a lower but not the next-lower layer is called *layer bridging*. If many of these are present, the system is poorly structured, at least with respect to the portability and modifiability goals that layering helps to achieve. Systems with upward usages are not, strictly according to the definition, layered. However, in such cases, the layered style represents a close approximation to reality and also conveys the ideal design that the architect was trying to achieve.

Layers are intended to provide a virtual machine, and one use of a virtual machine is to promote portability. For this reason, it is important to scrutinize the interface of a layer to ensure that portability concerns are addressed. The interface should not expose functions that are dependent on a particular platform; these functions should be hidden behind a more abstract interface that is independent of platform.

FOR MORE INFORMATION

See Coming to Terms: Virtual Machines on page 93.

Because the ordering relationship among layers has to do with "implementation allowed to use," the lower the layer, the fewer the facilities available to it. That is, the "worldview" of lower layers tends to be smaller and more focused on the computing platforms. Lower layers tend to be built using knowledge of the computers, communications channels, distribution mechanisms, process dispatchers, and the like. These areas of expertise are largely independent of the particular application that runs on them, meaning that they will not need to be modified if the application changes. Conversely, higher layers tend to be more independent of the platform; they can afford to be, because the existence of the lower layers has given them that freedom. The higher layers can afford to be more concerned only with details of the application.

Layers cannot be derived by examining source code. The source code may disclose what uses what, but the relation in layers is *allowed to use*. As a trivial example, you can tell by code inspection that a "double" operation was implemented using multiplication by 2, but you cannot tell from the code whether

- It would have been equally acceptable to implement double(x) by adding x to itself or by performing a binary left shift—that is, what double(x) was allowed to use

- Addition, double, and multiplication are in the same or different layers

A layer may provide services that are not used by other modules. This occurs when the layer was designed to be more general than is strictly necessary for the application in which it finds itself. This in turn often occurs when the layer is imported from another application, purchased as a commercial product, or designed to be used for subsequent applications. This result, of course, can occur in styles other than the layered style.

2.4.2 Elements, Relations, and Properties

Table 2.4 summarizes the discussion of the characteristics of the layered style.

Table 2.4: Overview of the layered style

Elements	Layers.
Relations	*Allowed to use,* which is a specialization of the module viewtype's generic *depends-on* relation. P_1 is said to use P_2 if P_1's correctness depends on a correct implementation of P_2 being present.
Properties of elements	• Name of layer.
	• The units of software the layer contains.
	• The software a layer is allowed to use. This property is documented in two parts. The first part gives the inter- and intra-layer usage rules; such as "a layer is allowed to use software in any lower layer," and "software is not allowed to use other software in the same layer." The second part names any allowable exceptions to those rules.
	• The cohesion of the layer: a description of the virtual machine represented by the layer.
Properties of relations	As for the module viewtype.
Topology	If layer A is above layer B, then layer B cannot be above layer A. Every piece of software is allocated to exactly one layer.

Elements

The elements of a layered diagram are *layers*. A layer is a cohesive collection of modules, each of which may be invoked or accessed. Each layer should represent a virtual machine. This definition admits many possibilities: from classes to assembly language subroutines to shared data. A requirement is that the units have an interface by which their services can be triggered or initiated or accessed.

Relations

The relation among layers is *allowed to use*. For two layers having this relation, any module in the first is allowed to use any module in the second. Module A is said to *use* module B if A's correctness depends on B being correct and present.

The endgame of a layer diagram is to define the binary relation *allowed to use* among modules. Just as $y = f(x)$ is mathematical shorthand for enumerating all the ordered pairs that are in the function f, a layer diagram is notational shorthand for enumerating all the ordered pairs (A,B) such that A is allowed to use B. A clean layer diagram is a sign of a well-structured relation; a layer diagram that is not clean will be rife with exceptions and appear chaotic.

Properties

Layers have the following properties, which should be documented in the element catalog accompanying the layer diagram.

- *Name:* Each layer is given a name.
- *Contents:* The catalog for a layer's view lists the software units contained by each layer. This document assigns each module to exactly one layer. Layers typically have labels that are descriptive but vague, such as "network communications layer" or "business rules layer"; a catalog is needed that lists the complete contents of every layer.
- *The software a layer is allowed to use:* Is a layer allowed to use only the layer below, any lower layer, or some other? Are modules in a layer permitted to use other modules in the same layer? This part of the documentation must also explain exceptions, if any, to the usage rules implied by the geometry. Exceptions may be upward, allowing something in a lower layer to use something above, or downward, either prohibiting a specific usage otherwise allowed by the geometry or allowing downward usage that "skips" intermediate layers normally required. Exceptions should be precisely described.
- *Cohesion:* An explanation is required of how the layer provides a functionally cohesive virtual machine. A layer provides a cohesive set of services, meaning that the services as a group would likely be useful as a group in a context other than the one in which they were developed.

> **FOR MORE INFORMATION**
> Element catalogs are described in Section 10.1.

> **FOR MORE INFORMATION**
> See Perspectives: Upwardly Mobile Software on page 94.

Suppose that module P_1 is allowed to use module P_2. Should P_2 be in a lower layer than P_1, or should they be in the same layer? Layers are not a function of just who uses what, but are the result of a conscious design decision that allocates modules to layers, based on such considerations as coupling, cohesion, and the likelihood of changes. In general, P_1 and P_2 should be in the same layer if they are likely to be ported to a new application together or if together they provide different aspects of the same virtual machine to a usage community.

The preceding is an operational definition of cohesion. The cohesion explanation can also serve as a *portability guide*, describing the changes that can be made to each layer without affecting other layers.

2.4.3 What the Layered Style Is For and What It's Not For

Layers help to bring quality attributes of modifiability and portability to a software system. A layer is an application of the principle of information hiding: in this case, the virtual machine. The theory is that a change to a lower layer can be hidden behind its interface and will not impact the layers above it. As with all such theories, both truth and caveats are associated with it. The truth is that this technique has been used with great success to support portability. Machine, operating system, or other low-level dependencies are hidden within a layer; as long as the interface for the layer does not change, the upper levels that depend only on the interface will work successfully.

FOR MORE INFORMATION

See Coming to Terms: Signature, Interface API on page 245.

The caveat is that *interface* means more than just the API (application programming interface) containing program signatures. An interface embodies *all* the assumptions that an external entity—in this case, a layer—may make. Changes in a lower layer that affect, say, a performance assumption will leak through its interface and may affect a higher layer.

A common misconception is that layers introduce additional runtime overhead. Although this may be true for naive implementations, sophisticated compile/link/load facilities can reduce additional overhead.

We have already mentioned that in some contexts, a layer may contain unused services. These unused services may needlessly consume a runtime resource, such as memory to store the unused code or a thread that is never launched. If these resources are in short supply, a sophisticated compile/link/load facility that eliminates unused code will be helpful.

Layers are part of the blueprint role that architecture plays for constructing the system. Knowing the layers in which their software resides, developers know what services they can rely on in the coding environment. Layers might define work assignments for development teams, although not always.

Layers are part of the communication role played by architecture. In a large system, the number of modules and the dependencies among them rapidly expand. Organizing the modules into layers with interfaces is an important tool for managing complexity and communicating the structure to developers.

Finally, layers help with the analysis role played by architecture. They support the analysis of the impact of changes to the design by enabling some determination of the scope of changes.

2.4.4 Notations for the Layered Style

Informal Notations

Stack
Layers are almost always drawn as a stack of rectangles. The *allowed-to-use* relation is denoted by geometric adjacency and is read from the top down, like this:

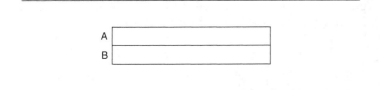

Layering is thus one of the few architectural styles in which connection among components is shown by geometric adjacency and not an explicit symbology, such as an arrow, although arrows can be used, like this:

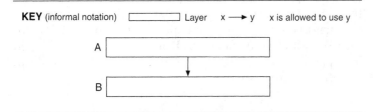

Segmented Layers
Sometimes layers are divided into segments denoting a finer-grained aggregation of the modules. Often, this occurs when a preexisting set of units, such as imported components or

components from separate teams, share the same *allowed-to-use* relation. When this happens, it is incumbent on the creator of the diagram to specify what usage rules are in effect among the segments. Many usage rules are possible, but they must be made explicit. Segmented layers essentially make the *allowed-to-use* relation a partial ordering of the elements. The following diagram specifies that A is allowed to use B and C, which are in turn allowed to use D *and each other.*

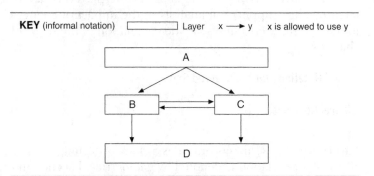

From the strict point of view of layers, the preceding diagram is completely equivalent to the following, where layer BC is the union of the contents of layers B and C:

A
BC
D

The *allowed-to-use* relation depicted by the two diagrams is the same. The decomposition of the middle layer into B and C brings to the diagram additional information that has nothing to do with layering; perhaps B and C have been developed by separate teams or represent separate modules or will run on different processors.

Rings

The most common notational variation is to show layers as a set of concentric circles, or rings. The innermost ring corresponds to the lowest layer; the outermost ring, the highest layer. A ring may be subdivided into sectors, meaning the same thing as the corresponding layer being subdivided into parts.

There is no semantic difference between a layer diagram that uses a stack of rectangles and one that uses rings paradigm, except when segmented layers have restrictions on the *allowed-to-use* relation within the layer. We now discuss this special case.

In the following figure, assume that ring segments that touch are allowed to use one another and that layer segments that touch are allowed to use one another.

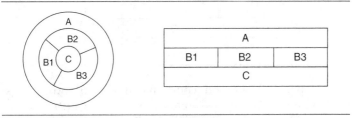

There is no way to "unfold" the ring diagram to produce a stack diagram, such as the one on the right, with exactly the same meaning, because circular arrangements allow more adjacencies than do linear arrangements. (In the layer diagram, B1 and B3 are separate; in the ring diagram they are adjacent. Cases like this are the only ones in which a ring diagram can show a geometric adjacency that a stack picture cannot.

Segmented Layers, 3-D Toaster Models
Sometimes, layers are shown as three-dimensional models to emphasize that segments in one or more layers can be easily replaced or interchanged. Sometimes these are called *toaster models* because the interchangeable pieces are shown in the shape and orientation of pieces of bread dropped into slots, as in a toaster:

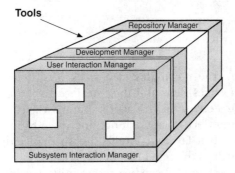

Layers with a Sidecar
Many architectures called *layered* look something like the following:

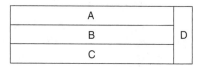

This type of notation could mean one of two things: (1) Modules in D can use modules in A, B, or C. (2) Modules in A, B, or C can use modules in D. (Technically, the diagram might mean that both are true, although this would arguably be a poor layered architecture.) It is incumbent on the creator of the diagram to specify which usage rules pertain. A variation like this makes sense only for single-level usage rules in the main stack, that is, when A can use only B and nothing below. Otherwise, D could simply be made the topmost—or bottommost, depending on the case—layer in the main stack, and the "sidecar" geometry would be unnecessary.

Contents
The modules that constitute a layer can be shown graphically, as follows:

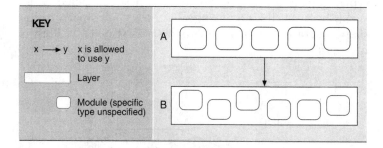

Interfaces
Sometimes, the rectangles in a stack are shown with thick horizontal edges denoting the interface to the layer. This is intended to convey the restriction that interlayer usage occurs only via interface facilities and not directly to any layer's "internals." If a layer's contents are so depicted, a lollipop scheme, such as the one in Figure 2.9, which is similar to Figure 1.1(b) on page 45, can be used to indicate which modules' interfaces make up the interface to the layer.

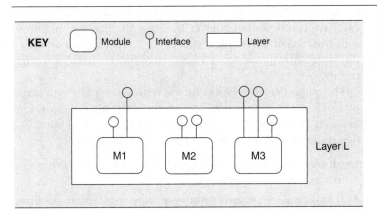

Figure 2.9
Notation to show which
interfaces of which internal
modules constitute the
interfaces of layers

Size and Color

Sometimes, layers are colored to denote which team is responsible for them or to denote another distinguishing feature. Size is sometimes used to give a vague idea of the relative size of the modules constituting the various layers. If they carry meaning, size and color should be explained in the key accompanying the layer diagram.

UML

Sadly, UML has no built-in primitive corresponding to a layer. However, nonsegmented layers can be represented in UML using *packages,* as shown in Figure 2.10. A package is a general-purpose mechanism for organizing elements into groups. UML has predefined kinds of packages for systems and subsystems. We can introduce an additional package for layers by defining it as a stereotype of package. A layer can be shown as a UML

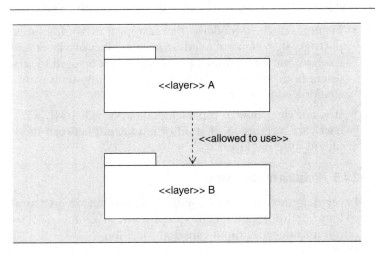

Figure 2.10
A simple representation of
layers in UML

package with the dependency between packages "allowed to use." We can designate a layer by using the package notation, with the stereotype name <<layer>> preceding the name of the layer or by introducing a new visual form, such as a shaded rectangle.

The *allowed-to-use* relation can be represented as a stereotype of UML *access dependency,* one of the existing dependencies between packages. This dependency permits the elements of one package to reference the elements of another package.

- An element within a package is allowed to access other elements within the package.

- If a package accesses another package, all elements defined with public visibility in the accessed package are visible within the importing package.

- Access dependencies are not transitive. If package 1 can access package 2 and package 2 can access package 3, it does not automatically follow that package 1 can access package 3.

If the *allowed-to-use* relation is loop free, you may wish to add the additional constraint that the defined dependency is antisymmetric. This dependency stipulates that if A is allowed to use B, we know that B is not allowed to use A.

UML's mechanism to define the visibility of classes and packages can be used to define the interface to a layer. The mechanism is to prefix the name of the package with + for public—which is the default—# for protected, and – for not visible outside the package. By appropriate tagging, then, we can define a layer's interface to be a subset of the interfaces of its elements.

Figure 2.11 shows alternatives for representing segmented layers in UML. Architects should be aware of the following problems when using UML packages to represent layers:

FOR MORE INFORMATION

Callbacks are discussed in Perspectives: Upwardly Mobile Software on page 94.

- Elements can be owned by—that is, appear in—only a single package. If an element needs to be a member of a layer and a subsystem, for example, packages cannot be used to represent both; recall that UML represents subsystems with a stereotyped package.

- It is not clear how to represent callbacks with UML. Callbacks are a common method of interaction between modules in different layers.

2.4.5 Relation to Other Styles

Layer diagrams are often confused with other architectural styles when information orthogonal to the *allowed-to-use* relation is introduced without conscious decision.

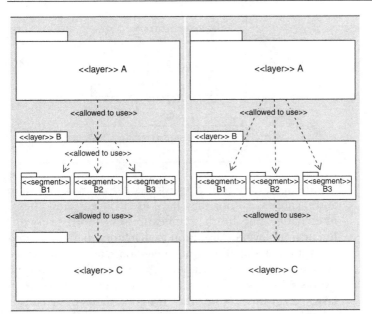

Figure 2.11
Documenting segmented layers in UML. The segments must be explicitly included in the dependencies. If segments in a layer are allowed to use each other, then <<allowed to use>> dependencies must be added among them as well (not shown). The two alternatives shown in this figure are equivalent.

1. *Module decomposition:* There is a tendency to regard layers as identical to modules in a decomposition view. A layer may in fact be a module, but it is not necessarily always so. One reason this one-to-one mapping often fails is that modules are decomposed into other modules, whereas layers are not decomposed into smaller layers. Segmented layers are often introduced to show mappings to modules. If a module spans layers, colors or fill patterns are often used (see Figure 2.12).

   In this example, once again borrowing from the A-7E architecture described previously, the mapping between layers and modules is not one-to-one. In this architecture, the criterion for partitioning into modules was the encapsulation of likely changes. The shading of the elements denotes the coarsest-grain decomposition of the system into modules; that is, Function Driver and Shared Services are both submodules of the behavior-hiding module. Hence, in this system, layers correspond to parts of highest-level modules. It's also easy to imagine a case in which a module constitutes a part of a layer.

2. *Tiers:* Layers are often confused with the tiers in an *n*-tier client-server architecture, such as is shown in the following figure:

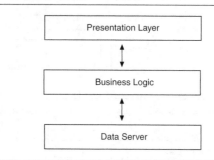

Although the figure above looks like a layer diagram, and a careless author may have used "layers" and "tiers" interchangeably, this diagram expresses concerns very different from layers. Allocation to machines in a distributed environment, data flow among elements, and the presence and use of communication channels all tend to be expressed in tier pictures, and these are indiscernible in layer diagrams. Note the two-way arrows. Whatever relations are being expressed here—and as always, a key should tell us—they're bidirectional, or symmetric, and we know that's bad news in a layer diagram. Further, assignment of a module to one of these elements is based on runtime efficiency: locality of processing, maintaining the ability to do useful work in case of network or server failure, not overloading the server, wise use of network band-

Figure 2.12
A diagram showing layers and modules from a decomposition view

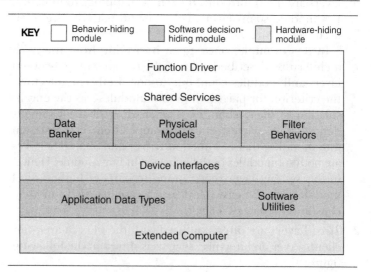

width, and so on. In contrast, layers are about the ease of making changes and building subsets.

Layers are not tiers, which in fact belong in a hybrid view combining styles in the component-and-connector and allocation viewtypes. Even in an architecture in which layers and tiers have a one-to-one correspondence, you should still plan on documenting them separately, as they serve different concerns.

3. *Module "uses" style:* Because layers express the *allowed-to-use* relation, there is a close correspondence to the uses style. It is likely, but not always the case, that if an architect chooses to include one style in the documentation suite, the other style will be included as well. Of course, no *uses* relation is allowed to violate the *allowed-to-use* relation. If incremental development or the fielding of subsets is a goal, the architect will begin with a broad *allowed-to-use* specification to guide the developers during implementation. That specification should permit any subset of interest to be built efficiently and without having to include scores of superfluous programs. Later, actual uses can be documented.

4. *Subsystems:* Layers cross conceptual paths with the concept of *subsystem*. The air traffic control system shown on page 63 was depicted using a segmented layers diagram; we reproduce it here, adding layer labels:

Position Display	Collision Avoidance	Simulation	Recording & Playback	Monitoring	Subsystem Layer
Display Generation			Workstation Scheduler		Application Support Layer
Network Communications					Communications Layer
Operating System					Platform Layer

In this context, a subsystem consists of a segment from the top layer and any segments of any lower layers it's allowed to use.

2.4.6 Examples of the Layered Style

Figure 2.13 shows the primary presentation of a layered view from the NASA ECS system. The use of the layered approach allows for the design of the application architecture independently of the communication architecture. The ECS system architecture is layered, in that higher-layer services are allowed

FOR MORE INFORMATION

Section 6.3.5 shows how the classic *n*-tier client-server architecture can be an example of a hybrid style.

FOR MORE INFORMATION

The uses style is covered in Section 2.2.

FOR MORE INFORMATION

See Coming to Terms: Subsystem on page 62.

Figure 2.13
A layered view from the ECS system documented in Appendix A. Here, software in a layer is allowed to use software in any layer it touches from above. For example, software in the Application Domain layer is allowed to use software in the Datalink/Physical layer but is not allowed to use software in the Network layer. Such rules of interpretation need to be explained in supporting documentation.

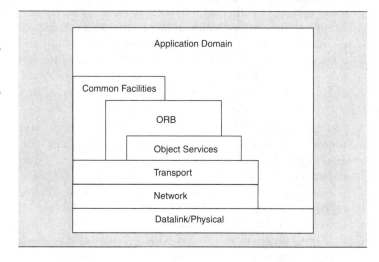

to use services in the layers below. Each layer can be thought of as an aggregation of services that form a specific service-layer class. These classes are evolving around market-driven segmentation, such as flight operations segment (FOS) and science data processing segment (SDPS). The segmentations are being grouped around the user disciplines most likely to use the services. This coupling of technical service descriptions with market-driven forces helps to encourage vendor devel–opment of products based on these services in specific horizontal or vertical market segments. The ECS architecture will be able to take advantage of all these points during the design process, including, but not limited to, standards and COTS selection.

The application domain layer contains all the subsystems' services of two out of the three segments in which the ECS is decomposed: FOS and SDPS. Three service classes are shown in the three intermediate layers of Figure 2.13: the object services, the object request broker (ORB) [OMG 93], and the common facility. From an OSI [ISO 93] perspective, these service classes could be related to layers 5 to 7: the session, presentation, and application layers, respectively. These three layers constitute the communication subsystem. The set of services within this subsystem are functionally dependent on the services provided by the internetworking subsystem. The set of services provided by these layers are the fundamental communications interfaces for the FOS and the SDPS.

The lowermost three layers are the physical/datalink, network, and transport layers. These system components are part of the internetworking subsystem. The services provided by the internetworking subsystem are functionally independent of any other services outside themselves. The transport services rely solely on the network services that, in turn, rely on the datalink/physical services.

Virtual Machines

A virtual machine, sometimes called an *abstract machine,* is a collection of modules that together provide a cohesive set of services that other modules can use without knowing how those services are implemented. C++ is a programming language that meets this definition: Although the ultimate result is machine code that executes on one or more processors somewhere, we regard the instruction set provided by the language as the ultimate lingua franca of our program. We forget, happily, that without other virtual machines underneath C++—the operating system, the microcode, the hardware—our program would be a collection of alphanumeric characters that wouldn't do anything.

Any module that has a public interface provides a set of services but does not necessarily constitute a virtual machine. The set of services must be *cohesive* with respect to a criterion. The services might all appeal to a particular area of expertise, such as mathematics or network communication. Or they might be native to an application area, such as maintaining bank accounts or navigating an aircraft. The goal of layering is to define virtual machines that are small enough to be well understood but comprehensive enough so that the number of layers is intellectually manageable. Some of the criteria used in defining the layers of a system are an expectation that they will evolve independently on different time scales, that different people with different sets of skills will work on different layers, and that different levels of reuse are expected of the different layers.

A program divided into a set of subprograms may be said to be hierarchically structured, when the relation "uses" defines levels.... The term "abstract machine" is commonly used, because the relation between the lower level programs and the higher level programs is analogous to the relation between hardware and software.

—D. L. Parnas (1974, p. 337)

Upwardly Mobile Software

We have been downright pedantic about saying that upward uses invalidate layering. We made allowances for documented exceptions but implied that too many of those would get you barred from the Software Architect's Hall of Fame.

Seasoned designers, however, know that in many elegantly designed layered systems, all kinds of control and information flow upward along the chain of layers, with no loss of portability, reusability, modifiability, or any of the other qualities associated with layers. In fact, one of the purposes of layers is to allow for the "bubbling up" of information to the units of software whose scope makes them the appropriate handlers of the information.

Error handling exemplifies this upward flow. The idea behind the now classic stack-based error propagation scheme, is that the software that caused the error is the best place to handle the error, because the scope and the information are available there to do so. When a layer is ported to another application or environment, not only the functionality transfers but also the ability to handle any errors that might be precipitated by that functionality. It makes a nice matching set.

Suppose that we have a simple three-layer system:

| A |
| B |
| C |

Say that program Pa in A uses program Pb in B, which uses program Pc in C. If Pc is called in a way that violates its specification, Pc needs a way to tell Pb, "Hey! You called me incorrectly!" At that point, (1) Pb can either recognize its own mistake and call Pc again, this time correctly, or take another action; or (2), Pb can realize that the error resulted because it was called incorrectly—perhaps sent bad data—by Pa. In the latter case, Pb needs a way to tell Pa, "Hey! You called me incorrectly!"

Callbacks are a mechanism to manifest the protestation. We do not want Pc written with knowledge about programs in B or Pb written with knowledge about programs in A, as this would limit the portability of layers C and B. Therefore,

...upon detecting a UE [undesired event, or error] in a hierarchically structured piece of software, the UE is first reflected and control passed to the level where it originated. At this point it is either corrected or reflected still higher.... At every level, either recovery is attempted or the UE is reported still higher.

D. L. Parnas and
H. Wuerges (2001)

the names of higher-level programs to call in case of error are passed downward as data. Then the specification for, say, Pb includes the promise that in case of error, it will invoke the program whose name has been made available to it.

So there we have it: data and control flowing downward *and upward* in an elegant error-handling scheme that preserves the best qualities of layers. So much for our prohibition about upward uses. Right?

Wrong. Upward *uses* are still a bad idea, but the scheme we just described doesn't have any. It has upward data flow and upward invocation but not uses. The reason is that once a program calls its error handler, its obligation is discharged. The program does not *use* the error handler, because its own correctness depends not a whit on what the error handler does.

Although this may sound like a mere technicality, it is an important distinction. *Uses* is the relation that determines the ability to reuse and to port a layer. "Calls" or "sends data to" is not. An architect needs to know the difference and needs to convey the precise meaning of the relations in his or her architecture documentation.

—P.C.C.

PERSPECTIVES

Levels of Distraction

Our definition of layers is not the only one you're likely to encounter. (It goes without saying, of course, that ours is the best one.) The following definition, which is fairly typical, is taken from a well-known contemporary book on software architecture: "The Layers architectural pattern helps to structure applications that can be decomposed into groups of subtasks in which each group of subtasks is at a particular level of abstraction." We would like to gently take exception to this definition in order to illuminate and to emphasize some concepts that are at the heart of layers.

First, the definition does not mention usage relationships. Suppose that we can agree on what a subtask is and can decompose our application into groups of subtasks that meet that definition's abstraction criterion. Do we have layers? According to the definition, yes. But we disagree. A system in which every group of subtasks is allowed to use every other group is by no stretch of the imagination layered. The essence of a layered system is that lower layers do not have unrestricted access to higher layers. Otherwise, the system will have none of the portability or maintainability benefits that layering is designed to provide and so does not deserve to be called layered.

Second, "levels of abstraction" makes us shudder. Layers are often bound up with that widely used unfortunate and intellectually bankrupt phrase, which often pops up in shallow viewgraph presentations next to "synergistic" or "value-add," and probably snuck into this book once or twice while the censors were at lunch. But we try to eschew it. Is 2 a valid level of abstraction? Is 3.14159? How about "medium low"? The phrase suggests that abstractions can be measured on a discrete numeric scale, but no such scale has ever been identified; nor is one likely to be. As Parnas (1974) peevishly wrote: "It would be nice if the next person to use the phrase...would define the hierarchy to which he refers." Indeed. The phrase reveals a basic misunderstanding about abstractions, suggesting that any two can be compared to each other to see which one is lower. This is rubbish. An abstraction is, at its core, a one-to-many mapping. The "one" is the abstraction; the "many" is the set of things for which the abstraction is a valid generalization. Mappings, which are a kind of relation, are not "higher" or "lower" than one another. They merely differ from one another.

We wrote that layers toward the bottom of the *allowed-to-use* relation *tend to* cover details of the hardware platform, whereas layers toward the top of the *allowed-to-use* relation *tend to* cover details of the application. The reason is that applications tend to use platforms and not the other way around. But neither abstraction is "lower" or "higher." The application layer is completely ignorant of the machine but is knowledgeable about the application. The machine layer is completely ignorant of the application but is knowledgeable about the platform. The two layers complement each other in an elegant symmetry, which is not to be confused with synergy.

People tend to say that the machine abstraction is "lower" because they have a layer (that is, an *allowed-to-use*) picture already in mind; there's nothing inherently "low" about a platform-encapsulating layer otherwise. Thus, the definition we're pillorying makes sense only if you already know what layers are.

The definition is repairable. We might have offered something like this: "The Layers architectural pattern structures software systems that can be decomposed into groups of subtasks in which each group of subtasks constitutes a cohesive abstraction of an aspect of the system—and no two groups constitute the same abstraction of the system—and in which an *allowed-to-use* relation among the groups imposes a strict ordering or a partial ordering. Thus, some layers would consist of more than one group, which are allowed to use one another."

Abstractions are not inherently ordered and do not have levels, except in the presence of a relation. Without that, you don't have layers. You just have groups of subtasks milling about, waiting to be told how to arrange themselves into a useful formation. Some might say the ordering brings a synergistic value-add to the groups.

But I wouldn't. The censors are back from lunch.

—P.C.C.

PERSPECTIVES

UML Class Diagrams: Too Much, Too Little

Throughout this chapter, you may have noticed that UML class diagrams are given as a notation of choice for each of the styles of the module viewtype, and you might conclude that a single class diagram can represent all the styles of the module viewtype, and maybe more.

In fact, it can. UML class diagrams are a veritable semantic smorgasbord, able to show specialization and generalization, dependency, *is-part-of* or decomposition, general entity-relationship information, and even the *realizes* relation between an interface and the element that implements it (see Figure 2.14). Specializing these semantics with stereotypes allows an even more precise expression of just about any relation among modules that one can imagine. The general *depends-on* relation can be stereotyped to become *uses,* for example, with precisely the meaning defined in the Coming to Terms: Uses sidebar, page 68.

Good, right? Class diagrams sound like the Rosetta Stone of architectural diagrams. What else do we need?

Well, plenty. First of all, using a single class diagram to represent all possible information undercuts the primary usefulness of views. Views separate concerns, and one of the greatest sources of confusion in architectural diagrams is the unplanned, haphazard amalgamation of various kinds of information in the same diagram. Muddy views are a sign of muddy architectures, which inevitably lead to design errors late in the game.

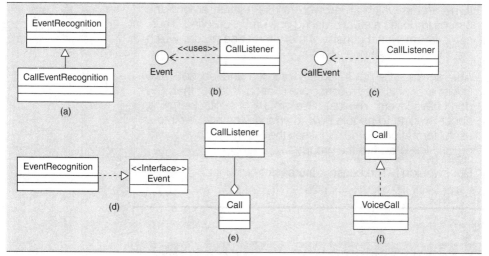

Figure 2.14
UML class diagrams can show many types of relations. (a) Class CallEventRecognition is a specialization of class EventRecognition, (b) class Call Listener uses interface Event, (c) class CallListener depends on the interface CallEvent, (d) class EventRecognition realizes the interface Event, (e) class Call contains the class CallListener, (f) class VoiceCall realizes the class Call.

Of course, not every view needs to be primitive or elementary. A source of great clarity and insight in architecture documentation comes when a small number of views are carefully and consciously chosen to be wed, showing various kinds of information at once and how they overlap and interplay. Section 6.3 explains how to choose and to document combined views, an important part of the architect's craft.

But what is produced by using all the class diagram's relations in a single view? The result would be the *"inherits/ depends-on/uses/ER/realizes/decomposition"* view, which— unless your system were very small—would probably be too busy to read and too bewildering to understand. Instead, document the module views separately, using restricted forms of the class diagram for each, as appropriate: stereotyped *depends on* for the uses and layered views, *is part of* for the decomposition view, *inheritance* for the generalization view, and so on. Combine two views only if it makes sense to do so.

But even if we use class diagrams separately, aren't they still rich enough to give us all we need?

No. If your architecture is object oriented, it's natural to think of it first and foremost in those terms: a collection of classes instantiated as objects that interact at runtime. You might be wondering whether you really need to document your architecture as anything but that. Maybe, when push comes to shove, the only thing you need to give your architectural stakeholders is a set of UML class diagrams. Certainly, many books on object-oriented design concentrate on how to represent the designs with class diagrams. But you need more.

First, take it from the people who brought you UML: If only class diagrams were necessary, UML would not have use case diagrams, sequence diagrams, collaboration diagrams, statechart diagrams, or activity diagrams. Second, class diagrams—even as rich as they are—are fundamentally about code relations. Class diagrams have no way to represent temporal information. None of the component-and-connector styles you'll see in Chapters 3 and 4 can be represented using them. Nor can the allocation styles of Chapter 5, except possibly by some bizarre use of annotations. Trying to represent behavior with a class diagram is out of the question.

UML class diagrams are a foundational piece of notation for module-based views. But like all good tools, they aren't for every job.

—D.G.

2.5 Summary Checklist

- The decomposition style shows how responsibilities are allocated across modules.
- The decomposition style is especially suitable to show newcomers and for performing change-impact analysis.
- The uses style shows how modules depend on one another.
- The uses style helps achieve incremental development and the building of useful subsets of the system.
- The generalization style relates modules by showing how one is a generalization or specialization of the other.
- The generalization style is widely used in object-oriented systems. It shows inheritance, and is used to exploit commonality among modules.
- The layered style divides a system into a set of virtual machines, related by the *allowed-to-use* relation.
- The layered style helps a system achieve portability and modifability.

2.6 Discussion Questions

1. Can you think of a system that cannot be described using a layered view? If a system is not layered, what would this say about its *allowed-to-use* relation?

2. How does a UML class diagram relate to the styles given in this chapter? Does that diagram show decomposition, uses, generalization, or another combination? (*Hint:* We'll discuss this in some detail in Section 11.2.)

3. We consciously chose the term *generalization* to avoid the multiple meanings that the term *inheritance* has acquired. Find two or three of these meanings, compare them, and discuss how they are both a kind of generalization. (*Hint:* You may wish to consult books by Booch and Rumbaugh, respectively.)

4. Suppose that a portion of a system is generated with, for example, a user interface builder tool. Using one or more views in the module viewtype, how would you show the tool, the input to the tool—the user interface specification—and the output from the tool?

2.7 For Further Reading

Each of the styles in this chapter can be traced to a foundational paper in the annals of the software engineering literature. An architect interested in the roots of the discipline may find the original ideas refreshing in their simplicity and purposefulness. These papers, seen as a group, express the then-revolutionary idea that there is more to a computer program than getting the right answer: how it is structured also matters.

Edsger Dijkstra wrote about designing an operating system as a set of abstract virtual machines, giving us the concept of layers, in 1968 [Dijkstra 68]. David Parnas showed how decomposing a system into modules based on likely changes, as opposed to steps in the processing, resulted in systems vastly easier to modify [Parnas 72]. Parnas also introduced the "uses" relation, and showed how it could lead to software that was easy to extend or to develop incrementally [Parnas 79].

In the early 1960s the fundamental concepts of object-oriented programming, including objects, inheritance, and dynamic binding were invented by Ole-Johan Dahl and Kristen Nygaard at the Norwegian Computing Center in Oslo [NygaardDahl 81]. The concepts were introduced in the programming language Simula-67, which, although never widely used itself, laid the foundation for the development of popular object-oriented languages such as Smalltalk and C++. In 1986–1987, two widely influential papers by Alan Snyder and Barbara Liskov, respectively, tied together two concepts that had been drifting apart—inheritance and encapsulation [Snyder 86] [Liskov 87]. Liskov in particular argued convincingly that undisciplined inheritance that violated objects' abstractions was harmful. Between them, they set the object-oriented community on its present path.

A software engineering demonstration project that paid special attention to the use of separate architectural structures was the A-7E avionics system built by the U.S. Navy in the 1980s. A case study of the A-7E avionics software system is presented in [Bass+ 98]. The example employs decomposition (using information-hiding as the criterion), layers, uses, and *allowed-to-use* relations, and shows how a subset is built from the uses relation.

The information-hiding-based decomposition of the A-7E system is the focus of a paper showing how that view is documented using a hierarchically structured document, called a module guide. The paper includes an extract from a software module guide [Clements+ 85], from which the A-7E decomposition example in this chapter is drawn.

More details of the UML notation can be found in [Booch+ 99]. Classes, packages, subsystems, and their relationships are especially relevant to styles in the module viewtype.

The Component-and-Connector Viewtype

3.1 Overview

Component-and-connector (C&C) views define models consisting of elements that have some runtime presence, such as processes, objects, clients, servers, and data stores. Additionally, component-and-connector models include as elements the pathways of interaction, such as communication links and protocols, information flows, and access to shared storage. Often, these interactions are carried out using complex infrastructure, such as middleware frameworks, distributed communication channels, and process schedulers.

A C&C view provides a picture of runtime entities and potential interactions. Such a view may contain many instances of the same component type. For example, you might have a Web client component type that is instantiated many times within the same view. Drawing on an analogy from object-oriented systems, C&C views are similar to object, or collaboration, diagrams, as opposed to class diagrams, which define the types of the elements.

Choosing the appropriate forms of interaction between computational elements is a critical aspect of an architect's task. These interactions may represent complex forms of communication. For example, a connection between a client component and a server component might represent a complex protocol of communication, supported by sophisticated runtime infrastructure. Other interactions might represent multiparty forms of communication, such as event broadcast, or n-way data synchronization. These interactions are captured as connectors in the C&C viewtype.

C&C views are commonly used in practice; indeed, box-and-line diagrams depicting these views are often the graphical medium of choice as a principal first-look explanation of the architecture of a system. But these informal C&C views can be misleading, ambiguous, and inconsistent. Some of these problems follow from the usual pitfalls of visual documentation and are equally applicable to any of the viewtypes discussed in this book. But other problems are more specifically related to the use of components and connectors to portray a system's execution structure. In this chapter, we try to bring some clarity to the picture by describing guidelines for documenting C&C views and by highlighting common pitfalls.

Let us begin with an informal examination of the C&C viewtype by means of a simple example. Figure 3.1 illustrates a primary presentation of a C&C view as one might encounter it in a typical description of a system's runtime architecture.

What is this diagram, backed up by its supporting documentation, attempting to convey? We are being shown a bird's-eye–view of the system as it might appear during runtime. The system contains a shared repository of customer accounts

FOR MORE INFORMATION

Supporting documentation is discussed in Section 10.2.

Figure 3.1
A bird's-eye–view of a system as it might appear during runtime. This system contains a shared repository that is accessed by servers and an administrative component. A set of client tellers can interact with the account repository servers and communicate among themselves through a publish-subscribe connector.

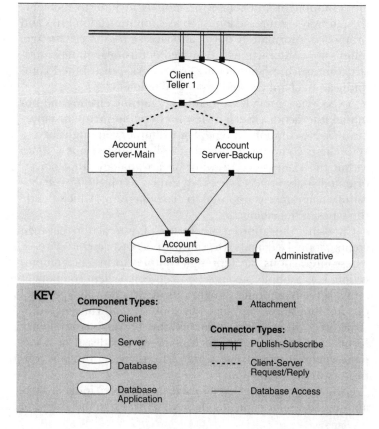

(Account Database) accessed by two servers and an administrative component. A set of client tellers can interact with the account repository servers, embodying a client-server style. These client components communicate among themselves by publishing and subscribing to events. We learn from the supporting documentation that the purpose of the two servers is to enhance reliability: If the main server goes down, the backup can take over. Finally, a component allows an administrator to access, and presumably maintain, the shared-data store.

Each of the three types of connectors shown in Figure 3.1 represents a different form of interaction among the connected parts. The client-server connector allows a set of concurrent clients to retrieve data synchronously via service requests. This variant of the client-server style supports transparent failover to a backup server. The database access connector supports authenticated administrative access for monitoring and maintaining the database. The publish-subscribe connector supports asynchronous event announcement and notification.

Each of these connectors represents a complex form of interaction and will likely require nontrivial implementation mechanisms. For example, the client-server connector type represents a protocol of interaction that prescribes how clients initiate a client-server session, constraints on ordering of requests, how/when failover is achieved, and how sessions are terminated. Implementation of this connecter will probably involve runtime mechanisms that detect when a server has gone down, queue client requests, handle attachment and detachment of clients, and so on. Note also that connectors need not be binary: Two of the three connector types in Figure 3.1 can involve more than two participants.

It may also be possible to carry out both qualitative and quantitative analyses of such system properties as performance, reliability, and security. For instance, the design decision that causes the administrative interface to be the only way to change the database schema would have a positive impact on the security of the system. But it also might have implications on administratability or concurrency. For example, does the use of the administrative interface lock out the servers? Similarly, by knowing properties about the reliability of the individual servers, you might be able to produce numeric estimates of the overall reliability of the system, using some form of reliability analysis.

Some things to note about Figure 3.1 are that it

- Acts as a key to the associated supporting documentation, which is not shown
- Is simple enough to be comprehended in a single bite

FOR MORE INFORMATION

The system illustrated in Figure 3.1 is built from an amalgamation of different styles: client-server is described in Section 4.4; the shared-data style is described in Section 4.2; and publish-subscribe is described in Section 4.3. Combining views is covered in Section 6.3.

- Is explicit about its vocabulary of component and connector types
- Provides a key to discussions about the number and kind of interfaces on its components and connectors
- Uses for its components and its connectors abstractions that concentrate on application functionality rather than on an implementation mechanism

FOR MORE INFORMATION

Supporting documentation is discussed in Section 10.2.

The documentation accompanying the figure elaborates on the elements shown. Such supporting documentation should explain how Account Server—Backup provides reliability for the total system. An expanded C&C figure, not shown here, might focus on the main account server, its backup, and the client-server connection.

3.2 Elements, Relations, and Properties of the C&C Viewtype

We start by considering the C&C viewtype in its most general form. In Chapter 4, we identify a few common C&C styles. Table 3.1 summarizes the elements, relations, and properties that can appear in the C&C viewtype. As we describe the constituents of a C&C viewtype, we also list guidelines about effective use of them in documenting software architecture.

Table 3.1: Summary of the C&C viewtype

Elements	• *Component types:* principal processing units and data stores. • *Connector types:* interaction mechanisms.
Relations	• *Attachments:* component ports are associated with specific connector roles, a component port, *p,* attached to a connector role, *r,* if the component interacts over the connector, using the interface described by *p* and conforming to the expectations described by *r.*
Properties of elements	*Component.* • *Name:* should suggest its functionality. • *Type:* defines general functionality, number and types of ports, and required properties. • *Other properties:* depend on type of component, including things such as performance and reliability values.

Table 3.1: Summary of the C&C viewtype (continued)

	Connector. • *Name:* should suggest the nature of its interactions. • *Type:* defines the nature of interaction, the number and types of roles, and required properties. • *Other properties:* depending on the type of connector may include protocol of interaction and performance values.
Topology	The C&C viewtype has no inherent topological constraints.

3.2.1 Elements

The elements of a C&C viewtype are *components* and *connectors*. Each element in a C&C view of a system has a runtime manifestation, consuming execution resources and contributing to the execution behavior of that system. The relations of a C&C view associate components with connectors to form a graph that represents a runtime system configuration.

These runtime entities are instances of component and connector *types*. The available types are either defined by choosing a specific architectural style that prescribes a set of C&C building blocks (see Chapter 4), or they may be custom defined. In either case, the types are chosen because of significant commonality among several components or connectors in the architecture. Defining or using a set of component-and-connector types provides a means for capturing this commonality, provides a specialized design vocabulary targeted to specific domains, and introduces constraints on how that vocabulary is used.

Components

Each **component** in a C&C view has a name. The name should indicate the intended function of the component. More important, the name allows you to relate the graphical element with supporting documentation.

Each component in a C&C view has a type. Examples of generic component types are clients, servers, filters, objects, and databases. More domain-specific component types might be a controller component type, used in a process control architecture, or a sensor component type, used in some avionics application. A component type is defined in terms of its general computational nature and its form. For example, a component having the type *filter* transforms data that is

DEFINITION

Components are the principal computational elements and data stores that execute in a system.

received on its input channel interfaces and transmits the result on its output channel interfaces. Similarly, a component having the type *server* must have an interface providing a set of service calls that clients may invoke and have as its main computational role to service those requests. A component's type description includes the number and kinds of interfaces it supports and required properties.

The relationship between architectural component types and their instances is similar but not identical to that between classes and instances in an object-oriented world. A component instance might define additional ports not required by its type or associate an implementation in the form of additional structure that is not part of the instance's definition.

FOR MORE INFORMATION

Chapters 2, 4, and 5 present the styles we cover in this book. Each section in those chapters is an example of a style guide. Section 6.5 explains how to devise and to document a style of your own.

The set of component types that contribute to a C&C view should be explicitly enumerated and defined. This may be done in a style guide for the style that you're using, if one exists. Or it may be done by defining the type in the properties of the component. For instance, the intended semantics of component types, such as filter or server, would need to be defined.

In some cases, the set of types used in a C&C view is provided by using a particular C&C architectural style. For example, a C&C view defined in the pipe-and-filter style will use pipe connector types and filter component types, as prescribed by that style.

FOR MORE INFORMATION

The pipe-and-filter C&C style is discussed in Section 4.1.

Although components have types, a C&C view contains component instances; that is, no component types should appear in the view itself. A C&C view may have many components of the same type. For example, a view may have many instances of the same server type. If the designer does not want to commit to a particular number of a replicated component or if that number changes dynamically as a system operates, it is possible to indicate a variable number of a component type. This can be done in a number of ways. However, the meaning of any replication should be clearly documented. In particular, the documentation should specify whether the variability is resolved at design time, system configuration/deployment time, or runtime.

FOR MORE INFORMATION

Conventions for documenting replication and other variability options are discussed in Section 6.4.

Components have interfaces. Given the runtime nature of C&C views, an interface is a specific point of potential interaction of a component with its environment. Component interfaces are referred to as *ports* to emphasize their runtime nature and to distinguish them from the interfaces of other kinds of architectural design elements, such as classes.

A component's ports should be explicitly documented. When documenting a component in a C&C view, it is important to be clear about the number and type of the component's ports. Note the use of plural: A component may have many ports of the same or different types. For example, the database in Figure 3.1 has two server-oriented ports and an administrative port.

Components may represent a complex execution structure, which in turn may be described as a collection of components and connectors. This component decomposition refinement may be represented in a style different from that in which the component is described.

FOR MORE INFORMATION

Refinement is described in Section 6.1

Connectors

Connectors are the other kind of element in a C&C viewtype. Simple kinds of connectors are procedure calls between two objects or between a client and a server, asynchronous messages, event multicast among components that communicate with one another by using publish-subscribe, and pipes that represent asynchronous, order-preserving data streams. But connectors often represent much more complex forms of interaction, such as a transaction-oriented communication channel between a database server and a client. These more complex forms of interaction may in turn be decomposed into collections of components and connectors that typically describe the runtime infrastructure that makes the more abstract form of interaction possible. For example, a decomposition of the failover client-server connector of Figure 6.1 would probably include components that are responsible for buffering client requests, determining when a server has gone, and rerouting requests.

As with components, each connector in a C&C view should have a type, which defines the nature of the interaction supported by the connector. The type also makes clear what form the connector can take, such as how many components can be involved in its interaction, the number and kinds of interfaces it supports, and required properties. Often, the interaction represented by a connector is best described as a protocol. A protocol describes what patterns of events or actions can take place for an interaction.

The set of connector types that contribute to a particular C&C view should, like component types, be explained by referring to the appropriate style guide that enumerates and defines them.

Part of the description of a connector type should be a characterization of the number and kinds of roles that instances of that type can have. A connector's roles can be thought of as interfaces of the connector, insofar as they define the ways in which the connector may be used by components to carry out interactions. For example, a client-server connector might

DEFINITION

A **connector** is a runtime pathway of interaction between two or more components.

FOR MORE INFORMATION

See Perspectives: Are Connectors Necessary? on page 112.

FOR MORE INFORMATION

Behavioral models for documenting protocols are described in Section 8.5.

FOR MORE INFORMATION

Style guides are described in Section 6.5. A standard organization for a style guide, used in the chapters of this book that explain styles, is given in Section 1.2. Section 6.5 covers creating and documenting a new style.

FOR MORE INFORMATION

See Perspectives: Choosing Connector Abstractions on page 114.

have *invokes-services* and *provides-services* roles. A pipe might have *writer* and *reader* roles. A publish-subscribe connector might have many *publisher* and *subscriber* roles. A role typically defines the expectations of a participant in the interaction. For example, an *invokes-services* role might require that the service invoker initialize the connection before issuing any service requests.

3.2.2 Relations

The relation of the C&C viewtype is *attachment*. An attachment relation indicates which connectors are attached to which components, thereby defining a system as a graph of components and connectors. Formally, this is done by associating component ports with connector roles: A component port, p, is attached to a connector role, r, if the component interacts over the connector, using the interface described by p and conforming to the expectations described by r.

ADVICE

Use the following guidelines when defining a graph of components and connectors using attachments:

- Refer to an appropriate style guide to clarify which style you are using.
- Always attach a connector to a particular port of a component.
- If it is not clear that it is valid to attach a given port with a given role, provide a justification in the rationale section for the view. For example, if an *invokes-services* role requires the service invoker to initialize the connection before issuing any service requests, you should explain why the port obeys this rule. In many cases, the justification can be done by appealing to the use of standard interfaces and protocols. For example, a client port might be said to be consistent with a role of an HTTP client-server connector simply by arguing that the port respects that protocol. In other cases, however, a more detailed and connector-specific argument may be needed.
- Make clear which ports connect the system to its external environment. For example, if an external user interface, outside the system, provides input to some components, they should have ports for that external connection. In other words, every interface that appears in a system's context diagram should also appear in at least the top-level C&C view packet of the system.

ADVICE

To illustrate what *not* to do, Figure 3.2 presents an example of a poorly documented C&C view.

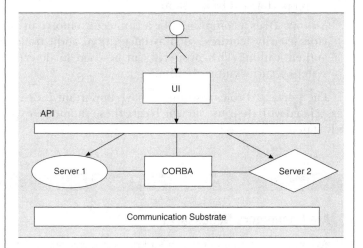

Figure 3.2
A poorly documented C&C view. There is no key; it portrays an API as a component; it uses different shapes for the same types of element; it uses the same
shape for different types of elements; it confuses the context with the system to
be built; its use of arrows is not explained; it has no explicit interface points.

3.2.3 Properties

A particular element may have various kinds of associated
properties, including the name and type of the element.
Other properties are possible and should be chosen to support the usage intended for the particular component-and-
connector view. For example, different properties might be
chosen depending on whether the view is to be used as a basis
for construction, analysis, or communication. Following are
some examples of typical properties and their uses:

- *Reliability:* What is the likelihood of failure for a given component or connector? This property might be used to help
  determine overall system reliability.
- *Performance:* What kinds of response time will the component provide under what loads? What kinds of latencies and
  throughputs can be expected for a given connector? This
  property can be used with others to determine such system
  properties as latencies, throughput, and buffering needs.
- *Resource requirements:* What are the processing and storage
  needs of a component or a connector? This property can be

used to determine whether a proposed hardware configuration will be adequate.

- *Functionality:* What functions does an element perform? This property can be used to reason about overall computation performed by a system.

- *Security:* Does a component or a connector enforce or provide security features, such as encryption, audit trails, or authentication? This property can be used to determine system security vulnerabilities.

The ports and roles also might have important properties associated with their use, in which case these should be explicitly stated.

PERSPECTIVES

Are Connectors Necessary?

We argue that connectors should be first-class design elements for documenting execution-based views: Connectors can represent complex abstractions; they have types and interfaces, or roles; and they require detailed semantic documentation. But couldn't one simply use a mediating component for a complex connector? For example, in the following diagram, the complex connector Connector-1 gets replaced by the component Component-1:

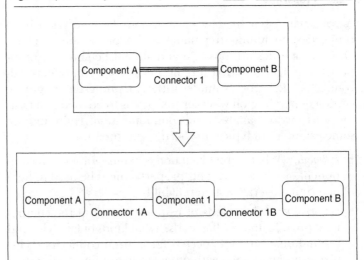

In other words, are connectors needed? The answer is emphatically yes! Connectors are needed. Here's why.

First, connectors are rarely realizable as a single mediating component. Although most connector mechanisms do involve runtime infrastructure that carries out the communication, that is not the only thing involved. In addition, a connector implementation requires initialization and finalization code; special treatment in the components that use the connector, such as using certain kinds of libraries; global operating system settings, such as registry entries; and others.

Second, connector abstractions support rich reasoning. For example, reasoning about a data flow system is greatly enhanced if the connectors are pipes rather than procedure calls or another mechanism, because well-known calculi are available for analyzing data flow graphs. Additionally, allowing complex connectors provides a single home where one can talk about the semantics. For example, in the preceding figure, I could attach a single description of the protocol of interaction to the complex connector. In contrast, the lower model would require me to combine the descriptions of two connectors and a component to figure out what is going on.

Third, using connectors more clearly indicates the architect's intent. When components are used to represent complex connectors, it is often no longer clear which components in a diagram are essential to the application-specific computation and which are part of the mediating infrastructure.

Fourth, we need connector abstractions because avoidance of complex connectors can significantly clutter an architectural model with unnecessary detail. Few would argue that the lower of the two diagrams is easier to understand. Magnify this many times in a more complex diagram, and it becomes obvious that clarity is served by using connectors to encapsulate details of interaction.

Fifth, shifting the description as in the preceding diagram begs the question, as the new depiction also has connectors. So we haven't eliminated them.

"Oh, but these are much *simpler* connectors," you say. Maybe. But even simple interactions, such as message sending or procedure calls, become complex in their own right in most distributed settings. Moreover, why should one think that the particular choice of simple connector for one system will be the same for another? In one case, a simple connector might be a message send; in another, a procedure call; in another, an event announcement. Because no universal "simplest" connector exists, we always need to be clear about exactly what we are modeling when we describe an interaction.

—D.G.

Choosing Connector Abstractions

Choosing how to document connector abstractions is often one of the most difficult jobs of producing effective architectural documentation using the C&C viewtype. It may be difficult to map from the C&C views to more implementation-oriented views if the view documents only early, coarse-grained decisions and includes abstract connector types. The view becomes cluttered if it documents connectors and components that are logically part of the connector mechanism. Deciding on connector abstractions is a matter of taste and is influenced by the needs of the architecture stakeholders and architectural analysis. More than one view may be necessary. In today's systems, documentation tends to err on the side of being too implementation oriented.

FOR MORE INFORMATION

The publish-subscribe style is described in Section 4.3.

To illustrate alternative choices in abstraction and representation with respect to connectors, consider the two forms of a simple publish-subscribe system shown in Figure 3.3. The first version shows five components communicating through an event bus, which describes an interaction that ensures that each published event is delivered to all subscribers of that event. The second version shows the same five components communicating with the assistance of a centralized dispatcher component responsible for distributing events via procedure calls to the other components.

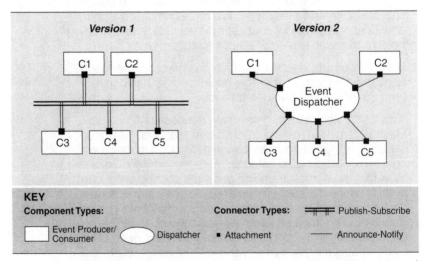

Figure 3.3
Two potential versions of a publish-subscribe system. In Version 1, all communication takes place over an event bus; in Version 2, communication occurs with the assistance of a dispatcher component.

How do they compare? Version 1 clearly indicates the *n*-ary nature of the interaction: events announced by one component may be delivered to multiple subscribers. The connector encapsulates the underlying mechanism. This abstraction allows alternative implementations, such as a centralized dispatcher, multiple dispatchers, or even point-to-point distribution of events between components, and it simplifies the diagram. For some purposes, on the other hand, it may be important to show the underlying infrastructure. For example, to calculate event throughput, it might be necessary to reason about the properties of a centralized dispatch mechanism that carries out the communication. Version 2 provides these details and could be an implementation refinement of Version 1. Which mechanism you choose depends on the context.

—D.G.

ADVICE

Because picking connector abstractions is a difficult job, it is worth listing some guidelines to keep in mind.

* Connectors need not be binary. As indicated in the preceding examples, connectors may have more than two roles. Even if the connector is ultimately implemented using binary connectors, such as a procedure call, it can be useful to adopt *n*-ary connector representations in a C&C view.

* If a component's primary purpose is to mediate interaction between a set of components, consider representing it as a connector. Such components are often best modeled as part of the communication infrastructure, as we illustrated.

* Connectors can—and often should—represent complex forms of interaction. Even a semantically simple procedure call can be complex when carried out in a distributed setting, involving runtime protocols for timeouts, error handling, and locating the service provider—for example, as provided by a CORBA (common object request broker architecture) implementation.

* Connectors embody a protocol of interaction. When two or more components interact, they must obey conventions about order of interactions, locus of control, and handling of error conditions and timeouts. When providing a detailed description of a connector, the documentation should attempt to capture this detail.

3.3 What the C&C Viewtype Is For and What It's Not For

The C&C viewtype is used to reason about runtime system quality attributes, such as performance, reliability, and availability. In particular, a well-documented view allows architects to predict overall system properties, given estimates or measurements of properties of the individual elements and interactions. For example, to determine whether the overall system can meet its real-time scheduling requirements, you usually need to know the cycle time of each process in a process-oriented view. Similarly, knowing the reliability of individual elements and communication channels supports an architect when estimating or calculating overall system reliability. In some cases, this kind of reasoning is supported by formal, analytical models and tools. In others, it is achieved by judicious use of rules of thumb and past experience.

C&C views allow you to answer the following questions.

- What are the system's principal executing components, and how do they interact?
- What are the major shared-data stores?
- Which parts of the system are replicated, and how many times?
- How does data progress through a system as it executes?
- What protocols of interaction are used by communicating entities?
- What parts of the system run in parallel?
- How can the system's structure change as it executes?

C&C views are not appropriate for representing design elements that do not have a runtime presence. For example, a good rule of thumb is that if it doesn't make sense to characterize the interface(s) of an element, it probably isn't a component. However, the inverse is not necessarily true: some things with interfaces are not components.

Data Flow and Control Flow Projections

Two views that have long been used to document software systems—for so long, in fact, that we might consider them archaic today—are the data flow and control flow views. These views show how data and control, respectively, flow around a system during execution, and each view is useful for performing a particular kind of analysis. Understanding control flow, for instance, helps programmers track down the source of a bug.

Both of these are examples of *projections* of a C&C view. Each highlights certain aspects of a view in order to simplify discussion or to analyze specific properties of the view. A data flow projection can be derived by examining the connector protocols to determine in which direction data can flow between components. One can then project a data flow view from a C&C view by replacing connectors with one- or two-headed arrows indicating flow of data and by eliminating connectors that have no data component. A similar approach works for control flow. Of course, you need to be clear what you mean by control flow and how that relation is derived from knowledge about the connectors in a C&C view.

When attempting to extract a data flow or a control flow relation from a more general connector, you need to be aware of several pitfalls. For instance, consider the very simple but typical situation illustrated in Figure 3.4, which shows components C1 and C2, which interact via a procedure call connector, P. Assume that procedure P takes some arguments and returns a value. How would we project a data flow relation? In particular, which way should the arrow go? Because C1 passes data to C2 in the form of procedure parameters, you might argue that data flows from C1 to C2. But because C2 returns a value, perhaps the arrow should go the other way. Or should it go both ways?

FOR MORE INFORMATION

See also Perspectives: Quivering at Arrows on page 28.

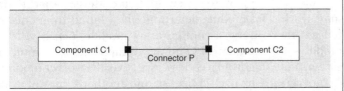

Figure 3.4
A component-and-connector fragment showing that C1 calls C2. To turn this into a data flow or a control flow projection, which way should the respective arrows point?

The same confusions apply to control flow. C1 invokes C2, so you might argue that control flows from C1 to C2. But C1 must block when C2 is performing its invoked operation, suggesting that C2 controls C1 during that period of invocation. And, of course, when C2 is finished, it returns control to C1.

And this is one of the most simple forms of interaction! Most connectors are more sophisticated, perhaps involving multiple procedure calls, rules for handling exceptions and timeouts, and callbacks.

FOR MORE INFORMATION

Data flow and control flow views are discussed in Section 11.7.

Two main conclusions can be drawn. First, when creating a data flow or a control flow projection, be explicit about the semantic criteria being used. Second, recognize that data flow and control flow projections are at best approximations to the connectors, which define the interactions between components.

—D.G.

3.4 Notations for the C&C Viewtype

Notations for the C&C viewtype are discussed in Section 4.7.

3.5 Relation to Other Viewtypes

FOR MORE INFORMATION

The correspondence between the elements in a system's module views and the elements in its C&C views should be documented as part of the documentation that applies to more than one view. This mapping between views is described in Section 10.3.

The relationship between a system's C&C views and its module views may be complex. The same code module might be executed by many of the elements of a C&C view. Conversely, a single component of a C&C view might execute code defined by many modules. Similarly, a C&C component might have many points of interaction with its environment, each defined by the same module interface. Figure 3.5 shows both a module view and a C&C view of the same system.

The module view represents a typical implementation that one might find in C under UNIX. In this view, the relation between modules is *uses*, as described in Chapter 2. A main module is used to start things off, invoking the facilities of four modules—To-upper, To-lower, Split, and Merge—that do the main work. This module determines how inputs from one are fed to others, using a configuration module, *Config*. All the modules use a standard I/O library to carry out the communication. Note that from a code perspective, the worker modules do not directly invoke services of one another—but rather do so only via the I/O library.

FOR MORE INFORMATION

The pipe-and-filter style is described in Section 4.1.

In the C&C view, we have a system described in the pipe-and-filter style. Each of the components is a filter that trans-

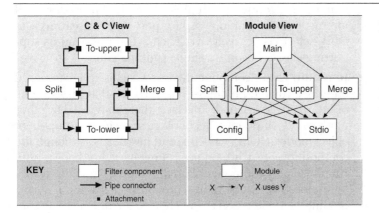

Figure 3.5
C&C and module views of the Capitalize System. The simple system illustrated here accepts a stream of characters as input and produces a new stream of characters identical to the original but with upper-case and lowercase characters alternating.

forms character streams. Pathways of communication between the components are explicit, indicating that during runtime, the pipe connectors will mediate communication of data streams among those components.

It should be clear even with this simple example that the two descriptions differ wildly in what they include and how they partition the system. Hence, there is no simple mapping between them. For example, some of the modules in the module view do not even appear in the C&C view. Conversely, the pipe connector does not appear in the module view, although one might argue that it is most closely associated with the module *Stdio*.

Although not illustrated in this example, the same code module might be mapped to several execution components: for example, if we used *Merge* twice. Also, the mapping of interfaces is not at all obvious. For example, the stream input/output interfaces on the filters have no clear mapping to the use of *Stdio*, which implements the communication interface of the code module.

In some situations, however, module and C&C views have a much closer correspondence.

• In one such situation, each module has a single runtime component associated with it, and the connectors are restricted to *calls procedure* connectors. Ignoring shared libraries, this would typically be the case with an Ada program, with each package representing a runtime entity and interactions occurring via procedure calls.

• In a second case, each class in the architectural model of an object-oriented system has a single instance at runtime, and one portrays the C&C view in terms of a peer-to-peer style;

that is, the connectors represent method/procedure call interactions. A variation used for performance reasons is to mark select classes as active. Each active class and its supporting classes become a single runtime entity.

- In a third case, "component-based systems" are composed out of executable modules—object code—that provide one or more service-oriented interfaces that can be used by other modules. Component technologies include component object model (COM), CORBA, and JavaBeans. Although the composition of such modules is in general not known until runtime, many component-based systems have a known configuration that can be represented in similar ways in both a module view and a C&C view. Here again, however, the connector types are restricted to *call procedure* connectors and, in some cases, publish-subscribe.

Finally, even in these types of cases, some correspondences are worth noting. In particular, there is a natural relationship between the components—*Split, To-upper, To-lower,* and *Merge*—and the modules that carry out the bulk of the computation. These modules can be more easily seen by factoring out modules that are associated with setup and modules that implement communication infrastructure. Because a C&C view describes an executing system, no parts relate to setup. In the example, we have *Main* and *Config.* Communication infrastructure is represented as connectors in a C&C view. In the example, this is the module *Stdio.* After removing these modules, the ones left are those that have a clear mapping to the C&C view.

3.6 Summary Checklist

- Component-and-connector (C&C) views define models consisting of elements that have some runtime presence, such as processes, objects, clients, servers, and data stores. Additionally, component-and-connector models include as elements the pathways of interaction, such as communication links and protocols, information flows, and access to shared storage.
- Components have interfaces, which are called ports.
- Connectors have interfaces, which are called roles.
- Connectors need not be binary, meaning that they may have more than two roles. Even if the connector is ultimately implemented using binary connectors, such as a procedure call, it can be useful to adopt *n*-ary connector representations at an architectural level.

- If a component's primary purpose is to mediate interaction between a set of components, consider representing it as a connector instead.

- Connectors can and often should represent complex forms of interaction. Even a semantically simple procedure call can be complex when carried out in a distributed setting, involving runtime protocols for timeouts, error handling, and locating the service provider.

- Connectors embody a protocol of interaction. When two or more components interact, they must obey conventions about order of interactions, locus of control, and handling of error conditions and timeouts. When providing a detailed description of a connector, the documentation should attempt to capture this detail.

- Be clear about which style you are using, by referring to an appropriate style guide.

- Make clear which port is used when attaching a component to a connector.

- If it is not clear that it is valid to attach a given port with a given role, provide a justification in the rationale section for the view.

- Make clear which ports are used to connect the system to its external environment.

- Data flow and control flow diagrams are projections of C&C models. When creating such diagrams, be explicit about the semantic criteria being used to determine where the arrows go. Data flow and control flow projections are at best approximations to the connectors, which define the components' interactions.

3.7 Discussion Questions

1. It is said that a C&C view illustrates a system in execution. Does this mean that it shows a snapshot of an execution, a trace of an execution, the union of all possible traces, some combination, or something else?

2. As we have mentioned, *component* is an overloaded term. Discuss the relationship between a component in a C&C view and (a) a UML component and (b) a component in the sense of the component-based software engineering community.

3. A communication framework, such as Enterprise Java-Beans (EJB), CORBA, or .NET, can be viewed as a connec-

tor among components or as a component with its own substructure. Which is appropriate, and why?

4. A user invokes a Web browser to download a file. Before doing so, the browser retrieves a plug-in to handle that type of file. How would you model this scenario in a C&C view?

5. Figure 3.6 shows an overview architecture diagram for an electronic commerce store. Assume that you are new on the job, without the background of the symbology the organization uses, or perhaps you wrote this some time ago but now have to go back and review the system. Critique the diagram. List places where you think it is misleading, and list the questions that need to be asked—and that the diagram fails to answer—before you can understand its meaning.

6. After you have critiqued Figure 3.6 and have enumerated the information you believe is missing, augment the diagram to make it tell a coherent story. Did you decide that the diagram is describing code-based entities, runtime entities, or both? Did you decide that the boxes called layers are, in fact, layers, or something else? What did you decide the arrows mean?

Figure 3.6
An overview architecture diagram. Where is it misleading? What questions does the diagram fail to answer?

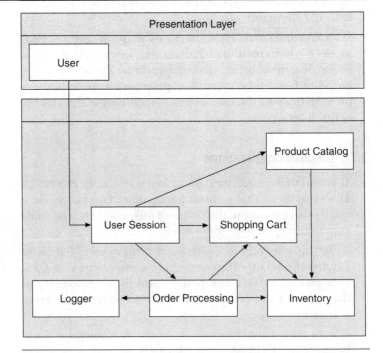

3.8   For Further Reading

Here in the early days of what some are calling the age of component-based software engineering, we are awash in stories where the architect thought he or she could plug two components together with a connector, only to find out that the component didn't implement the right protocol, or was otherwise badly matched with the expectations of that connector. This is why we prescribe writing a justification where the match-up is less than obvious. For a thoughtful treatment of element mismatch, see [Garlan+ 95].

It is tempting to treat architecture as an assembly of components, but there are great conceptual advantages to be gained from elevating connectors to a first-class architectural status as well. Mary Shaw makes an eloquent argument for doing so in [Shaw 96b]. Shaw and Garlan [ShawGarlan 96] treat software architecture in terms of components and connectors and address concerns such as constructing systems as assemblies of components. For a more thorough discussion of connector mechanisms see [Shaw+ 96]. Allen and Garlan lay out the semantic foundations for connectors as first-class entities [AllenGarlan 97].

Styles of the Component-and-Connector Viewtype

C&C styles specialize the C&C viewtype by introducing a specific set of component-and-connector types and by specifying rules about how elements of those types can be combined. Additionally, given that C&C views capture runtime aspects of a system, a C&C style is typically also associated with a pattern of interaction that prescribes how computation, data, and control flow through systems.

Any particular component or connector may be documented in multiple C&C views, because it may interact with other components or connectors in several ways. For example, a component may be a server in a client-server system. The same component may also act as a respository for data. Thus, assuming that both client-server and shared-data styles are important to understanding the system, views in both styles will include the same component, showing different patterns of interaction.

The component-and-connector viewtype is specialized by numerous styles. The style chosen to represent a C&C view of the system usually depends on both the nature of the runtime structures in the system and the intended use of the representation. For example, if the view documents early, coarse-grained design decisions that will be refined later, it will probably include abstract connector types that will need to be refined later. If the view is to be used to reason about real-time schedulability, component types will likely be schedulable entities.

Many C&C styles exist, and we discuss only a few of them in this chapter. We discuss six—pipe-and-filter, shared-data, publish-subscribe, client-server, peer-to-peer, and communicating-processes—that apply to a wide variety of systems and provide enough semantic richness to illustrate documentation principles.

FOR MORE INFORMATION

In Section 4.10, we provide references for reading about dozens of styles. We discuss notation for C&C styles in Section 4.7.

4.1   The Pipe-and-Filter Style

4.1.1   Overview

The pattern of interaction in the pipe-and-filter style is characterized by successive transformations of streams of data. Data arrives at a filter, is transformed, and is passed through pipes to the next filter. A single filter can pass data through multiple ports. Examples of such systems are signal-processing systems and systems built using UNIX pipes.

4.1.2   Elements, Relations, and Properties

The pipe-and-filter style, summarized in Table 4.1, provides a single type of component—the *filter*—and a single type of connector—the *pipe*. A filter transforms data that it receives through one or more pipes and transmits the result through one or more pipes. A pipe is a connector that conveys streams of data from the output port of one filter to the input port of another filter. Pipes act as unidirectional conduits, providing an order-preserving, buffered communication channel to transmit data generated by filters. Pipes change none of the data content. In the pure pipe-and-filter style, filters interact only through pipes.

Table 4.1: Summary of the pipe-and-filter style

Elements	• *Component types:* filter. Filter ports must be either input or output ports.
	• *Connector types:* pipe. Pipes have data-in and data-out roles.
Relations	*Attachment* relation associates filter output ports with data-in roles of a pipe and filter input ports with data-out roles of pipes and determine the graph of interacting filters.
Computational model	• Filters are data transformers that read streams of data from their input ports and write streams of data to their output ports.
	• Pipes convey streams of data from one filter to another.
Properties	Same as defined by the C&C viewtype.
Topology	Pipes connect filter output ports to filter input ports. Specializations of the style may restrict the association of components to an acyclic graph or a linear sequence.

Because pipes buffer data during communication, filters can act asynchronously, concurrently, or independently. Moreover, a filter need not know the identity of its upstream or downstream filters. For this reason, pipe-and-filter systems have the nice property that the overall computation can be treated as the functional composition of the compositions of the filters.

Constraints on composition of elements in this style dictate that pipes must connect output ports to input ports. Specializations of the pipe-and-filter style may also impose other constraints, such as that the architectural graph be acyclic or that the configuration define a linear sequence, or a *pipeline*.

ADVICE

Useful properties to document for pipes include whether pipes are buffered, how they treat end-of-data, and their blocking behavior when writing to buffered pipes that are filled up or reading from pipes that are empty. Properties of filters can include whether or not each filter is a separate process, and the stream transformation each achieves.

4.1.3   What the Pipe-and-Filter Style Is For and What It's Not For

Systems with a pipe-and-filter style are heavily oriented toward data transformation. Often, pipes and filters constitute the front end of signal-processing applications. These systems typically receive a large amount of data at the initial filter from sensors; the filter compresses the data and performs initial filtering. The next filters reduce the data further and do synthesis across different sensors. The final filter typically allows the application of the data, such as providing input to modeling tools, providing input to visualization tools for user exploration, or providing input to further application. Analyses that are associated with pipe-and-filter systems include deriving the aggregate transformation provided by a graph of filters and reasoning about system performance: input/output stream latency, pipe buffer requirements, and schedulability.

4.1.4   Relation to Other Styles

A C&C view in a pipe-and-filter style is not the same as a data flow projection or a data flow view. In the pipe-and-filter style, "lines" between components represent connectors, which have a specific computational meaning: They transmit streams of data from one filter to another. In data flow projections, the

FOR MORE INFORMATION

Data flow views are discussed in Section 11.7.

lines represent relations indicating the communication of data between components. The latter have little computational meaning: They simply mean that data flows from one element to the next. This flow might be realized by a connector, such as a procedure call, the routing of an event between a publisher and a subscriber, or data transmitted via a pipe. The reason that these views might be confused is that the data flow projection of a pipe-and-filter style looks almost identical to the original view.

4.1.5 Examples of the Pipe-and-Filter Style

ECS

Figure 4.1, taken from Appendix A, shows a pipe-and-filter primary presentation for the ECS system.

String-Processing Application

Figure 4.2 shows a simple string-processing application in a pipe-and-filter style. The system is described hierarchically: The filter

Figure 4.1
ECS viewed as a pipe-and-filter system. Data enters from satellites on the left, is processed and refined, and is made available for distribution to the science community on the right. The steps are explained in the view's supporting documentation, which is given in Appendix A but not repeated here.

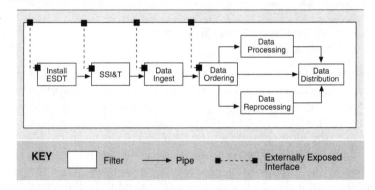

Figure 4.2
A system in the pipe-and-filter style. The refinement of MergeAndSort is itself in this style.

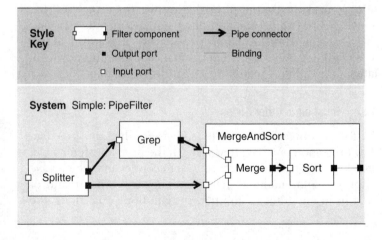

MergeAndSort is defined by a refinement that is itself a pipe-and-filter system. Properties of the components and connectors are not shown but would list, for example, performance characteristics used by a tool to calculate overall system throughput.

4.2 Shared-Data Style

4.2.1 Overview

In the shared-data style, the pattern of interaction is dominated by the exchange of persistent data. The data has multiple accessors and at least one shared-data store for retaining persistent data.

Database systems and knowledge-based systems are examples of this style. One feature of a shared-data style is the method by which the data consumer discovers that data of interest is available. If the shared-data store informs data consumers of the arrival of interesting data, the shared-data style is called a *blackboard*. If the consumer has responsibility for retrieving data, the shared-data style is called a repository. In modern systems, these distinctions have been blurred, as many database management systems that were originally repositories now provide a triggering mechanism that turns them into blackboards.

4.2.2 Elements, Relations, and Properties

The shared-data style, summarized in Table 4.2, is organized around one or more shared-data stores, which store data that other components may read and write. Component types include shared-data stores and *data accessors*. The general computational model associated with shared-data systems is that data accessors perform calculations that require data from the data store and writing results to one or more data stores. That data can be viewed and acted on by other data accessors. In a pure shared-data system, data accessors interact only through the shared-data store(s). However, many shared-data systems also allow direct interactions between nonstore elements. The data-store components of a shared-data system provide shared access to data, support data persistence, manage concurrent access to data, provide fault tolerance, support access control, and handle the distribution and caching of data values.

The stylistic specializations differ along two dimensions: the nature of stored data and the control model. In the *blackboard style*, data accessors are sometimes called *knowledge sources*, and the shared-data store is called the *blackboard*. The computational model for such systems is that knowledge sources are "triggered," or invoked, when certain kinds of data appear in

Table 4.2: Summary of the shared-data style

Elements	• *Component types:* shared-data repositories and data accessors.
	• *Connector types:* data reading and writing.
Relations	*Attachment* relation determines which data accessors are connected to which data repositories.
Computational model	Communication between data accessors is mediated by a shared-data store. Control may be initiated by the data accessors or the data store.
Properties	Same as defined by the C&C viewtype and refined as follows: types of data stored, data performance-oriented properties, data distribution.
Topology	Data accessors are attached to connectors that are attached to the data store(s).

the database. The computation of a triggered knowledge source will typically change the data in the blackboard, thereby triggering the actions of other knowledge sources. Blackboard systems differ in how the data is structured within the blackboard and in the mechanisms for prioritizing the invocation of knowledge sources when more than one is triggered.

One of the first systems to employ the blackboard style was a speech-understanding system called Hearsay II [Nii 1986]. A more modern variation is provided by "tuple spaces," as exemplified by Linda and JavaSpaces. A tuple space is a repository that contain *tuples,* or lists of values. Clients communicate with one another by releasing data—a tuple—into tuple space. Clients can also register to be notified of changes in a tuple space. Other forms of such triggered databases are sometimes called *continuous-query* databases.

A particular portion of a system will be either a blackboard or a pure repository, depending on where the initiative lies in accessing data. Trigger mechanisms are common in systems that use work-flow management to inform data accessors of the modification of particular types of data making that use a blackboard. In other portions of such systems, the data accessor is responsible for initiating a query. Thus, it is important to identify those data accessors that can initiate a query and those that are triggered by actions on particular data. If data accessors are triggered by the respository, the circumstances under which the triggers are activated are important to document.

ADVICE

Useful properties to document about data stores include restrictions on the number of accessors, whether or not new accessors can be added at runtime, access control enforcement policies, whether or not the data is persistent, whether control is initiated by data accessors or by the data store, whether concurrent access is permitted, and if so, what kinds of synchronization mechanisms are used. Other properties can capture administrative concerns: Can one modify the types of data stored in the data store? if so, who has access, when can those changes be performed, and via what interface?

4.2.3   What the Shared-Data Style Is For and What It's Not For

The shared-data style is used whenever various data items have multiple accessors and persistence. Use of this style has the effect of decoupling the producer of the data from the consumers of the data; hence, this style supports modifiability, as the producers do not have direct knowledge of the consumers.

Analyses associated with this style usually center on performance, security, privacy, reliability, and compatibility with, for example, existing repositories and their data. In particular, when a system has more than one data store, a key architectural concern is the mapping of data and computation to the data stores and their local data accessors. For example, distributing data or providing redundant copies may improve performance but often at the cost of added complexity and a decrease in reliability and security.

4.2.4   Relation to Other Styles

This style has aspects in common with the client-server style, especially the n-tiered client-server form. In information management applications that use this style, the data store is often a relational database, providing relational queries and updates using client-server interactions. In other cases, the data store and its associated servers may provide an object-oriented data model, in which object methods become the main form of interaction with the data. Enterprise JavaBeans is a good example of an architectural framework in this style.

The publish-subscribe style is similar to the blackboard style except it lacks persistence of the data.

Figure 4.3
The primary repository
of the ECS system. The
gateways and maintenance
tool are data accessors;
SYBASE and DS are
components of the data
repository.

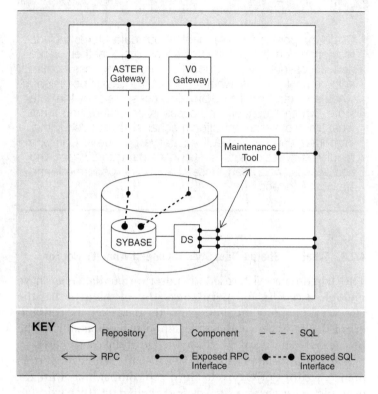

4.2.5 Example of the Shared-Data Style

Figure 4.3, taken from Appendix A, shows part of a shared-data view of the ECS system.

4.3 Publish-Subscribe Style

4.3.1 Overview

In the publish-subscribe style of the C&C viewtype, summarized in Table 4.3, components interact via announced events. Components may subscribe to a set of events. It is the job of the publish-subscribe runtime infrastructure to make sure that each published event is delivered to all subscribers of that event. Thus, the main form of connector in these styles is a kind of event bus. Components place events on the bus by announcing them; the connector then delivers those events to the appropriate components.

The publish-subscribe style is commonly used to decouple producers and consumers of messages. This decoupling therefore supports the modification of these producers and consumers.

Table 4.3: Summary of the publish-subscribe style

Elements	• *Component types*: any C&C component type with an interface that publishes and/or subscribes to events.
	• *Connector types*: publish-subscribe.
Relations	*Attachment* relation associates components with the publish-subscribe connector.
Computational model	A system of independent components that announce events and react to other announced events.
Properties	Same as defined by the C&C viewtype but refined as follows: which events are announced by which components and which events are subscribed to by which components, and when components are allowed to subscribe to events.
Topology	All components are connected to an event distributor that may be viewed as either a bus—connector—or a component.

4.3.2 Elements, Relations, and Properties

The computational model for the publish-subscribe style is best thought of as a system of largely independent processes or objects that react to events generated by their environment and in turn cause reactions in other components as a side effect of their event announcements. Because the developer of a component in this style cannot know in advance the number of recipients of the component's announced events, the correctness of the component cannot, in general, depend on those recipients. This fundamental property of publish-subscribe systems decouples the components and greatly enhances the ability to modify one part of a system without affecting other parts of it.

The publish-subscribe style can take several forms. In the most common one, often called *implicit invocation,* the components have procedural interfaces, and a component registers for an event by associating one of its procedures with each subscribed type of event. When an event is announced, the associated procedures of the subscribed components are invoked in an order usually determined by the runtime infrastructure. User interface frameworks, such as Visual Basic, are often driven by implicit invocation: User code is added to the framework by associating user code fragments with predefined events, such as mouse clicks.

In another publish-subscribe form, events are simply routed to the appropriate components. It is the component's job to figure out how to handle the event. Such systems put more of a burden on individual components to manage event streams but also permit a more heterogeneous mix of components than implicit invocation systems do.

ADVICE

Useful properties to document for components include whether they can subscribe to new events dynamically, whether new event types can be created dynamically, and whether one can add new publishers dynamically. Connector properties can describe the dispatch mechanism: How are published events handled? Are they synchronous or asynchronous? Do events have priorities? What kinds of temporal or causal ordering is enforced? Is event delivery reliable? What are the semantics of each event? Does the connector support other distributed component management, such as starting and stopping publish-subscribe components at the same time?

4.3.3 What the Publish-Subscribe Style Is For and What It's Not For

The publish-subscribe style is used to send events and messages to an unknown set of recipients. Because the set of recipients is unknown, new recipients can be added without modification to the producers.

4.3.4 Relation to Other Styles

When used to distribute messages, the publish-subscribe style can be regarded as a shared-data blackboard without persistence. When the components have independent threads of control, the publish-subscribe style is a refinement of communicating-processes style.

Implicit invocation is often combined with a peer-to-peer style, in which components may interact either explicitly, using procedure or function invocation, or implicitly, by announcing events. For example, in the distributed object setting, CORBA and EJB provide event announcement capabilities that may be combined with remote procedure calls. In other object-based systems, the same effect is achieved by using the MVC (Model-View-Controller), or Observer pattern.

4.3.5 Examples of the Publish-Subscribe Style

Section 7.6.3 describes a portion of the infrastructure used to support a publish-subscribe system. In the HLA (High Level Architecture) publish-subscribe mechanism (HPSM), the concept of *publish* is split into two notions: intent and action. Within the HLA, *publish* means the announcement of an intent to provide data. When it publishes an HLA class, a component announces the intent to provide, at a later time, data values for instances of that class. Conversely, a component can subscribe to an HLA class. The subscription indicates the subscribing component's wish to be notified of new data values of instances of the HLA classes to which the component subscribes.

The action of providing the data is called *update* in the HPSM. Once it publishes a class, a component may then update instances of that class, whereby the component provides the data values for instances to the HPSM infrastructure. It is the job of the HLA runtime infrastructure (RTI) to ensure that each update is delivered to all subscribers of the relevant class. The update notification is a "pull" event for the subscribing components; a subscribing component must query the HPSM infrastructure for available object instance updates.

The HPSM notions of publish and update are similar to the multiple definitions of the term *publish* in the newspaper industry. A newspaper publisher announces the intent to provide, or publish, issues of a newspaper. The publisher also provides, or publishes, individual issues of the newspaper. HLA recognizes this duality, teasing the concepts apart and giving them individual names.

4.4 Client-Server Style

4.4.1 Overview

In the client-server style of the C&C viewtype, components interact by requesting services of other components. The essence of this style is that communication is typically paired and initiated by the client. A request for service from a client is normally paired with the provision of that service. Servers in this style provide a set of services through one or more interfaces, and clients use zero or more services provided by other servers in the system. There may be one central server or several distributed ones. Examples of the client-server style are (1) window systems that partition the system according to client application and screen server; (2) name directory services that partition according to name resolver and name server;

(3) two-tier database systems that partition the system according to clients and data; and (4) distributed Web-based information systems that partition the system according to such concerns as client applications, business logic, and data management services.

4.4.2 Elements, Relations, and Properties

In the client-server style, summarized in Table 4.4, component types are *clients* and *servers*. The principal connector type for the client-server style is the request-reply connector used for invoking services. When more than one service is indicated on a connector, a protocol is often used to document ordering relationships among the invocable services. Servers have interfaces that describe the services they provide. Servers may in turn act as clients by requesting services from other servers, forming a hierarchy of service invocation.

Table 4.4: Summary of the client-server style

Elements	• *Component types: client,* which requests services of another component, and *server,* which provides services to other components.
	• *Connector types:* request/reply, the asymmetric invocation of server's services by a client.
Relations	*Attachment* relation associates clients with the request role of the connector and servers with the reply role of the connector and determines which services can be requested by which clients.
Computational model	Clients initiate activities, requesting services as needed from servers and waiting for the results of those requests.
Properties	Same as defined by the C&C viewtype but refined by the server: the numbers and types of clients that can be attached and performance properties, such as transactions per second.
Topology	In general, unrestricted. Specializations may impose restrictions:
	• Numbers of attachments to a given port or role
	• Allowed relationships among servers
	• Tiers

   The computational flow of pure client-server systems is asymmetric: Clients initiate actions by requesting services of servers. Thus, the client must know the identity of a service to invoke it, and clients initiate all interactions. In contrast, servers do not know the identity of clients in advance of a service request and must respond to the initiated client requests.

One form of service invocation is synchronous: The requester of a service waits, or is blocked, until a requested service completes its actions, possibly providing a return result. Variants of the client-server style may introduce other connector types. For example, in some client-server forms, servers are permitted to initiate certain actions on their clients. This might be done by announcing events or by allowing a client to register notification procedures, or callbacks, that the server calls at specific times.

Constraints on the use of the client-server style might limit the number of clients that can be connected to a server or impose a restriction that servers cannot interact with other servers. A specialization case in client-server style is an n-tiered client-server model. In this case, clients and servers form an n-level hierarchy, upper tiers consisting of clients that invoke servers in tiers below. N-tiered systems are typically found in business processing applications, and n is usually 3: The first tier consists of client applications; the second tier, business logic services; the third tier, data management services, such as data persistence, concurrency control, and query support. Enterprise JavaBeans is a good example of this kind of architectural style.

> **FOR MORE INFORMATION**
>
> Section 6.3.5 discusses the n-tier client-server style as a hybrid between the client-server and the deployment styles.

> **ADVICE**
>
> Useful properties to document about components include whether new clients and servers can be introduced dynamically, as well as any limitations on the number of clients that can interact with a given server. Connector properties deal with the reply-respond protocol: How are errors handled? How are client-server interactions set up and taken down? Are there sessions? How are servers located? What kinds of middleware, if any, are relied upon?

4.4.3 What the Client-Server Style Is For and What It's Not For

The client-server style presents a system view that decouples clients applications from the services they use. This style supports system understanding by separating out common services. The grouping of functionality in this style provides a useful basis for deploying the system to the hardware platform or for interoperating with services on legacy systems. The partitioning of functionality into clients and servers allows them to be independently assigned to tiers, thereby supporting performance scalability and reliability.

Client-server system analyses include determining whether the system's server provides the client-required services and whether clients use the services appropriately, such as respecting ordering constraints on service invocations. Other analyses include those for dependability—for example, to understand whether a system can recover from a service failure; security—for example, to determine whether information provided by servers is limited to clients with the appropriate privileges; and performance—for example, to determine whether a system's servers can keep up with the volume and rates of anticipated service requests.

4.4.4 Relation to Other Styles

Like many C&C styles, the client-server style decouples producers of services and data from consumers. The client-server style is a generalization of procedure/function/method call found in programming languages. Another style that involves a round-trip form of communication is the peer-to-peer style, but it does not have the asymmetry found in the client-server style.

Clients and servers are often grouped and deployed to different machines in a distributed environment to form an n-tier hierarchy.

As discussed in Section 2.4.5, layers and tiers in an n-tiered client-server architecture are not the same. Layering is a particular style of the module viewtype; n-tiered client-server is a constrained form of the client-server style of the C&C viewtype. The main difference is that the relation in the former case is *allowed-to-use;* in the latter case, the interactions are expressed as request-reply connectors. A tiered diagram can be easily confused for a layered diagram when each layer is realized as a tier.

4.4.5 Examples of the Client-Server Style

The World Wide Web is a hypertext-based system that allows clients to access information from servers distributed across the Internet. Clients access the information, written in Hypertext Markup Language (HTML), provided by a Web server using Hypertext Transfer Protocol (HTTP). HTTP is a form of request-reply invocation. HTTP is a stateless protocol; the connection between the client and the server is terminated after each response from the server.

For example, a client making a simple request will ask for an HTML page. The client knows the identity of the server, and uses a uniform resource location (URL) to locate and access the server. The client sends a server a request in the form of a header that specifies the method used for the request and the properties of the client. Client properties include user name, browser, and supported document types. Some of these are communicated in the request so that the server can send the data in a document format that the client understands. The server sends the client a response in the form of a header that specifies the status of the transaction and the type of data to be sent followed by the data.

4.5 Peer-to-Peer Style

4.5.1 Overview

In the peer-to-peer style of the C&C viewtype, components directly interact as peers by exchanging services. Peer-to-peer communication is a kind of request/reply interaction without the asymmetry found in the client-server style. That is, any component can, in principle, interact with any other component by requesting its services. Thus, connectors in this style may involve complex bidirectional protocols of interaction, reflecting the two-way communication that may exist between two or more peer-to-peer components.

Examples of peer-to-peer systems include architectures that are based on distributed object infrastructure, such as CORBA, COM+, and Java RMI. Runtime architectural views of object systems, using notations such as collaboration diagrams, are often examples of this C&C style. Note, however, that a system designed in a non-peer-to-peer style could be *implemented* using object-based implementations and a distributed object/component infrastructure.

4.5.2 Elements, Relations, and Properties

Table 4.5 summarizes the discussion of the characteristics of the peer-to-peer style. The component types in this style are peers, such as objects, distributed objects, and clients. The principal connector type is the *invokes-procedure* connector. Unlike client-server, the interaction may be initiated by either party. Peers have interfaces that describe the services they request from other peers and the services they provide. The computational flow of peer-to-peer systems is symmetric: Peers initiate actions to achieve their computation by cooperating with their peers by requesting services from one another.

Table 4.5: Summary of the peer-to-peer style

Elements	*Component types:* peers. *Connector types:* invokes procedure.
Relations	The *attachment* relation associates peers with *invokes-procedures* connectors and determines the graph of possible component interactions.
Computational model	Peers provide interfaces and encapsulate state. Computation is achieved by cooperating peers that request services of one another.
Properties	Same as defined by the C&C viewtype, with an emphasis on protocols of interaction and performance-oriented properties. Attachments may change at runtime.
Topology	Restrictions may be placed on the number of allowable attachments to any given port, or role. Other visibility restrictions may be imposed, constraining which components can know about other components.

Constraints on the use of the peer-to-peer style might limit the number of peers that can be connected to a given peer or impose a restriction about which peers know about which other peers. The form of data may be a reference or a value. The propagation of requests from peer to peer can also be constrained.

4.5.3 What the Peer-to-Peer Style Is For and What It's Not For

The peer-to-peer style presents a view of the system that partitions the application by area of collaboration. Peers interact directly among themselves and can play the role of both clients and servers, assuming whatever role is needed for the task at hand. This partitioning provides flexibility for deploying the system across a distributed system platform. Because peers have access to the latest data, the load on any given component acting as a server is reduced, and the responsibilities that might have required more server capacity and infrastructure to support it are distributed. This can decrease the need for other communication for updating data and for central server storage but at the expense of storing the data locally.

Peer-to-peer computing is used in distributed computing applications. Using a suitable deployment, the application can make efficient use of CPU and disk resources by distributing computational-intensive work across a network of computers and by taking advantage of the resources available to the clients. The results can be shared directly among participating peers.

4.5.4 Relation to Other Styles

The absence of hierarchy means that peer-to-peer systems have a more general topology than client-server systems do.

4.5.5 Examples of the Peer-to-Peer Style

The Gnutella open source project provides software registered under the GNU License to support bidirectional information transfer using the peer-to-peer style. The topology of the system changes at runtime as users enter the system or change their connections. A user becomes a Gnutella site by installing Gnutella software that functions as a peer in the Gnutella system. A user configures the software to communicate directly with a small number of sites belonging to friends or with public Gnutella sites; these are its peers.

Gnutella supports protocols for peers to discover other peers, to search for information, and to exchange information. The Gnutella protocol among peers for obtaining information uses HTTP and is based on request and reply. If a Gnutella site A requests information from one of its peers B, that peer will respond with any information of interest. It will also pass the request to its peers, keeping a record of the request. When its peers return with information, B knows to return it to A. One property of the request is whether the information or its source is returned. Clients have the option of setting this property so that a source is returned if information might be a large piece of data. The requestor then could initiate a data exchange directly with the source through another protocol, such as client-server.

Figure 4.4 shows a small Gnutella system of four peers. The figure shows the configuration of the system, but not its behavior.

FOR MORE INFORMATION

Documentation of behavior is discussed in Chapter 8.

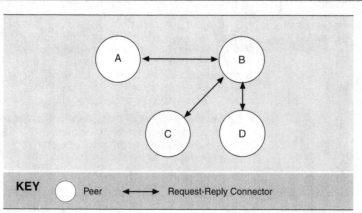

Figure 4.4
A system in the peer-to-peer style. A, C, and D are peers of B but not of each other.

KEY   ◯ Peer   ◄——► Request-Reply Connector

4.6 Communicating-Processes Style

4.6.1 Overview

The communicating-processes style is characterized by the interaction of concurrently executing components through various connector mechanisms. Examples of the connector mechanisms are synchronization, message passing, data exchange, start, stop, and so forth.

Communicating processes are common in most large systems and necessary in all distributed systems. Thus, for most systems, the communicating-processes style is an appropriate one to use to understand any behavior associated with concurrency.

4.6.2 Elements, Relations, and Properties

Table 4.6 summarizes the discussion of the characteristics of the communicating-processes style. This style represents a system as a set of concurrently executing units together with their interactions. A concurrent unit is an abstraction of more concrete software platform elements, such as tasks, processes, and threads. Connectors enable data exchange between concurrent units and control of concurrent units, such as start, stop, synchronization, and so on.

Table 4.6: Summary of the communicating-processes style

Elements	• *Component types:* concurrent units, such as tasks, processes, and threads
	• *Connector types:* data exchange, message passing, synchronization, control, and other types of communication
Relations	The *attachment* relation, as defined in the C&C viewtype
Computational model	Concurrently executing components that interact via the specific connector mechanisms
Properties of elements	• *Concurrent unit: preemptability,* which indicates that execution of the concurrent unit may be preempted by another concurrent unit or that the concurrent unit executes until it voluntarily suspends its own execution; *priority,* which influences scheduling; *timing parameters,* such as period and deadline
	• *Data exchange: buffered,* which indicates that messages are stored if they cannot be processed immediately, or *protocol,* used for communication
Topology	Arbitrary graphs

4.6.3 What the Communicating-Processes Style Is For and What It's Not For

This style is used to understand which portions of the system could operate in parallel, the bundling of components into processes, and the threads of control within the system. Therefore, this style can be used for analyzing performance and reliability. This style is also useful in design stages, when decisions are being made about which components should be assigned to which processes.

The essence of this style is that elements operate relatively independently, and concurrency is an important part of understanding how the system works. However, just because your system has processes doesn't mean that the communicating-processes style is for you. Maybe you want to instead use another style and overlay it with process boundaries later.

4.6.4 Relation to Other Styles

In practice, this style is rarely used in its pure form but instead is usually combined with another style. For example, if you want to show the concurrency aspects of a client-server system, you may want to explicitly mark the concurrent units that are servers and those that are clients. Additionally, this style is often specialized to provide watchdog information, such as a process that monitors the execution time of other processes or resource synchronization.

It is often of interest to know which communicating processes reside on which processors. The deployment style is used to allocate processes to hardware elements.

> **FOR MORE INFORMATION**
> Combined views are discussed in Section 6.3.

> **FOR MORE INFORMATION**
> The deployment style is described in Section 11.3.

4.6.5 Examples of the Communicating-Processes Style

Figure 4.5, taken from Appendix A, demonstrates one use of communicating processes within the ECS system.

4.7 Notations for C&C Styles

Practitioners document C&C architectures in various ways, although most depend on informal box-and-line diagrams. In this section, we present more rigorous strategies for documenting C&C views in Acme, an architecture description language, and in UML. Focusing on architectural structure, we explain how to document a C&C view in terms of the core concepts: components, connectors, systems, properties, and styles.

Figure 4.5
Part of the communicating-processes view from the ECS system. The Ingest subsystem deals with the initial reception of all data received at a facility and triggers subsequent archiving and processing of the data. The subsystem makes data ingest schedules available to users and programs and reports deviations from the schedules as exceptions so they can be handled through intervention by operations or science users.

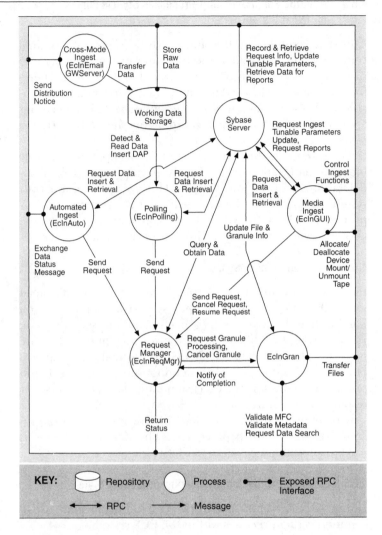

4.7.1   Informal Notations

Most informal box-and-arrow diagrams of architectures are in fact attempts to represent C&C views, although C&C views are not merely boxes and lines but rather represent computational models and the basis for analytical methods. Following some guidelines, however, can lend rigor to the process.

Within a graphical depiction, each component type should be given a separate presentation form. Similarly, each connector type should be given a separate visual form. In both cases, the types should be listed in a key. However, it is important to specify what those visual forms mean. A common source of ambiguity in most existing architectural documents is the meaning of connectors, especially the use of arrows on connectors. What exactly does the "directionality" mean? Flow of data? Flow of control?

FOR MORE INFORMATION

See Perspectives: Quivering at Arrows on page 28.

4.7.2   Formal Notations

While informal notations are often useful in the early stages of working out the documentation of a C&C architectural view, they have a number of limitations. Most importantly, different people may interpret their meaning in quite different ways. Moreover, they are usually not a good basis for detailed analytical evaluation, or tool-supported creation, maintenance, and analysis. In the remainder of this section we consider alternative, more formal notations.

ADLs and Acme

Listing 4.1 shows a partial textual description of the simple pipe-and-filter system of Figure 4.1 written in Acme, a typical **architecture description language (ADL)**. Acme is representative of a family of ADLs that treat an architecture as an annotated graph of components and connectors. Each of the top-level component and connector instances has a corresponding definition containing its type, instance name, and substructure. The types are declared in the PipeFilter family, which is Acme's name for a C&C style. The attachments of ports to roles are also described explicitly. Components and connectors may be associated with a set of properties, each of which has a name and a value. Details of the style definition, the substructure of the pipes, properties of the pipes and connectors, and the details of the MergeAndSort component are not included here; Section 4.10 cites references to that information.

DEFINITION

An **architecture description language (ADL)** is a language (graphical, textual, or both) for describing a software system in terms of its architectural elements and the relationships among them.

FOR MORE INFORMATION

For a definition of the Acme language, see [Garlan+ 2000].

```
Family PipeFilter = {
   Port Type OutputPort;
   Port Type InputPort;
   Role Type Source;
   Role Type Sink;

   Component Type Filter;
   Connector Type Pipe = {
      Role src : Source;
      Role snk : Sink;
      Properties {
         latency : int;
         pipeProtocol: String = . . . ;
      }
   };
```

Listing 4.1
Partial textual description of the simple Pipe-and-Filter system

```
};
System simple : PipeFilter = {
  Component Splitter : Filter = {
      Port pIn : InputPort = new InputPort;
      Port pOut1 : OutputPort = new OutputPort;
      Port pOut2 : OutputPort = new OutputPort;
      Properties { . . . }
  };
  Component Grep : Filter = {
      Port pIn : InputPort = new InputPort;
  Port pOut : OutputPort = new OutputPort;
  };
  Component MergeAndSort : Filter = {
      Port pIn1 : InputPort = new InputPort;
      Port pIn2 : InputPort = new InputPort;
      Port pOut : OutputPort = new OutputPort;
      Representation {
          System MergeAndSortRep : PipeFilter = {
              Component Merge : Filter = { . . . };
              Component Sort : Filter = { . . . };
              Connector MergeStream : Pipe = new Pipe;
              Attachments { . . . };
          }; /* end sub-system */
          PropertybindingNote="Bindings associate a com-
          ponent's external interfaces with interfaces of
          components internal to it."
          Bindings {
              pIn1 to Merge.pIn1;
              pIn2 to Merge.pIn2;
              pOut to Sort.pOut;
          };
      };
  };
  Connector SplitStream1 : Pipe = new Pipe;
  Connector SplitStream2 : Pipe = new Pipe;
  Connector GrepStream : Pipe = new Pipe;

  Attachments {
      Splitter.pOut1 to SplitStream1.src;
      Grep.pIn to SplitStream1.snk;
      Grep.pOut to GrepStream.src;
      MergeAndSort.pIn1 to GrepStream.snk;
      Splitter.pOut2 to SplitStream2.src;
      MergeAndSort.pIn2 to SplitStream2.snk;
  };
}; /* end system */
```

Connectors are first-class entities in Acme, having types,
such as *Pipe*. They may also have nontrivial semantics—for
example, as defined by a protocol of interaction, represented
in Acme as a particular type of connector property. Moreover,

connectors have "interfaces," which identify the roles in the interaction and may associate semantics with those interfaces. The *Filter* and *Pipe* types have many instances. Note that different instances of a component or connector type may have quite different behavior: Here we have five components of type *Filter,* each performing a different kind of computation. The *Splitter* filter has two output ports. Bindings associate the input and output ports of the *MergeAndSort* filter with the input ports of *Merge* and the output port of *Sort,* respectively. The purpose of a binding is to provide a logical association—not a communication path—as a binding does not have any specific runtime behavior of its own.

Comparing the Acme description to the informal graphical diagram shown earlier, one might wonder whether there are advantages to using such a text-based approach. Although the textual format tends to make the topological and graphical nature of the architecture less perspicuous, it has a number of advantages. Most important, the text is inherently more expressive. While, in principle, you can say anything you want using graphical forms, to do this for complex system properties requires a lot of special-purpose symbolic notation that is typically hard to learn and use, and that clutters the visual depiction. Consequently what people typically do is take a shortcut, allowing free-form annotations—which is (surprise!) after all a textual form, and not a very good one at that. In particular, such free-form notations are difficult to use as the basis of formal analysis.

Using a textual form, such as Acme, does not preclude the complementary use of graphical renditions. Indeed, virtually all ADLs have accompanying tools that allow one to view and modify C&C architectural views through a graphical interface.

Finally, comparing C&C documentation in an ADL (such as Acme) to the use of other more generic graphical and textual notations (such as UML, described below) reveals that the ADL provides a much more constrained world for describing architectural models. This has the advantage of providing concepts and notation tailor-made to architectures. For example, Acme allows one to explicitly define C&C styles and to treat connectors as first-class design entities. On the other hand, general-purpose design notations allow more flexibility in terms of the kind of elements and relations one can model, are usually better supported by commercial tools, and are often more widely understood in the software engineering community.

UML

There is no single preferred strategy in UML to document C&C views. Rather, UML offers a number of alternatives for documenting C&C views, and each alternative has its own advantages and disadvantages. Here we present three strategies for using UML to model components and connectors. We organize the presentation around the choices for representing component types and instances, as the components are typically the central design elements of an architectural description. For each choice, we consider subalternatives for the other architectural elements.

The three strategies are (1) representation of component types by UML classes and component instances by objects, (2) representation of component types as UML subsystems and component instances as subsystem instances, and (3) use of a UML profile providing a variant on the first strategy. Each of the strategies has strengths and weaknesses, depending on how well it supports the selection criteria.

- *Semantic match:* The strategy should respect documented UML semantics and the intuitions of UML modelers. The interpretation of the encoding UML model should be close to the interpretation of the component-and-connector viewtype description so the model is intelligible to both designers and UML-based tools. In addition, the mapping should produce legal UML models.

- *Visual clarity:* The resulting architectural descriptions in UML should bring conceptual clarity to a system design, avoid visual clutter, and highlight key design details.

- *Completeness:* The component-and-connector types, as well as the computational model, should be representable in the UML model.

Also there is typically a trade-off between completeness and legibility. Encodings that emphasize completeness, by providing a semantic home for all the aspects of architectural design, tend to be verbose, whereas graphically appealing encodings tend to be incomplete. Hence, the strategy you pick will depend on what aspects of architectural design need to be represented. In restricted situations, such as if there is only one type of connector, it may be preferable to use an incomplete but visually appealing encoding.

Strategy 1: Using Component Types as Classes and Component Instances as Objects
A natural candidate for representing component-and-connector types in UML is the class concept. Classes describe the con-

ceptual vocabulary of a system just as component-and-connector types form the conceptual vocabulary of an architectural description in a particular style. Additionally, the relationship between classes and objects is similar to that between architectural types and their instances. Figure 4.6 illustrates the general idea.

We now take a closer look at this strategy. The type/instance relationship in architectural descriptions is a close match to the class/object relationship in a UML model. UML classes, like component types in architectural descriptions, are first-class entities and are rich structures for capturing software abstractions. The full set of UML descriptive mechanisms is available to describe the structure, properties, and behavior of a class, making this a good choice for depicting detail and using UML-based analysis tools.

Properties of architectural components can be represented as class attributes or with associations, behavior can be described using UML behavioral models, and generalization

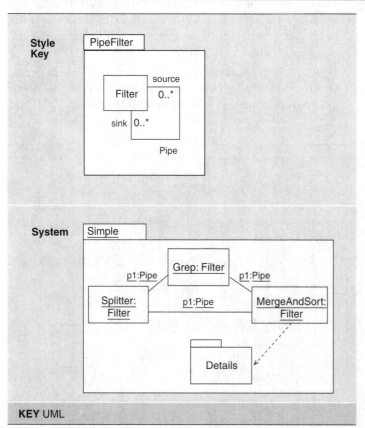

Figure 4.6
Types as classes and instances as objects. The *Filter* architectural type is represented as the UML class *Filter*. Instances of filters, such as *Splitter*, are represented as corresponding objects in an object—instance—diagram. To provide a namespace boundary, we enclose the descriptions in packages. The representation of MergeAndSort, denoted *Details*, is shown as another package and will be discussed in more detail later.

can be used to relate a set of component types. The semantics of an instance or a type can also be elaborated by attaching one of the standard stereotypes; for example, the «process» stereotype can be attached to a component to indicate that it runs as a separate process. Note that the relationship between MergeAndSort and its substructure is indicated using a dependency relation. Note also that the typical relationship between classes and instances in UML is not identical to that between architectural components and their instances. A component instance might define additional ports not required by its type or might associate an implementation in the form of additional structure that is not part of its type's definition. In UML, an object cannot include parts that its class does not also define.

With strategy 1, ports can be represented in five ways, as shown in Figure 4.7.

1. *Option 1: No explicit representation.* Leaving ports out leads to the simplest diagrams but suffers from the obvious problem that there is no way to characterize the names or the properties of the ports. However, this choice might be reasonable if the components have only a single port or if the ports can be inferred from the system topology, or if the diagram is refined elsewhere.

2. *Option 2: Ports as annotations.* Representing ports as annotations provides a home for information about ports, although annotations have no semantic value in UML and

Figure 4.7
Five ways to represent ports. Option 1 is to avoid the issue by not representing ports explicitly. Option 2 uses annotations and is a minor extension to option 1. Option 3 treats ports as an attribute of a class or an object. Option 4 treats ports as interfaces. Option 5 turns ports into classes.

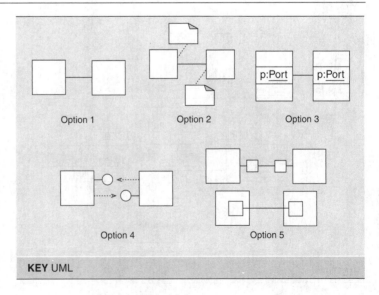

Option 1　　　Option 2　　　Option 3

Option 4　　　Option 5

KEY UML

hence cannot be used as a basis for analysis. Again, if the detailed properties of a port are not of concern, this approach might be reasonable.

3. *Option 3: Ports as class/object attributes.* Treating ports as attributes of a class/object makes them part of the formal structural model, but they can have only a simple representation in a class diagram: essentially, a name and a type. This restriction limits the expressiveness of this option.

4. *Option 4: Ports as UML interfaces.* Describing port types as UML interfaces has three advantages. First, both the interface and the port concepts characterize aspects of the ways in which an entity can interact with its environment. Second, the UML "lollipop" notation provides a compact description of a port in a class diagram depicting a component type. In an instance diagram, a UML association role, corresponding to a port instance, qualified by the interface name—the port type—provides a compact way to designate that a component instance is interacting through a particular port instance. Finally, this approach provides visually distinct depictions of components and ports, in which ports can clearly be seen as subservient to components. However, although the two concepts are similar, they are not identical. An interface exposes a set of operations that can be invoked by the environment of a component. In contrast, the description of a port in an ADL often includes both the services *provided* by the component and those it *requires* from its environment. Furthermore, it is meaningful for a component type to have several instances of the same port type, but it is not meaningful to say that a class realizes several versions of the same UML interface. For example, there is no easy way to define a "splitter" filter type that has two output ports of the same "type" using this technique. Finally, unlike classes, UML interfaces do not have attributes or substructure.

5. *Option 5: Ports as classes.* Describing ports as classes contained by a component type overcomes the lack of expressiveness of the previous alternatives: We can now represent port substructure and indicate that a component type has several ports of the same type. A component instance is modeled as an object containing a set of port objects. But by representing ports as classes, we not only clutter the diagram but also lose clear discrimination between ports and components. We could use a notational variation in which the ports are contained classes, as shown in the lower part of option 5 in Figure 4.7. Indicating points of interaction

is counterintuitive, however, as containment usually indicates that a class owns other classes whose instances may or *may not* be accessible through instances of the parent class.

Strategy 1 offers three reasonable options for representing connectors.

1. *Option 1: Connector types as associations and connector instances as links.* In an architectural box-and-line diagram of a system, the lines between components are connectors. One tempting way to represent connectors in UML is as associations between classes or links between objects. The approach is visually simple, provides a clear distinction between components and connectors, and makes use of the most familiar relationship in UML class diagrams: association. Moreover, associations can be labeled, and a direction associated with the connector can be indicated with an arrow in UML. Unfortunately, connectors and associations have different meanings. A system in an architectural description is built up by choosing components with behavior exposed through their ports and connecting them with connectors that coordinate their behaviors. A system's behavior is defined as the collective behavior of a set of components whose interaction is defined and limited by the connections between them. In contrast, although an association, or link, in UML represents a potential for interaction between the elements it relates, the association mechanism is primarily a way of describing a conceptual relationship between two elements. In addition, associations are relationships *between* UML elements, so an association cannot stand on its own in a UML model. Consequently, a connector type cannot be represented in isolation. Instead, one must resort to naming conventions or the use of stereotypes whose meaning is captured by description in UML's object constraint language. Further, the approach does not allow one to specify the interfaces to the connector, that is, its roles.

2. *Option 2: Connector types as association classes.* One solution to the lack of expressiveness is to qualify the association with a class that represents the connector type. In this way, the attributes of a connector type or a connector can be captured as attributes of a class or an object. Unfortunately, this technique still does not provide any way of explicitly representing connector roles. The approach is similar to the one taken in the UML Real-Time profile, which we consider later.

3. *Option 3: Connector types as classes and connector instances as objects.* One way to give connectors first-class status in UML is to represent type as class and connector instances as objects. Using classes and objects, we have the same options for representing roles as we had for ports: not at all, as annotations, as interfaces realized by a class, or as child classes contained by a connector class. Given a scheme for representing ports and roles, an attachment between a port and a role may be represented as an association or a dependency.

In addition to representing individual components and connectors and their types, we also need to encapsulate graphs of components and connectors: systems. Three options are available.

1. *Option 1: Systems as UML subsystems.* The primary mechanism in UML for grouping related elements is the package. In fact, UML defines a standard package stereotype, called «subsystem», to group UML models that represent a logical part of a system. The choice of subsystems is appropriate for *any* choice of mappings of components and connectors and works particularly well for grouping classes.

   One of the problems with using subsystems, as defined in UML 1.4, is that although subsystems are both a classifier and a package, the meaning is not entirely clear. Some people have argued that we should be able to treat a subsystem as an atomic classlike entity at certain stages in the development process and later be able to refine it in terms of more detailed substructure. Having the ability to do this would make the subsystem construct more appropriate for modeling architectural components.

2. *Option 2: Systems as contained objects.* Object containment can be used to represent systems. Components are represented as instances of contained classes, and connectors are modeled using one of the options outlined earlier. Objects provide a strong encapsulation boundary and carry with them the notion that each instance of the class will have the associated "substructure."

   However, this approach has problems. The most important one is that associations, used to model connectors between contained classes, are not scoped by the class. That is, it is not possible to say that a pair of classes interacts via a particular connector, modeled as an association, only in the context of a particular system. So, for example, indicating that two contained classes interact via an association is valid for instances of those classes used anywhere else in the model.

3. *Option 3: Systems as collaborations.* A set of communicating objects connected by links is described in UML using a collaboration. If we represent components as objects, we can use collaborations to represent systems. A collaboration defines a set of participants and relationships that are meaningful for a given set of purposes, which in this case is to describe the runtime structure of the system. The participants define classifier roles that objects play, or conform to, when interacting. Similarly, the relationships define association roles that links must conform to.

Collaboration diagrams can be used to present collaborations at either the specification or the instance level. A specification-level collaboration diagram shows the roles, defined within the collaboration, arranged in a pattern to describe the system substructure. An instance-level collaboration diagram shows the objects and links conforming to the roles at the specification level and interacting to achieve the purpose. Therefore, a collaboration presented at the instance level is best used to represent the runtime structure of the system.

Figure 4.8 illustrates this approach. Although this is a natural way to describe runtime structures, it leaves no way to explicitly represent system-level properties. There is also a semantic mismatch; a collaboration describes a representative interaction between objects and provides a partial description, whereas an architectural configuration is meant to capture a complete description.

Strategy 2: Using Subsystems
The second strategy for using UML to model components and connectors is to use UML subsystems. This approach is appealing because packages are an ideal way to describe coarse-grained elements as a set of UML models. Also the package construct is already familiar to UML modelers as a way of bundling pieces or views of a system. Figure 4.9 shows the filter type as a package, and filter instances as package instances.

The subsystem construct is used in UML to group, or encapsulate, a set of model elements that describe a logical piece of a system, similar to components in architectural descriptions. Subsystems—indeed, any package—can include structures based on any of the UML models. The advantage over describing components and connectors as classes is that by identifying a component or a connector with a package, we can include structure as classes, or objects *and* behavioral models. This approach also has a visual appeal; substructure

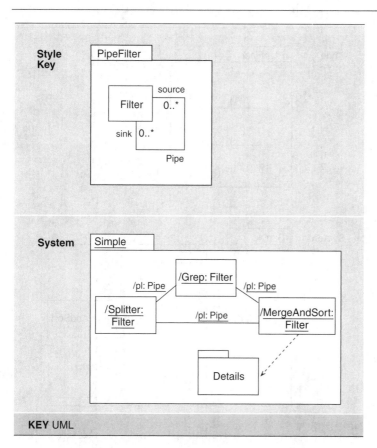

Figure 4.8
Systems as collaborations.
The *Filter* architectural type
is represented as previously. Instances of *Filters*
and *Pipes* are represented
as corresponding classifier
roles—for example, */Splitter* indicates the *Splitter*
role—and association
roles, and the objects and
links conforming to those
roles are shown in the collaboration diagram at the
instance level, indicated by
underlines on the names.

can be depicted as "embedded" in the package. Components and component types would be modeled in essentially the same way, although one could also take advantage of the UML template mechanism when defining a type.

However, the use of subsystems to model components suffers from a number of problems. In UML, a subsystem has no behavior of its own, so all communications sent to a closed subsystem must be redirected to instances inside the subsystem, and UML leaves that redirection unspecified as a semantic variation point. Second, subsystem interfaces raise the same set of issues mentioned for class interfaces. (That is, it is impossible to model several interfaces of the same type on the same subsystem.) Third, representing substructure, such as ports, as elements contained by a subsystem is arguably counterintuitive. The fact that certain elements correspond to ports, others to properties, and others to representations is likely to be misleading.

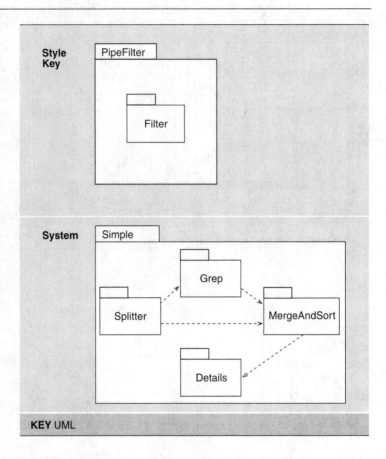

Figure 4.9
Components as sub-systems

This scheme provides two natural choices for representing connectors: as dependencies—visually simple but lacking expressiveness—or as subsystems themselves. Dependencies have visual appeal, but they do not provide a way to define more detailed aspects of a connector. Using subsystems to model connectors—similar to using objects or classes to model connectors in the previous two approaches—suffers from the problem that components and connectors are not distinguishable.

Strategy 3: Using the UML Real-Time Profile
Thus far, we have examined ways to encode architectural concepts in generic UML. We now consider a different approach. Rather than using *generic* UML, we start by leveraging the work done in defining a specific UML profile—namely, the UML Real-Time (UML-RT) profile. A UML profile is a collection of stereotypes, constraints, and tagged values that can be bundled to form a domain-specific language specialization.

UML-RT, a profile originally developed by the telecommunication industry to meet its software development needs, benefits from a rich pool of commercial experience. In particular, UML-RT adopts the notion of a connector between components as a protocol. Unlike generic UML, the profile provides a natural home for expressing runtime structures, and supplies a semantic mapping to UML. It also is supported by commercial tools.

In UML-RT, the primary unit for encapsulating computation is the *capsule*. Capsules can have interfaces and can be hierarchically decomposed. Component types map to UML capsule-stereotyped classes; component instances map to capsule-stereotyped objects—in a collaboration diagram.

Component ports map to UML-RT ports, because both serve as interfaces that define points of interaction between the computational elements and the environment. Port instances map to UML port-stereotyped objects. Port types could likewise be mapped to port-stereotyped implementation classes, but a UML-RT protocol role defines the *type* of the port. Instead, we can map port types to protocolRole-stereotyped classes in UML.

Connectors map to UML-RT connectors because both represent interactions between the computational units. Connector types map to the UML AssociationClasses, and connector instances map to UML links, instances of UML association. UML-RT protocols represent the behavioral aspects of UML-RT connectors.

Systems describe the structural configuration, as do UML-RT collaborations. Thus, systems map to collaborations.

Table 4.7 summarizes the relationship between UML-RT and the concepts of the C&C viewtype. To illustrate this mapping, Figure 4.10 shows the simple pipe-and-filter system of Figure 4.1, but now drawn in UML-RT, using the strategy just outlined. In Figure 4.10, the filters become capsules of type *Filter*, each with input and output ports. A slash prepending the name denotes a role in a collaboration. The pipes become connectors that conform, in this case, to a pipe protocol (*ProtPipe*) with a *source* and a *sink* protocol role. The output and input Acme ports, joined by the connector, therefore play the *source* and *sink* protocol roles, respectively. Because a UML-RT port plays a specific role in some protocols, the protocol role defines the type of the port, which simply means that the port implements the behavior specified by that protocol role. Thus, *pOut*'s type is *ProtPipe::source*, and *pIn*'s type is *ProtPipe::sink*. For visual simplicity, only two of the port instances are labeled.

Table 4.7: Summary of mapping from C&C to UML-RT (ordered by instance, then type, if present)

C&C	UML-RT
Component	«Capsule» instance
Type	«Capsule» class
Port	«Port» instance
Type	«ProtocolRole» class
Connector	«Connector» (link)
Type	AssociationClass
(Behavioral constraint)	«Protocol» class
Role	No explicit mapping; implicit elements: LinkEnd
Type	AssociationEnd
System	Collaboration

Figure 4.10
UML-RT description for system simple. The filter type is defined as a capsule, a class stereotype. The system consists of three top-level capsule instances, one of which is further decomposed into two sub-capsules.

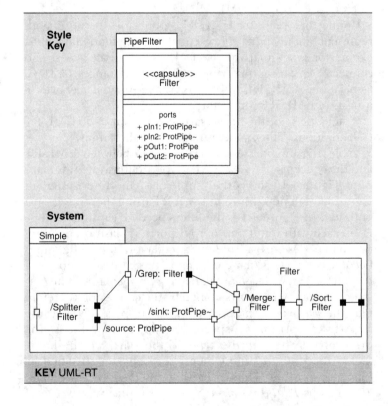

For binary protocols, UML-RT provides notational conventions for the port icon and the type name. The role selected as the base protocol role—in this case, the *source* role—is shown as a black-filled box, with the type denoted only by the protocol name; the other, conjugate role is shown as a white-filled box, with the type denoted by appending ~ to the protocol name, as shown in Figure 4.10.

The collaboration diagram is presented at the specification level to indicate how the capsules participate in the system. The filter representing MergeAndFilter is shown as a capsule class instead of a capsule role for a similar reason: to convey a pattern of interaction for the internal capsules. Finally, the bindings from the external port to the internal port are shown as normal connectors.

Because only one *Filter* type is in the *simple PipeFilter* system, only one class is in the class diagram shown in Figure 4.10. In UML-RT, all elements contained by a capsule are considered attributes of that capsule class, and all attributes have protected visibility except ports, which have public visibility, indicated by + on the port attribute. Additionally, ports are listed in a separately named compartment. The «capsule»-stereotyped *Filter* class has four ports: two as *sources* and two as *sinks*. The reason is that each *Filter* has either one or two ports of each type, so two are defined to accommodate all *Filter* instances, whereas only the used ports are shown in the collaboration diagram. The connectors in the collaboration diagram do not have a counterpart in the class diagram, because the connectors associate the *Ports*, not the *Filter*.

PERSPECTIVES

Using Classes to Represent Component Types and Instances

A sometimes-used variation of the strategy to use classes and objects is to use classes to represent *both* component types and instances. By representing both component types and instances as classes, we have the full set of UML features to describe them. We can also capture patterns at both the type—as part of a description of an architectural style—and instance levels, supporting the description of a dynamic architecture whose structure evolves at runtime.

Figure 4.11 illustrates this approach, defining both the *Filter* type and instances of *Filters*, such as *Splitter,* as classes. Unfortunately, this variation on strategy 1 suffers from several problems. Representing both types and instances as

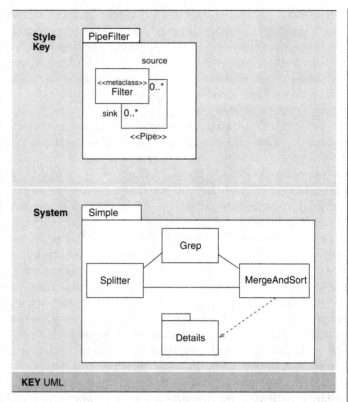

Figure 4.11
Types and instances as classes

classes blurs the distinction between type and instance. However, the major problem with this approach is that, owing to the semantics of classes, it is unable to handle situations characterized by multiple instances of the same component type. Consider system description a1 in Figure 4.12. Although it suggests two distinct instances of component A, there is, in fact, only *one* instance because a1 and a2 are equivalent. It is also worth noting that the class diagram b1 in Figure 4.12 does not require A to be shared in the object instance level. Either of the instance diagrams in b2 is a legal representation of b1.

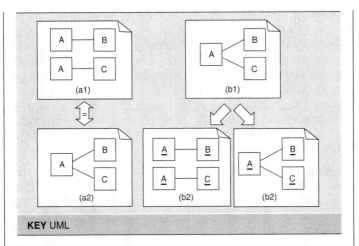

KEY UML

Figure 4.12
Representing component instances as classes doesn't work when a component appears multiple times in a system. Class diagram a1 has the same meaning as a2, even though class A appears twice in a1. Conversely, both object diagrams shown in b2 are consistent with the class diagram b1, even though class A appears only once in b1.

—D.G.

COMING TO TERMS

Components Versus UML Components

UML's component modeling element is used to describe *implementation* artifacts of a system and their deployment. A UML component diagram is often used to depict the topology of a system at a high level of granularity and plays a similar function, although at the implementation level, as an architectural description of a system.

At first glance, UML components appear to be natural candidates for representing architectural components. Components have interfaces, may be deployed on hardware, and commonly carry a stereotype and are depicted with a custom visualization. UML components are often used as part of diagrams that depict an overall topology, and just as it is natural to talk about mapping architectural components to hardware, components are assigned to nodes in UML deployment diagrams. For some architectural styles, the identification of abstract components with implementation-level components is a reasonable choice.

But in UML, components are defined as concrete chunks of implementation—for example, executables, or dynamic link libraries—that realize abstract interfaces. In the C&C view-type, the notion of components is unlike the more abstract, frequently having only an indirect relationship to a deploy-able piece of a system. Nonetheless, the concepts share more than a name. As with classes, components expose interfaces and can be used to represent the ports exposed by a component, just as they were used in the strategy based on classes and objects.

However, the rich set of class associations available to relate classes is not available for components, limiting how we can describe ports, represent patterns, and indicate connection. (Moreover, UML behavioral models cannot reference components.)

This scheme has two natural choices for representing connectors: as dependencies between a component and the ports/interfaces realized by a component—visually simple but lacking expressiveness—or as components themselves. If we represent connector instances as dependencies between components, we have the option of representing connector types as stereotypes, with consequences we addressed in previous sections. Unfortunately, although dependencies are visually appealing, the built-in dependency notion in UML does not adequately capture the idea of architectural connection or provide an explicit descriptive capability. Representing a connector as a UML component addresses this problem but blurs the distinction between components and connectors.

Conclusions

The current definition of UML does not favor a single best way to document C&C views. Each strategy has certain strengths and weaknesses, and in practice you are likely to see all of them. All of the strategies exhibit some form of semantic incompleteness or mismatch. The key stumbling blocks are difficulties in faithfully representing ports, connectors, and substructure. With respect to ports the primary difficulty is to support the definition of multiple ports of the same type. With respect to connectors, the primary difficulty is to support definition of connector types independent of any particular use of them. With respect to substructure, the primary difficulty is to be able to limit the scope of the substructure definition to the element being elaborated.

In the final analysis, UML can be made to work, typically by sacrificing completeness in the diagram, and making up for it in supporting documentation. A reasonable alternative is to use a profile, such as UML-RT, which, although nonstandard, provides a better match to the architectural documentation task.

4.8 Summary Checklist

- C&C styles specialize the C&C viewtype by introducing a specific set of component-and-connector types and by specifying rules about how elements of those types can be combined. A C&C style is typically associated with a pattern of interaction that prescribes how computation, data, and control flow through systems in this style.

- Several dozen C&C styles have been described in design books. This chapter presents six generally useful ones.

- In the pipe-and-filter style, the pattern of interaction is characterized by successive transformations of data. Data arrives at a filter, is transformed, and is passed through the pipe to the next filter or filters in the pipeline.

- Analyses associated with pipe-and-filter systems include deriving the aggregate transformation provided by a graph of filters and reasoning about system performance.

- In the shared-data style, the pattern of interaction is dominated by the retention of persistent data. There are multiple accessors of the data and at least one repository where the persistent data is retained.

- Analyses associated with the shared-data style usually center on performance, security, privacy, reliability, and compatibility with, for example, existing repositories and their data.

- In the publish-subscribe style, components interact by announcing events. Components may subscribe to a set of events. It is the job of the publish-subscribe runtime infrastructure to make sure that each published event is delivered to all subscribers of that event.

- The publish-subscribe style is used to send events and messages to an unknown set of recipients. Because the set of recipients is unknown, a new recipient can be added without modification to the producers.

- The client-server style shows components interacting by requesting services of other components. The essence of this style is that communication is typically paired. A request for service from a client is normally paired with the provision of that service.

- The client-server style supports learning about the system in terms of separating out common services. The partitioning of functionality into clients and servers allows them to be independently assigned to tiers, based on runtime criteria. Client-server system analyses include determining whether the system's servers provide the client-required services, dependability analyses, security analyses, and performance.

- Peer-to-peer systems provide for the exchange of services by direct exchange among components. Peer-to-peer is a kind of call/return style without the asymmetry found in the client-server style. Any component can in principle interact with any other component by requesting its services.

- The peer-to-peer style provides flexibility of deploying the system across a global system platform.

- The communicating-processes style is characterized by the interaction of concurrently executing components through various connector mechanisms, such as synchronization, message passing, data exchange, start, stop, and so forth.

- For most systems, the communicating-processes style is an appropriate one to use to understand any behavior associated with concurrency, especially for analyzing performance and reliability.

- C&C styles are sometimes the subject of confusion with one another and with styles in other viewtypes.

- Informal box-and-line notations are often used to document C&C styles. UML provides several strategies for representing C&C styles, each of which has shortcomings. Principal strategies include (1) using classes and objects; (2) using subsystems, and (3) using the UML Real-Time Profile.

4.9   Discussion Questions

1. Publish-subscribe, client-server, and other call-and-return styles all involve interactions between producers and consumers of data or services. If an architect is not careful when using one of these styles, he or she will produce a C&C view that simply shows a request flowing in one direction and a response flowing in the other. What means are at the architect's disposal to distinguish among these styles?

2. Some forms of publish-subscribe involve runtime registration; others allow only pre-runtime registration. How would you represent each of these cases?

3. If you wanted to show a C&C view that emphasizes the system's security aspects, what kinds of properties might you

associate with the components? With the connectors? (*Hint:* This topic is discussed in Chapter 9.)

4. Suppose that the middle tier of a three-tier system is a data repository. Is this system a shared-data system, a three-tier system, a client-server system, all of them, or none? Justify your answer.

4.10   For Further Reading

The reader interested in finding out more about a particular style can look in one of the many style catalogs available. Style catalogs can be found in Shaw and Garlan [ShawGarlan 96], Buschmann et al. [Buschmann+ 96], and Schmidt et al. [Schmidt+ 00]. In addition, a description of blackboards can be found in Nii [Nii 86]. A description of communicating processes can be found in CSP [Hoare 85].

There is not widespread agreement about what to call styles or how to group them. While this might seem like an issue of importance only to the catalog purveyors, it has documentation ramifications as well. For instance, suppose you choose a client-server style for your system. In theory, that should free you of some documentation obligations, because you should be able to appeal to a style catalog for details. However, Shaw and Clements are able to identify not one but three different varieties of client-server style, and they assign each to a different style family [ShawClements 97].

Details of the PipeFilter system used in the example are described in [GarlanKompanek 00]. Acme is described in [Garlan+ 00]. Acme is representative of a family of architectural description languages that treat an architecture as an annotated graph of components and connectors. Other languages in the Acme family include ADML [OpenGroupADML 00] and xArch [Dashofy+ 01]. UML-RT is described in [SelicRumbaugh 98].

The Allocation Viewtype and Styles

5.1   Overview

In previous chapters, we discussed various aspects of software architecture and how to document them. Hardware, file systems, and team structure all interact with the software architecture, and this interaction must also be documented. It is through the mapping of the software architecture onto hardware that the performance of the system can be analyzed; it is through the mapping of the software architecture onto the team structure that project management activities can proceed; and it is through the mapping of the software environment onto a file structure that the management of the system's development can be done. This chapter focuses on the viewtype and styles that represent these interactions.

We begin by considering the most general form of the mapping of the software architecture onto its environment. We call this general form the *allocation viewtype*, which presents a mapping from the elements of either a module or a component-and-connector style onto elements of the environment. We then identify three common styles, as shown in Figure 5.1:

- The deployment style describes the mapping of the components and connectors onto the hardware on which the software executes.

- The implementation style describes the mapping of modules onto a file system that contains these modules.

- The work assignment style describes the mapping of modules onto the people, groups, or teams tasked with the development of the modules.

Figure 5.1
Three styles of the allocation viewtype are deployment, or mapping software architecture to a hardware environment; implementation, or mapping it to a file management system; and work assignment, or mapping it to an organization of teams.

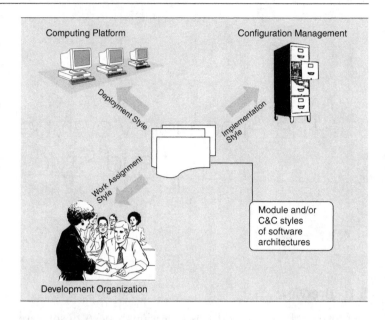

5.2 Elements, Relations, and Properties of the Allocation Viewtype

Table 5.1 summarizes the discussion of the characteristics of the allocation viewtype. The elements of the allocation viewtype are software elements and environmental elements. An environmental element represents a piece of an environmental structure, such as a processor, a disk farm, a configuration item, or a development group. The software elements in a style of the allocation viewtype come from a style in either the module or the C&C viewtype. The elements, not relations, from the module or C&C styles are emphasized in an allocation style.

The relation in an allocation viewtype is the *allocated-to* relation, with the direction from the software element to the environmental element. A single software element can be allocated to multiple environmental elements, and multiple software elements can be allocated to a single environmental element. If these allocations change over time—both during development and execution of the system—the techniques of specifying architectural dynamism can be brought to bear.

Software elements and environmental elements have properties. What the specific properties are depends on the purpose of the allocation. Allocating software to an environmental element always means matching required properties of the software element to the provided properties of the environmental element. If that property match cannot be made, an *allocated-to* relation would not be valid. For example, to ensure the required response

FOR MORE INFORMATION

Documenting dynamic architectures is covered in Section 6.4.

time of a component, it has to execute on a sufficiently fast processor. This might be a simple comparison: An IEEE 754 single-precision floating-point multiply must execute in 50 microseconds. You can look at the instruction timings for the target processor to verify that this requirement will be met. These comparisons might be more complicated: The task cannot use more than 10 kilobytes of virtual memory. In this case, an execution model of the software element in question must be performed, and then the virtual memory usage can be determined.

Table 5.1: Summary of the allocation viewtype

Elements	Software element and environmental element.
Relations	*Allocated-to.* A software element is allocated to an environmental element.
Properties of elements	A software element has *required* properties. An environmental element has *provided* properties that need to be matched.
Properties of relations	Dependent on the particular style.
Topology	Varies by style.

The specific uses and notations for styles of the allocation viewtype are style specific and are covered in their respective sections. Even though the notation constituents are different for each style, the styles are dominated by the environmental elements; the software elements take a secondary role.

We now look at some of the more common styles of the allocation viewtype. Each of these styles constrains the basic allocation viewtype, perhaps adding specialized versions of elements and relation types.

5.3 Deployment Style

5.3.1 Overview

In the deployment style, elements of a C&C style—usually the communicating-processes style—are allocated to execution platforms. The constraints for any particular allocation are the requirements expressed by the software elements and how those requirements are met by characteristics of the relevant hardware element(s).

5.3.2 Elements, Relations, and Properties

Table 5.2 summarizes the discussion of the characteristics of the deployment style. Environmental elements in the deployment style are entities that correspond to physical units that store, transmit, or compute data. Physical units include processing nodes (CPUs), communication channels, memory stores, and data stores.

Table 5.2: Summary of the deployment style

Elements	• *Software element,* usually a process from the C&C viewtype
	• *Environmental elements:* computing hardware—processor, memory, disk, network, and so on
Relations	• *Allocated-to,* showing on which physical units the software elements reside
	• *Migrates-to, copy-migrates-to,* and/or *execution-migrates-to* if the allocation is dynamic
Properties of elements	• *Required* properties of a software element: the significant hardware aspects, such as processing, memory, capacity requirements, and fault tolerance
	• *Provided* properties of an environmental element: the significant hardware aspects that influence the allocation decision
Properties of relations	*Allocated-to* relation: either static or dynamic, as discussed in Section 6.4
Topology	Unrestricted

The software elements in this style are usually derived from elements in a C&C view corresponding to processes. When represented in the deployment style, the software elements are assumed to run on a computer with operating system support. Therefore, software elements in this style are likely operating system processes.

The typical relation depicted in the deployment style is a special *allocated-to* form that shows on which physical units the software elements reside. The relation can be dynamic; that is, the allocation can change as the system executes. In this case, additional relations, such as the following, may be shown.

- *Migrates-to:* A relation from a software element on one processor to the same software element on a different processor, this relation indicates that a software element can move from processor to processor but does not simultaneously exist on both processors.

- *Copy-migrates-to:* This relation is similar to the *migrates-to* relation, except that the software element sends a copy of itself to the new process element while retaining a copy on the original processing element.

- *Execution-migrates-to:* Similar to the previous two, this relation indicates that execution moves from processor to processor but that the code residency does not change. A copy of a process exists on more than one processor, but only one is active at any particular time. The execution of the process "migrates" when the active process is changed.

It is also possible for the allocation to change over time as a result of manual reconfiguration. In this case, the possibilities represent variation points.

FOR MORE INFORMATION
Documenting variability and dynamism is discussed in Section 6.4.

The important properties of the elements, both software and physical, of the deployment style are those that affect the allocation of the software to the physical elements. How a physical element satisfies a software element requirement is determined by the properties of both. For example, if a software element FOO requires a minumum storage capacity, any environment element that has at least that capacity is a candidate for a successful allocation of FOO.

Moreover, the types of analyses performed based on a deployment style also detemine the particular properties the elements must possess. For example, if a memory capacity analysis is needed, the necessary properties of the software elements must describe memory consumption aspects, and the relevant environment element properties must depict memory capacities of the various hardware entities.

Following are some environmental element properties relevant to physical units.

- *CPU properties:* A set of properties relevant to the various processing elements may be specified. These properties include processor clock speed, number of processors, memory capacity, bus speed, and instruction execution speed.

- *Memory properties:* A set of properties relevant to the memory stores may be specified. These properties include memory size and speed characteristics.

- *Disk or other storage unit capacity:* This property specifies the storage capacity and access speed of disk units: individual disk drives, disk farms, and RAID [redundant array of inexperience disks] units.

- *Bandwidth:* This property indicates the data transfer capacity of communication channels.

- *Fault tolerance:* Multiple hardware units may perform the same function, and these units may have a failover control mechanism.

Properties that are relevant to software elements include

- *Resource consumption:* For example, computation takes 32,123 instructions.
- *Resource requirements and constraints that must be satisfied:* For example, a software element must execute in 0.1 second.
- *Safety critical:* For example, a software element must always be running.

The following property is relevant to the allocation:

- *Migration trigger:* If the allocation can change as the system executes, this property specifies what must occur for a migration of a software element from one processing element to another.

5.3.3   What the Deployment Style Is For and What It's Not For

The deployment style is used for analyses of performance, reliability, and security. It is also used as a portion of cost estimation.

Performance is tuned by changing the allocation of software to hardware. Optimal or improved allocation decisions are those that eliminate bottlenecks on processors or that distribute work more evenly so that processor utilization is roughly even across the system. Often performance improvement is achieved by colocating deployment units that have frequent and/or high-bandwidth communications with one another. The volume and the frequency of communication among deployable units on different processing elements, which takes place along the communication channels among those elements, is the focus for much of the performance engineering of a system.

Reliability is directly affected by the system's behavior in the face of degraded or failed processing elements or communication channels. If it is assumed that a processor or a channel will fail without warning, copies of deployable units are placed on separate processors. If it is assumed that a warning will precede a failure, deployable units can be migrated at runtime when a failure is imminent.[1] Typical users of this structure are performance engineers, who use this structure to design and

---

1. If every processing element has enough memory to host a copy of every deployable unit, runtime migration need not occur. When a failure occurs, a different copy of the no-longer-available deployable unit becomes active, but no migration of code occurs.

to predict system performance; testers, who use this structure to understand runtime dependencies; and integraters, who use this view to plan integration and integration testing.

The cost of deploying a system depends on the hardware elements of that system. Therefore, the deployment view is used to display the hardware elements of a particular configuration and their purposes. The purposes are given by the processes deployed on the various hardware elements.

Modern software architectures seek to make allocation decisions transparent and thus changeable. Therefore, for example, interprocess communication should be coded in exactly the same fashion whether the two processes reside on the same or on different processors. So the deployment style may contain information that implementers should not be allowed to assume or to use. When allocation decisions are dynamic, the *migrates-to* relation in its various forms must be used to indicate the dynamism.

Additionally, allocations can capture enterprise deployments, whereby the allocation of subsystems is dependent on an organization in the enterprise. Each organization can use its own policies and standards to control the deployment.

An incorrect use of a deployment style is to treat it as the software architecture of a system. A single view of this style, in isolation, is not a complete description of a software architecture. Although this observation is true of every style, no matter what its viewtype, allocation styles seem especially susceptible. When asked for their software architecture, people sometimes present an impressive diagram that shows a network of computers with all their properties and protocols used and the software components running on those computers. Although these diagrams fulfill an important role by helping to organize the work and to understand the software, they do not fully represent the software architecture.

Design errors involving the deployment style usually center on forcing other units of software to conform to the deployable units allocated to a single processor. For example, it is usually not the case that a processor's resident software should correspond to a module or a layer; these are typically spread among several processors.

5.3.4 Notation for the Deployment Style

Informal Notations

Informal graphical notations contain boxes, circles, lines, arrows, and so on. Boxes and circles are used to represent the software and environmental elements and the lines and arrows are used to represent the *allocated-to* relation. In many cases, stylized symbols or icons are used to represent the environmental elements. The symbols are frequently pictures of the hardware devices in question. Additionally, shading, color, border types, and fill patterns are often used to indicate the type of element. Software elements can be listed inside or next to the hardware to which they're allocated. If the deployment structure is simple, a table that lists the software units and the hardware element on which each executes may be adequate. Figure 5.2 shows an example of informal notation for the deployment style.

UML

Figure 5.3 shows an example of UML notation for the deployment style.

In UML, a deployment diagram is a graph of nodes connected by communication associations. Nodes correspond to processing elements, usually having a memory and a processing capability. Nodes may contain component instances, indicating that the component resides on the node. Components can be connected to each other by dependency arrows. In a UML deployment diagram, components may contain objects, meaning that the objects are part of those components. Migration of components from node to node (or objects from component to component) is shown by the <<becomes>>

Figure 5.2
Example view of the deployment style in an informal notation. This example uses distinctive symbols for different types of hardware. The connecting lines are physical communication channels that allow the processes to communicate with one another. The line between the DNS Server and the FTP Server also has a property—Trusted— assigned with it. The allocation of the processes is done by writing their names below the symbol. Note that the "processes" mentioned, such as FTP and Office Suite, are not processes in the operating system sense but rather are applications or components as defined by the C&C viewtype.

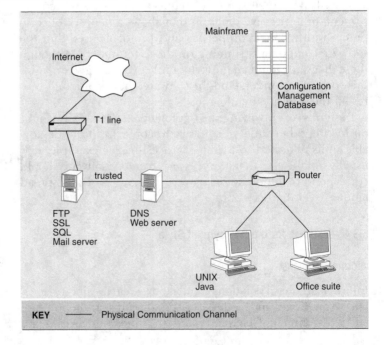

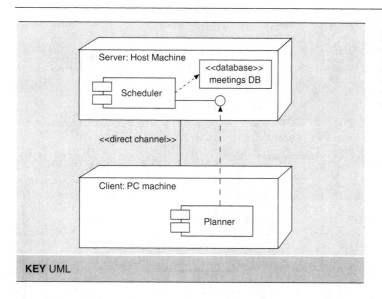

Figure 5.3
A deployment view in UML, showing a client-server system in which the server has a scheduler that maintains a meeting database and the client has planner software (Rumbaugh, Jacobson, and Booch 1999, p. 253)

stereotype of dependency. A node is shown using a symbol that looks like a 3-D box, with an optional name inside. Nodes are connected by associations that stand for communication paths. The precise nature of the communication path can be indicated by a stereotype on the association.

5.3.5 Relation to Other Styles

Clearly, the deployment style is related to the C&C style(s) that provided the software elements that are allocated to the physical environment.

5.3.6 Examples of the Deployment Style

Figure 5.4, taken from Appendix A, shows part of the deployment view of the ECS system.

5.4 Implementation Style

5.4.1 Overview

The implementation style maps modules of a module viewtype to a development infrastructure. Implementing a module always results in many separate files, such as those that contain the source code, files that have to be included and usually contain definitions, files that describe how to build an executable, and files that are the result of translating, or compiling, the module. Those files need to be organized so as not to lose control and integrity of the system. Configuration management

Figure 5.4
Primary presentation from the ECS deployment view. The elements are subsystems, host computers, routers, switches, and networks. The subsystems are the software elements, and they are defined in the ECS decomposition view. The remainder are environmental elements defined in the deployment view's supporting documentation.

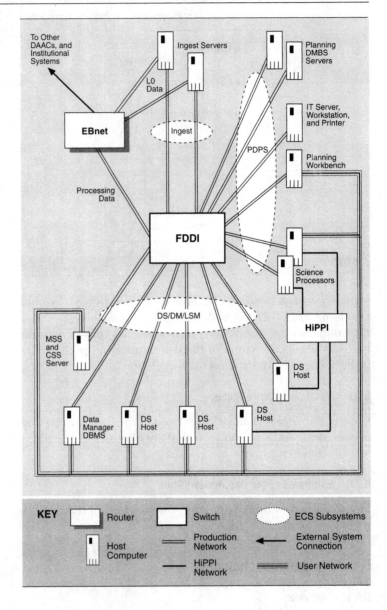

techniques usually do this job: in the simplest case, a hierarchy of directories in a file system.

A view in the implementation style can also be much more elaborate, perhaps showing special configuration items for various kinds of modules, such as those items that need a specific test procedure. This usually requires a more sophisticated configuration management system that allows the definition of new configuration items and complex processes necessary to create new items in the structure.

5.4.2 Elements, Relations, and Properties

Table 5.3 summarizes the discussion of characteristics of the implementation style. Environmental elements in the implementation style are configuration items: files in a file system or primitives managed by the configuration management system. In the simplest case, those configuration items are directories for organizational purposes and files as containers for the information. The software elements are modules of any style of module viewtype, such as functions or classes.

Two relations in the implementation style are

- *Allocated-to:* A relation between modules and configuration items. This relation connects a module with the configuration item that implements that module and is mostly a one-to-one relationship. However, the configuration item can be composed of multiple items.

- *Containment:* A relation between configuration items. This relation indicates that a configuration item contains other configuration items. One configuration item can be contained in multiple other configuration items. Examples include directory structures and version branches.

Table 5.3: Summary of the implementation style

Elements	• Software element: a module
	• Environmental element: a configuration item, such as a file or a directory
Relations	• *Containment,* specifying that one configuration item is contained in another
	• *Allocated-to,* describing the allocation of a module to a configuration item
Properties of elements	• *Required* properties of a software element, if any: usually, requirements on the developing environments, such as Java or a database
	• *Provided* properties of an environmental element: indications of the characteristics provided by the development environments
Properties of relations	None
Topology	Hierarchical configuration items: *is-contained-in*

As with the deployment style, the important properties of the software and enviromental elements of the implementation style are those that affect the allocation of the software to configuration items. For example, how a configuration management system deals with histories and branches is a configuration item property; a specific version of a Java compiler to use might be a property of a software module. A dependency that requires one module to be compiled before another is a property of a software module.

5.4.3 What the Implementation Style Is For and What It's Not For

The implementation style is used during development and at build time to manage and to maintain the files that correspond to software elements. Developers use this style to identify files that they can check for updating, testing, or system building; and to check back in new releases.

The implementation style can be used to specify the version differences of a particular system. This style can also be used to highlight those elements that are used for special purposes, such as testing, or to analyze the configuration management for a system.

5.4.4 Notation for the Implementation Style

Any notation for the implementation style must have modules, the configuration items, and the mapping between them. Ideally, icons are used to distinguish the configuration items from the modules. The decomposition of the configuration items should also be shown. Figure 5.5 shows an example of a

Figure 5.5
Implementation view in an informal notaticn. The configuration items are directories and files. The lines show containment. The allocation relation is shown as a name convention, not as an explicit line. Allocations as a name convention are frequently used and usually indicate missing tool support.

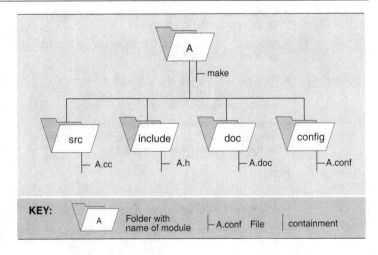

small implementation view, rendered in an informal notation specialized to the style.

5.4.5 Relation to Other Styles

The implementation style is naturally most strongly related to the module styles that provide the software elements for the allocation.

5.4.6 Example of the Implementation Style

An implementation style is included in the NASA ECS example in Appendix A.

5.5 Work Assignment Style

In the 1960s, Conway [1968] formulated a law that the architectural structure mirrors the organizational structure. He based his law on ease of communication within as opposed to across groups. This law is an organizational articulation of coupling and coherence. Software work breakdown structures have always been based on some decomposition of the system being built into parts: a software architecture. More recently, Paulish [2001] has observed that accurate time and budget estimates depend on basing them on the software architecture. Paulish's observation has a strong intuitive base, as the time and budget estimates depend on the work breakdown structure, which in turn depends on the software architecture.

Because work assignments represent a mapping of the software architecture onto groups of humans, it is an important allocation style. Teams—and hence work assignments—are not simply associated with building software that will run in the final system. Even if software is purchased in its entirety as a commercial product without the need for any implementation work, someone has to be responsible for procuring it, testing it, and understanding how it works, and someone has to "speak" for it during integration and system testing. The team responsible for that has a place in the work assignment view. Also, software written to support the building of the system—tools, environments, test harnesses, and so on—and the responsible team have a first-class place in the work assignment style.

5.5.1 Elements, Relations, and Properties

Table 5.4 summarizes the discussion of the characteristics of the work assignment style. The elements of this style are software modules and people elements.

Table 5.4: Summary of the work assignment style

Elements	• Software element: a module • Environmental element: an organizational unit, such as a person, a team, a department, a sub-contractor, and so on
Relations	*Allocated-to*
Properties of elements	Skills set: *required* and *provided*
Properties of relations	None
Topology	In general, unrestricted; in practice, usually restricted so that one module is allocated to one organizational unit

- The production, acquisition, testing, and/or integration of software modules are the responsibility of an individual or a team of people. Documentation of the work assignment style must include information about each module to bound its scope and responsibilities: in essence, to give its team its charter.

- The people elements denote organizational units or specific teams of people or personnel roles. People within a people element may belong to multiple teams for multiple purposes. For example, a common practice is for a person to have one reporting relationship for personnel matters, such as reviews, and other reporting relationships for development. Within the work assignment style, we are concerned only with those teams that have developmental responsibilities.

In this style, the *allocated-to* relation maps from software elements to people elements.

A well-formed work assignment relation has the property of completeness—all work is accounted for—and no overlap—no work is assigned to two places. Properties of the software elements may include a description of the required skill set, whereas properties of the people elements may include provided skill sets.

5.5.2 What the Work Assignment Style Is For and What It's Not For

The work assignment style shows the major units of software that must be present to form a working system and who will produce them, as well as the tools and environments in which the software is developed. This style is well suited for managing team resource allocations and for explaining the structure of a project—to a new hire, for example. This style is the basis for work breakdown structures and for detailed budget and schedule estimates.

The work assignment style does not show runtime relations, such as *calls* or *passes-data-to*. Nor does it show dependency relations among the modules.

5.5.3 Notations for the Work Assignment Style

No special notations for architectural work assignments exist.

5.5.4 Relation to Other Styles

The work assignment style is strongly related to and uses the module decomposition style as the basis for its allocation mapping. This style may extend the module decomposition by adding modules that correspond to development tools, test tools, configuration management systems, and so forth, whose procurement and day-to-day operation must also be allocated to an individual or a team.

> **FOR MORE INFORMATION**
>
> The Module decomposition style is discussed in Section 2.1.

The work assignment style is often combined with other styles. For example, team work assignments could be the modules in a module decomposition style, the layers in a layered diagram, the software associated with tiers in an *n*-tier architecture, or the tasks or processes in a multiprocess system. Although this style is a conflation of conceptually different views, it sometimes works well enough. The creation of a work assignment style as a separate style—whether maintained separately or carefully overlaid onto another—enables the architect and the project manager to give careful thought to the best way to divide the work into manageable chunks and keeps explicit the need to assign responsibility to software, such as the development environment, that will not be part of the deployed system. A danger of combining work assignments with other styles is that the work assignments associated with tool building may be lost.

> **FOR MORE INFORMATION**
>
> Combining views is discussed in Section 6.3.

Be careful about combining the work assignment style with another one. Remember that decomposing work assignments yields the same kind of element. The same is not true of processes, tiers, layers, and many other architectural elements. If it is based on decomposition, the work assignment structure will not map well to those kinds of elements. On the other hand, mapping to a module decomposition obtained under the principle of information hiding or encapsulation is a natural fit. The compartmentalization of information within modules is greatly aided by a compartmentalization of information among teams.

5.5.5 Example of the Work Assignment Style

Figure 5.6, taken from Appendix A, shows a portion of the work assignment view for the ECS system.

Figure 5.6
Primary presentation for the ECS work assignment view. The software elements are modules defined in the decomposition view. The environmental elements are teams, which are elaborated in the view's supporting documentation (not shown here).

ECS Element (Module)		
Segment	**Subsystem**	**Organizational Unit**
Science Data Processing Segment (SDPS)	Client	Science team
	Interoperability	Prime contractor team 1
	Ingest	Prime contractor team 2
	Data Management	Data team
	Data Processing	Data team
	Data Server	Data team
	Planning	Orbital vehicle team
Communications and System Management Segment (CSMS)	System Management	Intrastructure team
	Communications	
	Internetworking	
Flight Operations Segment (FOS)	Planning and Scheduling	Orbital vehicle team
	Data Management	Database team
	Command Management	Orbital vehicle team
	Commanding	Orbital vehicle team
	Resource Management	Prime contractor team 3
	Telemetry	Orbital vehicle team
	User Interface	User interface team
	Analysis	Orbital vehicle team

5.6   Summary Checklist

- Styles in the allocation viewtype map software structures to structures in the environment of the software.

- The software architecture and environmental structures influence each other. The available computing assets environmental structures may exert a strong influence on the software architecture, and software architecture most likely influences the structure of the configuration management system.

- The deployment style describes the mapping of runtime software elements to the hardware on which the software executes.

- The implementation style describes the mapping of modules on a configuration management scheme and helps the organization of the files that implement the modules.

- The work assignment style describes the aggregation of modules according to the people, groups, or teams tasked with the development of the modules.

5.7   Discussion Questions

1. Construct an allocation style that assigns the runtime files to a file system. Although this style carries important information, seven of the authors voted not to include it in the allocation viewtype. Why do you suppose that was? Although we will not identify the lone supporter, what do you suppose her reasons were?

2. Suppose that you needed to map the modules under test to the test harness that generates inputs, exercises the modules, and records the outputs. Sketch an allocation style that addresses this concern.

3. In one project, short identifiers were assigned to every module. A module's full name consisted of its identifier, prefixed by its parent's identifier, separated by a period (.). The project's file structure was defined by a short memorandum stating the pathname of a root directory and further stating that each module would be stored in the directory obtained by changing each period in the module's full name to a slash (/). Did this memorandum constitute an implementation view for this system? Why or why not? What are the advantages and disadvantages of this scheme?

4. Suppose that your system can be deployed on a wide variety of hardware platforms and configurations. How would you represent that?

5.8 For Further Reading

For more information about documenting the deployment style using UML, visit http://www.rational.com/uml.

Architectured-based management of software projects is discussed in [Paulish 01]. This is the place where the work assignment style comes into play. The relationship between the structure of systems and the structure of organizations that build them was first observed by Conway [Conway 68].

The implementation style is closely aligned with the very broad topic of software configuration management (CM). An in-depth treatment of CM is far beyond the scope of this book, but you can begin investigating the topic by visiting http://www.stsc.hill.af.mil/crosstalk/1999/mar/cmsites.asp, which contains links to other CM-related sites and resources.

Software Architecture Documentation in Practice

PART II

Part I laid the foundations for software architecture documentation by providing a repertoire of styles from which to choose and build views for a system; Part II presents information to complete the picture and to put the ideas into practice.

- Chapter 6 explores advanced documentation techniques that apply to many real systems: refinement and chunking of information, context diagrams, creating and documenting combined views, documenting variability and dynamism, and documenting a new style.

- Chapter 7 tells how to document the interfaces of architectural elements.

- Chapter 8 explores another advanced but essential technique: documenting the behavior of an element or an ensemble of elements.

- Chapter 9 provides detailed guidance for choosing the set of views to incorporate into a documentation suite, explores examples of sets of views, and gives two short examples for illustrating how to decide which views to use.

- Chapter 10 prescribes templates and detailed guidance for documenting views and documenting information that applies to more than one view.

- Chapter 11 examines other well-known prescriptions of software architecture documentation and places them in the context of the material in this book.

Advanced Concepts

This chapter covers the following topics:

1. *Chunking information: view packets, refinement, and descriptive completeness.* Documentation for a view cannot show all its information at once; the result would be hopelessly complex and confusing. Architects break their information up into digestible chunks called *view packets*. Section 6.1 discusses view packets and how they let a stakeholder move around the documentation of the system, up and down in levels of granularity, and from view to view, all while maintaining a coherent picture of the whole.

2. *Using context diagrams.* A context diagram establishes the boundaries for the information contained in a view packet. A context diagram for the entire system defines what is and is not in the system, thus setting limits on the architect's tasks. Context diagrams are discussed in Section 6.2.

3. *Documenting combined views.* Prescribing a given set of rigidly partitioned views is naive; there are times and good reasons for combining two or more views into a single combined view. Indeed, combined views are often responsible for an architecture's conceptual integrity, because only views that resemble one another in fundamental ways can be fruitfully merged. On the other hand, combined views, especially views that unintentionally mix concerns, are also the source of the vast majority of confusion in carelessly documented architectures. These topics are discussed in Section 6.3.

4. *Documenting variability and dynamism.* Some architectures incorporate built-in *variability* to let a group of similar but architecturally distinct systems be built from them. Other

architectures are *dynamic,* in that the systems they describe change their basic structure while they are running. Section 6.4 discusses documenting views of variable and dynamic architectures.

5. *Creating and documenting new styles.* Just as a fixed set of views is naive, so too is a fixed set of styles. Styles, like design patterns, are a growing body of knowledge, and new and useful ones are emerging all the time. What are the architect's obligations when creating or documenting a new or modified style? Section 6.5 discusses these obligations.

6.1 Chunking Information: View Packets, Refinement, and Descriptive Completeness

6.1.1 View Packets

Views of large software systems can contain hundreds or even thousands of elements. Showing these elements in a single presentation, along with the relations among them, can result in a blizzard of information that is indecipherable and contains far too much information for any stakeholder, who is concerned only with a certain part of the system. Architects need a way to present a view's information in digestible "chunks." We call these chunks **view packets**. Each view packet shows a fragment of the system. The documentation for a view, then, consists of a set of view packets, each showing a small portion of the system.

> **DEFINITION**
>
> A **view packet** is the smallest cohesive bundle of documentation that you would give to a stakeholder, such as a development team or a subcontractor.

Same-View View Packets

The view packets that constitute a view are related to one another as either siblings or children.

- Sibling view packets document different parts of the same system. These view packets form a mosaic of the whole view, as if each partial view were a photograph taken by a camera that panned and tilted across the entire view.

- Children view packets document the same part of the system but in greater detail. These view packets come into focus when our hypothetical camera zooms in on a particular part of the system.

View packets from the same view are related to one another as are the nodes of a tree structure; they document elements of the system that are siblings or parents and children of one another. To "move" from one view packet to another requires a series of operations that pan and tilt or zoom in and zoom out. View packets allow the architect to document a view—and a reader to understand a view—in

- Depth-first order: that is, choosing an element, document-ing its substructure, choosing a subelement, documenting its substructure, and so on
- Breadth-first order: for all elements, documenting their substructures and then, for all those elements, document-ing their substructures, and so on
- Some combination of the two, based on what the architect knows at the time

View Packets from Different Views

View packets from different views may be related to one an-other as well. In our Prologue discussion of styles, we said that no system is built from a single style. We used three cases; let's see how the concept of view packets lets us handle each one.

1. *Case 1: Different "areas" of the system exhibit different styles.* For example, a system might use a pipe-and-filter style to pro-cess input data but then route the result to a database that is accessed by many elements. This system would be a blend of pipe-and-filter and shared-data styles. Documen-tation for this system would include a pipe-and-filter view that showed one part of the system and a shared-data view that showed the other part.

   In a case like this, one or more elements must occur in both views and have properties of both kinds of elements. (Otherwise, the two parts of the system could not commu-nicate with each other.) These **bridging elements** provide the continuity of understanding from one view to the next and likely have multiple interfaces, each providing the mechanisms for letting the element work with other ele-ments in each of the views to which it belongs.

   To document this system, we would have a pipe-and-filter view packet that shows the pipe-and-filter portion of the system and a shared-data view packet that shows the shared-data part of the system. Bridging elements would appear in both, and the supporting documentation—particularly a mapping between views—would make the correspondence clear, perhaps by showing the combined picture, as in Figure 6.1. Each view packet might be supple-mented by view packets showing finer-grained parts of the system. In this example, neither top-level view packet shows the "whole" system, and each refers to the other as a cross-view sibling.

Figure 6.1
A system of pipe-and-filter and shared-data styles. Here, the bridging element, or element common to both, is the connector that takes the data stream from the last filter and translates it into a form deliverable to the database's interface. That connector will have a role that works with a filter's port and another that works with a database port.

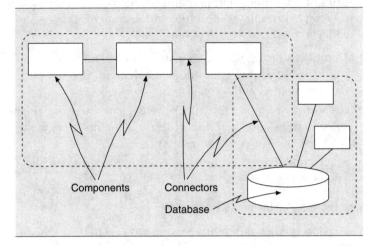

Components   Connectors

Database

2. *Case 2: An element playing a part in one style is itself composed of elements arranged in another style.* For example, a server in a client-server system might—unknown to the other servers or to its own clients—be implemented using a pipe-and-filter style. Documentation for this system would include a client-server view showing the overall system, as well as a pipe-and-filter view documenting that server, as shown in Figure 6.2. To document this system, one view packet in the client-server view will show the overall system whose elements are the clients, the server, and the connectors linking them. A view packet in the pipe-and-filter view will document that server. The pipe-and-filter view will not show the whole system but rather the part(s) to which it applies. The whole-system client-server view packet will refer to the server-as-pipe-and-filter view packet and vice versa as a cross-view child (parent).

Figure 6.2
A decomposition of an element in one style reveals substructure in a different style. Here, the server in this client-server system is designed as a pipe-and-filter system.

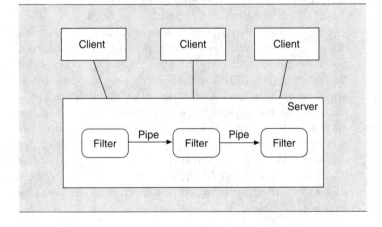

3. *Case 3: The same system may simply be seen in different lights, as though you were looking at it through filtered glasses.* For example, the filters in a pipe-and-filter system each access a common data repository in the course of their processing, as shown in Figure 6.3. If we look through glasses that hide the pipes, the system exhibits the shared-data style. But if we look through glasses that hide the repository and the connectors to it, the system is clearly in the pipe-and-filter style. The glasses you choose will determine the style that you "see." Here, view packets in different views will show the same region of a system and at the same level of granularity. Each may have child view packets in its own view, as needed. The top-level view packets will refer to one another as siblings, showing the same information in a different view. Systems like this are also excellent candidates to be documented using combined views, in which the view packets show both kinds of information.

Not all view packets from different views are related so cleanly to one another as shown in these three cases. If understanding the relation is important, however, they need to be documented.

FOR MORE INFORMATION

Section 10.2 prescribes the precise contents of view packets and how to document their relationship to one another.

FOR MORE INFORMATION

Combined views are discussed in Section 6.3.

6.1.2   Refinement

View packets that represent a zoom-in operation are **refinements** of their parent. Architects use *refinement*—the gradual disclosure of information across a series of descriptions—to represent the information in a view.

A **decomposition refinement**, or simply decomposition, elaborates a single element to reveal its internal structure and then recursively refines each member of that internal structure (see Figure 6.4). The text-based analogy of this is the outline, whereby major sections, denoted by roman numerals, are decomposed into subsections, denoted by capital letters, are decomposed into subsubsections, denoted by arabic numerals, and so forth.

DEFINITION

Refinement is the process of gradually disclosing information across a series of descriptions.

Decomposition refinement is a refinement in which a single element is elaborated to reveal its internal structure, and then each member of that internal structure is recursively refined.

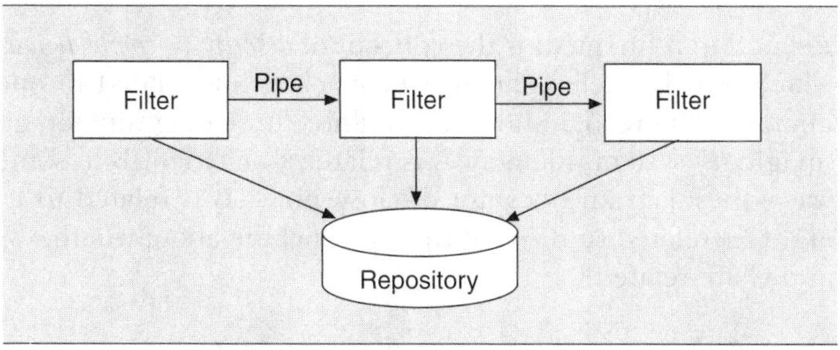

Figure 6.3
A system of pipes and filters with a shared database might be seen as exhibiting either of two styles.

Figure 6.4
(a) A hypothetical system consisting of three related elements: A, B, and C.
(b) Element B consists of elements B1, B2, B3, and B4. Element B1 has responsibility for handling communication with the "outside" world, which here means outside of B.

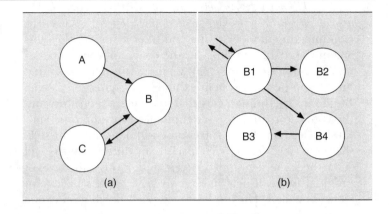

(a) (b)

Using decomposition refinements in a view carries an obligation to maintain consistency with respect to the relation(s) native to that view. For example, suppose that the relation shown in Figure 6.4(a) is *send-data-to*. Because element B is shown as both receiving and sending data, the refinement of B in Figure 6.4(b) must show where data can enter and leave B: in this case, via B1.

Another kind of refinement, called an **implementation refinement**, shows the same system—or portion of the system—in which many or all the elements and relations are replaced by new, typically more implementation-specific, ones. For example, imagine two views of a publish-subscribe system. In one view, components are connected by a single event bus. In the refined view, the bus is replaced by a dispatcher to which the components make explicit calls to achieve their event announcements. By replacing the connector, we also have to change the interfaces of the components: Hence, we have implementation refinement. An implementation refinement is a case of a parent-child relation between view packets that belong to different views—where learning more detail about a system takes a reader from one view to another. In Figure 6.2, the pipe-and-filter system is an implementation refinement of the server.

6.1.3 Descriptive Completeness

Related to refinement is the concept of *descriptive completeness*, which tells how elements in view packets are related to one another. Figure 6.5 shows an architectural diagram for an imaginary system. Element A is related to element B in some way—the diagram does not disclose how—B is related to C, and C is related to B. What can we conclude about whether A and C are related?

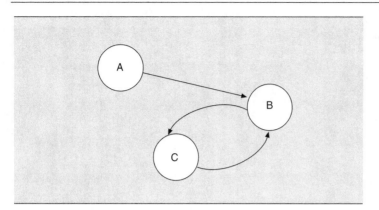

Figure 6.5
Element A is related to B, B is related to C, and C is related to B. What is the relation between A and C?

One possible answer is straightforward: A and C are not related, because the diagram shows no arrow between A and C. A second possible answer is a bit more complicated: This diagram reveals no relationship between A and C, but it is possible that this information was considered too detailed or tangential for the view packet in which this diagram appears. Therefore, the question cannot be answered at this time. Another view packet may subsequently reveal that A and C share this relation.[1]

Either answer is acceptable, as each represents a different strategy for documentation. The first strategy says that the view packets are written with **descriptive completeness**. This strategy tends to be used for packets that convey instructions or constraints to downstream designers or implementers. For instance, the layered view shows implementers what other elements they are allowed to use—and, by extension, what elements they are prohibited from using—when coding their work assignments. If we gave Figure 6.5 to the coder of element A, we would want him or her to interpret the absence of an arrow between A and C as carrying meaning: namely, a prohibition from using element C.

The second strategy tends to be used for view packets intended to convey broad understanding. Suppose that we want to picture a system's data flow, so that a new project member can gain insight into how a result is computed or an important transaction is carried out. In that case, we might not want to show all data flow but only the data flow in the nominal, usual, or high-frequency cases. We might defer to

> **DEFINITION**
>
> **Descriptively complete** view packets show all elements and relations within the view they document.

---

1. A third answer is possible as well. If we happen to know that the relation—whatever it might be—is transitive, we could deduce that it holds between A and C because it holds between A and B and between B and C. That case is not relevant for the discussion at hand, however.

Figure 6.6
A supplement to Figure 6.5, showing alternative relationships among the elements. Under the assumption that descriptive completeness does not hold, this figure supplements Figure 6.5. Under the assumption of description completeness, the two figures taken together represent a conflict and hence an error.

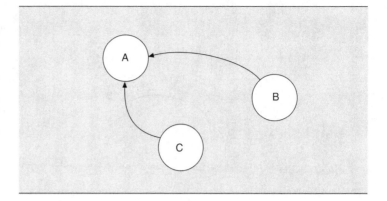

another view packet, the data flow, when the system is doing, say, error detection and recovery. Suppose that Figure 6.5 shows that nominal case. Figure 6.6 might show the error case. A new programmer would eventually want to see both diagrams but not at once. Under this interpretation, Figure 6.6 does not contradict Figure 6.5 but augments it, whereas under the assumption of completeness, Figures 6.5 and 6.6 are contradictory; both cannot document the same system.

So far, we've discussed these strategies in terms of relationships among elements, but we could also ask an element-related question. Suppose that Figure 6.5 purports to show an entire system or a specific portion of it. Can we then presume that A, B, and C are the only elements involved? That is, is every piece of software in A or in B or in C? The same two strategies apply. The first tells us, "Yes, you can presume that with impunity. All software within the scope of this view packet is shown in this view packet." The second says, "We don't know yet. Perhaps in a refinement or an augmentation of this view, another element will be shown."

If an error-logging element comes into play during error detection, a diagram like Figure 6.7 might apply. Again, both strategies are correct and have their place. In Section P.6, we admonished you to explain your notation. The issue of descriptive completeness is a special case of that. You simply need to specify which of the two strategies your documents follow. And, as we suggested, some documents may follow one, whereas others may follow the other. That is not a problem, as long as the reader is informed. So, if you adopt the completeness strategy, include one of the following statements in your documentation, as part of the notation key.

- If no relationship is shown beween two elements, that relationship either does not or is not allowed to exist between those two elements.

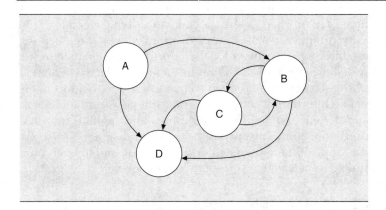

Figure 6.7
A refinement to Figure 6.5,
showing an additional
element, D

- The elements shown in this diagram account for all software in the system.

If you adopt the noncompleteness strategy, include one of the following statements in your key:

- Subsequent refinements or other renditions of this view may show relationships among elements that are not shown here.

- Subsequent refinements or other renditions of this view may depict additional elements not shown here.

Earlier, we dealt with the issue of refinement. The issue of descriptive completeness is related. View packets that convey descriptive completeness also convey obligations on refinements. If a view packet shows no relationship (of whatever kind) between, say, elements A and C, no refinement of that view packet is allowed to subsequently show that relationship between A and C. If a view packet shows a set of elements, no new elements that are not part of those are allowed to be introduced later.

Descriptive completeness makes consistency checking among view packets much more straightforward but at the cost of making the diagrams and their explanation more cluttered and arguably more difficult to understand. As in many issues of architecture, this one brings with it an inherent trade-off.

6.2   Using Context Diagrams

In Section 6.1, we introduced the notion of walking through a view by visiting discrete chunks, which we document with view packets. We need a way to help the reader establish his or her bearings each time the scope of documentation changes, such as when we narrow our focus as the result of taking a refinement step or when we shift laterally to a sibling element at the same granularity. A **context diagram** serves this purpose, establishing the context for the information contained in the rest of the view packet. Unlike the architectural documentation whose scope is limited to an element of interest and its internal architecture, a context diagram is a view of that element and the environment in which it lives and contains information about both. The purpose of a context diagram is to depict the scope of the subsequent documentation and to bound the problem the element is responsible for solving.

6.2.1 Top-Level Context Diagrams

A distinguished context diagram is one for which the "element" being defined is the system. A *top-level context diagram* (TLCD) establishes the scope for the system whose architecture is being documented, defining the boundaries around the system that show what's in and what's out. A TLCD shows how the system under consideration interacts with the outside world. Entities in that outside world may be humans, other computer systems, or physical objects, such as sensors or controlled devices. A TLCD identifies sources of data to be processed by the system, destinations of data produced by the system, and other systems with which it must interact.

ADVICE

Use TLCDs as the first ingredient of architectural information presented to a reader. These TLCDs should be the reader's first introduction to a system and its architecture description. They can serve as the jumping-off point for delving into deeper architectural detail in any number of directions.

A TLCD is useful because it clarifies what constitutes the system of interest. Sometimes, an organization is asked to develop a system that is part of a larger system, and a TLCD depicts that. Sometimes, the supporting tools and environment, some off-line-processing software in a system, or some other tangential software is considered outside the scope of the system being developed. A TLCD clarifies what is in and what is out.

A system does not have just one TLCD but potentially one TLCD for each view, because the system's context can be described using the different vocabularies of the various views. A context diagram in one of the component-and-connector views shows interactions between the system of concern and its environment. A context diagram in a layered view shows which layers are within the project's scope and which are not. A TLCD for a view is associated with the view packet of that view that shows the entire system, if there is one. (Recall from Section 6.1 that not all views begin at a granularity showing the entire system.)

6.2.2 Content of a Context Diagram

Context diagrams show

- A depiction of the entity—the element or the system—whose architecture is being documented, given with a clear delineation that distinguishes it from those entities external to it
- Sources and destinations of data or stimuli or commands processed and produced by the entity, shown outside the symbol for the entity being described and expressed in the vocabulary of the view of which the context diagram is a part
- A key that explains the notation and symbology used in the context diagram, as is the case for all graphical figures
- Other entities with which the entity being documented must interact

A pure context diagram does not disclose any architectural detail about an entity, although in practice, most context diagrams show some internal structure of the entity being put in context. Context diagrams do not show any temporal information, such as order of interactions or data flow. They do not show the conditions under which data is transferred, stimuli fired, messages transmitted, and so on.

6.2.3 Context Diagrams and Other Supporting Documentation

Context diagrams are part of the view packet's supporting documentation. As such, they impart some obligations on the other supporting documentation.

- The view packet's element catalog must explain the entities shown in the diagram. The catalog should include the interfaces between the entity being documented and the environmental entities with which it interacts, as well as behavioral descriptions of the entities and their properties. The context diagram must be accompanied by a data dictionary that describes the syntax and the semantics of the

> **FOR MORE INFORMATION**
>
> Element catalogs are described in Section 10.2

data and commands shown in the diagram. If all the entities are not fully explained in the catalog, it should be accompanied by a list of references where a reader can turn for further information about any of the entities shown in the diagram.

ADVICE

Every view packet should have a context diagram. This requirement is satisfied in most cases by a pointer to a context diagram elsewhere that establishes the context for that packet.

- The view packet's variability guide should account for variability depicted in the context diagram. Context diagrams can be used to identify unchanging, or core, elements of a product family and, by implication, the variable parts of the family. The meaning conveyed by accompanying documentation is that to build a system, one augments the core parts with instances of the noncore parts. Thus, a context diagram is a reasonable way to explain the concept of a framework.

- The view packet's rationale should explain the reasons for drawing the boundary where it is.

6.2.4 Notations for Context Diagrams

Informal Notations

Informally, context diagrams consist of a circle-and-line drawing, with the entity being defined depicted in the center as a circle, the entities external to it with which it interacts depicted as various shapes, and lines depicting interactions connecting the entities as appropriate. Because context diagrams are often used to explain systems to people who know more about the externals of the application than the internals, such diagrams can be quite elaborate and use all sorts of idiomatic symbols for entities in the environment.

UML

UML does not have an explicit mechanism for a context diagram. UML's means for showing system context are *use case diagrams.* Elements in a use case diagram are actors, use cases, and associations between them. Actors denote external systems and agents, such as the user. The use case icon denotes system functions. The basic symbology is shown in Figure 6.8.

One actor may be associated with several use cases. Figure 6.9 shows the UML use case diagram for a hypothetical patient monitoring system. The external entities are the patient, the nurse, and a patient log. Patient and nurse provide input to the system, and the system produces a patient log. Although this diagram provides a good overview of the functionality of the system and the external entities that interact with the system, the diagram can easily get out of control if *all* the possible functionality is put into this diagram.

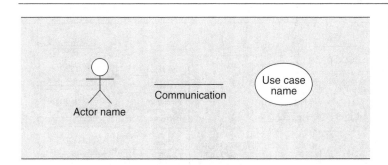

Figure 6.8
Symbology of use case diagrams showing actors, associations, and use cases

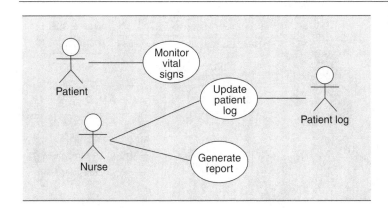

Figure 6.9
A few use cases in a UML use case diagram, showing some context of a patient monitoring system

Other context diagrams use UML class diagrams. Figure 6.10 shows the patient monitoring system again, using a class diagram. This style of diagram contains less information, containing no description of the functionality of the system. But for more complex environments, this way of documenting the system context gives a better overview. If this style of context diagram is used, you still would expect more detailed specifications about the expected functionality of the system. Therefore, use

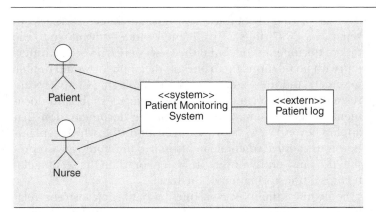

Figure 6.10
Description of a system context, using a UML class diagram. The class stereotyped as «system» depicts the system whose context is shown; Patient, Nurse, and PatientLog are external entities. Different symbols are used here to distinguish people from technical things.

Figure 6.11
A context diagram from the ECS Science Data Processing Segment as documented in Appendix A. The thick-lined rectangle in the middle depicts the system; the thin-lined rectangles around it show the external entities: people or other systems. In this context diagram, people and systems are differentiated only by the name of the box, not the shape. Replication is depicted by repeated boxes. The arrows show data flow between the system and the external entities. The external systems need to be explained in the element catalog in this diagram's view packet.

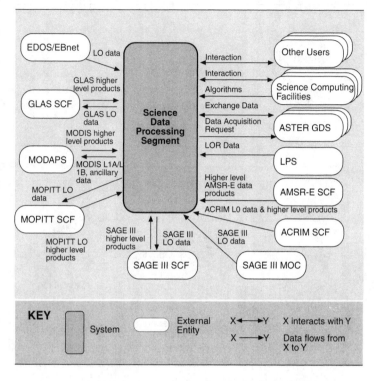

case diagrams as shown in Figure 6.9 more naturally occur as part of the behavior description of the whole system.

6.2.5   Example of a Context Diagram

Figure 6.11 shows a context diagram for the ECS system detailed in Appendix A.

FOR MORE INFORMATION

Section 10.3 describes documentation that maps separately documented views to each other. Section 6.5 later in this chapter explains the documentation obligations associated with creating a new style.

6.3   Combined Views

The basic principle of documenting an architecture as a set of separate views brings a divide-and-conquer advantage to the task of documentation, but if the views were irrevocably different, with no relationship to one another, nobody would be able to understand the system as a whole. Managing how views are related is an important part of the architect's job, and documenting it is an important part of the documentation that applies beyond views, as we see in Section 10.3, which explains how to recognize when elements in two different views represent the same entity within the system or when the second element is a transformation of the first.

Sometimes, the most convenient way to show a strong relationship between two views is to collapse them into a single

combined view. Combinations can be among views or among
styles. The choice of whether to combine a particular set of
views or styles is partially dependent on the importance, persistence, and ongoing usefulness of the resulting new view or
style. Defining a new style imposes certain obligations with
respect to the documentation. A new style must be documented
in the same fashion as one of the styles we have described in
this book. Creating these materials is important if the style is
used throughout a particular system and multiple stakeholders
need to be familiar with it. Sometimes, however, a combined
view is created for a single, short-term purpose: to do analysis
or communicating, for example. For these short-term purposes, creating the required documentation for a new style is
burdensome overhead. To differentiate these two cases of combined views, we introduce the terms **hybrid style**, and **overlay**.

So now an architect has three ways to establish a mapping
between otherwise standalone styles or views:

- Document a mapping between separate views. Do this as
  part of the documentation suite that applies beyond views.

- Create an overlay that combines the information in what
  would otherwise have been two separate views. Do this if
  the relationship between the two views is strong, the mapping from elements to elements in the other is clear, and
  documenting them separately would result in too much
  redundant information.

- Create a hybrid style by combining two existing styles and
  creating a style guide that introduces the result and the
  relationship among elements in the constituent styles. Do
  this if the style is important and will be used in a variety of
  analyses and communication contexts in the system at hand
  or in other systems you expect to build.

6.3.1   When to Combine Views

Producing a useful combined view depends on understanding
the mapping among the constituent views or styles. A combined
view can be produced from different views of the same overarch-
ing viewtype. For example, the modules defined in a module
uses view can be mapped to layers described in a layered diagram because both belong to the module viewtype. A combined
view also can be produced from views of different viewtypes. For
example, layers of a layered style, which belongs to the module
viewtype, can be mapped to processes in the communicating-
processes style, which belong to the C&C viewtype.

The styles we have presented in this book are each intended
to deal with a small set of coherent and common concerns. In

DEFINITION

A **combined view** is a
view that contains ele-
ments and relationships
that come from two or
more other views.

DEFINITION

A **hybrid style** is the
combination of two or
more existing styles. It
introduces the same
documentation obliga-
tions as any of the
styles introduced earlier
in this book. In addition,
the mapping between
the styles that consti-
tute the hybrid must
also be documented.
Hybrid styles, when ap-
plied to a particular system, produce views.

DEFINITION

An **overlay** is a combination of the primary
presentations of two or
more views. It is in-
tended for short-term
use. An overlay has the
same documentation
requirements as a pri-
mary presentation of
a normal view; for ex-
ample, a key must be
provided. But an over-
lay introduces no addi-
tional documentation
obligations beyond
those of a primary pre-
sentation and a defini-
tion of the mapping
among the constituent
views.

order to accomplish many of the uses of an architectural description, an architect must understand concerns from several of these "atomic" styles. During a performance analysis, for example, both the set of responsibilities from a view based on a module viewtype style and the synchronization behavior of the processes derived from those modules provide important information. The set of responsibilities are useful in order to derive the resource requirements. These two sets of information combine to enable a schedulability analysis. When the architecture is being communicated to stakeholders, multiple views are necessary to provide sufficient information to enable complete understanding. When the architectural documentation serves as a blueprint, the developer must understand the prescriptions included in various views in order to correctly implement the system. Keeping these concerns separate facilitates clarity of presentation and enhances understanding.

ADVICE

Many Separate Views or a Few Combined Ones?

- When considering a combined view, make sure that the mapping among the constituents is clear and straightforward. Otherwise, these views are probably not good candidates to be combined, as the result will be a complex and confusing view. In this case, it would be better to manage the mapping in a table—in the documentation that applies beyond views—that relates the views while keeping them separate. A mapping table has the space to make the complex relationships among the constituents clear and complete.

- Large systems tend to require more views. In large systems, it is important to keep concerns separate, as the impact of an error caused by mixing concerns is much greater than in a small system. Also the relationships among views in large systems tend to be more complicated, which, according to the first rule of thumb, argues for maintaining separate views. Furthermore, reasoning about the properties of the system is simplified when it is clear where in the documentation the input into the reasoning framework can be found. Consequently, the larger the system, the more it makes sense to keep views distinct.

- Too many different concepts clutter up combined views. Keys and the plethora of relations shown in the primary presentation all become difficult to understand. Before committing to a combined view, sketch it to see whether it passes the "elevator speech" test: Could you explain the idea behind it to someone in the time it takes to ride an elevator up a dozen or so floors?

- Different groups of workers need different types of information. Make your choice of views responsive to the needs of your stakeholders. Before committing to a combined view, make sure that there is a stakeholder "market" for it.
- Tool support influences the choice and number of views. The cost of maintaining multiple views is partially a function of the sophistication of the available tool support. If your tool understands how a change in one view should be reflected in another view, it is not necessary to manage this change manually. The more sophisticated the tool support, the more views can be supported.
- If the the mapping is clear and straightforward, the combined view won't be overly complex, a consumer group for the combined view has been identified, and is the same group as for the constituent views, it makes sense to adopt the combined view in place of the separate constituents.

On the other hand, the developer incurs the mental overhead of having to use separate documents and keeping the relationships among them straight. Such a developer might grumble, with some justification, that the information needed to do his or her particular job is scattered over several places. Additionally, there is a cost for maintaining multiple views. Multiple views tend to get out of synch as they evolve, and a change to one now precipitates a change to *three* documents: the two affected views and the mapping between them. Hyperlinking the documents helps, but the developer still has to visit all the places and make appropriate adaptations. Thus, there are good reasons to keep the number of views to a minimum.

The set of views used for a system, then, is the result of a trade-off between the clarity of many views, each of which has a small number of concepts, and the reduced cost associated with having a small number of views, each dealing with multiple concepts.

Use caution in combining views. Remember, views that can be mapped to one another *should* be so mapped, whether or not you create a hybrid or an overlay to do it. At a minimum, simply produce the mapping prescribed in Section 10.3, and leave the views separate.

6.3.2   Types of Mapping

In a *many-to-one* mapping (see Figure 6.12), multiple elements in one view are mapped to a single element in another view. Modules are frequently mapped to processes in this fashion. The mapping should make clear which module maps to which process.

Figure 6.12
Many-to-one mapping.
Multiple elements from
one view can be mapped
to a single element of
another view. As shown
here, two modules from a
decomposition view are
designed to run in a single
process, shown in the
communicating-processes
view.

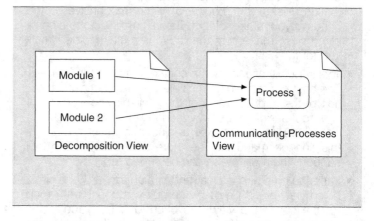

In a *one-to-many* mapping (see Figure 6.13), a single element can be mapped from one view to multiple elements in another view. For example, a communications module may be mapped to multiple processes in an *n*-tier client-server style.

A one-to-many mapping could denote replication, as shown in Figure 6.13, or a splitting of elements, whereby parts of the functionality of element 1 of view A map to element 2 of view B, and the rest of the functionality of element 1 maps to element 3. In this case, it must be clear which parts of the split element map to which elements of view B. The split functionality might introduce additional dependencies among the parts. These dependencies introduce additional relationships between elements 2 and 3, which may not have been considered.

As much as we would like to have a one-to-many or a many-to-one mapping, it is more likely that a *many-to-many* mapping occurs, with a set of elements in one view mapping to a set of

Figure 6.13
One-to-many mapping. An
element of one view can be
mapped to multiple ele-
ments in another view.
Although the architect
must make it clear, this
normally implies that the
complete functionality of
element 1 is replicated
when mapped to Elements
2 and 3 of View B. This
mapping may mean that
several instances of Ele-
ment 1 are created or that
a functionality is used by
several elements of View B.

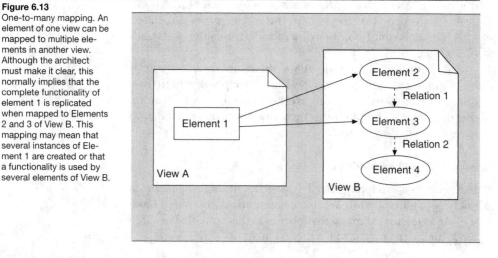

elements in another. Here, element splitting abounds. These mappings reflect the inherent complexity in relating two views to each other, each of which was crafted to show a few important aspects that in many ways might be orthogonal.

At this point, the first rule of thumb given previously applies: A complex mapping suggests keeping the views apart and maintaining their mapping separately. However, given compelling reasons to override this rule and produce a combined view, you can make your task easier by redrawing the constituent views first to split the elements into carefully defined pieces that will then map to their counterparts straightforwardly.

6.3.3   Elements, Relations, and Properties

In hybrid styles, elements and relations of the constituent styles can "melt" into new element types with new properties; in overlays, elements and relations are put together in a view without changing the type. Therefore, hybrid styles require the definition of the resulting element and relation types, but overlays do not.

Hybrid Style

The element types of a hybrid style often include a composite of the element types of the constitutents. So, for example, if the combined view is a mapping from a layered style to a communicating-processes style—a common practice—the element type could be *layered process,* and this type would need to be defined as the element of the hybrid style.

The relations of a hybrid view are derived from the relations of the constituent styles and the mapping among the styles. Not all relations of the constituent styles need be shown.

Deriving relations in a hybrid view can result in the definition of connectors. Using again the hybrid of a layered style and a communicating-processes style, the allowed-to-use relation between layers defines a connector type between the processes. This connector ensures the correct communication pattern between layered processes.

Properties of the elements and the relations of a hybrid style will usually be a subset of the properties of the elements and the relations of the constituent styles, along with the properties that derive from the mapping. Which properties need to be shown in a mapping depend on which aspect of the architecture will be documented or analyzed. If the mapping is used to analyze performance, all performance-related properties from elements and relations of all the views that are mapped need to be available.

Overlay

In an overlay, the elements and the relations keep the types as defined in their constituent styles. Usually, an overlay view shows only a subset of the combined elements and relations with a mapping added. What is included in the view depends on what the overlay is intended to present. The same is true for the properties of elements and relations. What is included depends on what should be uncovered.

6.3.4 Documenting Combined Views

Figure 6.12 showed how multiple modules might map to a single process. Figure 6.14 shows how that mapping might be documented using a combined view.

In Figure 6.13, we showed how an element of one view mapped to more than one element of a second view. In Figure 6.15, we show how to represent this as a hybrid view. If elements 2, 3, and 4, for example, are components of a C&C view and element 1 is the functionality to store and to retrieve data within a component, designed as a class in a decomposition view, mapping element 1 onto elements 2 and 3 makes those elements "persistent components." In fact, element 1 of the decomposition view became a property of an element in the hybrid view. As you can see, hybrid views can be very useful as long as you do not try to overload them with too many mappings.

Figure 6.14
Multiple elements from one view can be mapped to a single element of another view. Here module Elements 1 and 2 from a module view are designed to run in a single process—Element 3—shown in the communicating-processes view. The resulting combined view shows all three elements, of the module and communicating-processes views, and their *containment* relation.

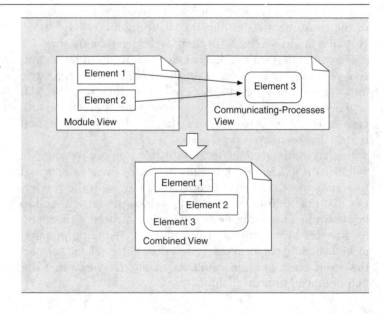

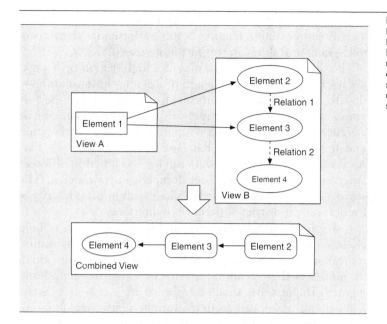

Figure 6.15
In this example, mapping
Element 1 of View A onto
Elements 2 and 3 of View B
resulted in a new type of
element, depicted as a new
shape. This required the
definition of a new type in a
style.

6.3.5   Examples of Combined Views

N-Tier Client-Server

In Chapter 4, *n*-**tier** client-server was discussed as a component-
and-connector style. In some contexts, however, the term refers
to a combination of that style with the deployment style—in
other words, a hybrid style.

The *n*-tier client-server architecture, a mainstay of business
and Internet data processing systems, was created as the natural descendant of mainframe systems supporting scores of
users on dumb terminals. Later, those terminals were replaced
by PCs, which inherited some of the systems' processing
responsibilities, such as user interface management. This
freed the mainframe to do more work and therefore support
more users. Two-tier systems divided functionality between
the computation necessary to support users with graphical
user interfaces on the PCs, or clients, and the computation
necessary to store and compute data as necessary on more
powerful machines, or servers.

The three-tier architecture that emerged in the 1990s to
overcome the limitations of the two-tier architecture features
a middle tier between the user interface, or client, and the
data management, or server, components. This middle tier,
where process management resides and business rules are executed, provides a further separation of concerns in the overall

DEFINITION

A **tier** is a mechanism
for system partitioning.
Usually applied to
client-server-based
systems, where the var-
ious parts (tiers) of the
system (user interface,
database, business ap-
plication logic, etc.) execute on different
platforms.

system, making it easier to change these things in isolation. The three-tier design features better performance than a two-tier system and thus can support more users.

The three-tier system also provides high flexibility by making it straightforward to reassign processing responsibilities—that is, move software—from tier to tier to enhance performance. For example, an underutilized middle tier might be assigned to handle database staging, queuing, transaction management, distributed database integrity, and the like. Also, software on different tiers can be developed in different languages, using different development environments. The segregation to different machines helps enforce modularity of the software and strict adherence to interfaces.

It should be clear by now that in this context we are talking about an architectural style in which a hardware configuration is inextricably bound up with a division of software functionality into tiers that communicate in the client-server fashion. Figure 6.16 illustrates this. The essence of n-tier systems is the ability to move software from platform to platform to enhance performance, failure recovery, functionality, or scalability.

6.3.6 Other Examples

Figure 2.11 shows an overlay that combines the module decomposition and layered styles. Figure 6.1 shows an overlay combining the shared-data and pipe-and-filter views.

Figure 6.16
A three-tier system showing it to be an overlay between a client-server view and a deployment view

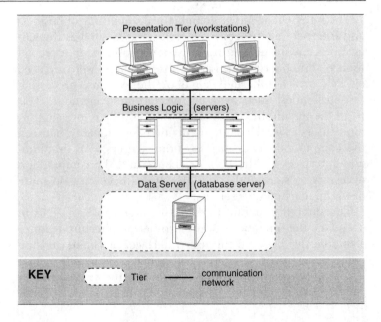

Presentation Tier (workstations)

Business Logic (servers)

Data Server (database server)

KEY   Tier   —— communication network

6.4 Documenting Variability and Dynamism

In some situations, decisions about some aspects of an architecture have not yet been made, but the options still need to be documented. We distinguish two cases: variability and dynamism.

6.4.1 Variability

Variability in an architecture can occur because

- Some set of decisions has not yet been made during the design process for a single system, but options have been explored
- The architecture is for a family of systems, and the option taken will depend on the specifics of the particular member of the family to be constructed
- The architecture is a framework for a collection of systems and contains explicit places where extensions to the framework can occur

In the first two cases, three kinds of information need to be documented.

1. *The variation points.* A **variation point** is the place in the architecture where variation can occur. The options within a variation point are a list of alternatives. Each alternative has, in turn, a list of elements impacted if that option is chosen.

2. *The elements affected by the option.* Each option will affect the existence of an element, its interface, the properties of that element, or the relations among the elements. An element can exist in one option and not in another. An element can exist in two options but compute different functions or have different properties. For example, multiple elements may realize a particular interface. Two elements can be related in one fashion in one option and in another fashion or not at all in another option. The elements and relations affected by an option need to be documented.

3. *The binding time of an option.* Choosing different binding times for elements affects their properties. For example, deciding to bind two components during initial load time will yield different system properties than deciding to bind these two components through a dynamic link mechanism. Possible binding times include design time, compile time, link time, or runtime; if it is runtime, many options are possible. Binding can be done when the program starts or restarts, when the program containing the option starts, or at any other time during execution.

There were a hundred and forty-two staircases at Hogwarts: wide, sweeping ones, narrow, rickety ones; some that led somewhere different on a Friday; some with a vanishing step halfway up that you had to remember to jump. Then there were doors that wouldn't open unless you asked politely, or tickled them in exactly the right place, and doors that weren't really doors at all, but solid walls just pretending. It was also very hard to remember where anything was, because it all seemed to move around a lot....

And the ghosts didn't help, either.

—J. K. Rowling, *Harry Potter and the Sorcerer's Stone* (Scholastic Press, 1998, p. 122)

DEFINITION

Variability refers to the decisions that will be made by a member of the development team prior to system deployment.

A **variation point** is a place in the architecture where a specific decision has been narrowed to several options but the option to be chosen for a particular system has been left open.

FOR MORE INFORMATION

See Perspectives: What Time Is It? on page 213.

In the case of documenting a framework, extension points need to be documented. An extension point is a place in the architecture where additional elements can be added. Each extension point is documented by an interface description of what the framework provides and the extension requires.

So-called reference architectures provide a collection of categories for elements. The type of the elements is specified and some indication of how they relate, but the specification for the elements is not sufficient to give more than an indication of their responsibilities. Figure 6.17 shows the ECMA "toaster" model for the integration of development tools.

Regardless of the type of variation, the documentation suite should include a variability guide where points of variation are identified, rationale for choosing one option over another are given, and the APIs are identified for extensions. The variability guide also describes what needs to be done—ranging from editing a configuration file to implementing new modules—in order to choose an alternative that fulfills certain interfaces.

6.4.2 Dynamism

Architectures change during runtime in response to user requirements or to better enable the achievement of particular quality attributes. An architecture can change dynamically by creating or deleting components and connectors, including replicas. Components or connectors can be created or deleted either in a fine-grained (e.g., object) or a coarse-grained (e.g., client) fashion. For example, when a new user enters an environment and wants new services, components to provide those

Figure 6.17
The ECMA toaster model for integrating development tools. This multidimensional layered diagram shows that services are provided within the integration framework for data integration, control integration, and process integration. Tools provide the layers, and a single user interface applies to all the tools (NIST special publication 500-201, ECMA, Technical Report ECMA TR/55, 2d Edition, 12, 1991, p 23).

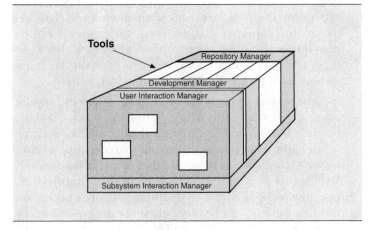

services would be created. When the user leaves the environment, the components would be deleted. The created component or connector may be a replica or a singleton. In any case, the number of allowable replicas, the conditions under which the creation or deletion occurs, and the connectors or components that are created must be documented.

Another way in which an architecture can change dynamically is by reallocation of resources or responsibilities. Components may be moved from one processor to another to offer better performance. Responsibilities may be shifted among components; perhaps a backup could assume primary status in the event of a failure. Other resources that affect the architecture could also be reallocated. Again, the circumstances under which resources are reallocated and the particular reallocation that will occur must be documented.

6.4.3 Recording the Information

Fortunately, the same work is involved in documenting dynamism and variability in architectures. We provide a few simple rules for documenting architectures with those characteristics:

ADVICE

Document variability and dynamism using the same styles you normally would choose for that architecture. Show what is constant and what is not. For the latter, describe the range of options and when the option is bound.

1. Choose from the same styles you normally would. That is, there is no special style that you must use specifically to document dynamism or variability. If your possible architectures differ logically, choose a module view to show the variation. If they differ in the processes they contain, choose a communicating-processes view to show the variation, and so forth. On the other hand, if there are many variation points, it may be useful to have a specific view that shows just the variation points. This view would appear in the variability guide.

2. Show what's constant and what's not. Each view you choose should indicate places where the architecture is the same across all possibilities and where it may vary.

3. Denote when the change can take place. When you document variability, indicate whether the alternatives apply at design time, at build time, at runtime or at some finer shading of one of these (such as compile time or link time).

4. Document dependencies among options. When variabilities or dyanamic options are linked, show that linkage.

5. Use scenarios of building different types of systems as a portion of the variability guide. Begin with constructing a simple system and progress to more complicated ones. Scenarios should show dependencies among options.

6.4.4 Notations for Variability and Dynamism

Informal Notations

Variation Point

Variation points contain information needed to choose a variant. Some of the attributes that may be used to characterize the variation point are name, description, optional or mandatory, binding time for variation decision, number of possible occurrences of the variants, and the rules for choosing the option(s) listed. Variation points can be represented graphically by any symbol that represents options. Each option is then attached to this symbol.

A variation point is a place in the architecture where a specific decision has been narrowed to several options but the option for a particular system has been left open. Figure 6.18 shows a variation point.

A broadly based variation point is one in which very few of the decisions have been made (see Figure 6.17). Intentionally, only some decisions are made here to support integration into the process and user interface environment. A variability guide in this case should include specifications that have to be fulfilled and perhaps some design or implementation rules.

Figure 6.18
A narrowly based variation point. This example is derived from a radio display software system. The display will show a station by displaying either a frequency or a station name. The ovals show a variation point and the possible options with a specific rule—choose 1—that guides the selection process. Depending on the choice, particular modules, depicted as rectangles, will be included in the architecture (Bachmann and Bass 2001, p. 131).

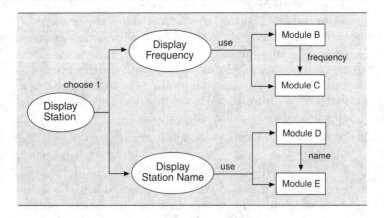

Component Replication

In an informal graphical notation, component replication is almost always documented showing shadow boxes:

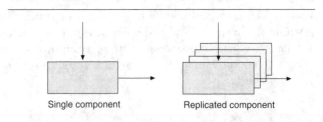

Single component   Replicated component

Almost always lacking are an indication of the possible range of replication and when the actual number is bound. Make sure to include both. For example:

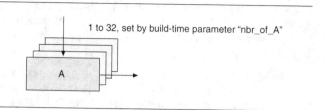

1 to 32, set by build-time parameter "nbr_of_A"

A

Creation and Deletion of Components or Connectors
Chapter 8 describes notations that can be used to indicate the creation and deletion of components or connectors. An example is a UML sequence diagram, in which a line on a time-line scale is used to indicate the existence of a component or a connector.

Reallocating Resources
Some forms of reallocation of resources, such as the migration of objects, can be described by the UML construct *become*. This is represented by a dashed arrow whose tail is on the original location of an object and whose head is on the subsequent location.

PERSPECTIVES

What Time Is It?

When I was a student first learning to program, a concept that gave me fits was compile time versus runtime information. Put in post-Watergate terms: What does the software know, and when does it know it? I struggled with this until, of all things, I took a written multiple-choice exam one year to renew my driver's license. One of the questions was about signage. The question asked the meaning of a sign like this:

The possible answers were (a) road slippery when wet, (b) dangerous curve, (c) reduce speed, (d) drunk driver ahead.

The last choice made me laugh out loud. The attendants supervising the exam smiled, having no doubt which question I was on. But I was laughing because the concept of runtime versus compile time was no longer a mystery: A slippery road is slippery every time it gets wet, but a drunk driver comes and goes, and no static sign, which was installed *before* the road's "runtime," can be correct all the time.

Since then, I've learned that those two "times" are but a few of the possible stages of a software system's life at which bindings occur that can affect its behavior. Other times of importance are

- *Program write time,* when most design decisions are frozen into code, including the decisions *not* to bind certain decisions, which are inserted into the code as points of variation to be bound at one of the later times.

- *Compile time,* when variation points that can be understood by a compiler are bound. Through macro facilities, such as #ifdef, alternative versions of the code can be selected. Parameters, often numbers, can be assigned their value. Compile-time parameters are used to achieve the effect of multiple copies of the source code that differ in slight ways but without having to maintain actual copies.

- *Link time,* when the system build environment looks around for all the files and external definitions it expects to have available at runtime. Some late-binding parameters are bound at link time, especially those having to do with versions of external files—components—with which the main program expects to interact.

- *Program start-up time,* when programs take special actions, which may be made to vary, the first time or each time they are powered up. For example, a large air traffic control system reads a massive file of *adaptation data* each time it starts. The data is a rich compendium of directions to the software, telling it the displays and display formats chosen by its human users, what the geography is like where it's been installed, how to divide the local sky into sectors, and a host of other tailoring information. Another example is the worm that, on finding itself infiltrated into your computer, consults your address book to see where to send itself.

- *Runtime,* when many decisions in modern infrastructures are bound. Browsers patiently wait while their users obtain necessary plug-ins on demand; middleware oversees the negotiation of compatible interfaces among components written in almost total ignorance of one another. And architectures that we call dynamic change their shape and connectivity.

Why is all this relevant? Because documenting *when* things can change is as important as documenting *what* things can change. Take care to consider all the possible times at which you want variabilities to be available, and specify the mechanisms by which the available choices are made.

—P.C.C.

6.5 Creating and Documenting a New Style

In Section 6.3, we discussed the need to define a new style when combining two or more existing styles and the result was expected to be of enduring value to the current or future projects. There are also other reasons to define new styles. Style catalogs are by their nature incomplete. They grow as practitioners discover new styles that solve new problems or solve old problems in new ways. An architect designing the software for a system is likely to realize that he or she has used a new style or made a new twist on an existing style. What are the obligations for documenting a new style?

In broad terms, documenting a new architectural style is done by writing a *style guide* specifying a vocabulary of design—as a set of element and relationship types—and rules for how that vocabulary can be used as a set of topological and semantic constraints. A second way is to define one or more *architectural patterns*. This is usually done by defining parameterized architectural fragments, or templates, which can be instantiated by filling in the missing parts.

Existing style catalogs prescribe different ways to catalog a style, but four key decisions must be made and documented.

1. *Vocabulary:* What are the types of elements in the style? What relationships do they have? What are their properties? What are the rules of composition that determine how the vocabulary can be used?

2. *Semantics:* What computational model do these elements support?

3. *Analyses:* What forms of analysis are supported by the style?

4. *Implementation:* What are the implementation strategies that allow one to produce an executable system?

In this book, Chapters 2, 4, and 5 use a slightly different catalog approach geared to the documentation of views discussed in those styles. The vocabulary section became Elements, Relations, and Properties, a good match. Semantics and analyses are manifested in What It's For and Not For, with a passing mention of computational models. Implementation was omitted from our descriptions as being of little interest in this context; in its place, we added a section on notations for the style.

ADVICE

When writing your own guide to a new style, you will probably want to pay more attention to implementation and computational models, as you will be writing for an audience that will be unfamiliar with the style and its usage. You may also want to follow our lead and indicate what the relationship is between the new style and other styles that have already been cataloged. This relationship information could include similarities to other styles, styles that are particularly useful for the new style to map to, or styles that the new style might be confused with.

Usually, the answers to the questions imposed by the style guide are interdependent. The choice of element vocabulary and the required properties may be driven by the kinds of analysis that one wants to perform. For instance, queuing-theoretic analysis depends on the use of connectors that support asynchronous, buffered messages, together with properties that indicate buffering capacity, latencies, and so on. Implementation strategies may exploit the fact that the architecture satisfies certain topological constraints. For example, a linear pipeline of filters can be optimized by combining the functions performed by several filters into one larger equivalent filter.

Getting all this working together is not an easy proposition. Consequently, architects often use three techniques to develop new styles.

1. *Combining styles:* An architect mixes and matches elements from several existing styles to produce a new one. For example, you might combine the features of a peer-to-peer style and a publish-subscribe style, so that components can either synchronously invoke other components' methods or asynchronously publish events. Combining styles has the advantage of reuse. However, one must be careful that the features of one style do not violate the semantic assumptions and constraints of another. Consider, for example, combining repository and a pipe-and-filter style. In the new style, filters can communicate via either pipes or a shared database. Unfortunately, doing this means that filters can no longer be treated as asynchronous processes, as they may need to synchronize on shared-data access. Is this a problem? It depends on the kinds of analyses that

you intend to perform and the implementation techniques you intend to use.

2. *Style specialization:* Refining an existing style can be done in several ways. You can provide a more detailed, domain-specific vocabulary. For example, you might define a new style by specializing pipes and filters for process control by adding a set of special filter types for monitoring the environment and regulating set points. You might add new constraints. For example, you might define topological constraints in the process control style to enforce a closed-loop organization of the filters. You might add new properties to enable new forms of analysis.

3. *Analysis-driven styles:* Choose a style to permit a particular form of analysis. Suppose that you want to be able to analyze a system for a certain quality attribute. You have a queuing theory that can do this. This analytic framework makes certain assumptions about the elements and their interactions, such as independent processes with buffered message queues. Embody those assumptions in the definition of the style.

COMING TO TERMS

Styles, Patterns

It must be clear by now that the concept of styles is fundamental to the engineering and documentation of an architecture. In the early 1990s, some in the software architecture community observed recurring coarse-grained problem solutions involving the use of specific kinds of elements arranged in specific kinds of relationships with each other. These architectural *styles,* as they were called, were recognized as providing glimpses into how architects went about their craft; they represented the results of early and fundamental design decisions. Except in matters of detail, architectural solutions to vastly different application problems—layering the system, employing clients and servers with message-passing, assigning the work to loosely coupled communicating processes, introducing a central data repository, delivering the data through pipes to be processed by filters—could be seen as identical.

At about the same time, the object-oriented programming community was discovering that they, too, could observe recurring solutions to problems in their realm. In 1995, the so-called "gang of four" design patterns book was published [Gamma+ 95], and is still the Bible of object-oriented design. Model-view-controller, abstract factory, adapter, builder, and other patterns entered our design vocabulary, and an entire community devoted to finding and describing patterns arose.

Both the style and the design patterns communities shared a common virtue. The goal, they made clear, was not to make up solutions but to capture solutions that were already in use. Various venues for describing these things had their own rules: Before being eligible for inclusion, the pattern or style has to occur in at least two systems, or in two different organizations, and so on. This mercifully headed off any temptation to catalog solutions for solutions' sake, and to concentrate instead on capturing provably useful design knowledge.

To its credit, the design patterns community became interested (if not obsessed) with more than just the patterns, but how the patterns should be described. They took their inspiration from Christopher Alexander, a building (not a software) architect who is at least as well known in our field as he is in his own. In 1977, Alexander published a book entitled *A Pattern Language: Towns, Buildings, Construction* (Oxford University Press, 1977). In it, he tried to codify rules for large-scale and small-scale building architecture that would result in homes, public buildings, and towns that people would find aesthetically and functionally pleasing. Computer scientists who read the book recognized an entire grammar for building architecture. Balconies should be at least 10 feet wide, or else people won't spend time on them. Entrances and public squares should be on the south side of buildings in the Northern Hemisphere, so as to be sunny. Breathtaking views shouldn't be squandered, but revealed suddenly and unexpectedly. Each rule was laid out in a prescribed form, giving its use, justification, and the circumstances in which it applied.

The gang of four used their own pattern language, a 13-part template with sections including "Name and classification," "also known as," "motivation," "applicability," "structure," "sample code," "known uses," and "related patterns." The template, wrote the authors, "lends a uniform structure to the information, making design patterns easier to learn, compare, and use."

In 1996, Buschmann, Meunier, Rohnert, Sommerlad, and Stal arranged the inevitable marriage between the two worlds. In *Pattern-Oriented Software Architecture, Volume 1: A System of Patterns* (John Wiley & Sons, 1996), they gave us a set of well-known architectural styles documented in a very design-pattern-like fashion—that is to say, using a pattern language. Thus came the first widely published catalog of architectural styles that was of general use to the in-the-trenches software architect.

So is there a difference between a style and a pattern? Yes
and no. They are alike in that both are cataloged partial
design solutions, captured in practice, and must be instantiated and completed before application to an actual system. They are different in that a style *tends* to refer to a
coarser grain of design solution than a pattern, which *tends*
to refer to a design solution localized within a few (or one)
of a system's many architectural components. But many
people treat architectural styles simply as patterns writ
large. We concur.

6.6 Summary Checklist

- Views are usually too complex to be understood all at once. Chunking information helps convey it more effectively. View packets are the documentation units that chunk view information.

- View packets are related to one another by child-parent relationships, which correspond to zooming in and out, and sibling relationships, which correspond to panning to different areas of the system.

- Because systems almost always exhibit multiple styles, view packets in different views can be parents, children, or siblings.

- Refinement, the gradual disclosure of more detailed infor-mation, is another chunking mechanism. Decomposition refinement reveals internal substructure. Implementation refinement replaces elements with different elements show-ing an implementation.

- Views can exhibit descriptive completeness. Descriptively complete views show all elements and relations; views that are not descriptively complete suppress some elements and relations.

- A context diagram shows what's in and what's out of the sys-tem under consideration and the external entities with which the system interacts. A pure context diagram shows no internal structure, but in practice, many do.

- A system does not show a single top-level context diagram, but rather one in each view. Each such diagram shows the interactions with the environment in the vocabulary for that view. All show what's in and what's out.

- Other context diagrams are used to establish the scope of a view packet.

- Combining views often yields useful insights about the architecture, when the combination is carefully considered. A combined view comes about either as a hybrid style or an overlay.
- Views with a high correspondence are good candidates for combining.
- Document variability and dynamism using the same styles you normally would choose for that architecture. Show what's constant and what's not. For the latter, describe the range of options and when the option is bound.
- To document a new style, write a style guide. Include vocabulary, semantics, analyses, and implementation strategies.

6.7   Discussion Questions

1. A user invokes a Web browser to download a file. Before doing so, the browser retrieves a plug-in to handle that type of file. Is this an example of a dynamic architecture? How would you document it?

2. Suppose that communication across layers in a layered system is carried out by signaling events. Is event signaling a concern that is part of the layered style? If not, how would you document this system?

3. Consider a shared-data system with a central database accessed by several components in a client-server fashion. What are your options for documenting the two-style nature of this system? Which option(s) would you choose, and why?

4. A bridging element is one that can appear in view packets in two separate views. Both views will have room for documenting the element's interface and its behavior. Assuming that we do not wish to document information in two places, how would you decide where to record that information? Suppose that the bridging element is a connector with one role for one style and one role for another. Where would you record the information then?

5. Sketch a top-level context diagram for a hypothetical system as it might appear in the following views, assuming in each case that the view is appropriate for that system: (a) uses, (b) layered, (c) pipe-and-filter, (d) client-server, (e) deployment.

6.8   For Further Reading

As noted in the Prologue, the notion of multiple views as a way to partition descriptions of complex systems has been around for some time. Recently there has been considerable interest from the software engineering community in identifying mechanisms for combining those concerns in systematic ways. One branch of this subarea is sometimes referred to as "aspect-oriented programming" or "multi-dimensional separation of concerns." Work in this area is represented by [Kiczales+ 97]. A good source of current information is http://www.aosd.net.

In a similar vein, Michael Jackson's book on problem frames has a good chapter on combining multiple problems frames [Jackson 01]. Although it is cast in terms of the problem space, rather than the solution space of architectures, many of the ideas carry over.

A number of researchers have considered the question of how to define architectural styles formally. One of the first papers to address the issue is [PerryWolf 92]. Chapters 6 and 8 in [ShawGarlan 96] also tackle the problem, using formal specifications languages like Z and CSP. For examples of defining architectural styles in an object-oriented framework, consider [Buschmann+ 96] and [Schmidt+ 00].

Documenting Software Interfaces

7.1 Overview

Early treatments of architecture and architecture description languages devoted loving attention to the elements of the system and their interactions but tended to overlook the interfaces to those elements. It was as though interfaces were not part of the architecture. Clearly, however, interfaces are supremely architectural, for one cannot perform analyses or system building without them. Therefore, a critical part of documenting a view includes documenting the interfaces of the elements shown in that view.

The characteristics of an interface depend on the viewtype of its element. If the element is a component, the **interface** represents a specific point of potential interaction of a component with its environment. If the element is a module, the interface is a definition of services. There is a relation between these two kinds of interfaces, just as there is a relation between components and modules.

By the element's *environment,* we mean the set of other entities with which it interacts. We call those other entities **actors.** In general, an actor is an abstraction for external entities that interact with the system. Here, we focus on elements and expand the definition of interaction to include anything one element does that can impact the processing of another element. This interaction is part of the element's interface. Interactions can take a variety of forms. Most involve the transfer of control and/or data. Some are supported by standard programming language constructs, such as local or remote procedure calls, data streams, shared memory, and message passing.

DEFINITION

An **interface** is a boundary across which two independent entities meet and interact or communicate with each other.

DEFINITION

An element's **actors** are the other elements, users, or systems with which it interacts.

223

These constructs, which provide points of direct interaction with an element, are called *resources*.

Other interactions are indirect. For example, the fact that using resource X on element A leaves element B in a particular state is something that other elements using the resource may need to know if it affects their processing, even though they never interact with A directly. That fact about A is a part of the interface between A and the other elements in A's environment.

An interaction extends beyond merely what happens. For example, if element X calls element Y, the amount of time that Y takes before returning control to X is part of Y's interface to X because it affects X's processing.

Let's establish some principles about interfaces.

- *All elements have interfaces.* All elements interact with their environment.

- *An element's interface contains view-specific information.* Because an element can occur in more than one view, aspects of its interface can be documented in each view, using the vocabulary of that view. For instance, an interface to a module in a uses view might describe which methods are provided, but an interface to the same module in a work assignment view would not include this information. In fact, some views may have little interface information to document. (Whether an architect chooses to document an element's interface separately in different views or in a single treatment is a packaging issue. An interface that transcends views can be documented in the package of documentation that applies to more than one view.)

FOR MORE INFORMATION
Chapter 10 discusses packaging issues.

- *Interfaces are two-way.* When considering interfaces, most software engineers first think of a summary of what an element provides. What methods does the element make available? What events does it process? But an element also interacts with its environment by making use of resources or assuming that its environment behaves in a certain way. Without these resources, or absent an environment behaving as expected, the element can't function correctly. So an interface is more than what is *provided* by an element; an interface also includes what is *required* by an element. The requires part of an element's interface typically comes in two varieties:

  - Resources on which an element builds. This kind of resource is something that is used in the implementation of the element, such as class libraries or toolkits, but often it is not information that other elements use in interacting with the element. This type of resource requirement is typically documented by naming the library, version, and platform of the resource. A build will generally quickly uncover any unsatisfied interface requirements of this kind.

– Assumptions that the element makes of other elements with which it interacts. For example, an element could assume the presence of a database using specific schema over which it can make SQL (Structured Query Language) queries. Or an element may require its actors to call an init() method before it allows queries. This type of information is critical to document—after all, the system won't work if the requirement is not met—and not easily uncovered if not satisfied.

When we say that an interface includes what is required, we're focusing on what interactions an element requires from its environment to complete an interaction it provides.

• *An element can have multiple interfaces.* Each interface contains a separate collection of resources that have a related logical purpose, or represent a role that the element could fill, and serves a different class of elements. Multiple interfaces provide a separation of concerns, which has obvious benefits. A user of the element, for example, might require only a subset of the functionality provided by the element. If the element has multiple interfaces, perhaps the developer's requirements line up nicely with one of the interfaces, meaning that the developer would have to learn only the interface that mattered to him or her rather than the complete set of resources provided by the element. Conversely, the provider of an element may want to grant users different access rights, such as read or write, to prevent resource contention or to implement a security policy. Multiple interfaces support different levels of access.

Multiple interfaces also support evolution in open-market situations. If you put an element in the commercial market and the element's interface changes, you can't recall and fix everything that uses the old version. So you can support evolution by keeping the old one but adding the new interface.

• *An element can interact with more than one actor through the same interface.* Document any limits on the number of actors that can interact with an element via a particular interface. For example, Web servers often restrict the number of simultaneously open HTTP connections.

• *Sometimes, it's useful to have interface types, as well as interface instances.* Like all types, an interface type is a template for a set of instances. Some notations support this concept, which we noted in some of the view examples in the C&C viewtype.

Many times, all the interfaces you're designing will include a standard set of resources, such as an initialization program; a set of standard exception conditions, such as failing to have called the initialization program; a standard way to handle exceptions, such as invoking a named error handler; or a standard statement of semantics, such as persistence of stored information. It is convenient to write these standard interface "parts" as an interface type. Sometimes, an element has multiple interfaces that are identical: A component that merges two input streams might be designed with two separate but identical interfaces. It is convenient to write these identical interfaces as an interface type. An interface type can be documented in the architecture's beyond view documentation.

7.2 Interface Specifications

An **interface specification** is a statement of what an architect chooses to make known about an element in order for other entities to interact or communicate with it.

An interface is documented with an **interface specification**. Although an interface constitutes every interaction an element has with its environment, what we choose to disclose about an interface—that is, what we document in an interface specification—is more limited. Writing down every aspect of every possible interaction is not practical and almost never desirable. Rather, the architect should expose only what users of an element *need* to know in order to interact with it. Put another way, the architect chooses what information is permissible and appropriate for people to assume about the element and unlikely to change.

The interface specification documents what other developers need to know about an element in order to use it in combination with other elements and provides a statement of other visible properties. Note that a developer might observe element properties that are an artifact of how the element is implemented but that are not in the interface specification. Because these are not in the interface specification, they are subject to change, and developers use these at their own risk.

Documenting an interface is a matter of striking a balance between disclosing too little information and disclosing too much. Disclosing too little information will prevent developers from successfully interacting with the element. Disclosing too much will make future changes to the system more difficult and widespread and makes the interface complicated for people to understand.

Also recognize that different people need to know different kinds of information about the element. The architect may have to provide separate sections in the interface document or

Guidelines for Writing an Interface Specification

- Focus on how elements interact with their environments, not on how elements are implemented. Restrict the documentation to phenomena that are externally visible.

- Expose only what actors in an element's environment need to know. Including a piece of information in the documentation is an implicit promise to the element's stakeholders that the information is reliable and stable. Once information is exposed, other elements may rely on it, and changes will have a more widespread effect.

- If you don't want people to rely on a piece of information, don't include it in the interface documentation. Make it clear that information that "leaks" through an interface but is not included in its interface documentation can be used only at the peril of the actors that exploit it and of the system as a whole.

- Keep in mind who will be using the interface documents and what types of information they will need. Avoid documenting more than is necessary.

- Be as specific and as precise as you can, remembering that an interface specification that two different parties can interpret differently is likely to cause problems and confusion.

multiple interface documents to accommodate different stakeholders of the element.

Interface specifications are documented as part of a view. When similar interface information occurs in more than one place, choose one to hold the interface specification and refer to it in the other.

For example, elements in a module view often correspond directly to one or more elements in a C&C view, and the module and C&C elements are likely to have similar, if not identical, interfaces. Documenting them in both places would produce needless duplication. To avoid that, the interface specification in the one view can point to the interface specification in the other view and contain only the information specific to its view.

Another example is that a set of C&C components might all provide instances of the same interface type, except that the resource names are prefixed with the name of the component and two of the components have a couple of extra resources. Document these interfaces by documenting the interface type in one place: either with one of the components or, perhaps, with the corresponding module. Document the deltas with each component.

FOR MORE INFORMATION

Section 10.2 provides a documentation template for views, with a section reserved for element interfaces.

Similarly, a module may appear in more than one module view: decomposition and uses, for example. Again, choose one view to hold the interface specification and refer to it in the other.

As in all architectural documentation, the amount of information conveyed in an interface specification may vary, depending on the stage of the design process captured by the documentation. If the interface is part of an element that is being developed in the system, the interface might be partially specified early in the design process; for example, module A provides the following services. Later, when the responsibilities of the the elements become stable, the interface specification is more fully elaborated; for example, module A provides method X with signature Y and semantics Z. Remember that an important rule for sound documentation prescribes using a standard organization, such as the one suggested in the next section. A standard organization lets you fill in what you know now and indicate TBD for what you don't yet know, thus providing a to-do list for the remaining work.

7.3 A Standard Organization for Interface Documentation

This section suggests a standard organization for interface documentation (see Figure 7.1). Like all templates and organizational layouts in this book, you may wish to modify this one to remove items not relevant to your situation or to add items unique to your business. More important than which standard organization you use is the practice of using one. Use what you need to present an accurate picture of the element's externally visible interactions for the interfaces in your project.

1. *The identity of the interface:* When an element has multiple interfaces, identify the individual interfaces to distinguish them from one another. The most common means of doing this is to name an interface. Some programming languages, such as Java, or frameworks, such as COM, even allow these names to be carried through into the implementation. In some cases, merely naming an interface is not sufficient, and the version of the interface must be specified as well. For example, in a framework with named interfaces that has evolved over time, it could be very important to know whether you mean the v1.2 or v3.0 persistence interface.

2. *Resources provided:* The heart of an interface document is the set of resources that the element provides to its actors. Define these resources by giving their syntax, their seman-

Figure 7.1
Documentation for an
interface consists of nine
parts

Element Interface Specification

Section 1.   **Interface identity**
Section 2   **Resources provided**
  Section a. Resource syntax
  Section b. Resource semantics
  Section c. Resource usage restrictions
Section 3.   **Locally defined data types**
Section 4.   **Error handling**
Section 5.   **Variability provided**
Section 6.   **Quality attribute characteristics**
Section 7.   **What the element requires**
Section 8.   **Rationale and design issues**
Section 9.   **Usage guide**

---

tics—what happens when they're used—and any restrictions on their usage.

a. *Resource syntax:* This is the resource's signature, which includes any information that another program will need to write a syntactically correct program that uses the resource. The signature includes the name of the resource, names and logical data types of arguments, if any, and so forth.

b. *Resource semantics:* What is the result of invoking this resource? Semantics come in a variety of guises, including

  i. Assignment of values to data that the actor invoking the resource can access. The value assignment might be as simple as setting the value of a return argument or as far-reaching as updating a central database.

  ii. Changes in the element's state brought about by using the resource. This includes exceptional conditions, such as side effects from a partially completed operation.

  iii. Events that will be signaled or messages that will be sent as a result of using the resource.

  iv. How other resources will behave differently in the future as the result of using this resource. For example, if you ask a resource to destroy an object, trying to access that object in the future through other resources will produce quite a different outcome—an error—as a result.

  v. Humanly observable results. These are prevalent in embedded systems; for example, calling a program

Guidelines for Writing Down the Semantics of a Resource

- Write down only those effects that are visible to a user: the actor invoking the resource, another element in the system, or a human observer of the system. Ask yourself how a user will be able to verify what you have said. If your semantics cannot be verified, the effect you have described is invisible, and you haven't captured the right information. Either replace it with a statement about something that the user will be able to observe, or omit it. Sometimes the only visible effect of a resource is to disable certain exceptional conditions that might otherwise occur. For instance, a program that declares a named object disables the error associated with using that name before the object is declared.

- Make it a goal to avoid prose as the only medium of your description. Instead, try to define the semantics of invoking a resource by describing ways other resources will be affected. For example, in a stack object, you can describe the effects of push(x) by saying that pop() returns x and that the value returned by g_stack_size() is incremented by 1.

- If you use prose, be as precise as you can. Be suspicious of all verbs. For every verb in the specification of a resource's semantics, ask yourself exactly what it means and how the resource's users will be able to verify it. Eliminate vague words, such as *should, usually,* and *may.* For operations that position something in the physical world, be sure to define the coordinate system, reference points, points of view, and so on, that describe the effects.

- Avoid giving example use in place of specifying the semantics. Usage is a valuable part of an interface specification and merits its own section in the documentation, but it is given as advice to users and should not be expected to serve as a definitive statement of resources' semantics. Strictly speaking, an example defines the semantics of a resource for only the single case illustrated by the example. The user might be able to make a good guess at the semantics from the example, but we do not wish to build systems based on guesswork. We should expect that users will use an element in ways the designers did not envision, and we do not wish to artificially limit them.

- Avoid giving an implementation in place of specifying the semantics. Do not use code to describe the effects of a resource.

that turns on a display in a cockpit has a very observable effect: The display comes on.

In addition, the statement of semantics should make it clear whether the execution of the resource will be atomic or may be suspended or interrupted.

c. *Resource usage restrictions:* Under what circumstances may this resource be used? Perhaps data must be initialized before it can be read, or perhaps a particular method cannot be invoked unless another is invoked first. Perhaps there is a limit on the number of actors that can interact via this resource at any instant. Perhaps there is a limit of one actor that has ownership and is able to modify the element, whereas others have only read access. Perhaps only certain resources or interfaces are accessible to certain actors to support a multilevel security scheme.

Notions of persistence or side effects can be relevant here. If the resource requires other resources to be present or makes certain other assumptions about its environment, these should be documented. Some restrictions are less prohibitive; for example, Java interfaces can list certain methods as *deprecated,* meaning that users should not use them, as they will likely be unsupported in future versions of the interface. Usage restrictions are often documented by defining *exceptions* that will be raised if the restrictions are violated.

3. *Locally defined data types:* If any interface resources use a data type other than one provided by the underlying programming language, the architect needs to communicate the definition of that data type. If the data type is defined by another element, a reference to the definition in that element's documentation is sufficient. In any case, programmers writing elements using such a resource need to know (a) how to declare variables and constants of the data type, (b) how to write literal values in the data type, (c) what operations and comparisons may be performed on members of the data type, and (d) how to convert values of the data type into other data types, where appropriate.

4. *Error handling:* Describe error conditions that can be raised by the resources on the interface. Because the same error condition might be raised by more than one resource, it is often convenient to simply list the error conditions associated with each resource; define them in a dictionary collected separately. This section is that dictionary. Common error-handling behavior can also be defined here.

ADVICE

Consider using preconditions and postconditions for documenting both resource usage restrictions and resource semantics together. A precondition states what must be true before the interaction is permitted; a postcondition describes any state changes resulting from the interaction.

5. *Any variability provided by the interface:* Does the interface allow the element to be configured in some way? These *configuration parameters* and how they affect the semantics of the interactions in the interface must be documented. Examples of variability include capacities—such as of visible data structures—that can be easily changed. Name and provide a range of values for each configuration parameter, and specify the time when its actual value is bound.

6. *Quality attribute characteristics of the interface:* The architect needs to document what quality attribute characteristics, such as performance or reliability, the interface makes known to the element's users. This information may be in the form of constraints on implementations of elements that will realize the interface. The qualities you choose to concentrate on and make promises about will depend on the context.

7. *What the element requires:* What the element requires may be specific, named resources provided by other elements. The documentation obligation is the same as for resources provided: syntax, semantics, and any usage restrictions. Two elements sharing this interface information—one providing it and the other requiring it—might each reference a single definition. If the element is being developed as an independent reusable component, that information needs to be fully documented. What the element requires may be expressed as something more general, such as "The presence of a process scheduler that will schedule in a priority-based fashion." Often, it is convenient to document such information as a set of assumptions that the element's designer has made about the system. In this form, they can be reviewed by experts who can confirm or repudiate the assumptions before the design has progressed too far.

8. *Rationale and design issues:* Like rationale for the architecture or architectural views at large, the architect should also record the reasons behind the design of an element's interface. The rationale should explain the motivation behind the design, constraints and compromises, alternative designs that were considered and rejected and why, and any insight the architect has about how to change the interface in the future.

9. *Usage guide:* Sections 2b and 7 in Figure 7.1 document an element's semantic information on a per resource basis. This sometimes falls short of what is needed. In some cases, semantics need to be reasoned about in terms of how

a broad number of individual interactions interrelate. Essentially, a *protocol* of interaction is involved that is documented by considering multiple interactions simultaneously. These protocols could represent the complete behavior of the interaction or patterns of usage that the element designer expects to be used repeatedly. In general, if interacting with the element via its interface is complex, the interface documentation might include a static behavioral model, such as a state machine or examples of carrying out specific interactions in the form of trace-oriented scenarios.

> **FOR MORE INFORMATION**
>
> Documentation mechanisms to help with protocols include connectors (Chapter 3 and Chapter 4) and behavioral models (Section 8.5).

COMING TO TERMS

Exceptions and Error Handling

When designing an interface, architects naturally concentrate on documenting how resources work in the nominal case, when everything goes according to plan. The real world, of course, is far from nominal, and a well-designed system must take appropriate action in the face of undesired circumstances. What happens when a resource is called with parameters that make no sense? What happens when the resource requires more memory, but the allocation request fails because there isn't any more? What happens when a resource never returns, because it has fallen victim to a process deadlock? What happens when the software is supposed to read the value of a sensor, but the sensor has failed and either isn't responding or is responding with gibberish?

Terminating the program on the spot seldom qualifies as "appropriate action." More desirable alternatives, depending on the situation, include various combinations of the following:

- Returning a status indicator: an integer code—or even a message—that reports on the resource's execution: what, if anything, went wrong and what the result was.
- Retrying, if the offending condition is considered transient. The program might retry indefinitely or up to a preset number of times, at which point it returns a status indicator.
- Computing partial results or entering a degraded mode of operation.
- Attempting to correct the problem, perhaps by using default or fallback values or alternative resources.

These are all reasonable actions that a resource can take in the presence of undesired circumstances. If a resource is designed to take any of these actions, that should simply be documented as part of the effects of that resource. But many times, something else is appropriate. The resource can, in effect, throw up its hands and report that an error condition existed and that it was unable to do its job. This is where old-fashioned programs would print an error message and terminate. Today, they often raise an *exception,* which allows execution to continue and perhaps accomplish useful work.

Making a strong distinction between detecting an error condition and handling it provides greater flexibility in taking corrective action. The right place to fix a problem raised by a resource is usually the actor that invoked it, not in the resource itself. The resource detects the problem; the actor handles it. If we're in development, handling it might mean terminating with an error message so the bug can be tracked down and fixed. Perhaps the actor made the mistake because one of its own resources was used incorrectly by another actor. In that case, the actor might handle the exception by raising an exception of its own and bubbling the responsibility back along the invocation chain until the actor ultimately responsible is notified.

Modern programming languages provide facilities for raising exceptions and assigning handlers. Program language reference manuals take a language-oriented view in classifying the world of exceptions. The C++ programming language, for instance, has built-in exceptions classes dealing with memory allocation failure, process failure, tasking failures, and the like. Those are exceptions that the compiled program is likely to encounter from the operating system.

But many other things can go wrong during execution of software, and it is incumbent on the architect to say what they are. An architecture-oriented classification of exceptions is summarized in Figure 7.2. In the context of an element's interface, exception conditions are one of the following:

1. *Errors on the part of an actor invoking the resource.*

    a. An actor sent incorrect or illegal information to the resource, perhaps calling a method with a parameter of the wrong type. This error will be detected by the compiler, and an exception is not necessary unless types can change dynamically, in which case things aren't so clear-cut. If your compiler does not generate code to do runtime type checking, associating an exception with the resource is the prudent thing to do. Other exceptions of this variety

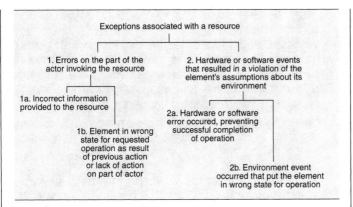

Figure 7.2
A classification of exceptions associated with a resource on an element's interface

describe a parameter with an illegal or out-of-bounds value. Division by zero is the classic example of this, with array-bounds violations a close runner-up. Other examples are a string that has the wrong syntax or length; in a pair of parameters defining a range, the minimum exceeds the maximum; an uninitialized variable was input; and a set contains a duplicate member.

b. The element is in the wrong state for the requested resource. The element entered the improper state as a result of a previous action or lack of a previous action on the part of an actor. An example of the latter is invoking a resource before the element's initialization method has been called.

2. *Software or hardware events that result in a violation in the element's assumptions about its environment.*

a. A hardware or software error occurred that prevented the resource from successfully executing. Processor failures, inability to allocate more memory, and memory faults are examples of this kind of exception.

b. The element is in the wrong state for the requested resource. The element's improper state was brought about by an event that occurred in the environment of the element, outside the control of the actor requesting the resource. An example is trying to read from a sensor or write to a storage device that has been taken offline by the system's human operator.

Exceptions and effects produce a three-way division of the state space for every resource on an interface.

"Exceptional" does not mean "almost never happens" or "disastrous." It is better to think of an exception as meaning "some part of the system couldn't do what it was asked to do."

—(Stroustrup 1997, p. 358)

1. First, effects promise what will happen in a certain portion of the state space, what Parnas (Parnas and Wuerges, 2001) has called the *competence set* of the program: the set of states in which it is competent to carry out its function. A resource invoked in a state that is a member of its competence set will execute as promised in the interface document.

2. Second, exceptions specify the semantics in a different region of the state space, corresponding to error conditions that the architect has had the foresight to anticipate. If a resource is invoked in a state corresponding to an exception, the effects are simply that the exception is raised. (Remember, handling the exception is not in the purview of the resource but in the actor that invoked it. Raising the exception gives the actor the chance to do so.) We'll call this set of states the *exception set.*

3. Third, there is everything else: the region of the state space where what happens is completely undefined if a resource is invoked. The architect may not even know and maybe even has never considered the possibility. We'll call this set of states the *failure set*; we could as well have called it the cross-your-fingers-and-hope-for-the-best set. The behavior may be unpredictable and hence difficult to re-create and therefore eliminate, or it may be depressingly predictable: a very ungraceful software crash.

In a perfect world, the architect squeezes the failure set to nothingness by moving failure states to the competence set by expanding the statement of effects, or to the exception set by creating more exceptions. An equally valid approach is to make a convincing argument that the program cannot possibly get into a state in the failure set.

For example, suppose that element E needs to have complete control of a shared device during the execution of resource R on interface I. If the architect wasn't sure that this would always be the case when R was invoked, he or she would either (1) specify what the element would do if the device was already in use—return immediately with a failure code, retry a set number of times, wait a set period—or (2) define an exception for R that reported the condition back to the actor and made it the actor's responsibility to sort out. But perhaps the architect is certain that the device will never be in use, because element E is the only element that uses it. So the architect doesn't define behavior for the resource to account for that condition and doesn't define an exception for it, either. This puts the condition in the resource's failure set, but the architect can make a convincing argument that doing so is safe.

ADVICE

For each resource in an interface, do the following:

- Define what exceptions the resource detects, using the classification of Figure 7.2 to help you account for possible exceptions. Do so in terms of phenomena that are visible to an actor, not in terms of implementation details that should remain unknown to the actor and its programmer.
- Let the specification of effects and exceptions help each other, and make sure they're consistent with each other. The exception's definition implies preconditions that must be true before a resource can be invoked. Conversely, preconditions imply exceptions that should be raised if the preconditions are not met.
- Do your best to identify the resource's failure set, and try reducing it by expanding the resource's behavior to work in more states or by defining more exceptions. For those states that remain in the failure set, include in the element's design rationale an explanation of why the failure set is safe.

7.4 Stakeholders of Interface Documentation

In the Prologue, we talked about stakeholders having special needs and expectations from an architecture. In Chapter 10, we use those stakeholders as the basis for organizing a system's architectural documentation. Interfaces are a microcosm of this general situation. Some of the stakeholders of interface documentation and the kinds of information they require are as follows:

- *Builder of an element,* who needs the most comprehensive documentation of an interface. The builder needs to see any assertions about the interface that other stakeholders will see and perhaps depend on, so that he or she can make them true. A special kind of builder is the *maintainer,* who makes assigned changes to the element.

- *Tester of an element,* who needs detailed information about all the resources and functionality provided by an interface; this is what is usually tested. The tester can test only to the degree of knowledge embodied in the element's semantic description. If required behavior for a resource is not specified, the tester will not know to test for it, and the element may fail to do its job. A tester also needs information about what is required by an interface, so that a test harness can be built, if necessary, to mimic the resources required.

- *Developer using an element,* who needs detailed information about the resources provided by the element, including semantic information. Information about what the element requires is needed only if the requirements are pertinent to resources the developer uses.

- *Analyst,* whose information needs depend on the types of analyses conducted. For a performance analyst, for example, the interface document should give information that can feed a performance model, such as computation time required by resources. The analyst is a prime consumer of any quality attribute information contained in an interface document.

- *System builder,* who focuses on finding *provides* for each *requires* in the interfaces of elements going together to build a system. Often, the focus is more on syntactic satisfaction of requirements—Does it build?—not on semantic satisfaction of requirements. This role often uses information that is not of interest to most other stakeholders of an interface document, such as what version of the Java String class an element uses.

- *Integrater,* who also puts the system together from its constituent elements but has a stronger interest in the behavior of the resulting assemblage. Hence, the integrater is more likely to be concerned with semantic rather than syntactic matching of *requires* and *provides* among the elements' interfaces. A special kind of integrater is a *product builder,* who exploits the variability available in the elements to produce different instantiations of them, which can then be assembled into a suite of similar but differing products. Ease of integration is also a key factor for the customer, who takes on aspects of the integrater's role when comparing vendors' products.

- *Architect looking for assets to reuse in a new system,* who often starts by examining the interfaces of elements from a previous system. The architect may also look in the commercial marketplace to find off-the-shelf elements that can be purchased and do the job. To see whether an element is a candidate, the architect is first interested in the general nature and capabilities of the resources it provides to determine what aspects of the interface are pertinent to the design. The architect is also interested in a basic understanding of what resources are required. As the architect continues to qualify the element, he or she becomes more interested in the precise semantics of the resources, their quality attributes, and any variability that the element provides.

- *Manager,* who is likely to use interface documents for planning purposes. Managers can apply metrics to gauge the complexity and then infer estimates for how long it will take to develop an element that realizes the interface. Depending on the metrics, information might be required about the size of the interface and the contained functionality but not on further details. Managers can also spot special expertise that may be required, and this will assist them in assigning the work to qualified personnel.

7.5 Notation for Interface Documentation

7.5.1 Showing the Existence of Interfaces

The *existence* of interfaces can be shown in the primary presentations by using most graphical notations available for architecture. Figure 7.3 shows some examples using an informal notation.

The existence of an interface can be implied even without using an explicit symbol for it. If a relationship symbol joins

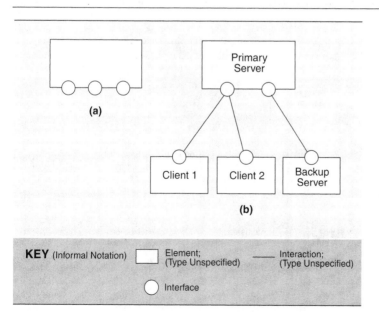

Figure 7.3
Graphical notations for interfaces typically show a symbol on the boundary of the icon for an element. Lines connecting interface symbols denote that the interface exists between the connected elements. Graphical notations like this can show only the existence of an interface, not its definition. (a) An element with multiple interfaces. For elements with a single interface, the interface symbol is often omitted. (b) Multiple actors at an interface. Clients 1 and 2 both interact with Primary Server via the same interface.

an element symbol and the relationship type involves an inter-action—as opposed to, say, *is a subclass of,* that implies that the interaction takes place through the element's interface.

ADVICE

Use an explicit interface symbol in your primary presenta-tions if

• Some elements have more than one interface.

• You wish to emphasize the interface for an element; for example, you are making provisions for multiple elements that realize the same interface.

Although it's never wrong to show interfaces explicitly, it is not necessary to do so if

• No element has more than one interface.

• You wish to reduce the visual clutter of the diagrams.

Sometimes, interfaces are depicted by themselves, without an associated element. When actors are shown interacting through this interface, it indicates that any element imple-menting the interface can be used. This is a useful means of expressing a particular kind of variability: the ability to substi-tute realizing elements, as shown in Figure 7.4(a). We say that an interface is *realized by* the element that implements it.

Figure 7.4
An interface can be shown separately from any ele-ment that realizes it, thus emphasizing the inter-changeability of element implementations. (a) Another version of Figure 7.3(b), showing the Primary Server interacting with the interfaces of Clients 1 and 2 and Backup Server, with-out showing those ele-ments. The emphasis here is on the interface. Else-where, the architect can show or list the possible elements that realize each interface. (b) An interface shown by itself emphasizes that many elements can realize it. If a specific set of possibilities has been iden-tified, their candidacy can be shown graphically by using a figure like this.

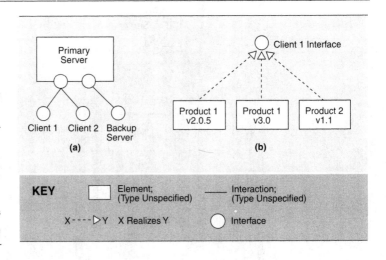

Graphically, this is shown as a line resembling relationships among elements, as shown in Figure 7.4(b).

Figure 7.5 illustrates how interfaces are shown in UML. Although it shows the existence of an interface, Figure 7.5 reveals little about the definition of an interface: the resources it provides or requires, or the nature of its interactions. This information must be provided in the supporting documentation that accompanies the primary presentation.

7.5.2 Conveying Syntactic Information

The Object Management Group (OMG) Interface Definition Language (IDL) is used in the CORBA community to specify interfaces' syntactic information. IDL provides language constructs to describe data types, operations, attributes, and exceptions. But the only language support for semantic information is a comment mechanism. An example of an IDL interface specification is given in Section 7.6.2.

Most programming languages have built-in ways to specify the signature of an element. C header (.h) files and Ada package specifications are two examples.

Finally, using the «interface» stereotype on a class in UML, as shown in Figure 7.5, provides the means for conveying some syntactic information about an interface. At a minimum, the interface is named; in addition, the architect can specify signature information.

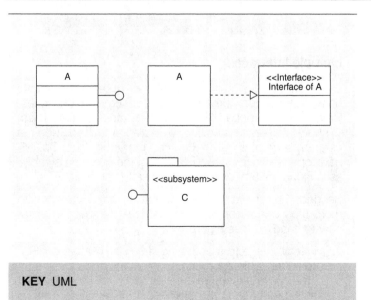

KEY UML

Figure 7.5
Showing syntactic information about interfaces in UML. UML uses a "lollipop" to denote an interface, which can be appended to classes and subsystems, among other things. UML also allows a class symbol, a box, to be stereotyped as an interface; the triangle dashed arrow shows that an element realizes an interface. The bottom part of the class symbol can be annotated with the interface's signature information: method names, arguments and argument types, and so on. The lollipop notation is normally used to show dependencies from elements to the interface; the box notation allows a more detailed interface description, such as the operations provided by the interface.

7.5.3 Conveying Semantic Information

Natural language is the most widespread notation for conveying semantic information. Boolean algebra is often used to write down preconditions and postconditions, which provide a relatively simple and effective method for expressing semantics. Traces are also used to convey semantic information by writing down sequences of activities or interactions that describe the element's response to a specific use.

Semantic information often includes the behavior of an element or one or more of its resources. In that case, any number of notations for behavior come into play.

FOR MORE
INFORMATION
Notations for behavior are detailed in Chapter 8.

7.5.4 Summary

No single notation adequately documents interfaces; practitioners have to use a combination. When showing the existence of interfaces in the views' primary presentations, use the graphical notation of choice. Use one of the syntactic notations to document the syntactic portion of an interface's specification. Use natural language, Boolean algebra for pre- and postconditions, or any of the behavior languages to convey semantic information. Document patterns of usage, or protocols, as rich connectors, or show usage scenarios accompanied by examples of how to use the element's resources to carry out each scenario.

PERSPECTIVES

Multiple Interfaces

Elements having multiple interfaces raise some subtle design issues and some important documentation issues. First, if an element has more than one actor, it's usually best to show interfaces explicitly in your diagrams. If you don't, a diagram such as Figure 7.6(a) can be ambiguous: Does E have one interface or two? Showing the interface symbol, as in Figures 7.6(b) or 7.6(c), resolves the ambiguity.

Second, if you have an element that needs to interact with more than one actor, you have at least three choices for how to handle it (see Figure 7.7).

1. Have all interactors operating via a single interface (Figure 7.7(a)). This approach compels the code in element E to handle any interactions among the actors. What, for instance, shall the element do if two actors try to

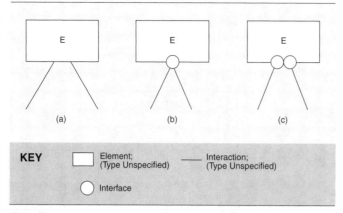

Figure 7.6
(a) Does element E have one interface or two? This diagram makes it difficult to determine at a glance. (b) By using the interface symbol, it's clear that this element has one interface and that (c) this element has two interfaces.

access its services simultaneously? Or what happens if one actor sets up a transaction with E—for example, calls an init() method in a particular way unique to it— but before it can request the transaction it set up, the second actor carries out a setup operation?

2. Have a separate interface dedicated for the use of each actor (Figure 7.7(b)).

3. Have mediation handled in the connector that ties element E to its interactors (Figure 7.7(c)). Figures 7.7(a) and (b) are view neutral, but Figure 7.7(c) shows a connector that handles the mediation and so is firmly rooted in the component-and-connector world. Here, the connector is more than a relation; it is a first-class element, with computational semantics of its own.

With respect to documentation, these three approaches determine where the semantics of mediation or conflict resolution should be explained. The approaches of Figures 7.7(a) and (b) both imply that the mediation among multiple actors is handled by element E. The approach of Figure 7.7(a) imposes on E's interface a documentation obligation that explains what happens when two or more actors try to access the interface simultaneously. The approach of Figure 7.7(b), on the other hand, implies that any one interface does not document mediation—because any interaction with its actor is going to be sequential—but that the element overall documents mediation among competing actors. The semantics of this interaction are documented in a behavioral specification of E or the ensemble consisting of E and its actors. Finally, the approach of Figure 7.7(c) requires an

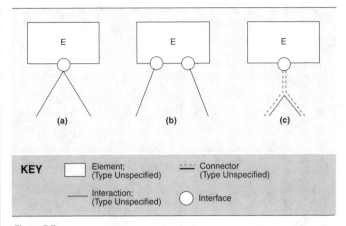

Figure 7.7
Three ways to handle multiple actors interacting with an element. (a) Element E has a single interface through which all its actors interact with it. (b) Element E has a separate interface for each actor. (c) Element E has a single interface attached to a connector that handles the mediation among actors. These three approaches imply different documentation obligations: The effects of contention among E's actors must be documented in, respectively, the interface specification, the behavior of E or the ensemble of E and its actors, and the behavior of the connector, which is an element in its own right.

explanation of the mediation in the behavioral model of the connector.

This discussion assumes that the interfaces we're discussing are instances of the same interface type: that all actors have the same kind of interactions available to them with the element in question. If you have different kinds of interactions, the approach in Figure 7.7(b) wins hands down; it's best to document those as different interfaces. For one thing, it will make detailed modeling of a system's execution behavior easier because each interface may have properties that characterize the runtime state of the interaction with a particular party. A good example is a client-specific session key maintained for each party interacting with a server.

What if your implementation is going to be in a language or programming system that does not support multiple interfaces? You can still document the elements as having multiple *logical* interfaces in an architectural design if it interacts with its environment in different ways. Suppose that you have an element that provides a set of services or methods that may be invoked synchronously by other elements, as well as a set of events that the element may announce asynchronously to other elements. Such an element can easily be documented as having at least two interfaces: one for its service-oriented point of interaction and one for its event-oriented point of interaction.

—P. C. C. and D. G.

Signature, Interface, API

Three terms people use when discussing element interactions are *signature, API,* and *interface.* Often, they use the terms interchangeably, with unfortunate consequences for their projects. We have already defined an interface to be a boundary across which two independent entities meet or communicate with each other, and we have seen that documenting an interface consists of naming and identifying it, documenting syntactic information, and documenting semantic information.

A signature deals with the syntactic part of documenting an interface. When an interface's resources are invokable procedures, each comes with a signature that names the procedure and defines its parameters. Parameters are defined by giving their order, data type, and, sometimes, whether their value is changed by the procedure. A procedure's signature is the information that you would find about it, for instance, in the element's C or C++ header file.

An API, or application programming interface, is a vaguely defined term that people use in various ways to convey interface information about an element. Sometimes, people assemble a collection of signatures and call that an element's API. Sometimes, people add statements about programs' effects or behavior and call that an API. An API for an element is usually written to serve developers who use the element.

Signatures and APIs are useful but are only part of the story. Signatures can be used, for example, to enable automatic build checking, which is accomplished by matching the signatures of different elements' expectations of an interface, often simply by linking different units of code. Signature matching will guarantee that a system will compile and/or link successfully. But it guarantees nothing about whether the system will operate successfully, which is, after all, the ultimate goal.

For a simple example, consider two elements: One provides a read() method, and the other wants to use a read() method. Let's assume that the signatures match as well. So a simple automated check would determine that the elements are syntactically compatible. But suppose that the read() method is implemented such that it removes data from its stream as read() is executed. The user, on the other hand, assumes that read() is free of side effects and hence can read and reread the same data. The semantic mismatch here will lead to errors and is why interfaces need to be specified beyond signatures.

As we have seen, a full-fledged interface is written for a variety of stakeholders, includes both *requires* and *provides* information, and specifies the full range of effects of each resource, including quality attributes. Signatures and low-end APIs are simply not enough to let an element be put to work with confidence in a system. A project that adopts them as a shortcut will pay the price when the elements are integrated, if they're lucky, but more than likely after the system has been delivered to the customer.

An analogy can be found in aviation. Every year in the United States, the Federal Aviation Administration and the National Transportation Safety Board spend millions of dollars tracking down counterfeit, low-quality aircraft parts. Jet engines, for example, are attached to aircraft by special bolts that have been engineered to have the right strength, durability, flexibility, and thermal properties. The next time you board a jet aircraft, imagine that the mechanic who reattached the jet engines after their last overhaul used whatever bolts were long enough and thick enough and happened to be lying around the parts bin. That's the mechanical engineering version of signature matching.

7.6 Examples of Interface Documentation

Following are a few examples of interface documentation. For each, we point out what it does and does not show.

7.6.1 SCR-Style Interface

The first example comes from a U.S. Navy software engineering demonstration project, called the Software Cost Reduction (SCR) project. One of the project goals was to demonstrate model software architecture documentation, including interfaces. The example shown here is for a module generator. The interface is shown for both the generator and the generated elements. The generated module lets actors create and manipulate tree data structures with characteristics determined by the generation step.

In the SCR style, each interface document begins with an introduction that identifies the element and provides a brief account of its function.

TREE.1: Introduction

This module provides facilities for manipulating ordered trees. A complete discussion of ordered trees (hereafter simply called trees) appears in [Knuth]; for the purposes of this specification, the following definitions will suffice:

A *tree* is a finite non-empty set T of nodes partitioned into disjoint non-empty subsets { {R}, T1, ..., Tn }, n>=0, where R is the *root* of T and each subset Ti is itself a tree (a *subtree* of R). The root of each Ti is a *child* of R, and R is its *parent*. The children of R (*siblings* of one another) are ordered, being numbered from 1 to n, with child 1 the *eldest* and child n the *youngest*. Every node also stores a *value*.

The *size* of the tree T is the number of nodes in T. The *degree* of a node is the number of children it has; a node of degree 0 is a leaf. The *level* of a node in a tree is defined with respect to the tree's root: the root is at level 1, and the children of a level N node are at level N+1. The *height* (sometimes also called *depth*) of a tree is the maximum level of any node in the tree.

Using the facilities defined in section TREE.2.1, a user provides (1) a name N for a type whose variables can hold values that denote tree nodes, and (2) the type D of values that a tree node can hold. This generates a submodule that defines the type N and implements the operations on variables of type N specified in section TREE.2.2. These operations include creating, deleting, and linking nodes, and fetching and storing the datum associated with each node.

SCR-style interfaces do not include a usage guide per se, but note how the introduction explains basic concepts and talks about how the element can be used.

The next part of an SCR interface is a table that specifies the syntax of the resources and provides a quick-reference summary of those resources: in this case, methodlike routines called *access programs*. The programs are named, their parameters are defined, and the exceptions detected by each are listed. Parameters are noted as I (input), O (output), I-OPT (optional input), or O-RET (returned as function results). This quick-reference summary, called an Interface Overview, provides the signature for the resources in a language-independent fashion.

TREE.2: Interface Overview (excerpt)

TREE.2.1: Generator access program

Program Name	Parameter Type	Parameter Info	Exceptions
++gen++	p1: id; I	value for !<ID>!	%%bad capacity%%
	p2: name; I	value for !<N>!	%%bad id%%
	p3: typename; I	value for !<D>!	%%bad max fanout%%

TREE.2.1: Generator access program (continued)

Program Name	Parameter Type	Parameter Info	Exceptions
	p4: integer; I	value for !<capacity>!	%%bad name%%
	p5: integer; I	value for !<max fanout>!	%%bad typename%%
	p6: string; I-OPT	exception handler command	%%cannot write%%
	p7: integer; O-RET	return code	%%conflict%%
			%%io error%%
			%%recursive%%
			%%system error%%
			%%too long%%

TREE.2.2: Access programs of generated module

Program Name	Parameter Type	Parameter Info	Exceptions
Programs that inquire about the universe of nodes			
+g_avail+	p1: integer; O_RET	!+avail+!	None
Programs that affect the structure of trees			
+add_first+	p1: !<N>!; I	reference node	%not a node%
+add_last+	p2: !<N>!; I	node to adopt	%already a child%
			%is root of tree%
			%too many children%

At this point, the syntax of the resources has been specified. Semantics are provided in two ways. First, for programs that simply return the result of a query—called *get* programs and prefixed with *g*—the returned argument is given a name, and its value is defined in the term dictionary. These programs have no effect on the future behavior of the element. Second, each of the other programs has an entry in an "effects" section to explain its results. You can think of this section as a precondition/postcondition approach to specifying semantics, except that the preconditions are implied by the exceptions associated with each resource. That is, the precondition is that the state described by the exception does *not* exist. In the following, note how each statement of effects is observable; that is, you could write a program to test the specification. For example, an effect of calling +s_datum+(p1,p2) is that an immediately following call to +g_datum+(p1) returns p2.

TREE.2.2.2 Effects (excerpt)

Note: Because +g_first+, +g_last+, and +g_is_null_node+ are defined completely in terms of other programs, the effects on these three programs are not listed below; they follow directly from the effects given on the programs in terms of which they are defined.

```
+add_first++g_num+(p1) = 1+'+g_num+'(p1)
          +g_nth+(p1,1) = p2
          For all i: integer such that (1<i and i<=1+'+g_num+'(p1)),
             +g_nth+(p1,i) = '+g_nth+'(p1,i-1)
          +g_num+(p1) > 1==>
             ( +g_next+(p2) = '+g_nth+'(p1,1)
               and +g_prev+('+g_nth+'(p1,1)) = p2
             )
          +g_parent+(p2) = p1
          For all n: !<N>!,
             '+g_is_in_tree+'(p1,n) ==>
                ( +g_size+(n) = '+g_size+'(n) + +g_size+(p2)
                and For all k: !<N>!,
                   '+g_is_in_tree+'(k,p2) ==>
                      +g_is_in_tree+(k,n)
                )
```

An SCR-style interface continues with a set of dictionaries that explain, respectively, the data types used, semantic terms introduced, exceptions detected, and configuration parameters provided. Configuration parameters represent the element's variability. Bracket notation lets a reader quickly identify which dictionary contains a term's definition: $data type literal$, !+semantic term+!, %exception%, and #configuration parameter#.

TREE.3: Locally defined data types (excerpt)

Type	Definition
integer	common type as defined in [CONV]
!<N>!	The set of values of this type is a secret of this module.

TREE.4: Dictionary (excerpt)

Term	Definition
!+avail+!	The number of new nodes that can be created without an intervening call to +destroy_tree+. Initially = #max_num_nodes#.

TREE.4: Dictionary (excerpt) (continued)

Term	Definition
!+equal+!	p1 and p2 denote the same node (that is, p1 and p2 contain the same value). Assignment of a to b makes a and b denote the same node.

TREE.5: Exceptions dictionary (excerpt)

Exception	Definition
%already a child%	+g_is_node+(+g_parent+(p2)).
%is root of tree%	+g_is_in_tree+(p1,p2).
%not a node%	For some input parameter pj of type !<N>!, ~+g_is_node+(pj).
%too many children%	For +add_first/last+: +g_num+(p1) = #max_num_children#.
	For +ins_next/prev+: +g_num+(+g_parent+(p1)) = #max_num_children#

TREE.6: System configuration parameters (excerpt)

Parameter	Definition
##max_capacity##	The maximum value of #max_num_nodes# for any generated submodule.
##max_max_fanout##	The maximum value of #max_num_children# for any generated submodule.
#max_num_children#	The maximum number of children that any node can have (= !<max fanout>!).
#max_num_nodes#	The maximum number of nodes that can exist at a time (= !<capacity>!).

Following the dictionaries, an SCR-style interface includes background information: design issues and rationale, implementation notes, and a set of so-called *basic assumptions* that summarize what the designer assumed would be true about all elements realizing this interface. Those assumptions form the basis of a design review for the interface.

TREE.7: Design Issues (excerpt)

1. How much terminology to define in the introduction.

   Several terms (leaf, level, depth) are defined in the introduction but not used anywhere else in this specification. These terms have been defined here only because they are expected to prove useful in the specifications of modules that use trees.

2. How to indicate a nonexistent node.

    How is the fact that a node has no parent, nth child, or older or younger sibling to be communicated to users of the module? Two alternatives were considered: (a) have the access programs that give the parent, and so on, of a node return a special value analogous to a null pointer; (b) have additional access programs for determining these facts.

    Option (a) was chosen because (1) it allows a more compact interface with no less capability, (2) it allows a user to make a table of nodes, some entries of which are empty, much more conveniently, and (3) it has the minor advantage of resembling the common linked implementation of trees, and thus may be viewed as more natural.

    Note that (a) may mimic (b) quite simply; comparing the result of the returned value with the special null value is equivalent to node has a parent, eldest child, or whatever. If the set of values of type !<N>! is defined to include a null value, then (b) may also mimic (a), since (b) is then a superset of (a).

3. How to move from node to node.

    "Moving from node to node" consists of getting the node that bears the desired relation to the first node. Several ways of accessing siblings were considered:

    (a) Sequentially, allowing moves to the next or previous sibling in the sequence.

    (b) By an index, allowing moves to the nth of the sequence of siblings.

    (c) Sequentially, but allowing moves of more than one sibling at a time.

    Option (c) seemed of marginal utility and was thus not included. Option (b) was included for generality. Although (a) is not strictly necessary if (b) is available, (a) was nevertheless also included because (a) can usually be implemented in a considerably more efficient manner.

TREE.8: Implementation Notes: none

TREE.9: Assumptions (excerpt)

1. The children of a node must be ordered.

2. It suffices that construction of trees be possible by a combination of creation of trees consisting of single nodes and attachment of trees as subtrees of nodes.

3. For our purposes, the following manipulations of trees are sufficient: (1) replication of a tree, (2) addition of a subtree at

either end of the list of subtrees of a node, (3) insertion of a subtree before or after a subtree in the list of subtrees of a node, (4) disassociation of a subtree from the tree that contains it.

Not shown in this example is an *efficiency guide* that lists the time requirements of each resource, the SCR analog to the quality attribute characteristics that we prescribe in our outline for an interface. Other quality attrtributes could be described here as well. The one piece of interface information that SCR-style interface specifications do not provide is what the element requires.

7.6.2   IDL

A small sample interface specified in OMG IDL is shown in Figure 7.8. The interface is for an element that manages a bank account.

Although syntax is specified unambiguously in this type of documentation, semantic information is largely missing. For example, can a user make arbitrary withdrawals? Withdrawals only up to the current account balance? Up to a daily limit? Up to a minimum balance? If any of these restrictions is true, what happens if it's violated? Is the maximum permissible amount withdrawn, or is the transaction as a whole canceled? IDL *by itself* is inadequate when it comes to fully documenting an interface, primarily because IDL offers no language constructs for discussing the semantics of an interface; without expression of the semantics, ambiguities and misunderstandings will abound.

Figure 7.8
An example of IDL for an element in a banking application (Bass, Clements, and Kazman 1998, p. 177). The element provides resources to manage a financial account. An account has attributes of "balance" and "owner." Operations provided are deposit and withdraw.

```
interface Account {
    readonly attribute string owner;
    readonly attribute float balance;
    void deposit (in float amount);
    void withdraw (in float amount);
};

interface CheckingAccount: Account {
    readonly attribute float overdraft_limit;
    void order_new_checks ();
};

interface SavingsAccount: Account {
    float annual_interest ();
};

interface Bank {
    CheckingAccount open_checking (in string name, in float starting_balance);
    SavingsAccount open_ savings (in string name, float starting_balance);
};
```

7.6.3 Custom Notation

The High Level Architecture (HLA) was developed by the U.S. Department of Defense (DoD) to provide a common architecture for distributed modeling and simulation. To facilitate intercommunication, HLA allows simulations and simulators, called *federates,* to interact with each other via an underlying software infrastructure known as the Runtime Infrastructure (RTI). The interface between federates and an RTI is defined in IEEE standard 1516.1 (IEEE 2000b).

The RTI provides services to federates in a way that is analogous to how a distributed operating system provides services to applications. The interface specification defines the services provided by the RTI and used by the federates.

This is an example in which the focus is on defining an interface that will be realized by a number of different elements. HLA was designed to facilitate interoperability among simulations built by various parties. Hence, simulations can be built by combining elements that represent different players into what is called a *federation.* Any element that realizes the HLA interface is a viable member of the simulation and will be able to interact meaningfully with other simulation elements that are representing other active parties.

Because of the need to ensure meaningful cooperation among elements that are built with little knowledge of one another, a great deal of effort went into specifying not just the syntax of the interface but also the semantics. The extract from the HLA Interface Specification presented in Figure 7.9 describes a single resource, a method, of the interface. Lists of preconditions and postconditions are associated with the resource, and the overview provides a context for the resource and explains its use within the context of the full HLA interface. The resource, a method, is called Negotiated Attributed Ownership Divestiture.

The full HLA interface specification contains more than 140 resources like the one in Figure 7.9, and the majority have some interaction with other resources. For example, using some resources will cause the preconditions of the presented resource to no longer be true with respect to specific arguments. There are a number of such restrictions on the order in which the resources can be used.

To facilitate an understanding of the implicit protocol of usage among the resources, the HLA interface specification presents a summary of this information. Figure 7.10 depicts the constraints on the order of use of a specific set of the resources. This type of summary information is valuable in

Figure 7.9
Example of documentation
for an interface resource,
taken from the HLA (IEEE
2000b, p. 104)

Negotiated Attribute Ownership Divestiture

Overview
The *Negotiated Attribute Ownership Divestiture* service shall notify the RTI that the joined federate no longer wants to own the specified instance attributes of the specified object instance. Ownership shall be transferred only if some joined federate(s) accepts. When the RTI finds federates willing to accept ownership of any or all of the instance attributes, it will inform the divesting federate using the *Request Divestiture Confirmation†* service (supplying the appropriate instance attributes as arguments). The divesting federate may then complete the negotiated divestiture by invoking the *Confirm Divestiture* service to inform the RTI of which instance attributes it is divesting ownership. The invoking joined federate shall continue its update responsibility for the psecified instance attributes until it divests ownership via the *Confirm Divestiture* service. The joined federate may receive one or more *Request Divestiture Confirmation†* invocations for each invocation of this service since different joined federates may wish to become the owner of different instance attributes.

A request to divest ownership shall remain pending until either the request is completed (via the *Request Divestiture Confirmation†* and *Confirm Divestiture* services), the requesting joined federate successfully cancels the request (via the *Cancel Negotiated Attribute Ownership Divestiture* service), or the joined federate divests itself of ownership by other means (e.g., the *Attribute Ownership Divestiture If Wanted* or *Unpublish Object Class Attributes* service). A second negotiated divestiture for an instance attribute already in the process of a negotiated divestiture shall not be legal.

Supplied Arguments
Object instance designator
Set of attribute designators
User-supplied tag

Returned Arguments
None

Pre-conditions
The federation execution exists.
The federate is joined to that federation execution.
An object instance with the specified designator exists.
The joined federate knows about the ojbect instance with the specified designator.
The joined federate owns the specified instance attributes.
The specified instance attributes are not in the negotiated divestiture process.
Save not in progress.
Restore not in progress.

Post-conditions
No change has occurred in instance attribute ownership.
The RTI has been notified of the joined federate's request to divest ownership of the specified instance attributes.

Exceptions
The object instance is not known.
The class attribute is not available at the known class of the object instance.

providing both an introduction to the complexities of an interface and a concise reminder to those already familiar with the interface. Without the summary, users would have to carefully read all the preconditions and postconditions of the 140 resources to reveal the restrictions. This is not trivial, and it is unrealistic to expect every user of the interface document to go through this kind of exercise.

Note that the one thing that the IDL example presented very clearly—the syntax of the resources—is lacking in what

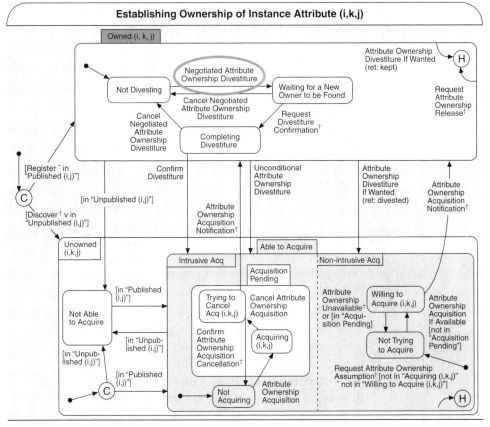

Figure 7.10
This statechart shows the constraints on the order of use of a specific set of resources. Statecharts like this show an entire protocol in which a resource is used. The method described earlier is in the top center, highlighted in a circle. This shows the states during which the method can be invoked, and the state that is entered when it is invoked (IEEE 2000b, p. 97).

has been shown so far in the HLA example. In fact, the HLA interface documentation distinguishes between what it calls an "abstract interface document" (Figure 7.9) and a number of different programming language representations of the interface, each of which is specified in a manner similar to the IDL example.

This separation is an example of how an interface document can be packaged into units that are appropriate for different stakeholders. The semantic specification is sufficient for architects examining the HLA for potential use. Developers of elements implementing the interface, on the other hand, need both the semantic specification and one or more of the programming language representations for syntactic information.

7.6.4 XML

Extensible Markup Language (XML) is a language for describing documents of structured information. As such, XML

FOR MORE INFORMATION

Statecharts are described in Section 8.5.2.

can be used to document the information that will be exchanged across an interface. Data elements can be defined as XML documents. A sample data element, a personal record, follows:

```
<person>
   <firstName>John</firstName>
   <lastName>Doe</lastName>
   <address>
      <street>123 Main St.</street>
      <city>anywhere</city>
      <state>somewhere</state>
      <zipCode>12345</zipCode>
      <country>US</country>
   </address>
</person>
```

In this example, person is the root-level element of the XML document and contains elements firstName, lastName, and address, which in turn is made up of five other elements.

Using XML to exchange information at runtime offers several benefits:

- All information is textual, making it easily readable by humans and portable across platforms.

- It is possible to include a description of what constitutes a valid document in an XML document itself; alternatively, a reference, identified by a uniform resource indicator (URI), to such a description can be supplied.

- Actors exchanging information via XML need not conform to exactly the same version of an interface. It is a simple task for one actor to read the subset of an XML document that it understands and ignore the rest of the document.

- Tool support, such as browsers and parsers, is readily available for a variety of commonly used programming languages.

Document type declarations (DTDs) or schemas can be used to document the types of elements allowed within a document and to constrain the order in which those elements can be arranged. Either form can be used for runtime validity checking or as a simple documentation aid.

However, DTDs provide only syntactic interface documentation at best. Just as when producing IDL-based interface documentation, the burden of specifying semantic information is left to the documenter of an XML interface. XML contains no effective language constructs for conveying semantic information.

The Simple Object Access Protocol (SOAP) describes a framework wherein XML documents are exchanged by actors as a means of implementing an RPC mechanism. The exact documents that are exchanged are left to be defined as part of any application using SOAP. So, although the standard does provide a bit of semantic information in terms of the role that the XML documents serve—requests and responses—it is still up to the documenter to provide application semantics to each document type, for example, what an "execute" document instructs an actor to do and what the permissible responses are.

XML is a useful means of representing data used in interfaces and provides a convenient way to specify the resource syntax portion of an interface. But XML does not absolve the documenter of the responsibility to fill in the resource semantics portion.

7.7   Summary Checklist

- All elements have interfaces.
- Interfaces are two-way, consisting of *requires* and *provides* information.
- An element can have multiple interfaces and multiple actors at each interface.
- An architect must carefully choose what information to put in an interface specification, striking a balance between usability and modifiability. Put information in an interface document that you are willing to let people rely on. If you don't want people to rely on a piece of information, don't include it.
- Follow the template given in Figure 7.1, making sure to address the needs of the interface specification's stakeholders.
- In graphical depictions, show interfaces explicitly if elements have more than one interface or if you want to emphasize the existence of an interface through which interactions occur. Otherwise, interfaces can be implicit.
- Many notations for interface documentation show only syntactic information. Make sure to include semantic information as well.

7.8   Discussion Questions

1. Think about your favorite Web browser. How many interfaces does it have, and what actors are served by those interfaces?

2. Sketch a picture of the Web browser, its interfaces, and its actors.

3. Who are the stakeholders for whom the specifications for those interfaces should be written?

4. For one of the interfaces you described in question 1, list a set of exceptions that the browser detects or, from your experience, fails to detect but should.

5. What's the difference between an interface and a connector?

7.9 For Further Reading

The SCR approach to interface specifications is based on a design approach pioneered by Parnas and others [Britton+ 81]. More information about the other interface examples documented in IDL, HLA, and XML is contained in [OMGIDL 02], [IEEEP1 516 00], and [W3GXML 02].

An excellent foundation paper on exceptions, which lays the groundwork for separating the concern of detecting an exception from the concern of handling an exception, is [ParnasWuerges 76].

Mary Shaw has made the observation that we can't have complete interface specifications, because the cast of stakeholders is too numerous and the range of information they need is too broad. And in the world in which we get our components from other sources and know precious little about them, good interface specifications are even more rare. However, she points out that we can and do accomplish useful work with such incomplete knowledge. This is so because we can assign confidence measures to individual units of information that we pick up about a component from various sources. She calls such a unit a "credential," and assigns it properties such as how we know it and what confidence we have in it [Shaw 96].

Interfaces seen as the set of assumptions that two components are allowed to make about each other dates from early work by Parnas [Parnas 71], echoed in more recent work about architectural mismatch [Garlan+ 95].

Documenting Behavior

8.1 Beyond Structure

In this chapter, we focus on the value of, and techniques for, documenting behavioral aspects of the interactions among system elements. Documenting behavior is a way to add more semantic information to elements and their interactions that have time-related characteristics.

Documentation of a view's behavioral aspects requires that a time line be provided along with structural information. Structural relationships provide a system view that reflects all potential interactions, few of which will be active at any given instant during system execution. It is the system behavior that describes how element interactions may affect one another at any point in time or when in a given system state. Every view can have an associated description that documents the behavior of the view's elements.

Some system characteristics can be analyzed entirely by using a system's structural description. For example, the existence of anomalies, such as required inputs for which no source is available, can be detected in a manner similar to the definition-use analysis performed by compilers. However, reasoning about such characteristics as a system's potential to deadlock or a system's ability to complete a task in the required amount of time requires that the architectural description contain information about both the behavior of the elements and constraints on the interactions among them. Behavioral documentation adds information that reveals

- The ordering of interactions among the elements
- Opportunities for concurrency

- Time dependencies of interactions, such as at a specific time or after a period of time

Interaction diagrams or statecharts as defined by UML are examples of behavioral documentation.

In this chapter, we provide guidance as to what aspects of behavior to document and how this documentation is used during the earliest phases of system development. In addition, we provide overviews and pointers to languages, methods, and tools that are available to help practitioners document system behavior.

8.2 Where to Document Behavior

Architects document behavior to show how an element behaves when stimulated in a particular way or to show how an ensemble of elements—up to and including the whole system—react with one another. In an architecture documentation package, where behavior is shown depends on what exactly is being shown. For example, in a view's supporting documentation, behavior

> **FOR MORE INFORMATION**
>
> Supporting documentation for a view is described in Section 10.2. Interface documentation, a particular kind of supporting documentation, is described in Chapter 7.

- Has its own section in the element catalog. Here, the behavior of the element is documented.
- Can be part of an element's interface documentation. The semantics of a resource on an element's interface can include the element's externally visible behavior that occurs as a result of using the resource. Or, in the usage guide section of an interface document, behavior can be used to explain the effects of a particular usage pattern, that is, a particular sequence of resources used.
- Can be used to fill in the design background section, which includes results of analysis. Behavior is often a basis for analysis, and the behaviors that were used to analyze the system for correctness or other quality attributes can be recorded here.

> **FOR MORE INFORMATION**
>
> Documentation beyond views is described in Section 10.3.

In the documentation that applies beyond views, the rationale for why the architecture satisfies its requirements can include behavioral documentation as part of the architect's justification.

8.3 Why to Document Behavior

Documentation of system analysis behavior is used for system analysis and communication among stakeholders during development activities. The types of analyses you perform and the extent to which you check the quality attributes of your system are based on the type of system you are developing. It is generally a good idea to do some type of trade-off analysis to determine the cost/risk involved with applying certain types of architectural analysis techniques. For any system, it is a good idea to identify and to simulate a set of requirements-based scenarios. If you are developing a safety-critical system, the application of more expensive, formal analysis techniques, such as model checking, is justified in order to identify possible design flaws that could lead to safety-related failures.

8.3.1 System Analysis

Behavioral documentation allows you to reason about the completeness, correctness, and other quality attributes of the system. Once the structure of an architectural view has been identified and the interactions among elements have been constrained, you need to look at whether the proposed system is going to be able to do its job the way it is supposed to. This is your opportunity to reason about both the completeness and the correctness of the architecture. It is possible to simulate the behavior of the proposed system in order to reason about the architecture's ability to support system requirements in terms of whether it supports the range of functionality that it is supposed to and to determine whether it will be able to perform its functions in a way that is consistent with its requirements.

Documenting system behavior provides support for exploring the quality attributes of a system early in the development process. Some techniques are available or are being developed that can be used to predict the architecture's ability to support the production of a system that exhibits specific measures related to such quality attributes as performance, reliability, and modifiability.

Architecture-based simulation is similar to testing an implementation in that a simulation is based on a specific use of the system under specific conditions and with expectation of a certain outcome. Typically, a developer identifies a set of scenarios based on the system requirements. These scenarios are similar to test cases in that they identify the stimulus of an activity and the assumptions about the environment in which the system is running and describe the expected result. These scenarios are played out against documented system models that support relating system elements and the constraints on their interactions. The results of "running the architecture" are checked against expected behavior.

Whereas simulation looks at a set of special cases, system-wide techniques for analyzing the architecture evaluate the system overall: analysis techniques for dependence, deadlock, safety, and schedulability. These techniques require information about the behavior of the system and its constituent elements in order to perform the appropriate analyses. Analysis of inter- and intra-element dependencies has many applications in the evaluation of system quality attributes. Dependence analysis is used as a supporting analysis to help evaluate quality attributes, such as performance and modifiability.

Compositional reasoning techniques—both those available today and those being developed in research laboratories—require information about the internal behavior of system elements and interactions among elements. This information is stated either as summarization of the behavior of existing elements or as derived requirements that the implemented element must satisfy in order to ensure the validity of analysis results. In either case, you will need to document internal element behavior in some way if you are to reap the benefits of early system analysis.

8.3.2 Driving Development Activities

Behavioral documentation plays a part in architecture's role as a vehicle for communication among stakeholders during system development activities. The process of designing the architecture helps the architect develop an understanding of the internal behavior of system elements and gross system structure and produces confidence that the system will be able to achieve its goals. This understanding can be captured in various types of behavioral documentation and later used to more precisely specify inter-element communication and intraelement behavior.

System decomposition results in identifying sets of subelements and defining both the structure and the interactions among the elements of a given set in a way that supports the required behavior of the parent element. In fact, the behavior defined for the parent element has important influence on the structure of its decomposition. As an example, consider an assignment to design a gateway. A gateway's responsibility is to receive messages from one protocol, translate them into another protocol, and then send them out again. For many protocols, unfortunately, this translation cannot be done message by message. A set of messages from one protocol may translate into a single message of the other protocol, or the content of a translated message may depend on earlier messages received. The specified behavior for the gateway documents which sequence of messages leads to a translated message and which information needs to be kept in order to produce the appropriate content of a message to send. This behavior will likely influence the decomposition in a way that reflects the fact that some elements have responsibility to deal with specific sequences of incoming messages and that other elements have responsibility to store the required information.

Additionally, you might want to use simulation during system development. Stimulus-oriented diagrams, such as sequence diagrams, offer a notation for documenting the results of running through system usage scenarios. Such simulation enables developers to gain early confidence that the system under development will fulfill its requirements or to quickly locate specific scenarios that the current architecture does not adequately handle. Simulation may even convince management that the developers are doing great stuff! In order to use simulation, a documented behavioral model of the system or parts of it is required. The scenarios used for this purpose can later be used to develop test cases to be applied during integration testing.

8.4   What to Document

As mentioned, documented behavioral models support exploring the range of possible orderings of interactions, opportunities for concurrency, and time-based interaction dependencies among system elements. In this section, we provide guidance as to what types of things you will want to document in order to reap these benefits.

The exact nature of what to model depends on the type of system that is being designed. For example, if the system is a banking system, you focus on the order of events—for example, atomic transaction and rollback procedures—whereas in a real-time embedded system, you need to say a lot about timing properties in addition to the order of events. Another factor is the stage of development, or scope, of current decision making.

In early stages of development, for example, you typically want to talk about the elements and how they interact; not about the details of how input data is transformed into outputs, although it may be useful to say something about constraints on the transformational behavior within elements, inasmuch as that behavior affects the global behavior of the system.

At a minimum, you should model the stimulation of actions and transfer of information from one element to another. In addition, you might want to model time-related and ordering constraints on these interactions. If correct behavior depends on restrictions on the order in which actions must occur or combinations of actions that must have occurred before a certain

ADVICE

At a minimum, model the stimulation of actions and transfer of information from one element to another.

FOR MORE INFORMATION

See Perspectives: What's the Difference Between Architecture and Design? on page 5.

action can be taken, these things must be documented. The more information that is documented and made explicit about the constraints on interactions, the more precise the analysis of system behavior can be, and the more likely that the implementation will exhibit the same qualities as those predicted during design.

8.4.1 Types of Communication

Looking at a structural diagram that depicts two interrelated elements, users of the documentation often ask, What does the line connecting the elements mean? Is it showing flow of data or control? A behavioral diagram provides a place to describe aspects of the transfer of information and the stimulation of actions from one element to another in more detail than you include in diagram keys.

Table 8.1 shows some common examples of various types of communication. In this table, we've classified types of communication along two axes. The first axis indicates the general purpose of the communication. In some cases, the primary purpose is to exchange data. In others, the primary purpose is to stimulate another element to signal that a task is completed or that a service is required. Often, however, a combination of the two is the main idea, as is the case when an element stimulates another to deliver data or when information is passed in messages or as parameters of events.

The second axis indicates the nature of the communication to some degree. In particular, whether elements communicate via synchronous or asynchronous communication is an important distinction. Remote procedure call is an example of synchronous communication. The sender and the receiver know about each other and synchronize in order to communicate. Messaging is an example of asynchronous communication. The sender does not concern itself with the state of the receiver when sending a message or posting an event. In fact, the sender and receiver may not be aware of each other's identity. Consider the telephone and e-mail as examples. If you make a phone call to someone, the person has to be at the phone in order for it to achieve its full purpose. That is synchronous communication. If you send an e-mail message and go on to other business, perhaps without concern for a response, the communication is asynchronous.

8.4.2 Constraints on Ordering

In the case of synchronous communication, you probably want to say more than that there is two-way communication. For instance, you may want to state which element initiated the

Table 8.1: Types of communication

	Synchronous	Asynchronous
Data		Database, shared memory
Stimulation	Procedure call, RPC without parameters	Interrupt, event without parameters
Both	Procedure call, RPC with parameters	Message, event with parameters

communication and which element terminates it; you may want to say whether the target of the original message uses the assistance of other elements before it can respond to the original request. Decisions about how much detail to include in a behavioral model depend on what types of information you want to be able to get out of the model. For instance, if you are interested in performance analysis, it is important to know that an element will reach a point in its calculation where it requires additional input, as the length of total calculation depends on not only the internal calculation but also the delay associated with waiting for required inputs.

You will probably want to be more specific about certain aspects of the way an element reacts to its inputs. You may want to note whether an element requires all or just some of its inputs to be present before it begins calculating. You may want to say whether it can provide intermediate outputs or only final outputs. If a specific set of events must take place before an action of an element is enabled, that should be specified, as should the circumstances in which a set of events or element interactions will be triggered or the environment in which an output of an element is useful. These types of constraints on interactions provide information that is useful for analyzing the design for functional correctness, as well as for quality attributes.

8.4.3 Clock-Triggered Stimulation

If any activities are specified to take place at specific times or after certain intervals of time, some notion of time needs to be introduced into your documentation. Using two types of clocks is helpful. One clock measures calendar time to whatever precision is required for the type of system under construction. This clock allows you to specify that certain things are to happen at certain times of the day or month. For instance, you may want to specify some behavior differently for weekends and holidays. The other clock counts tics or another, perhaps more precisely specified, measure of time. This clock allows you to specify periodic actions, such as directions to check every 5 minutes and determine how many people are logged on to the system. Although it is clearly possible to compute one clock from the other, it is simpler to use both mechanisms when creating your architectural documentation, as these are two different ways of thinking about time.

8.5　How to Document Behavior: Notations and Languages

Any language that supports documenting system behavior must include constructs for describing sequences of interactions. Because a sequence is an ordering in time, it should be possible to show time-based dependencies. Sequences of interactions are displayed as a set of stimuli and the triggered activities are ordered into a sequence by line, numbering, or ordering. Examples of stimuli are the passage of time and the arrival of an event. Examples of activities are computing and waiting. Languages that show time as a point—for example, timeout—and time as an interval—such as wait for 10 seconds—are normally also provided. As documentation of behavior implicitly refers to structure and uses structure, the structural elements of a view are an essential part of the language. In most behavioral documentation, therefore, you can find representations of

- Stimulus and activity
- Ordering of interactions
- Structural elements with some relationships the behavior maps to

Two groups of behavioral documentation are available, and the languages to support behavioral documentation tend to fall into one of two corresponding categories: traces and static models.

ADVICE

Use trace-oriented documentation if the goal is to analyze a difficult situation or to understand how the system behaves in a specific scenario.

- One type of documentation *traces* what happens through the structural elements of a system during a scenario. Those traces are complete only with regard to what happens in a system when a specific stimulus arrives while the system is in a specific state. Traces are by no means a complete behavioral model of a system. However, the union of all possible traces would generate a complete behavioral model, although this isn't remotely feasible in most systems. Traces are easier to design and communicate because they have a narrow focus.

- Another type of documentation, often state based, shows the complete behavior of a structural element or a set of elements. This is referred to as a *static model* of behavior because it is possible to infer all possible traces through a system, given this type of documentation. Static behavioral models support documentation of alternatives and repetitions to provide the opportunity of following different paths through a system, depending on runtime values. With this type of documentation, it is possible to infer the behavior of the elements for the arrival of any possible stimulus.

Not surprisingly, traces and static models document the behavior of elements in a system to different extents. In the documentation of a static behavioral model of a particular element, you typically find all the resources identified in the interfaces of that element: the complete behavior of the element. In the documentation of a trace, however, you find only the resources identified in the element interfaces that are involved in the execution of that particular scenario.

Another difference between the two approaches is the focus of the documentation relative to individual elements. Traces are typically scoped to include all the system elements that are involved in a particular scenario. However, as mentioned earlier, only a fraction of the behavior of any given element shows up in any particular trace. Each static model, on the other hand, is typically scoped to focus on all the behavior of a particular element. In order to reason about systemwide behavior, you must look at multiple static models side by side.

Many languages and notations are available for both types of behavioral documentation. These differ in the emphasis that is put on certain aspects of the behavior, such as how ordering is identified, how much support is available for documenting timing, what types of communication are easily modeled, and so on.

In the sections that follow, we provide cursory overviews of several notations within each of these categories. The discussions are intended to provide a flavor of the particular notations and to motivate their use. There are many ways in which the diagrams we present in this section may be used together to support the design process. Figure 8.1 shows a reasonable way to combine the strengths of several notations during the design processes.

Figure 8.1
Using various types of behavioral documentation together. Begin by documenting functional requirements with use cases (a), which helps clarify and understand the requirements and the system boundaries. Then produce use case maps (b) to document how the use cases work their way through the elements of the system. Next, produce sequence diagrams (c) from the use case maps to define the messages between the elements. Finally, once the message interfaces between elements are understood, produce statecharts (d) to completely document the behavior of the elements.

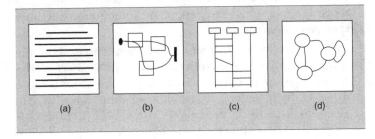

(a)   (b)   (c)   (d)

Each of the following notation sections is presented in terms of a common example, JavaPhone, an example meant to facilitate the development of telecommunication-aware applications on any platform supporting the standard. The JavaPhone example documents resources available for use in telephony, data communication, power management, and many other areas. We focus on a small portion of JavaPhone: making a point-to-point connection, or placing a call.

8.5.1 Traces

Traces are sequences of activities or interactions that describe the system's response to a specific stimulus when the system is in a specific state. These sequences document the trace of activities through a system described in terms of its structural elements and their interactions. Although it is conceivable to describe all possible traces through a set of elements to generate the equivalent of a static behavioral model, it is not the intention of trace-oriented documentation to do so. This would reduce the benefit of being readily comprehensible, owing to the resultant loss of focus.

In this section, we describe five notations for documenting traces: use cases, use case maps, sequence diagrams, collaboration diagrams, and message sequence charts. Although other notations are available, we have chosen these five as a reasonably representative sample of various types of trace-based notations.

Use Cases

A use case is a description of a unit of functionality performed by a single element. The functionality is described by documenting the sequence of interactions in which the element engages in order to provide the functionality. All interactions in a use case are interactions between the element and actors in its environment; no interactions within the element are shown. Use cases often include variants of the main sequence of interactions in order to document exceptional conditions.

Making a point-to-point connection

Main flow of events:
The use case starts when a user places a call via a terminal, such as a cell phone.
All terminals to which the call should be routed then begin ringing. When one of
the terminals is answered, all others stop ringing and a connection is made
between the call initiator's terminal and the terminal that was answered. When
either terminal is disconnected—someone hangs up—the other terminal is also
disconnected. The call is now terminated, and the use case is ended.

Exceptional flow of events:
The call initiator can disconnect, or hang up, before any of the ringing terminals
has been answered. If this happens, all ringing terminals stop ringing and are disconnected, ending the use case.

Figure 8.2
Example use case for
JavaPhone in an informal
notation. This use case
contains a main flow of
events and one exceptional
flow of events.

Use cases are frequently used to capture initial requirements
for a system by producing a use case for each system requirement. The element in these use cases represents the system
itself, and each interaction is an interaction with an actor in
the system's environment.

UML does not define any set notation for documenting use
cases, but notations used in practice are generally brief and
textual. Figure 8.2 uses one such ad hoc notation used to document a use case for JavaPhone.

Use Case Maps

The use case map notation was developed at Carleton University and has been used to document and to understand a wide
range of applications since 1992. Use case maps concentrate
on visualizing execution paths through a set of elements from
a bird's-eye view. The fairly intuitive notation helps communicate how a system works or is supposed to work, without getting lost in too much detail.

Use case maps can be derived from informal requirements
or from use cases, if they are available. Responsibilities need
to be stated or be inferred from these requirements. Separate
use case maps can be created for individual system functional-
ities or even for individual scenarios. However, the strength of
this notation resides mainly in the integration of related scenarios. In such cases, use case maps can be used to illustrate
concurrency, such as resource contention problems—multiple
paths using one element—or possible deadlock situations—
two paths in opposite directions through at least two of the
same elements.

If you ever followed a discussion of developers trying to
answer concurrency-related questions—Does an element need
to be locked? Is there potential for deadlock?—you may have
seen them drawing pictures like the sketch in Figure 8.3. This

Figure 8.3
Informal sketch of activities through some elements. The circles denote system elements; each line is a path of activity involved in a scenario.

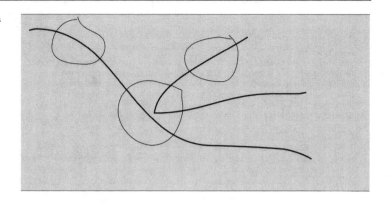

type of informal notation is useful in answering such questions and illustrates a need for the well-defined equivalent found in use case maps.

The basic idea behind use case maps is captured by the phrase "causal paths cutting across organizational structures." An execution path in a use case map is just that; it describes how elements are ordered according to the responsibilities they carry out. When it enters an element, a box, an execution path, or line, states that now this element does its part to achieve the system's functionality. A responsibility that is assigned to the path while within an element defines it as a responsibility of the element.

Figure 8.4 shows an example JavaPhone use case map that deals with establishing a point-to-point connection. Use case maps include a means to represent execution path decomposition, allowing step-by-step understanding of more and more details of the system. Figure 8.4 includes an example of this. The Callee service stub, shown in the Root use case map with a diamond-shaped symbol, can be decomposed into either of the other use case maps—Callee service: Basic call or Callee service: Call forwarding. In this specific case, the decomposition is showing variation. The use case map notation includes many other symbols for such features as timers and timeouts, data containers, interactions between execution paths—aborting—and goals, which are very useful when describing agent-oriented elements.

Sequence Diagrams

Sequence diagrams document a sequence of interactions, presenting a collaboration in terms of instances of elements defined in the structural documentation with superimposed interactions arranged in time sequence. In particular, a sequence diagram shows only the instances participating in

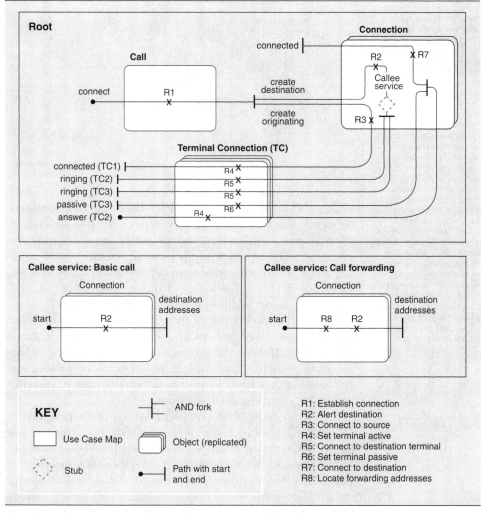

Figure 8.4
A use case map for JavaPhone. Execution paths are represented as sets of curvy lines. Execution paths have a beginning (large dot) and an end (thick straight line). Execution paths can split to show concurrent activities; they can be independent or join together again. Responsibilities assigned to a path are shown as annotated crosses on that path, and each is labeled in this example as Rn. The Root use case map contains two execution paths: one starting with connect and proceeding through Call with responsibility R1, and one starting with answer (TC2) and proceeding through the second Terminal Connection instance (TC2) with responsibility R4. Decomposition and variation are shown using a stub (diamond-shaped symbol) in the parent use case map, with incoming and outgoing execution paths. Child use case maps (Callee service: Basic call and Callee service: Call forwarding in this example) document in more detail what happens within the stub. In this example, the Callee service stub can be decomposed into either of the child use case maps, depending on the circumstances.

the scenario being documented. A sequence diagram has two dimensions: vertical, representing time, and horizontal, representing the various instances. In a sequence diagram, relationships among the objects—like those found in a module view—are not shown.

Figure 8.5
A UML sequence diagram. Instances have a "lifeline," drawn as a vertical line along the time axis. A lifeline can exist from the top of the time axis to indicate that an instance exists—instance ob1 of type C1—when the scenario begins. Or a lifeline can begin and end to show creation and destruction of an instance—instance ob2. The arrow labeled op depicts the message that creates instance ob2. A stimulus is shown as a horizontal arrow. The direction of the arrow defines the producer—start of the arrow—and the consumer—end of the arrow—of the stimulus. A stimulus usually has a name. The name describes the stimulus and usually maps to a resource in the interface of the consumer instance. A stimulus can be drawn as a dotted line to indicate that it describes a return of control to the sender.

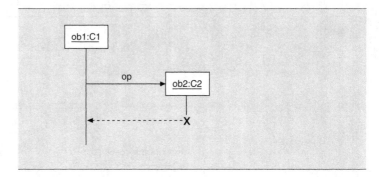

Sequence diagrams support picturing dependent interactions, showing which stimulus follows another stimulus. Sequence diagrams are not very explicit in showing concurrency, however. Although a sequence diagram shows instances as concurrent units, no assumptions can be made about ordering when a sequence diagram depicts an instance sending messages at the "same time" to different instances or, conversely, receiving multiple stimuli at the "same time."

It might be intended that the interactions shown in different sequence diagrams can be performed independently of one another. If this is the intention when documenting behavior using sequence diagrams, it should be noted somewhere. It is not appropriate to document independent behaviors within the same sequence diagram.

Figure 8.5 shows a very simple, UML sequence diagram.

Figure 8.6 shows a more interesting sequence diagram, one that documents a portion of our running JavaPhone example. UML's sequence chart notation supports more features than we have illustrated. For example, interactions can be documented using different types of arrows to indicate more specific semantics for the communication (e.g., synchronous, asynchronous, periodic, and aperiodic types of communication). There are also ways to depict forms of flow control (e.g., decisions and iteration).

A constraint language, such as UML's Object Constraint Language (OCL), can be used to add more precise definitions of conditions like guard or iteration conditions. OCL statements can be attached to the arrow and become recurrence values of the action attached to the stimulus. A return arrow departing the end of the focus of control maps into a stimulus that (re)activates the sender of the predecessor stimulus.

Collaboration Diagrams

Like other trace notations, a collaboration diagram shows ordered interactions among elements needed to accomplish a

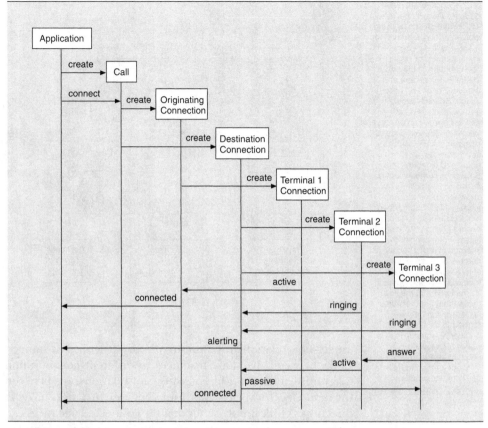

Figure 8.6
A UML sequence diagram for JavaPhone. A lifeline is shown as a vertical line to indicate the period during which the instance is active. The vertical ordering of interactions shows their relative ordering in time. Vertical distances between interactions may describe time duration in the sense that a greater distance stands for a longer time. However, this is not part of the standard UML semantics for sequence diagrams, and so any such use must be explicitly indicated. An informal extension to standard UML sequence diagrams is included; the answer interaction is shown without a source instance. This indicates that the interaction originates from the environment of the collection of elements found in the sequence diagram.

purpose. Whereas a sequence diagram shows order using a time-line-like mechanism, a collaboration diagram shows a graph of interacting elements and annotates each interaction with a number denoting order. Instances shown in a collaboration diagram are instances of elements described in the accompanying structural documentation. Collaboration diagrams are useful when the task is to verify that an architecture can fulfill the functional requirements. The diagrams are not useful if the understanding of concurrent actions is important, as when conducting a performance analysis.

A collaboration diagram also shows relationships among the elements, called links (see Figure 8.7). Links show important

Figure 8.7
A UML collaboration diagram for JavaPhone. Interactions are shown by using labeled arrows attached to links—the lines—between the instances, or boxes. The direction of the arrow identifies the sender and the receiver of each interaction. Special types of arrows, such as a half-headed arrow, can be used to depict different kinds of communication, such as asynchronous, synchronous, and timeout. Sequence numbers can be added to interactions to show which interactions follow which. Subnumbering can be used to show nested stimuli and/or parallelism. For example, the interaction with a sequence number 2.1a is the first stimulus sent as a result of receiving stimulus number 2. The letter *a* at the end means that another stimulus, 2.1b, can be performed in parallel. This numbering scheme may be useful for showing sequences and parallelism, but it tends to make a diagram unreadable.

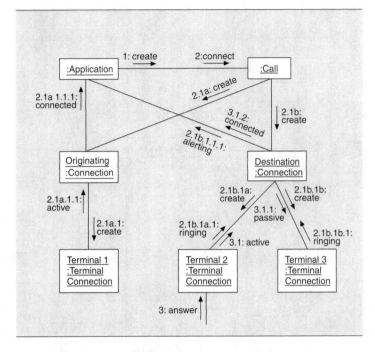

aspects of relationships among those structural instances. Links between the same instances in different collaboration diagrams can show different aspects of relationships between the same structural elements. Links between instances have no direction. A link simply states that the connected instances can interact. If a more accurate definition is required, additional documentation elements—perhaps textual description—have to be introduced.

Collaboration diagrams and sequence diagrams express similar information. Sequence diagrams show time sequences explicitly, making it easy to see the order in which interactions occur; collaboration diagrams indicate ordering by using numbers. Collaboration diagrams show element relationships, making it easy to see how elements are statically connected; sequence diagrams do not show these relations if connected elements do not interact in the scenario depicted in the sequence diagram.

Message Sequence Charts

A message sequence chart is a message-oriented representation containing the description of the asynchronous communication between instances. Simple message sequence charts look like sequence diagrams, but have a more specific definition and have a richer notation. The main area of application for a message sequence chart is as an overview specification of the communication behavior among interacting systems, especially telecommunication switching systems.

Message sequence charts may be used for requirement specification, simulation and validation, test-case specification, and system documentation. They allow documentation of traces through the system in the form of a message flow. A big advantage of a message sequence chart is that it defines a textual notation in addition to its graphical notation. This allows a more formalized model that can generate test cases that test an implementation against its specification.

Message sequence charts are often seen in conjunction with specification and description language (SDL), discussed later in this chapter. Whereas a message sequence chart focuses on representing the message exchange *between* elements, such as systems and processes, SDL focuses on documenting what does or should happen *in* an element. In that respect, message sequence charts and SDL diagrams complement each other.

Although message sequence charts look similar to sequence diagrams, they are used for different purposes. A sequence diagram is systemcentric in that it is used to track a scenario through the system, showing which elements are involved and how. A message sequence chart is elementcentric, and focuses on one element and how it interacts with its environment, without regard to the identity of other elements.

The most fundamental language constructs of message sequence charts are instances, or elements, and messages describing communication events, or interactions. Figure 8.8 shows how the JavaPhone layer interacts with its environment in establishing a point-to-point connection. In a message sequence chart, communication with outside elements is shown by message flow from and to the frame that marks the system environment. Figure 8.8 also documents actions—Alert and Establish Connection—and the setting and resetting of a timer.

The complete message sequence chart language has many other primitives, such as for local actions, timers—set, reset, and timeout—process creation, and process stop. Furthermore, message sequence charts have a means to show decomposition and so can be used to construct modular specifications.

8.5.2 Static Models

Static models show the complete behavior of structural elements. Given this type of documentation, it is possible to infer all possible traces through a system. The state machine formalism is a good candidate for representing the behavior of architectural elements because each state is an abstraction of

Figure 8.8

A message sequence chart for JavaPhone. An instance is shown as a box with a vertical line. Message flow is presented by arrows, which may be horizontal or with a downward slope to indicate the flow of time. Horizontal arrow lines may also be bent to indicate message crossing. The head of the message arrow indicates message consumption; the opposite end indicates message sending. Along the instance axis, a total ordering of the described communication events is assumed. Within a message sequence chart, the system environment is graphically represented by a frame, which forms the boundary of the diagram. Communication arrows from and to the frame show message exchange with elements outside the scope of the diagram.

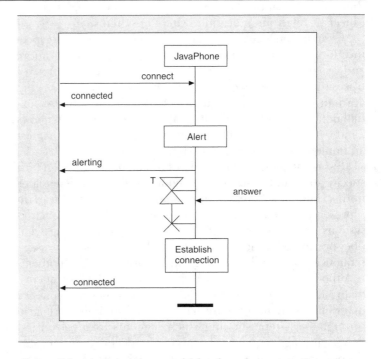

all possible histories that could lead to that state. Once a system is in a state, it doesn't matter how it got there, only that it is there; it will react to the occurrence of a given event in the same way, no matter the particular history of the system at the time the event occurs. Languages are available that allow you to also document the internal behavior of elements in terms of finite state machines and element-to-element interactions in terms of interprocess communication of various types. These languages allow you to overlay a structural description of the elements of the system with constraints on interactions and timed reactions to both internal and environmental stimuli.

In this section, we describe three state-based languages: statecharts, specification and description language (SDL), and Z. Although other languages are available, we have chosen these three because they allow you to describe the basic concepts of documenting behavior in forms that capture the essence of what you wish to convey to system stakeholders. The three are also used as base representations in tools that you are most likely to encounter. Each language has been incorporated into one or more development environments that allow you to design, simulate, and analyze your system early in the development process.

Statecharts

Statecharts, a graphical formalism developed by David Harel for modeling reactive systems, allow you to trace the behavior of your system, given specific inputs. Statecharts add a number of useful extensions to traditional state diagrams, such as the nesting of states, concurrency, and primitives to express communication among concurrent units. These extensions provide the expressive power to document behavior concisely and to effectively model abstraction and concurrency.

Statecharts extend the finite state machine formalism to support description of the transitions within a state in terms of nested states. The outer state is called the *superstate;* inner states, *substates.* The superstate defines the scope of a new statechart, and the substates are related by transitions, just as in a finite state machine. When the superstate is entered, the initial state within the superstate is also entered. Grouping substates into a superstate is often done to allow common behavior to be expressed concisely. Any behavior indicated at the superstate level—depicted as transitions from the superstate boundary rather than from any specific substate—applies to all substates. A good use of this technique is to indicate common error handling or termination behavior. Figure 8.9 shows an example of this; the alerting, failed, and connected states within the Connection state are grouped into an unnamed superstate so that common disconnection behavior can be expressed.

States can be nested in a different way to express concurrency. If the substates are separated by a concurrency boundary—a dotted line—rather than by transitions, each substate is also entered whenever the superstate is entered. Typically, this form of nesting is combined with the first. For example, a top-level superstate is composed of two or more concurrent substates. Each of the concurrent substates is in turn a superstate to substates that are connected by transitions.

This is, in fact, exactly the pattern followed in Figure 8.9. The top-level superstate, JTAPI, is composed of the three concurrent substates Call, Connection, and Terminal Connection. Each of these three substates is in turn a superstate to numerous other states, such as idle, active, and inactive in the Call state, connected by transitions. In Figure 8.9, the default start for each substate is depicted by an arrow coming from the initial state: a solid black circle. Initially, Call is in the idle state. As soon as the connect event arrives, Call generates a create event for Connection: the Connection.create action, which transitions Connection into the idle state. From there, events are exchanged with the telecommunication platform, and a

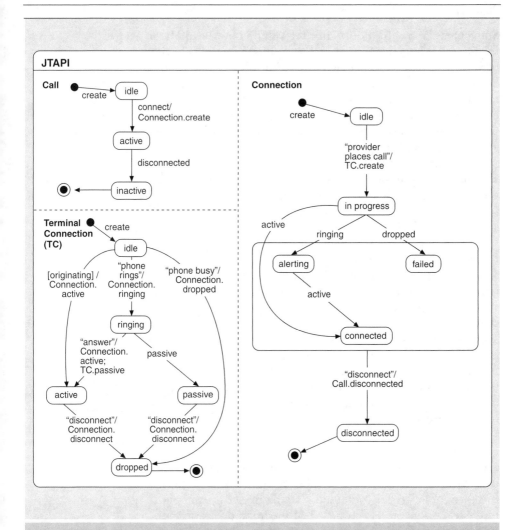

Figure 8.9
A UML statechart for JavaPhone. Sequence is shown by transitions and denoted by a single-headed arrow leading from the source state to the target state. Each transition is labeled with the event causing the transition. Alternatively, a transition could be triggered by the satisfaction of a guard condition, which is bracketed. Whenever the guard condition evaluates as *true*, the transition occurs. Transitions can also have consequences, called actions. When an action is noted, it indicates that the event following the slash will be generated when the transition occurs. Concurrency is represented by grouping sets of states into superstates and separating the superstates by dotted lines.

Terminal Connection is created. Terminal Connection receives events from the telecommunication platform, which lead to state changes. Those changes trigger state changes in Connection, which trigger state changes in Call. Ultimately, each concurrent state transitions to the end state, a solid black circle enclosed by another circle; for example, on reaching the inactive state, Call transitions to the end state.

With the introduction of concurrency to finite state machines came a need to express communication among states. For example, when an event generated in one concurrent substate is intended to cause a transition in another substate, it is useful to indicate which substate should consume the event. For example, in Figure 8.9, a create event within the Call state is generated and intended to be consumed by the Connection state; this is denoted by labeling the event as Connection. create. This type of communication among statecharts is also needed when documenting interactions between statechart models for different elements of a system.

The statechart in Figure 8.9 shows the states some of the JavaPhone objects—Call, Connection, and Terminal Connection—can be in when a phone connection is established and disconnected. The statechart shown contains important states and transitions but is by no means complete.

Statechart notation contains many other features not mentioned here, such as means of expressing choice, timing, and history and has been incorporated in UML.

SDL

Specification and description language (SDL) is an object-oriented formal language defined by the International Telecommunications Union (ITU)–Telecommunications Standardization Sector. The language is intended for the documentation of complex, event-driven, real-time, and interactive applications involving many concurrent elements that communicate by using discrete signals. The most common application is in the telephony area.

SDL is an accessible language that can be used in an environment that is constructed of tools that support documentation, analysis, and generation of systems. SDL's strength lies in describing what happens within a system. If the focus is on interaction between systems, then a message-oriented representation, such as message sequence charts, is more suitable. SDL specifications are often used in combination with message sequence charts to explore a system's behavior.

SDL uses a finite state machine formalism at its core to model behavior. Constructs for describing hierarchical structure and interelement behavior enhance the capability for modeling large-scale systems. Structure is described in terms of a hierarchy of blocks that are eventually refined into sets of processes, as shown in Figure 8.10. Flow of data and stimulation among blocks and processes are described as signals that

Figure 8.10
A hierarchical structure and inter-element behavior in SDL for JavaPhone. The structure of a system is decomposed into a hierarchy of named blocks. Blocks are sets of either other blocks or processes but not combinations of these.

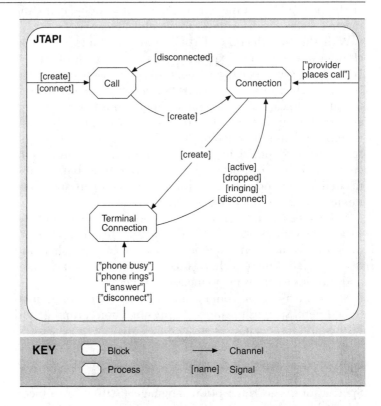

travel over named channels. *Signals* are the means of communication between blocks and processes. Communication is asynchronous and is specified textually as an annotation attached to a communication channel. Signals are visible to other blocks/processes at lower levels in the hierarchy, not to enclose blocks or other blocks at the same level.

Processes run concurrently and have no knowledge of one another's states. Processes can be instantiated at startup or while the system is running. The internal behavior of a process is documented using a finite state machine formalism resembling flowchart notation. SDL provides a rich set of flowchart symbols, some of which are used in Figure 8.11 to partially document how a Terminal Connection is formed.

SDL supports user-defined data types and provides several predefined types—Integer, Real, Natural, Boolean, Character, Charstring, PId, Duration, and Time—that have expected meanings. Variables, user-defined data types, and constant data values can be declared.

The hierarchy of blocks provides a structural view of the system; the flow among the blocks and processes, combined with process flowcharts, document system behavior. Once these

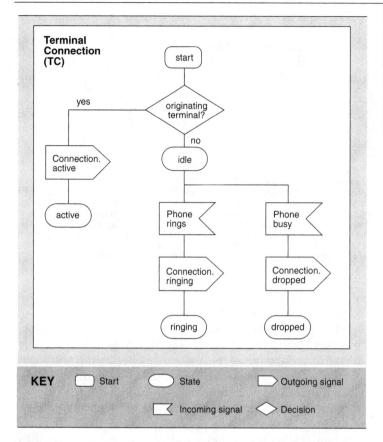

Figure 8.11
Intraprocess behavior in an SDL flowchart for Java-Phone. The various shapes represent specific aspects of behavior, including state changes, receiving input and sending output, decision, and so on: and lines represent the flow from one activity to the next. Flow is read from top to bottom.

aspects have been documented, it is possible to simulate the system and to observe control and data flow through the system as signals pass from block to block and into processes, where they move through the flowchart model of process behavior. This type of simulation allows you to visibly check how your system will react to various stimuli.

Z

Z, pronounced "*zed*," is a mathematical language based on predicate logic and set theory. As a language for formal specification, Z is used to produce precise behavioral models and permits rigorous analyses, such as type checking, model checking, and proofs. Z models document what behavior a system must exhibit, without constraining how it must be implemented. Z does so by focusing on data and operations involving the data.

Systems are specified as collections of *schemas*. Each schema documents a portion of the system; the two basic types of

Account _____

actual_balance: $\mathbb{Z}$
minimum_balance: $\mathbb{Z}$
_____

actual_balance $\geq$ minimum_balance

Withdraw _____

Δ Account
amount?: $\mathbb{Z}$
_____

actual_balance — amount? $\geq$ minimum_balance
actual_balance$'$ = actual_balance — amount?
minimum_balance$'$ = minimum_balance

Figure 8.12
Z schemas for a bank account. Schema Account, a state schema, defines the state space of an account to consist of two integers; $\mathbb{Z}$ is the symbol for an integer. This schema also documents an invariant, namely, that the account actual_balance must be greater than or equal to minimum_balance. In schema Withdraw, an operation schema, the first line above the dividing bar indicates that it is an operation that changes the state of an Account, the Δ indicating a state change. The amount? integer indicates an input parameter to the operation. Below the dividing line, the variables from Account appear in two different forms, with and without an accent ($'$). The form without an accent refers to the value of the variable before the operation begins; the form with an accent, to the value of the variable after the successful completion of the operation. The first line after the dividing line then is a precondition; it indicates that the operation can be completed only if enough money is in the account. The next two lines indicate the results, postconditions, of successfully completing the operation.

schema are often referred to as state schema and operation schema. A state schema contains a set of variables and invariants over those variables, the allowable combinations of which are permissible states of the system. An operation schema documents an operation over the state schema, documenting when it is allowed, via preconditions, and what is true when it is completed, via state changes. A simple banking example illustrating these schema types is shown in Figure 8.12.

Schemas allow the designer and other users of the specification to focus on one aspect of the system at a time and can also be combined using schema calculus to create complete behavioral models. The language supports a compositional approach to development, providing increased tractability when documenting large systems.

For example, Figure 8.12 could easily be extended using Z's schema calculus to deal with different aspects of a withdrawal. An additional operation schema could be written that focuses only on PIN verification at an ATM, and this operation could be combined with the Withdraw operation to express more complex behavior.

Figure 8.13 shows how we might document the running JavaPhone example in Z. However, we have restricted the example to the type of information conveyed in the other languages in this chapter, and so the figure doesn't contain the same kind of detail as in Figure 8.12. Essentially, Figure 8.13 uses the Z language to document when interactions are allowed but on a per interaction basis.

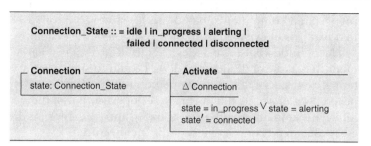

Figure 8.13
Z schemas for JavaPhone.
Outside of the two sche-
mas, the Connection_State
type is defined as an enumerated type. The Connec-
tion state schema has only
one state variable of type
Connection_State. Each
interaction over a Connection is modeled as an operation schema. The
operation schema for the
Active interaction is shown.
The precondition docu-
ments in which states
Active is a valid interaction
and in which state Connection will end as a result of
the Active interaction.

We've provided only a flavor of Z. Many other constructs are available for specifying more complex data types and relationships. Description of the schema calculus is beyond the scope of this presentation, as are the details of Z type checking and proof techniques. Additionally, a number of extensions to the Z notation, like Object Z and TCOZ, deal with such concepts as object orientation.

Z is particularly useful when you want to prove correct behavior in all cases, as when developing safety-critical systems. Additionally, commercial tools are available supporting development based on Z. Many practitioners who are experienced in the use of the language consider Z an invaluable tool because of these strengths. However, the language Z includes a large set of symbols, and expressions are written in terms of predicate logic, making it difficult for some designers to warm up to.

Other Notations

Other notations are emerging but not widely used yet. Some are domain specific, such as MetaH, and others are more general, such as Rapide. MetaH was designed specifically to support the development of real-time, fault-tolerant systems. Its primary emphasis is on avionics applications, although it has also been used to describe other types of systems. MetaH can be used in combination with ControlH, which is used to document and to analyze hardware systems. When used in combination, the system supports analysis of stability, performance, robustness, schedulability, reliability, and security.

Rapide has been designed to support the development of large, perhaps distributed, component-based systems. Rapide descriptions are stated in a textual format that can be translated into a box-and-arrow diagram of a set of connected components. System descriptions are composed of type specifications for component interfaces and architecture specifications for permissible connections among the components of a system. Rapide is an event-based simulation language that provides support for the dynamic addition and deletion of predeclared components, based on the observation of specified patterns of events during the execution of the system.

The Rapide toolset includes a graphical design environment that allows a designer to describe and to simulate a system. The result of a Rapide simulation is a *POSET,* a partially ordered set of events that form a trace of execution of the system. The simulation and analysis tools support exploring the correctness and completeness of the architecture.

8.6 Summary Checklist

- Documenting behavior adds semantic detail to elements and their interactions that have time-related characteristics. Behavioral models add information that reveals ordering of interactions among the elements, opportunities for concurrency, and time dependencies of interactions, such as at a specific time or after a period of time.

- Behavior documented in the element catalog of a view and in interface specifications can be used to fill in the design background section, which includes results of analysis.

- At a minimum, the stimulation of actions and transfer of information should be modelled from one element to another.

- Constraints on the interaction between elements in the form of synchronous or asynchronous communication should be documented. Document any ordering constraints on actions or interactions. Document a clock if your system depends on time.

- Most behavioral languages include representations of stimulus and activity, ordering of interactions, and structural elements with some relationships to which the behavior maps.

- Trace-oriented models consist of sequences of activities or interactions that describe the system's response to a specific stimulus when in a specific state. They document the trace of activities through a system described in terms of its structural elements and their interactions. Use cases, use case maps, sequence diagrams, collaboration diagrams, and message sequence charts are trace-oriented modeling languages.

- Static models, often state based, show the complete behavior of a structural element or set of elements. Statecharts, SDL, and Z are static behavior modeling languages.

8.7 Discussion Questions

1. Consider a car radio with seek, scan, power on/off, and preset station buttons, along with a manual tuning knob and volume control and a digital frequency display. Of the languages and notations for describing behavior presented in this chapter, which ones would be good candidates for describing the behavior of this radio? Why?

2. Using one of the languages you chose as a good candidate in the previous question, sketch the behavior of the car radio.

3. Suppose that you wanted to make sure that your car radio did not exhibit undesirable behavior in unusual circumstances, such as the display going blank when the driver turns the frequency knob while holding down a preset button. What languages would you likely use to help in that case, and why?

8.8 For Further Reading

A rich source for behavior descriptions can be found in the UML definition that is publicly available from the OMG. At http://www.omg.org/uml/ you can find definitions, descriptions, and examples of sequence and collaboration diagrams as well as example use cases and statecharts. You can also find several books that explain UML and its usage in detail. Two seminal books that you will find to be valuable references are *The Unified Modeling Language User Guide* by Booch, Jacobson, and Rumbaugh [Booch+ 99] and *The Unified Software Development Process* by Jacobson, Booch, and Rumbaugh [Jacobson+ 99].

A good reference for statecharts is *Modeling Reactive Systems with Statecharts: The Statemate Approach* by Harel and Politi [HarelPoliti 98].

Message sequence charts, especially combined with SDL diagrams, are broadly used by the telecommunication industry. Both languages are standardized by the International Telecommunication Union (ITU). Their Web site, http://www.itu.int, has all the references to resources, such as documentation and tool vendors, needed to understand and use MSC and SDL. Additional information and pointers to events, tools, and papers can be found at the SDL Forum Society's Web site: http://www.sdl-forum.org/. The SDL Forum Society currently recommends *SDL Formal Object-Oriented Language for Communicating Systems* by Ellsberger, Hogrefe, and Sarma [Ellsberger+ 97] as the best practical guide to the use of SDL.

Many books have been written about use cases. The book from Ivar Jacobson that started the whole use case discussion is *Object-Oriented Software Engineering: A Use Case Driven Approach* [Jacobson 92]. This book can serve as a starting point to understand what was originally meant by use cases and their underlying concepts.

Use case maps are still in the research domain, although there is a user group that tries to show the value of use case maps by applying the method to several projects. You can find much interesting information at their Web site at http://www.usecasemaps.org, including a free download of the book *Use Case Maps for Object-Oriented Systems* by Buhr and Casselman [BuhrCasselman 96]. At that Web site you can also find a free tool that supports use case maps.

Z was originally developed at Oxford University in the late 1970s and has been extended by a number of groups since then. A large number of support tools, to help create and analyze specifications, have been developed by various groups and are available freely over the Internet. A great resource for information and pointers is the Web archive found at http://archive.comlab.ox.ac.uk/z.html. There are a number of books available through your local bookseller to guide you in the use of J. M. Spivey's book, *The Z Notation: A Reference Manual*, 2d ed. [Spivey 88] is available both in print and online at http://spivey.oriel.ox.ac.uk/~mike/zrm/. It provides a good reference in terms of a standard set of features.

For more information on Object Z and TCOZ, extensions to the notation, see [Duket 95] and [Mahoney Dong 00].

A MetaH user manual, instructions for obtaining an evaluation copy of the tool for use on NT 4.0, and other associated information about MetaH is available at the MetaH Web site: http://www.htc.honeywell.com/metah/.

In addition to this site Honeywell has a Web site that describes both ControlH and MetaH in terms of their relationship to domain-specific software architecture. Publications that may be of interest include [Feiler+ 00], [Honeywell 00], and [Lewis 99].

A good Rapide tutorial along with other information and manuals associated with Rapide are available from the Rapide Web site at Stanford University: http://pavg.stanford.edu/rapide/. Publications containing information on specific aspects of Rapide include [Luckham+ 95], [LuckhamVera 95], and [PerrochonMann 99].

Architecture description languages (ADLs) have been developed within the research community to support description, in textual form, of both the structure and the behavior of software systems. See Stafford and Wolf [StaffordWolf 01] for a discussion of ADLs including a table containing references to and brief descriptions of several languages.

Useful Web Sites

This list of pointers below is alphabetized by diagram type for quick reference.

Collaboration Diagrams

OMG Web site: http://www.omg.org/uml/

Message Sequence Charts

International Telecommunication Union Web site: http://www.itu.int

SDL Forum Society's Web site: http://www.sdl-forum.org/

MetaH

Honeywell site for MetaH: http://www.htc.honeywell.com/metah/

Honeywell site for ControlH and MetaH: http://www.htc.honeywell.com/projects/dssa/dssa-tools.html

Rapide

The Rapide site at Stanford University: http://pavg.stanford.edu/rapide/

The Rapide online tutorial: http://pavg.stanford.edu/rapide/examples/teaching/dtp/index.html

Sequence Diagrams

OMG Web site: http://www.omg.org/uml/

SDL

SDL Forum Society's Web site: http://www.sdl-forum.org/

International Telecommunication Union Web site: http://www.itu.int

Statecharts

International Telecommunication Union Web site: http://www.itu.int

Use Case Maps

Use Case Maps Web site including manuscript of seminal book [BuhrCasselman 96]: http://www.usecasemaps.org

Z

J. M. Spivey's book [Spivey 88]: http://spivey.oriel.ox.ac.uk/~mike/zrm/

A collection of pointers: http://archive.com lab.ox.ac.uk/z.html

Choosing the Views

Before a view can be documented, it must be chosen by the
architect. And that is the topic of this chapter: how an architect
decides on the views to include in the documentation package.

In previous chapters, we explained how to represent all the
various aspects of a software architecture. We discussed views
that focus on coding aspects and on runtime aspects, and
views that document the relationship of the software with its
environment: module, C&C, and allocation viewtypes, respectively. Within a single development project, you will not document all the aspects of a software architecture. You will have to
make decisions on what to document and to what level of
detail. You also have to decide whether you want to define a
new style to better support your project needs or to overlay
two or more of the mentioned views.

But how many views are enough? How many are too many?
And how complete does each view have to be? As a reader, you
may be wondering whether we are going to impose an unrealistic documentation obligation on you, one that will produce
beautiful exemplary documents that will never be used
because the project will have run out of money at implementation time.

The reality is that all projects make cost/benefit trade-offs to
pack all the work to be done into the time and the resources allocated for that work. Architecture documentation is no different.

We have tried to explain the benefits of each kind of documentation and to make a compelling case for when you would want to produce it. If you can't afford to produce a particular part of the architecture documentation package, you need to understand what the long-term cost will be for the short-term savings.

Understanding which views to produce at what time and to what level of detail can be answered only in the concrete context of a project. You can determine which views are required, when to create them, and to what level of detail they have to be described in order to make the development project successful only if you know

- What people you will have: which skills are available
- What budget is on hand
- What the schedule is
- Who the important stakeholders are

This chapter is about helping you make those determinations. Once the entire documentation package has been assembled or at opportune milestones along the way, it should be reviewed for quality, suitability, and fitness for purpose by those who are going to use it.

9.1　Stakeholders and Their Documentation Needs

FOR MORE INFORMATION

Having decided on a nice set of views, you may want to ask your stakeholders whether the information shown is what they expect. Having a prototypical example helps tremendously. See Chapter 10 for more information about reviewing the documents.

To choose the appropriate set of views, you must identify the stakeholders that depend on software architecture documentation. You must also understand each stakeholder's information needs.

The set of stakeholders will vary, depending on the organization and the project. The list of stakeholders in this section is suggestive but is not intended to be complete.

The documents mentioned for those stakeholders are ones in which they probably are interested, but the need for other documentation will vary from case to case. For instance, a project manager might not be interested in any C&C view. But a product with a Web-based client-server architecture might have a C&C view showing parts of the client-server architecture that are of interest to the project manager. So take the following lists as a starting point and adapt them according to the needs of your project.

A project manager cares about schedule, resource assignments, and perhaps contingency plans to release a subset of the system for business reasons. This person is not interested in the detailed design of any element or the exact interface specifications beyond knowing whether those tasks have been completed. But the manager is interested in the system's overall purpose and constraints; its interaction with other systems, which may suggest an organization-to-organization interface that the manager will have to establish; and the hardware environment, which the manager may have to procure.

The project manager might create or help create the work assignment view, in which case he or she will need a decomposition view to do it but will certainly be interested in monitoring it. As shown in Figure 9.1, a project manager, then, will likely be interested in

- A top-level context diagram: module viewtype
- A decomposition, uses, and/or layered view: module viewtype
- A work assignment view: allocation viewtype
- A deployment view: allocation viewtype
- Overall purpose and constraints

A member of the development team, for whom the architecture provides marching orders, is given constraints on how that person does his or her job. Sometimes, a developer is given responsibility for an element he or she did not implement, such as a commercial off-the-shelf product. Someone still has to be responsible for that element, to make sure that it performs as advertised and to tailor it as necessary. This person will want to know

- The general idea behind the system. Although that information lies in the realm of requirements rather than architecture, a top-level context diagram can go a long way to provide the information.
- Which element the developer has been assigned, that is, where functionality should be implemented.
- The details of the assigned element.
- The elements with which the assigned part interfaces and what those interfaces are.

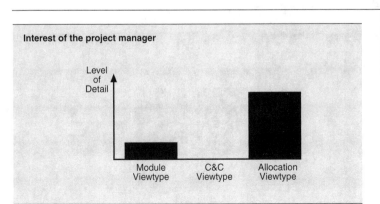

Figure 9.1
A project manager usually creates the work assignments and therefore needs some overview information of the software.

- The code assets the developer can make use of.
- The constraints, such as quality attributes, legacy systems interfaces, and budget, that must be met.

As shown in Figure 9.2, a developer, then, is likely to want to see

- A context diagram containing the module(s) he or she has been assigned: module viewtype
- A decomposition, uses, and layered view: module viewtype
- A view showing the component(s) the developer is working on and how they interact with other components at run-time: C&C viewtype
- A mapping between views, showing the module(s) as components: module viewtype, C&C viewtype
- The interface specification(s) of the developer's element(s) and the interface specifications of those elements with which they interact: module viewtype, C&C viewtype
- The variability guide to implement required variability: module viewtype
- An implementation view to find out where the assets he or she produces must go: allocation viewtype
- A generalization view showing other modules that the developer can use to accomplish his or her work assignment: module viewtype
- A deployment view: allocation viewtype
- The documentation that applies beyond views, including a system overview
- Rationale and constraints

Testers and integraters are stakeholders for whom the architecture specifies the correct black-box behavior of the pieces that must fit together. A unit tester of an element will want to see

Figure 9.2
Developers have interest mainly in the software itself, and therefore create detailed module and C&C views and have some interest in allocation viewtypes.

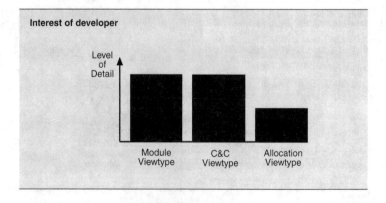

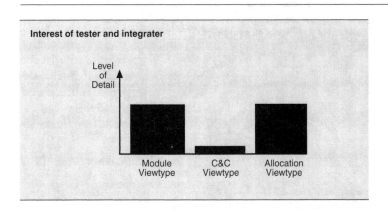

Figure 9.3
Testers and integraters need context and interface information, along with information about where the software runs and how to build incremental parts.

the same information as a developer of that element, with an emphasis on behavior specifications. A black-box tester will need to see the interface specification for the element. Integraters and system testers need to see collections of interfaces, behavior specifications, and a uses view so they can work with incremental subsets.

As shown in Figure 9.3, testers and integraters, then, are likely to want to see

- A context diagram showing the module(s) to be tested or integrated: module viewtype
- The interface specification(s) and behavior specification(s) of the module(s) and the interface specifications of those elements with which they interact: module viewtype, C&C viewtype
- An implementation view to find out where the assets that build the module are: allocation viewtype
- A deployment view: allocation viewtype

Designers of other systems with which this one must interoperate are stakeholders. For these people, the architecture defines the set of operations provided and required, as well as the protocols for their operation. As shown in Figure 9.4, these stakeholders will likely want to see

- A top-level context diagram: module viewtype and/or C&C viewtype
- Interface specifications for those elements with which their system will interact: module viewtype, C&C viewtype

Maintainers use architecture as a starting point for maintenance activities, revealing the areas a prospective change will affect. Maintainers will want to see the same information as developers, for they both must make their changes within the

Figure 9.4
Designers of other systems are interested in interface specifications and important system behavior.

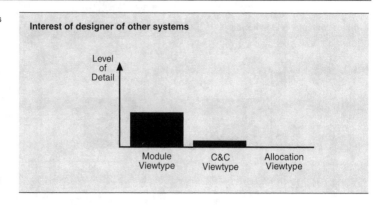

same constraints. But maintainers will also want to see a decomposition view that allows them to pinpoint the locations where a change will need to be carried out and perhaps a uses view to help build an impact analysis to fully scope out the effects of the change. Maintainers will also want to see design rationale that will give them the benefit of the architect's original thinking and save them time by letting them see already discarded design alternatives.

As shown in Figure 9.5, a maintainer, then, is likely to want to see

- The views as mentioned for the developers of a system
- A decomposition view: module viewtype
- A layered view: module viewtype
- Rationale and constraints

Application builders in a **software product line** tailor the core assets according to preplanned and built-in variability mechanisms, add whatever special-purpose code is necessary, and instantiate new members of the product line. Application build-

DEFINITION

A **software product line** is a set of software-intensive systems sharing a common, managed set of features that satisfy the specific needs of a particular market segment or mission and that are developed from a common set of reusable core assets in a prescribed way.

Figure 9.5
A maintainer has the same information needs as a developer but with a stronger emphasis on design rationale and variability.

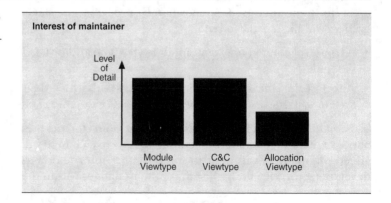

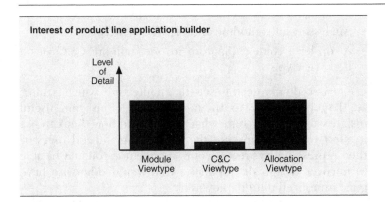

Figure 9.6
The product line application builder needs to understand what adaptations to make in order to build new products.

ers will need to see the variability guides for the various elements, to facilitate tailoring. After that, application builders need to see largely the same information as integraters do.

As shown in Figure 9.6, a product line application builder, then, is likely to want to see

- The views mentioned for an integrater
- A variability guide: module and/or C&C viewtype

Customers are the stakeholders who pay for the development of specially commissioned projects. Customers are interested in cost and progress and convincing arguments that the architecture and resulting system will meet the quality and functional requirements. Customers will also have to support the environment in which the system will run and will want to know that the system will interoperate with other systems in that environment.

As shown in Figure 9.7, the customer, then, is likely to want to see

- A work assignment view, no doubt filtered to preserve the development organization's confidential information: allocation viewtype

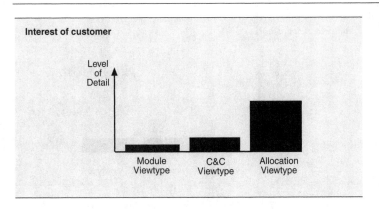

Figure 9.7
A customer is interested mainly in how the software works in the desired environment.

- A deployment view: allocation viewtype
- Analysis results: module and/or C&C viewtype
- A top-level context diagram in one or more C&C views: C&C viewtype

End users do not need to see the architecture, which is, after all, largely invisible to them. But they often gain useful insights about the system, what it does, and how they can use it effectively by examining the architecture. If end users or their representatives review your architecture, you may be able to uncover design discrepancies that would otherwise have gone unnoticed until deployment.

To serve this purpose and as shown in Figure 9.8, an end user is likely to be interested in

- A view emphasizing flow of control and transformation of data, to see how inputs are transformed into outputs: C&C viewtype
- A deployment view to understand how functionality is allocated to the platforms with which the users interact: allocation viewtype
- Analysis results that deal with properties of interest to them, such as performance or reliability: module and/or C&C viewtype

Analysts are interested in the ability of the design to meet the system's quality objectives. The architecture serves as the fodder for architectural evaluation methods and must contain the information necessary to evaluate such quality attributes as security, performance, usability, availability, and modifiability. For performance engineers, for example, architecture provides the model that drives such analytical tools as rate-monotonic real-time schedulability analysis, simulations and simulation generators, theorem provers, and model-checkers. These

Figure 9.8
An end user needs to have an overview of the software, how it runs on the platform, and how it interacts with other software.

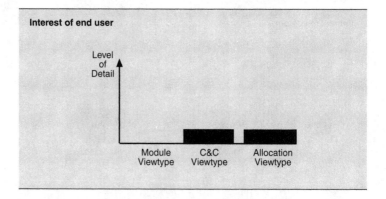

tools require information about resource consumption, scheduling policies, dependencies, and so forth.

Recently, architecture evaluation and analysis methods have emerged as repeatable, robust, low-cost ways to make sure that an architecture will deliver the required quality attributes before the project commits to implementation based on it. The Architecture Trade-off Analysis Method (ATAM) exemplifies this new breed of methods. ATAM relies on suitable architecture documentation to do its work. Although ATAM does not prescribe specific documents that are required, it does offer general guidelines.

As shown in Figure 9.9, an ATAM practitioner is likely to be interested in

- Views of the module viewtype family: module viewtype
- A deployment view: allocation viewtype
- A communicating-processes view: C&C viewtype
- Applicable component-and-connector views: C&C viewtype

In addition to generalized analysis, architectures can be evaluated for the following and other quality attributes, each of which suggests certain documentation obligations.

- *Performance:* To analyze for performance, performance engineers build models that calculate how long things take. Plan to provide a communicating-processes view to support performance modeling. In addition, performance engineers are likely to want to see a deployment view, behavioral documentation, and those C&C views that help to track execution.

- *Accuracy:* Accuracy of the computed result is a critical quality in many applications, including numerical computations, the simulation of complex physical processes, and many embedded systems in which outputs are produced that cause actions to take place in the real world. To analyze

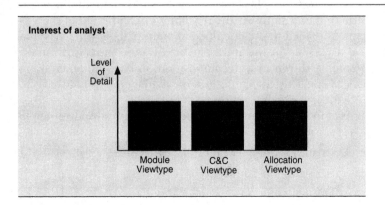

Figure 9.9
An analyst needs information from all viewtypes. Depending on the specific analysis, other, more detailed information might be required.

for accuracy, a C&C view showing flow and transformation of data is often useful because it shows the path that inputs take on their way to becoming outputs and help identify places where numerical computations can degrade accuracy.

- *Modifiability:* To gauge the impact of an expected change, a uses view and a decomposition view are most helpful. Those views show dependencies and will help with impact analysis. But to reason about the runtime effects of a proposed change requires a C&C view as well, such as a communicating-processes view, to make sure that the change does not introduce deadlock.

- *Security:* A deployment view is used to see outside connections, as are context diagrams. A C&C view showing data flow is used to track where information goes and is exposed; a module decomposition view, to find where authentication and integrity concerns are handled. Denial of service is loss of performance, and so the security analyst will want to see the same information as the performance analyst.

- *Availability:* A C&C communicating-processes view will help analyze for deadlock, as well as synchronization and data consistency problems. In addition, C&C views in general show how redundancy, failover, and other availability mechanisms kick in as needed. A deployment view is used to show possible points of failure and backups. Reliability numbers for a module might be defined as a property in a module view, which is added to the mix.

- *Usability:* A decomposition view will enable analysis of system state information presented to the user, help with determination of data reuse, assign responsibility for usability-related operations, such as cut-and-paste and undo, and other things. A C&C communicating-processes view will enable analysis of cancellation possibilities, failure recovery, and so on.

Infrastructure support personnel set up and maintain the infrastructure that supports the development and build of the system. You need to provide documentation about the parts that are accessible in the infrastructure. Those parts are usually elements shown in a decomposition and/or implementation view. Especially for configuration management, you have to provide a variability guide.

As shown in Figure 9.10, infrastructure support people likely want to see

- A decomposition view: module viewtype
- A uses view: module viewtype
- An implementation view: allocation viewtype

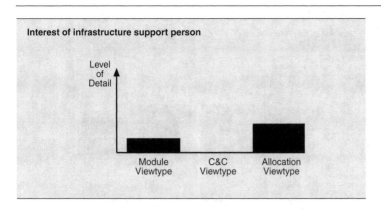

Figure 9.10
Infrastructure support people need to understand the software artifacts produced to provide tool support.

- A variability guide: module viewtype, C&C viewtype
- A deployment view, allocation viewtype

New stakeholders will want to see introductory, background, and broadly scoped information: top-level context diagrams, architectural constraints, overall rationale, and root-level view packets as shown in Figure 9.11. In general, anyone new to the system will want to see the same kind of information as his or her counterparts who are more familiar with the system but will want to see it in less detail.

Future architects are the most avid readers of architectural documentation, with a vested interest in everything. After the current architect has been promoted for producing the exemplary documentation, the replacement will want to know all the key design decisions and why they were made. As shown in Figure 9.12, future architects are interested in it all but will be especially keen to have access to comprehensive and candid rationale and design information.

To summarize, the views you choose depend on the views you expect to use. For most nontrivial systems, you should

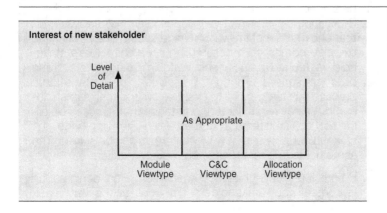

Figure 9.11
New stakeholders need to have the same information as their counterparts.

Figure 9.12
A future architect has strong interest in all the architecture documentation.

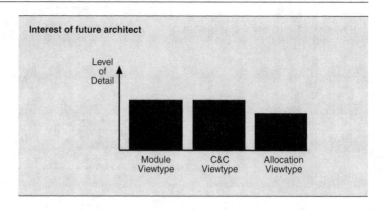

Interest of future architect

expect to choose at least one view from each of the three viewtypes presented in this book: module, component-and-connector, and allocation. Beyond that, choose specific views based on anticipated uses by your stakeholders. The guidelines presented in this section are rules of thumb with which to begin. Remember that each view you select comes with a benefit but also a cost. You will undoubtedly wish to combine some views or to have one view serve in another's place; for instance, a work assignment view includes the information in a decomposition view, so you may not need both. Table 9.1 summarizes these guidelines.

ADVICE

Ask the Stakeholders

It is asking a lot of an architect to divine the specific needs of each stakeholder, and so it is a very good idea to make the effort to communicate with stakeholders, or people who can speak for those roles, and talk about how they will best be served by the documentation you are about to produce. Practitioners of architecture evaluation almost always report that one of the most rewarding side effects of an evaluation exercise comes from assembling an architecture's stakeholders around a table and watching them interact and build consensus among themselves. Architects seldom practice this team-building exercise among their stakeholders, but a savvy architect understands that success or failure of an architecture comes from knowing who the stakeholders are and how their interests can be served. The same holds true for architecture documentation.

Before the architecture documentation effort begins, plan to contact your stakeholders. This will, at the very least,

Table 9.1: Summary of documentation needs

Stakeholder	Module Views				C&C Views	Allocation Views			Other					
	Decomposition	Uses	Generalization	Layered	Various	Deployment	Implementation	Work Assignment	Interface Specification	Context Diagrams	Mapping between Views	Variability Guides	Analysis Results	Rationale and Constraints
Project manager	s	s		s	d	d	s	d		o				s
Member of development team	d	d	d	d	d	s	s		d	d	d	d		s
Tester and integrater	d	d	d	d	s	s	s		d	d	s	d		s
Designer of other systems		d							d	o				
Maintainer	d	d	d	d	d	s	s		d	d	d	d		d
Product line application builder	d	d	s	o	s	s	s		s	d	s	s		s
Customer					s	o		o		o			s	
End user					s	s							s	s
Analyst	d	d	s	d	s	d	s		d	d	d	s	d	s
Infrastructure support personnel	s	s				s	d				s	s		
New stakeholder	x	x	x	x	x	x	x	x	x	x	x	x	x	x
Current and future architect	d	d	d	d	d	d	s	s	d	d	d	d	d	d

Key: d = detailed information, s = some details, o = overview information, x = anything compel you to name them. For a large project in which the documentation is a sizable line item in the budget, it may even be worthwhile to hold a half-day or full-day round table workshop. Invite at least one person to speak for each stakeholder role of importance in your project. Begin the workshop by having each stakeholder explain the kind of information he or she will need to carry out his or her assigned tasks. Have a scribe record each stakeholder's answer on a flip chart for all to see. Then present a documentation plan: the set of views you've chosen, the supporting documentation, and the cross-view information you plan to supplement them with. Finally, perform a cross-check to find requested but missing information and planned but unneeded documentation. Whether you hold a full-blown workshop or talk to your stakeholders informally, the result will be vastly increased buy-in for your documentation efforts and a clearer understanding on everyone's part of what the role of the architecture and its documentation will be.

PERSPECTIVES

Architecture Trade-off Analysis Method

Until recently, there were no reliable methods that would let us subject an architecture to a test to see whether it would deliver the required functionality and, at least as important, the required quality attributes of performance, modifiability, usability, security, availability, and so forth. The architect had to rely on his or her own past experience, styles and patterns in books, or, more likely, folklore. Only when code was developed, whether prototype or production, could the architecture be validated: Code testing served as architecture testing. But by then, changing the architecture was often prohibitively expensive.

Now, however, architecture evaluation methods have emerged that let us validate an architecture while it is still a paper design, before it has been hardened into code. As architecture evaluation matures to become a standard part of architecture-based development methods, architecture documentation takes on an additional use: serving as the fuel for an evaluation.

One of the most mature evaluation methods is the **Architecture Trade-off Analysis Method (ATAM)**. Under ATAM, a four- or five-person evaluation team is gathered along with a set of stakeholders for the system whose architecture is being evaluated: designers, maintainers, end users, system administrators, and so forth. The analysis phase consists of nine steps.

DEFINITION

ATAM (Architecture Tradeoff Analysis Method) is an architecture evaluation method developed by the Software Engineering Institute.

1. *Present the ATAM.* The evaluation team leader describes the evaluation method to the participants, tries to set their expectations, and answers questions they may have.

2. *Present business drivers.* A project spokesperson, usually the project manager or the system customer, identifies the business goals that are motivating the development effort and hence what will be the primary architectural drivers, such as high availability, time to market, or high security.

3. *Present the architecture.* The architect describes the architecture, focusing on how it addresses the business drivers.

4. *Identify architectural approaches.* ATAM focuses on analyzing an architecture by understanding the architectural styles and approaches that it embodies. Approaches and styles, including those described in this and other books, have known characteristics in terms of how they promote or preclude certain quality attributes. In this step, the team compiles a list by asking the architect to explicitly name any identifiable approaches used but also captures any other approaches mentioned during the architecture presentation in the previous step.

5. *Generate quality attribute utility tree.* The quality factors that comprise system utility—performance, availability, security, modifiability, usability, and so on—are elicited. Then refinements are added. For example, security might be refined to disclose that data confidentiality and data integrity are important. Finally, the refinements are made operational by eliciting detailed scenarios that express the qualities. The utility tree serves to make concrete the quality attribute requirements, forcing the architect and customer representatives to define the relevant quality requirements precisely. Participants prioritize the utility tree scenarios according to how important each scenario is to the system and by how difficult the architect expects it will be to achieve.

6. *Analyze architectural approaches.* At this point, a prioritized set of concrete quality requirements from step 5 and a set of architectural approaches used in the architecture from step 4 exist. Step 6 sizes up how well suited they are to each other. Here, the evaluation team can probe for the architectural approaches that realize the important quality attributes. This is done with an eye to documenting these architectural decisions and identifying their risks, nonrisks, sensitivity points, and trade-offs. The evaluation team probes for sufficient information about each architectural approach to conduct

a rudimentary analysis about the attribute for which the approach is relevant.

7. *Brainstorm and prioritize scenarios.* A larger set of scenarios is elicited from the group of stakeholders. Whereas the utility tree scenarios were generated using quality attributes as the context, here the evaluation team asks the stakeholders to contribute scenarios that speak to stakeholder roles. A maintainer will propose a scenario relevant to the architecture's ability to support maintenance, for example. These new scenarios are then prioritized by means of a facilitated voting process involving the entire stakeholder group.

8. *Analyze architectural approaches.* This step reiterates the activities of step 6, using the highly ranked scenarios from step 7. This analysis may uncover additional architectural approaches, risks, sensitivity points, and trade-off points, which are then documented.

9. *Present results.* Finally, the collected information from the ATAM needs to be summarized and presented back to the stakeholders. This presentation typically takes the form of a verbal report accompanied by slides but might also be accompanied by a more complete written report delivered subsequent to the ATAM. In this presentation, the evaluation leader recapitulates all the information collected in the steps of the method.

ATAM outputs are

- The documentation of architectural approaches
- The quality attribute utility tree, including the scenarios and their prioritization
- The set of attribute-based analysis questions
- The mapping from approaches to achievement of quality attributes
- The risks and nonrisks discovered, and how the risks might undermine the architecture's business drivers
- The sensitivity points and trade-off points found

A savvy architect can and should turn these outputs into part of the project's documentation legacy, which brings us full circle: The effort to prepare documentation to support an evaluation is paid back in full. Not only is the architecture validated or weaknesses discovered in time for repair, but also these outputs can be incorporated into the documentation as a part of the design rationale and analysis results.

—P. C. C.

9.2 Making the Choice

This section presents a procedure for choosing the views, and applies that procedure to two real-world systems.

Here is a simple three-step procedure for choosing the views for your project.

- **Step 1. Produce a candidate view list.** For this step, begin by building a stakeholder/view table for your project, like that in Table 9.1.

Enumerate the stakeholders for your project's software architecture documentation down the rows. Your stakeholder list is likely to be different from the one in Table 9.1; however, be as comprehensive as you can. For the columns, enumerate the views that apply to your system. As discussed in the Prologue, some views (such as decomposition, uses, and work assignment) apply to every system, while others (C&C views, the layered view) only apply to systems designed according to the corresponding styles.

Once you have the rows and columns defined, fill in each cell to describe how much information the stakeholder requires from the view: none, overview only, moderate detail, or high detail.

The candidate view list consists of those views for which some stakeholder has a vested interest.

- **Step 2. Combine views.** The candidate view list from step 1 is likely to yield an impractically large number of views. This step will winnow the list to manageable size.

First, look for views in the table that require only overview, or that serve very few stakeholders. See if the stakeholders could be equally well served by another view having a stronger constituency.

Next, look for views that are good candidates to become combined views. For small and medium projects, the work assignment and implementation views are often easily overlaid with the module decomposition view. The decomposition view also pairs well with the layered and uses views. Where different parts of a system exhibit different component-and-connector styles, the corresponding views might be easily overlaid. Finally, the deployment view usually combines well with whatever C&C view shows the components that are allocated to hardware elements—the communicating-processes view, for example.

> **FOR MORE INFORMATION**
>
> Combined views are discussed in Section 6.3.

- **Step 3. Prioritize.** After step 2 you should have the minimum set of views needed to serve your stakeholder community. At this point you need to decide what to do first. How you decide depends on the details specific to your project, but here are some things to consider:
  - You don't have to complete one view before starting another. People can make progress with overview-level information, so a breadth-first approach is often the best.
  - Some stakeholders' interests supersede others. A project manager, or the management of a company with which yours is partnering, often demand attention and information early and often.
  - If your architecture has not yet been validated or evaluated for fitness of purpose, then documentation to support that activity merits high priority.
  - Resist the temptation to relegate rationale documentation to the "do when we have time" category, because rationale is best captured when fresh.

9.3 Two Examples

This section provides two examples of applying the procedure in the previous section to select a set of views for a project.

9.3.1 A Small Project: A-7E

The U.S. Navy's A-7E avionics program, used as a source for some of the documentation examples in this book, was one of the first software engineering projects that paid special attention to engineering and documenting its architecture as a set of related but separate views. It was by most standards a small project, with staff size of ten or less for most of its duration. Here are A-7E architecture views under the three-step method outlined above.

Step 1: Produce a Candidate View List

Stakeholders include the current and future architects, the project manager, members of the development team, testers and integraters, and maintainers. The architecture was designed to deliver three primary qualities: modifiability, real-time performance, and the ability to be fielded in incremental subsets. Hence, it is important to analyze the architecture for these qualities, and so by extension, the analysts become stakeholders. The agency responsible for funding the project was also a stakeholder; their interest was in knowing how the architecture leads to a system more maintainable than other avionics programs of the same generation.

Applicable views in the module viewtype include the decomposition, uses, and layered views. Generalization is not employed in the A-7E architecture. The system is structured as a set of cooperating sequential processes, and so in the C&C realm the communicating-processes view applies. The system also has a central data store called a Data Banker; its function is to isolate producers and consumers of data from each other to enhance modifiability. Therefore, the shared-data C&C view also applies. In the allocation viewtype, the work assignment, implementation, and deployment view, all apply as well.

Table 9.2 shows the stakeholders for the A-7E architecture documentation and the views useful to each. At this point, the candidate view list contains eight views.

Table 9.2: A-7E stakeholders and the architecture documentation they might find most useful

Stakeholder	Module Views			C&C Views		Allocation Views		
	Decomposition	Uses	Layered	Communicating-processes	Shared-data	Deployment	Implementation	Work Assignment
Current and future architect	d	d	d	d	d	d	s	s
Project manager	s	s	s		o	d	o	d
Member of development team	d	d	d	d	d	s	s	d
Testers and integraters		d		d	s	s	d	
Maintainer	d	d	d	d	d	s	s	s
Analyst for performance	d	d	d	d	s	d		
Analyst for modifiability	d	d	d	s	s	d	o	o
Analyst for "subsettability"	d	d	d	s	s	d		o
Funding agency	o	o	o					

Key: d = detailed information, s = some details, o = overview information

Step 2: Combine Views

The A-7E's hardware environment features a uniprocessor, and so the deployment view can be dispensed with. By adopting modules (as defined in the module decomposition view) as the basic unit of work assignment and development file structure, the work assignment and implementation views can easily be combined with the decomposition view. These simple decisions quickly eliminate three of the eight views from the candidate list.

Consultations with stakeholders revealed that the shared-data view was unnecessary. Performance analysts can build performance and schedulability models using the communicating-processes view. Developers, testers, integraters, and maintainers can do their jobs with the module decomposition view[1] (which tells them what the systems' parts were) and the layered view (which tells them what those parts are allowed to use).

After this step, four views remain: decomposition, uses, layered, and communicating-processes.

Step 3: Prioritize

FOR MORE INFORMATION

An excerpt from the A-7E module decomposition view is given in Section 2.1.

Most of the stakeholders are served by the module decomposition view, and so that was chosen as the first undertaking. Because of the tight correspondence between modules and work assignments in this project, the creation of a module is also the commissioning of a work assignment. Before that work assignment can be carried out, the programmers need to know what other software they are allowed to use. Hence, the module decomposition and layered views proceeded hand in hand through successively finer levels of detail.

Communicating-processes views are created once the modules are decomposed to a sufficiently fine grain so that the communication and synchronization needs can be decided and then documented.

The uses view has the lowest priority, targeted for documentation only during the module implementation phase. The allowed-to-use information of the layered view constrains programmers but still leaves them with considerable latitude. As a trivial example, a programmer writing a "double(x)" routine is allowed to use multiplication (2x) or addition (x+x) to implement that function. The uses view reflects the programmers' actual choices. Since the uses view is not employed until it is time to begin fielding subsets, it is the last A-7E view to emerge.

9.3.2   A Large Project: ECS

ECS is a system for capturing, storing, distributing, processing, and making available extremely high volumes of data from a constellation of earth-observing satellites. By any measure, ECS is a very large project. Many hundreds of people are

---

1. The module decomposition view was able to partially supplant a C&C view in this case because in the A-7E architecture there is a straightforward, almost one-to-one mapping between modules and components.

involved in its design, development, deployment, sustainment, and use. Here is how the three-step view selection approach might have turned out, had it been applied to the ECS software architecture.

Step 1: Produce a Candidate View List

Stakeholders for the ECS architecture include the usual suspects: the current and future architect, developers, testers and integraters, and maintainers. But the size and complexity of ECS, plus the fact that it is a government system whose development is assigned to a team of contractors, add complicating factors. In this case, there is not one project manager, but several: one for the government, and one for each of the contractors. Each contractor organization has its own assigned part of the system to develop, and hence, its own team of developers and testers. ECS relies heavily on COTS components so the people responsible for selecting COTS candidate components, qualifying them, selecting the winners, and integrating them into the system play a major role. We'll call these stakeholders *COTS engineers*.

The important quality attributes for ECS begin with performance. Data must be ingested into the system to keep up with the rate at which it floods in from the satellites. Processing the raw data into more sophisticated and complex "data products" must also be done every day to stay ahead of the flow. Finally, requests from the science community for data and data analysis must be handled in a timely fashion. Data integrity, security, and availability round out the important list of quality attributes and make the analysts concerned with these qualities important architectural stakeholders.

ECS is a highly visible and highly funded project which attracts oversight attention. The funding authorities require at least overview insight into the architecture to make sure the money over which they have control is being spent wisely. Finally, the science community using ECS to measure and predict global climate change also require insight into how the system works, so they can better set their expectations about its capabilities.

At least five of the component-and-connector views discussed in Chapter 4 and all four of the module views of Chapter 2 apply to ECS. It is primarily a shared-data system. Its components interact in both client-server and peer-to-peer fashion. Many of those components are communicating processes. And while the system is not actually built using pipes and filters, the pipe-and-filter style is a very useful

FOR MORE INFORMATION

Implementation refinements are discussed in Section 6.1.2.

paradigm to provide an overview to some of the stakeholders. (Information more detailed than the overview will be in a different view, becoming an implementation refinement of the pipe-and-filter view.)

In addition to the five C&C views, all four of the module views discussed in Chapter 2 apply to ECS, as do all three of the allocation views discussed in Chapter 5.

Table 9.3 shows the stakeholders for the ECS architecture documentation and the views useful to each. At this point, the candidate view list contains 12 views.

Step 2: Combine Views

Because of the large size of this project and the number of different development organizations involved, the work assignment view (normally a good candidate for combination) would likely be kept separate. Similarly, because a large number of stakeholders interested in the module decomposition would not be interested in how the modules were allocated to files in the development environment, the implementation view would also be kept separate.

Three of the C&C views would prove good candidates for combination. Augmenting the shared-data view with other components and connectors that interact in client-server or peer-to-peer fashion allows those three views to become one. The pipe-and-filter view can be discarded; the shared-data view plus some key behavioral traces showing the data pipeline from satellite to scientist would provide the same intuitive overview to the less detail-oriented stakeholders.

Finally, recording uses information as a property of the decomposition view yields a combination of the decomposition and uses views.

After this step, eight views remain:

- In the module viewtype, decomposition, layered, and generalization
- In the C&C viewtype, shared-data and communicating-processes
- In the allocation viewtype, deployment, implementation, and work assignment.

Step 3: Prioritize

To let the project begin to make progress requires putting contracts in place, which in turn requires coarse-grained decomposition. Thus, the higher levels of the decomposition and work assignment views would likely receive the highest priority.

Table 9.3: ECS stakeholders and architecture documentation they might find most useful.

Stakeholder	Module Views				C&C Views					Allocation Views		
	Decomposition	Generalization	Uses	Layered	Pipe-and-filter	Shared-data	Client-server	Peer-to-peer	Communicating-processes	Deployment	Implementation	Work Assignment
Current and future architect	d	d	d	d	s	d	d	d	d	d	s	s
Government project manager	d	o	o	s	o	s	o	o	o	s		d
Contractors' project managers	s	o	s	s	o	s	s	s	o	d	s	d
Member of development team	d	d	d	d	o	d	d	d	d	s	s	d
Testers and integraters	s	s	d	s	o	d	d	d	s	s	d	
Maintainer	d	d	d	d	o	d	d	d	d	s	s	s
COTS engineers	d	s		d		d	d	d	s	d		d
Analyst for performance	d	s	d	s	o	d	d	d	d	d		
Analyst for data integrity	s	s	s	d	o	d	d	d	d	d		
Analyst for security	d	s	d	d	o	s	d	d	d	d	o	o
Analyst for availability	d	s	d	d				s	s	d		o
Funding agency	o				o	o				o		
Users in science community	o				o	o				o		

Key: d = detailed information, s = some details, o = overview information

In ECS, the layering in the architecture is very coarse-grained and can be quickly described. Similarly, generalization occurs largely in only one of the three major subsystems, is also coarse-grained, and can also be quickly described. Hence, these two views might be given next priority because they can be quickly dispatched.

The shared-data, communicating-processes, and deployment views would follow, nailing down details of runtime interaction only hinted at by the module-based views. During this phase, the architect can see if the communicating processes map straightforwardly to components in the shared-data view, in which case those two views could also be combined.

Finally, because the implementation view can be relegated to each contractor's own internal development effort, it would receive the lowest priority from the point of view of the overall system.

The result is four "full-fledged" views (decomposition, work assignment, shared-data/communicating-processes, and deployment), and three minor ones that stop at high levels or can be deferred.

9.4 Summary Checklist

ADVICE

Think twice if you need a new style. Perhaps an overlay is good enough. If existing styles are not sufficient for your purposes, define a new style and produce the necessary style guide for it.

- What views you choose depends on who the important stakeholders are, what budget is on hand, what the schedule is, and what skills are available.

- You should expect to choose at least one view from each of the three viewtypes: module, component-and-connector, and allocation.

- You will probably wish to combine some views or to have one view serve in another's place.

9.5 Discussion Questions

1. Suppose that your company has just purchased another company and that you've been given the task of merging a system in your company with a similar system in the purchased company. If you're given the resources to produce whatever architecture documentation you need, what views would you call for, and why? Would you ask for the same views for both systems?

2. Some architects speak of a "security view" or documentation of a "security architecture." What do you suppose they mean? What might this consist of?

3. How would you make a cost/benefit argument for the inclusion or exclusion of a particular view in an architecture documentation package? If you could summon up any data you needed to support your case, what data would you want?

9.6 For Further Reading

A central theme of [Hofmeister+ 00] is the coordinated use of separate (in their case, four) views to engineer and document software-intensive systems. Their treatment provides an excellent foundation for the philosophy behind choosing the views—providing information to stakeholders, and points of engineering leverage to the architect, based on expected needs of the system being built.

Building the
Documentation Package 10

You now have everything you need to begin building the complete documentation package. You have a repertoire of views and insights about how to document structure, behavior, and interfaces. This chapter shows you how to put it all together.

First, we return once again to our fundamental principle of documenting architectures: Documenting an architecture is a matter of documenting the relevant views and then adding documentation that applies to more than one view. Rule 4 for sound documentation, given in the Prologue, counsels us to use a standard organization for documents. Combining these two foundations, this chapter provides standard document organizations for documenting architectural views, along with the information that transcends views.

10.1   One Document or Several?

You can use the templates in this chapter to create either a single document with separate sections or a series of separate documents, each containing one or more parts of the template. Which option you choose will depend on the size of the system, how you wish to package it for its stakeholders, and your organization's standards and practices. The comprehensive example in Appendix A, for instance, structures the information as a two-volume set.

Document adornments, such as title pages, tables of contents, sign-off approvals, page formats, and the like are important but left largely to your discretion. However, you should make sure that each document you produce contains the following:

- Date of issue and status: draft, baseline, version number, and so on
- Name of issuing organization
- Change history
- Summary

FOR MORE INFORMATION

See Section 11.6 for further discussion of the ANSI/IEEE Standard on architecture documentation.

Also make sure that your documentation package includes a glossary of terms, a list of acronyms, and a list of references or at least a pointer to these things in the overall project documentation suite. These items are good things in themselves and will help your documentation be compliant with the recent ANSI/IEEE standard on architecture documentation, which requires them.

It depends on what the meaning of the word "is" is. If the—if he—if "is" means is and never has been, that is one thing. If it means there is none, that was a completely true statement.

—William Jefferson Clinton, August 17, 1998

PERSPECTIVES

What the Meaning of "Is" Is

Documentation in general, and software architecture documentation in particular, is chock-full of assertions: what the elements are, how they behave, what their interfaces are, and what relationships exist among them. There are assertions about why a design satisfies its requirements, what will change in the future, and, for product line architectures, what must be changed to get a product-ready instance of the architecture. There are assertions about who wrote the documentation, who approved it and when, and where you can find more information. An architecture document is basically a package of bald assertions.

In practice, however, not all assertions are created equal. Information has various pedigrees. Some information represents a constraint that the architect is obliged to honor. Some represents a heuristic that the architect can obey if convenient. Some information simply identifies properties.

When digesting all this information to document an architecture, the architect adds his or her own touch of "assertive freedom." Some of what the architect writes are facts, such as properties; for example, the bandwidth of a chosen network is what it is. Some of what the architect writes are requirements or constraints to be imposed on downstream developers, and no deviation is allowed. An element implementer must make sure that the element provides its advertised interface resources, period. Some assertions are nonbinding decisions: suggestions, if you will. Maybe some of those interface resources can be put off until later. Some assertions are placeholders for information not yet available, which is a class unto itself. Some placeholders are clearly marked TBD, but others show desired or possible values. For example, the architect may want to use version 6.4 of a vendor's database, but if it isn't ready by product-ship time, version 6.3 will have to do.

The result is documentation interlaced with insidious ambiguity. The problem is less pronounced in documentation that describes a fielded system rather than prescribes one under development. But even there, the system might not have all the features asserted in the documentation: assertions that were apparently just suggestions, even if the architect didn't think of them as such.

What to do? First, be aware of the problem. Second, for those key assertions whose pedigree is something short of stone tablets carried down a mountain, footnote them with a short explanation about what might cause them to change. It's good discipline to try to do this as you produce the documentation, but you can also make this check part of the documentation review process.

—P. C. C.

10.2   Documenting a View

Recall from Section 6.1 that a view consists of a set of view packets that are related by sibling and parent/child relationships. Documenting a view, then, becomes a matter of documenting a series of view packets. No matter what the view, the documentation for a view packet can be placed into a standard organization consisting of seven parts.

1. The *primary presentation* shows the elements and relationships among them that populate the portion of the view shown in this view packet. The primary presentation should contain the information you wish to convey about the system—in the vocabulary of that view—first. It should certainly include the primary elements and relations but under some circumstances might not include all of them. For example, you may wish to show the elements and relations that come into play during normal operation but relegate error handling or exception processing to the supporting documentation. What information you include in the primary presentation may also depend on what notation you use and how conveniently it conveys various kinds of information. A richer notation will tend to enable richer primary presentations.

    The primary presentation is usually graphical. If so, this presentation must be accompanied by a key that explains

FOR MORE INFORMATION

Descriptive completeness is discussed in Section 6.1.

ADVICE

Every diagram in the
architecture documen-
tation should include a
key that explains the
meaning of every sym-
bol used. The first part
of the key should iden-
tify the notation. If a
defined notation is
being used, the key
should name it and cite
the document that
defines the version
being used. Otherwise,
the key should define
the symbology and the
meaning, if any, of col-
ors, position, or other
information-carrying
aspects of the diagram.

or points to an explanation of the notation used in the presentation.

Sometimes, the primary presentation can be textual, as we saw in Figure 2.2 on page 58. If the primary presentation is textual instead of graphical, it still carries the obligation to present a terse summary of the most important information in the view packet. If that text is presented according to certain stylistic rules, they should be stated or incorporated by reference, as the analog to the graphical notation key.

2. The *element catalog* details at least those elements depicted in the primary presentation and perhaps others; see the discussion of descriptive completeness in Section 6.1. For instance, if a diagram shows elements A, B, and C, documentation is needed that explains in sufficient detail what A, B, and C are and their purposes or the roles they play, rendered in the vocabulary of the view. In addition, if elements or relations relevant to this view packet were omitted from the primary presentation, they should be is introduced and explained in the catalog. Specific parts of the catalog include

a. *Elements and their properties.* This section names each element in the view packet and lists the properties of that element. In Part I, each view we introduced listed a set of properties associated with elements in that view. For example, elements in a module decomposition view have the property of "responsibility"—an explanation of each module's role in the system—and elements in a communicating-processes view have timing parameters, among other things, as properties. Whether the properties are generic to the kind of view chosen or the architect has introduced new ones, this is where they are documented and given values.

b. *Relations and their properties.* Each view has specific relation type(s) that it depicts among the elements in that view. Mostly, these relations are shown in the primary presentation. However, if the primary presentation does not show all the relations or if there are exceptions to what is depicted in the primary presentation, this is the place to record that information.

c. *Element interfaces.* An interface is a boundary across which elements interact or communicate with each other. This section documents element interfaces. An element might occur in more than one view packet or even more than one view. Where its interface is docu-

**FOR MORE
INFORMATION**

Documenting inter-
faces is covered in
Chapter 7.

mented is a packaging question, decided on the basis of convenience and addressing the needs of stakeholders. Different aspects of the interface may be captured and documented in different views. Or you may wish to document the interfaces in a single document, in which case this section consists of a pointer.

FOR MORE INFORMATION
Documenting behavior is discussed in Chapter 8.

   d. *Element behavior.* Some elements have complex interactions with their environment. For purposes of understanding or analysis, it is often incumbent on the architect to specify element behavior.

3. A *context diagram* shows how the system or portion of the system depicted in this view packet relates to its environment.

FOR MORE INFORMATION
Context diagrams are discussed in Section 6.2.

4. A *variability guide* shows how to exercise any variation points that are a part of the architecture shown in this view packet.

5. *Architecture background* explains why the design reflected in the view packet came to be. The goal of this section is to explain why the design is as it is and to provide a convincing argument that it is sound. Architecture background includes

FOR MORE INFORMATION
Documenting variability is discussed in Section 6.4.

   a. *Rationale.* The architect explains why the design decisions reflected in the view packet were made and gives a list of rejected alternatives and why they were rejected. This information will prevent future architects from pursuing dead ends in the face of required changes.

   b. *Analysis results.* The architect should document the results of analyses that have been conducted, such as the results of performance or security analysis or a list of what would have to change in the face of a particular kind of system modification.

   c. *Assumptions.* The architect should document any assumptions he or she made when crafting the design. Assumptions are usually about either environment or need. Assumptions about the environment document what the architect assumes is available in the environment and what can be used by the system being designed. Assumptions are also made about invariants in the environment. For example, a navigation system architect might make assumptions about the stability of the earth's geographic and/or magnetic poles. Finally, assumptions about the environment can pertain to the development environment: tool suites available or the skill levels of the implementation teams, for example.

Assumptions about need state why the design provided is sufficient for what's needed. For example, if a navigation system's software interface provides location information in a single geographic frame of reference, the architect is assuming that it is sufficient and that alternative frames of reference are not useful.

Assumptions can play a crucial role in the validation of an architecture. The design that an architect produces is a function of these assumptions, and writing them down explicitly makes it vastly easier to review them for accuracy and soundness than trying to ferret them out by examining the design.

6. *Other information* provided will vary according to the standard practices of each organization or the needs of the particular project. If the view packet is maintained as a separate document, you can use this section to record document information (see Section 10.1). Or the architect might record references to specific sections of a requirements document to establish traceability. Information in this section is, strictly speaking, not architectural. Nevertheless, it is convenient to record such information alongside the architecture, and this section is provided for that purpose.

7. *Related view packets* are the parent, siblings, and any children. In some cases, a view packet's children may reside in a different view, as when an element in one style is decomposed into a set of elements in a different style.

Items 2–7, the *supporting documentation*, explain and elaborate the information in the primary presentation. Even if some items are empty for a given view packet—for example, perhaps no mechanisms for variability exist or no relations other than those shown in the primary presentation exist—include those sections, marked "none." Don't omit them, or your reader may wonder whether it was an oversight.

Every view packet, then, consists of a primary presentation, usually graphical, and supporting documentation that explains and elaborates the pictures (see Figure 10.1). To underscore the complementary nature of the primary presentation with its supporting documentation, we call the graphical portion of the view packet an **architectural cartoon**. We use the definition from the world of fine art: A cartoon is a preliminary sketch of the final work; it is meant to remind us that the picture, although getting most of the attention, is not the complete description but only a sketch of it. In fact, it may be considered merely an introduction to or a quick summary of the information provided by the supporting documentation.

Template for a View Packet

Section 1. Primary presentation of the view packet

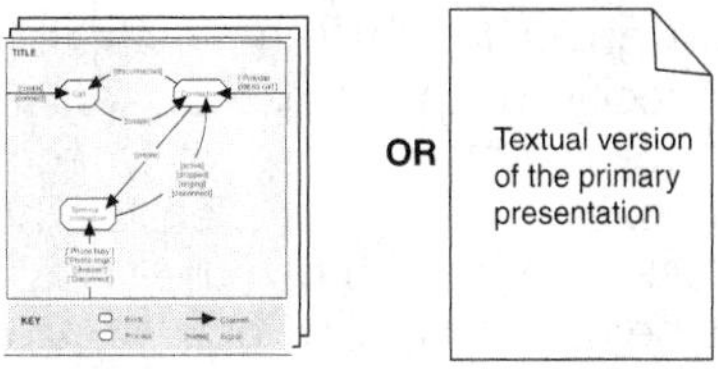

Section 2. Element catalog

- **Section 2.A Elements and their properties**
- **Section 2.B Relations and their properties**
- **Section 2.C Element interfaces**
- **Section 2.D Element behavior**

Section 3. Context diagram

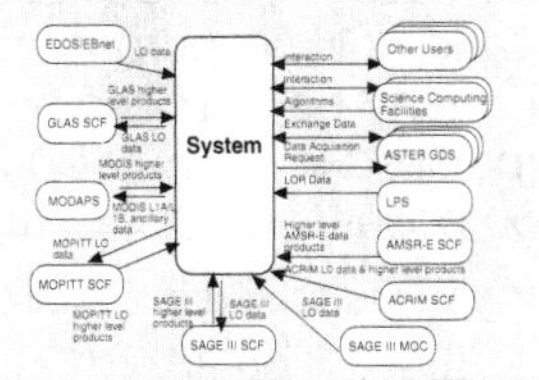

Section 4. Variability guide

Section 5. Architecture background

- **Section 5.A Design rationale**
- **Section 5.B Analysis results**
- **Section 5.C Assumptions**

Section 6. Other information

Section 7. Related view packets

Figure 10.1
Documenting a view packet consists of documenting seven parts: (1) the primary presentation; (2) the element catalog; (3) a context diagram; (4) a variability guide; (5) architecture background, including rationale, results of analysis, and assumptions made; (6) organization- or project-specific information; and (7) pointers to the view packet's siblings, parent(s), or children. If the primary presentation is graphical, we call it a *cartoon*. A cartoon must be accompanied by a key that explains the notational symbology used or that points to the place where the notation is explained.

PERSPECTIVES

Presentation Is Also Important

Throughout this book, we focus on telling you what to document. We do not spend much, if any, time on how it should look, although this is not because form is unimportant. Just as the best-designed algorithm can be made to run slowly by insufficient attention to detail during coding, so too the best-designed documentation can be made difficult to read by insufficient attention to presentation details. By presentation details, I mean such items as style of writing, fonts, types and consistency of visual emphasis, and the segmenting of information.

We have not spent time on these issues not because we do not think they are important but because presentation details are not our field of expertise. Universities offer master's degrees in technical communication, in information design, and in other fields related to the presentation of material. We have been busy being software engineers and architects and have never been trained in presentation issues. Having denied expertise, however, I am now free to give some rules of thumb.

- Adopt a style guide for the documentation. The style guide will specify such items as fonts, numbering schemes, conventions with respect to acronyms, captions for figures, and other such details. The style guide should also describe how to use the visual conventions discussed in the next several points.
- Use visually distinct forms for emphasis. Word processors offer many techniques for emphasis. Words can be **bold**, *italic,* large, or <u>underlined</u>. Using these forms makes **some** words more important than others.
- Be consistent in using visual styles. Use one visual style for one purpose, and do not mix purposes. That is, the first use of a word might be italicized, and a critical thought might be expressed in bold, but do not use the same style for both purposes, and do not mix styles.
- Do not go overboard with visuals. It is usually sufficient to use one form of visual emphasis without combining them. Is **bold** less arresting to you than <u>**underlined bold**</u>? Probably not.
- Try to separate different types of ideas with different visual backgrounds. In this book, we attempted to put the main thread in the body of the book, with ancillary information as sidebars. We also made the sidebars visually distinct so that you would know at a glance whether what you were reading was in the main thread or an ancillary thread.

The key ideas with respect to presentation are consistency and simplicity.

- Use the same visual language to convey the same idea: consistency.
- Do not try to overwhelm the user with visuals; you are documenting a computer system, not writing an interactive novel: shoot for simplicity.

The goal of the architecture documentation, as we have stressed throughout this book, is to communicate the basic concepts of the system clearly to the reader. Using simple and consistent visual and stylistic rules is an important aspect of achieving this goal.

—L.B.

It may take you months, even years, to draft a single map. It's not just the continents, oceans, mountains, lakes, rivers, and political borders you have to worry about. There's also the cartouche (a decorative box containing printed information, such as the title and the cartographer's name) and an array of other adornments—distance scales, compass roses, wind-heads, ships, sea monsters, important personages, characters from the Scriptures, quaint natives, menacing cannibal natives, sexy topless natives, planets, wonders of the ancient world, flora, fauna, rainbows, whirlpools, sphinxes, sirens, cherubs, heraldic emblems, strapwork, rollwork, and/or clusters of fruit.

—Miles Harvey, *The Island of Lost Maps: A True Story of Cartographic Crime* (Random House, 2000, p. 98)

10.3 Documentation Beyond Views

In many ways, an architecture is to a system what a map of the world is to the world. Thus far, we have focused on capturing the various architectural views of a system, which tell the main story. In the words of Miles Harvey, they are the "continents, oceans, mountains, lakes, rivers, and political borders" of the complete system map that we are drawing. But we now turn to the complement of view documentation, which is capturing the information that applies to more than one view or to the documentation package as a whole. Documentation beyond views corresponds to the adornments of the map, which complete the story and without which the work is inadequate.

Documentation beyond views consists of three major aspects, which we can summarize as how/what/why:

1. *How* the documentation is laid out and organized so that a stakeholder of the architecture can find the information he or she needs efficiently and reliably. This part consists of a documentation roadmap and a view template.

2. *What* the architecture is. Here, the information that remains to be captured beyond the views themselves is a short system overview to ground any reader as to the purpose of the system, the way the views are related to one another, a list of elements and where they appear, and a glossary and an acronym list for the entire architecture.

3. *Why* the architecture is the way it is: the background for the system, external constraints that have been imposed to shape the architecture in certain ways, and the rationale for large-scale decisions.

Figure 10.2 summarizes documentation beyond views.

Figure 10.2
Documenting information beyond views consists of how/what/why: *how* the documentation is laid out to serve stakeholders—a documentation roadmap and a view template; additional information beyond the views about *what* the architecture is—system overview, mapping between views, a directory, and a glossary; and *why* the architecture is the way it is—system background, design constraints, and rationale.

```
Template for Documentation Beyond Views

How the documentation is organized
        Section 1. Documentation roadmap
        Section 2. View template

What the architecture is:
        Section 3. System overview
        Section 4. Mapping between views
        Section 5. Directory
        Section 6. Glossary and acronym list

Why the architecture is the way it is:
        Section 7. Background, design constraints, and rationale
```

10.3.1 How the Documentation Is Organized to Serve a Stakeholder

Every suite of architecture documentation needs an introductory piece to explain its organization to a new stakeholder and to help that stakeholder access the information he or she is most interested in. The two kinds of *how* information to help an architecture stakeholder are a documentation roadmap and a view template.

Documentation Roadmap

The documentation roadmap introduces the reader to the information that the architect has chosen to include in the suite of documentation. When using the documentation as a basis for communication, a new reader needs to determine where particular information can be found. When using the documentation as a basis for analysis, a reader needs to know which views contain the information necessary for a particular analysis. A roadmap contains this information.

A roadmap consists of the following two sections:

1. *Description of the parts.* The roadmap begins with a brief description of each part of the documentation package. Each entry may contain document information, such as the author, location, and latest version. The major part of the roadmap describes the views that the architect has included in the package. For each view, the roadmap gives

   a. The name of the view and what style it instantiates.

   b. A description of the view's element types, relation types, and property types. These descriptions can be found in the style guide from which the view was built and can be included in the roadmap directly or by reference. They let a reader begin to understand the kind of information that he or she can expect to see presented in the view.

c. A description of what the view is for. Again, this information can be found in the corresponding style guide. The goal is to tell a stakeholder whether the view is likely to contain information of interest. The information can be presented by listing the stakeholders who are likely to find the view of interest, and by listing a series of questions that can be answered by examining the view.[1]

d. A description of language, modeling techniques, or analytical methods used in constructing the view.[2]

Figure 10.3 shows what a roadmap might say about a layered view for system S.

---

a. View name: layer view for system S
b. Elements, relations, properties
- Element types: layers
- Relation types: *allowed-to-use*
- Property types: name, contents, cohesion

c. What the view is for
- Stakeholders who might find this view useful:
  - Member of development team
  - Tester, integrater
  - Maintainer
  - Product line (family member) application builder
  - Analyst
  - New stakeholder looking for familiarization
  - Future architect
- Questions answerable by information in this view:
  - What elements is each particular element allowed to use?
  - What are the virtual machines provided for in the architecture?
  - What are the interfaces of each layer, and how do they relate to the interfaces of the elements they contain?
  - If an element is in a particular subset of the system, what other elements must also be in that subset?

d. Language, modeling tecniques, or analytical methods used
- UML packages used to represent the layers
- Scenario-based analysis used to help assign software to layers based on portability concerns

Figure 10.3
A roadmap for a layered view of system S

---

2. *How stakeholders might use the package.* The roadmap follows with a section describing how various stakeholders might

---

1. ANSI/IEEE-1471-2000, the ANSI/IEEE recommended practice for architectural description for software-intensive systems, requires that the selected views address the concerns of at least users, acquirers, developers, and maintainers. See Section 11.6 for more information.

2. This information is also required by ANSI/IEEE-1471-2000.

ADVICE

Use the organization shown in Figure 10.1 as the basis for your view template. Modify it as necessary to make it appropriate for your organization's standards and the special needs of the development project at hand. Be cautious about throwing out sections that you think you don't need; the presence of a section in the template can prod you to think about the issue across the system, whereas omitting the section will let you forget about it, perhaps to the detriment of the system. For each section, include a terse description of the contents of that section. It is possible, but unlikely, that different views will have different templates. If so, produce a view template for each case necessary, and note in each view the template it follows.

---

access the package to help address their concerns. This might include short scenarios, such as "A maintainer wishes to know the units of software that are likely to be changed by a proposed modification."

View Template

A view template is the standard organization for a view. Figure 10.1 and the material surrounding it provide a basis for a view template by defining the standard parts of a view document and the contents and rules for each part. The purpose of a view template is that of any standard organization: It helps a reader navigate quickly to a section of interest, and it helps a writer organize the information and establish criteria for knowing how much work is left to do.

10.3.2   What the Architecture Is

System Overview

This is a short prose description of the system's function, its users, and any important background or constraints. The purpose is to provide readers with a consistent mental model of the system and its purpose.

The system overview is, strictly speaking, not part of the architecture and does not contain architectural information but is indispensable for understanding the architecture. If an adequate system overview exists elsewhere, such as in the overall project documentation, a pointer to it is sufficient.

Mapping Between Views

Because all the views of an architecture describe the same system, it stands to reason that any two views will have much in common. Helping a reader or other consumer of the documentation understand the relationship between views will help that reader gain a powerful insight into how the architecture works as a unified conceptual whole. Being clear about the relationship by providing mappings between views is the key to increasing understanding and to decreasing confusion.

The mappings in a particular architecture are often complicated. For instance, each module may map to multiple runtime

FOR MORE INFORMATION

Section 6.3 discusses hybrid views. Also, the views in the allocation viewtype (Chapter 5) are related to the concept of view mappings because each one involves mapping a structure of software architecture onto a structure not in the realm of software architecture, such as a hardware environment, a file system, or a set of work units.

ADVICE

Documenting the Mapping Between Views

To document a mapping from one view to another, use a table that lists the elements of the first view in some convenient look-up order. For each element

- List the element or elements of the second view that correspond to it.
- Indicate whether the correspondence is partial or complete.
- If the element of the first view has an interface, list any interface or module in the second view that corresponds to it.

The table itself should be annotated or introduced with an explanation of the mapping that it depicts; that is, what the correspondence is between the elements across the two views. Examples include *is implemented by* for mapping from a component-and-connector view to a module view, *implements* for mapping from a module view to a component-and-connector view, *included in* for mapping from a decomposition view to a layered view, and many others.

For which views should you provide a mapping? The answer, of course, is that it depends, but begin with these rules of thumb:

- Ensure at least one mapping between a module view and a component-and-connector view.
- If your system uses more than one module view, map them to each other.
- If your system uses more than one component-and-connector view, map them to each other.

elements, such as when classes map to objects. Complications arise when the mappings are not one-to-one or when runtime elements of the system do not exist as code elements at all, such as when they are imported at runtime or incorporated at build or load time. These are relatively simple none- or one-to-many mappings. But in general, parts of the elements in one view can map to parts of elements in another view.

As discussed in Section 6.1, a view packet can sometimes point to another view packet in a different view. This is also part of the information that maps views.

Directory

The directory is an index of all the elements, relations, and properties that appear in any of the views, along with a pointer to its definition.

Glossary and Acronym List

The glossary and acronym list defines terms used in the architecture documentation that have special meaning. These lists, if they exist as part of the overall system or project documentation, may be given as pointers in the architecture package.

10.3.3 Why the Architecture Is the Way It Is: Background, Design Constraints, and Rationale

This section documents the reasoning behind decisions that apply to more than one view. Prime candidates include documentation of background or organizational constraints that led to decisions of systemwide import.

> To reuse the design, we must also record the decisions, alternatives, and trade-offs that led to it.
>
> —(Gamma+ 95, p. 6)

By now, you may realize that rationale is an important ingredient in the mix of architecture documentation, for this is the third place in the documentation package where it enjoys a reserved section. (The first place is in the documentation for an interface, see Chapter 7, and a second is in the template for a view, shown in Figure 10.1.) Having three places in the documentation package for rationale does indeed signal its importance but also results from the fact that these are different kinds of rationale, distinguished by the scope of the design decisions to which each pertains. Rationale can apply to a single view, to the design of an interface of an individual element, or to the entire design approach. No matter what the scope, the principles about what rationale should contain and when it should be included overlap all areas.

Rationale is the architect's chance to explain key decisions to a skeptical audience of peers, perhaps even a future archi-

ADVICE

Which Decisions to Justify

Which of the hundreds or thousands of design decisions comprising an architecture should be accompanied by rationale explaining them? Certainly not all of them. It's simply too time consuming, and many decisions do not warrant the effort. So how do you select which decisions are important enough to warrant documentation of rationale? Document the rationale behind a design decision in the following circumstances:

- The design team spent significant time evaluating options before making a decision.
- The decision is critical to the achievement of a requirement/goal.
- The decision seems to not make sense at first blush but becomes clear when more background is considered.
- On several occasions, you've been asked, "Why did you do that?"
- The issue is confusing to new team members.
- The decision has a widespread effect that will be difficult to undo.
- You think it's cheaper to capture it now than not capturing it will be later.

To understand all is to forgive all.

—Evelyn Waugh,
Brideshead Revisited
(Little, Brown, 1945,
© 1973)

tect. The goal is to convey why the architecture—or the piece of it to which the rationale applies—is in fact a good solution. The idea is to convey a vicarious appreciation of the thought process the architect went through to arrive at the decision.

Once you've decided to document a design decision, try to describe it with the following five-part outline:

1. *Decision:* a succinct summary of the design decision.

2. *Constraints:* the key constraints that ruled out other possibilities. The system's requirements constitute a large body of constraints but by no means all. Sometimes, a particular operating system must be used; other times, a particular middleware system; at other times, the components derived from legacy systems. Perhaps there were funding pressures, or a particular commercial component was chosen because of the organization's relationship with its vendor. Perhaps key stakeholders wielded influence that affected the design. Business goals, such as time to market, often influence an architecture, as do quality attribute goals, such as

modifiability, that are not always documented in a system's requirements. Some design choices result from constraints generated by other design decisions and from trade-offs with other solutions.

3. *Alternatives:* the options you considered and the reasons for ruling them out. The reasons need not be technical: A future architect will especially appreciate your insights about what dead ends to avoid, as well as your candor if you think you made the wrong decision or if you could just as well have adopted another approach.

4. *Effects:* the implications or ramifications of the decision. For example, what constraints does the decision impose on downstream developers, users, maintainers, testers, or builders of other interacting systems?

5. *Evidence:* any confirmation that the decision was a good one. For example, you can explain how the design choice meets the requirements or satisfies constraints. There are various frameworks for reasoning about quality attributes, such as rate-monotonic analysis and queuing models. Use cases and quality scenarios are also used to evaluate the architecture with respect to the requirements.

Like all documentation, rationale is subject to a cost/benefit equation. But know this: Most rationale is read and used by the person who wrote it in the first place, often after weeks rather than years. So if you're altruistic, write rationale as your legacy for the next generation. If you're more motivated by interests closer to home, remember that the time it saves may be your own.

ADVICE

Building an Architecture Overview Presentation

Sooner or later, every architect has to give an oral overview of an architecture, backed up by viewgraphs. Once built, the presentation is likely to be used often, introducing the architecture to managers, developers, sponsors, evaluaters, customers, and even visitors. What should such a presentation contain? The goal is to help the audience gain an appreciation of the problem, see the solution(s) chosen, understand why they were chosen, and gain confidence that the architecture is the right one for the job.

Here's an outline for a five-part, one-hour overview containing anywhere from 20 to 35 viewgraphs.

1. *Problem statement:* 2–3 slides. State the problem the system is trying to solve. List driving architectural require-

ments, the measurable quantities you associate with them, and any existing standards/models/approaches for meeting them. State any technical constraints, such as a prescribed operating system, hardware, or middleware.

2. *Architectural strategy:* 2 slides. Describe the major architectural challenges. Describe the architectural approaches, styles, patterns, or mechanisms used, including what quality attributes they address and a description of how the approaches address those attributes.

3. *System context:* 1–2 slides. Include one or two top-level context diagrams that clearly show the system boundaries and other systems with which yours must interact.

4. *Architectural views:* 12–18 slides. Use the views you've chosen as the backbone of the presentation. For each view, include the primary presentation from at least the top-level view packet and, depending on the amount of detail you want to include, perhaps a few second-level view packets. Naturally, each should include a notation key.

   An overview presentation is the one case for which a cartoon does not have to be accompanied by the supporting documentation, but you will want to have it available for answering questions.

   For each viewgraph showing a primary presentation, make a couple of accompanying viewgraphs that explain (a) how the architecture shown supports the functionality and achieves the system qualities that reside with that view and (b) the rationale for choosing that design. You may wish to annotate or color some of the cartoons to show programmatic information about the elements, such as which elements are provided by COTS products or other source, the state of an element's development, the amount of risk posed by an element, or the scheduled delivery or other milestone of an element. You need not include every view in the presentation, but you should include at least one view from each of the modules, C&C, and allocation viewtypes.

   Where views can be straightforwardly mapped to each other, include viewgraphs that do so. This will be very useful in conveying the overall picture.

5. *How the architecture works:* 3–10 slides. Trace up to three of the most important use cases. If possible, include the runtime resources consumed for each use case. You should be able to extract the traces from your behavioral documentation in the form of, for example, sequence diagrams or statecharts.

   Show the architecture's capacity for growth with a trace of up to three of the most important change scenarios. If possible, describe the change impact—estimated size/difficulty of the change—in terms of the changed elements, connectors, or interfaces.

Depending on the importance of each item, consider tracing a scenario that illustrates any of the following: concurrency, failure recovery, error propagation, or key end-to-end data flows. Again, you should be able to extract this information from your behavioral documentation.

You may wish to have the following viewgraphs available to answer questions or to help discussion but not make them part of the standard presentation:

- The set of stakeholders for the documentation and a sketch of the information needs of each (2–3 slides)
- Glossary (1–2 slides)

Preface the whole package with a title slide, sprinkle outline slides throughout to let the audience follow the outline of the presentation, and end with a "for further information" slide, and you're done.

If you're using an informal or ad hoc notation throughout your architecture, this overview presentation will be a good place to spot inconsistencies. Even something as minor as data flowing left to right in one diagram but right to left in another can be annoying and leave the audience puzzled.

A good presentation can help an architect in many ways. Put on videotape, it can free the architect from having to brief new hires or low-ranking visitors. It can be handed to junior designers as a way to groom them for technical leadership positions. And it helps establish a consistent vision of the architecture throughout an organization, which makes every architect's life easier.

PERSPECTIVES

Global Analysis

Global analysis is the first design activity for each view in the Siemens approach to architecture design. As seen in Figure 10.4, this activity documents the rationale for the design decisions critical to the achievement of some requirement or goal.

The analysis must be global because key issues transcend boundaries between development activities, subsystems, and architecture viewtypes. Successful architects note the flexibility of the influencing factors and their likelihood of change, characterize how factors interact and their impact, and select cost-effective design strategies and project strategies to reduce the expected impact.

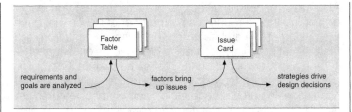

Figure 10.4
Global Analysis begins by documenting the factors, such as requirements and goals, that influence the architecture design of a system. Analyzing factors results in a set of key issues and corresponding global strategies that guide the architecture design and improve its changeability with respect to the factors identified. Linking factors to issues to design decisions in this way provides traceability and documents the rationale for the architecture design.

Factors include the constraints from the environment and the system requirements. Factors are documented in a factor table (see Table 10.1). A factor table describes the factor, characterizes its flexibility or changeability, and the impact that a change in the factor has on the system. For example, the organization places constraints on the system, such as requirements for time to market using available personnel and resources. These factors influence whether the system can be built. The requirements document the important features and quality attributes and may introduce constraints on technology. Factor tables record constraint-based rationale. Linking them to issue cards shows how they influence design decisions.

Organizational Factor	Flexibility and Changeability	Impact
01: (Factor Category)		
01.1 *(Factor Name)*		
(description of factor)	*(what aspects of the factor are flexible or changeable)*	*(components affected by the factor or changes to it)*
01.2: *(Factor Name)*		
(description of factor)	*(what aspects of the factor are flexible or changeable)*	*(components affected by the factor or changes to it)*
02: (Factor Category)		
02.1 *(Factor Name)*		
(description of factor)	*(what aspects of the factor are flexible or changeable)*	*(components affected by the factor or changes to it)*

(*Source:* C. Hofmeister, R. L. Nord, and D. Soni, *Applied Software Architecture* (Addison-Wesley, 2000, p. 31).

After documenting the factors in factor tables, you begin organizing them around a small number of issues that drive the design of the architecture. These issues arise from the factors that have little flexibility, a high degree of changeability, and a global impact on the rest of the system. For example, analyzing the factors: (1) "time-to-market is short"; (2) "delivery of features is negotiable"; and (3) "new features are added continuously over the lifetime of the product" produces the architectural issue "Easy Addition of Features." Making it easy to add features will help meet the aggressive schedule by trading off function with time.

Issues are documented in an Issue Card (see Figure 10.5). The solution to an issue is in the form of strategies that guide the architect in making the design decisions. Such strategies may advocate the adoption of an architecture style or pattern, provide design guidelines (encapsulation, separation of concerns), place constraints on elements of the system, or introduce additional structure. The solution description records the analysis-based rationale that illustrates that the strategies satisfy the issue.

Issue: *(name of the architecture design issue)*
(Description of the issue)
Influencing Factors
(List of the factors that affect this design issue and how)

Solution
(Discussion of a general solution to the design issue, followed by a list of the associated strategies)
Strategy: *(name of the strategy)*
(Explanation of the strategy)

Related Strategies
(References to related strategies and discussion of how they are related to this design issue)

Figure 10.5
Sample Issue Card (C. Hofmeister, R. L. Nord, and D. Soni, *Applied Software Architecture* (Addison-Wesley, 2000, p. 33)). An issue card describes the issue, the influencing factors that affect this issue, and the solution to the issue.

How strategies are used is documented in a table linking them to design decisions. Solutions are revisited and may change as issues are resolved during design. There will be conflicts among the issues and the resulting trade-offs need to be made and documented.

—R.N.

10.4 Validating Software Architecture Documentation

Validation is an essential part of engineering practice, and validation of documentation is no different. Recall the seventh rule of sound documentation: *Review documentation for fitness of purpose*. Validation enables you to make certain that the documentation you have put forth considerable effort to produce will in fact be useful to the communities you've aimed to serve. Validation is about making sure that the architecture you have designed is documented well enough so that people can understand and use it.

A review can answer a number of questions about the architecture documentation's consistency:

1. Is the architecture documentation consistent with the stakeholder community that's going to use it? This question leads to the following.

   a. Has the right set of stakeholders been identified?

   b. Have their concerns been met?

   c. Have the right views been chosen? For each stakeholder concern, is there at least one view that satisfies it?

   d. Is the documentation organized so that an answer can be looked up quickly?

2. Is the architecture documentation consistent with itself? That is, is it free from errors of ambiguity and contradiction?

   a. Are mappings among views provided?

   b. Are inconsistencies among views highlighted, explained, and justified?

   c. Are assertions identified as fact, heuristics, properties, requirements, nonbinding decisions, desire, range of possibilities, place holders, and so on?

   d. Are two terms introduced that mean essentially the same thing? Is one term used to mean two different things?

   e. Is information needlessly repeated in different places?

3. Is the architecture documentation consistent with good form?

   a. Does a template, or a standard organization, define each section of the documentation, such as the template for a view?

   b. Does it adhere to the standards and templates that it claims to follow?

   c. For each view, is the definition of the view—that is, what the elements, relations, and properties are—provided?

  d. Is the documentation clear? Are definitions crisp?

  e. Does it contain useful rationale, including constraints, background, and rejected alternatives?

  f. Are traces to requirements included?

  g. Does it explain how to exercise variabilities?

  h. Does the documentation contain extraneous nonarchitectural information?

4. Is the architecture documentation consistent with the architecture that it purports to describe?

  a. Is the documentation accurate?

  b. Is it up-to-date?

  c. Is it complete? Are TBDs waiting to be resolved?

A review requires reviewers. Reviewing for the first question—about consistency with stakeholder needs—requires stakeholders. Good architectural practice requires early identification of stakeholders, and their input can be solicited during the planning of the documentation suite. Ask them—individually, in small groups, or in a documentation planning workshop—what their documentation concerns are. They can articulate them, using scenarios. "I want to know how to exercise the variability in an architecture," a stakeholder might say, "so that I can field a product in a product line." Or, "I will need to know how to change the architecture to accommodate the next generation of middleware," another might say. You can use these scenarios to help plan the documentation package and then later to validate it by asking the stakeholders to exercise their scenarios by walking through the documentation to carry them out.

This technique is a form of *active design review*, whereby reviewers are actively engaged to exercise the artifact they are reviewing, not just look it over and scan for defects. For all the questions cited, active design reviews are recommended. Here is what David Weiss, one of the creators of active design reviews, has this to say about them:

> Starting in the early 1970s I have had occasion to sit in on a number of design reviews, in disparate places in industry and government. I had a chance to see a wide variety of software developers conduct reviews, including professional software developers, engineers, and scientists. All had one thing in common: the review was conducted as a (usually large) meeting or series of meetings at which designer(s) made presentations to the reviewers, and the reviewers could be passive and silent or could be active and ask questions. The amount, quality, and time of delivery of the design documentation varied widely. The time that the reviewers put in preparation varied widely. The participation by

the reviewers varied widely. (I have even been to so-called reviews where the reviewers are cautioned not to ask embarrassing questions, and have seen reviewers silenced by senior managers for doing so. I was once hustled out of a design review because I was asking too many sharp questions.) The expertise and roles of the reviewers varied widely. As a result, the quality of the reviews varied widely. In the early 1980s Fagin-style code inspections were introduced to try to ameliorate many of these problems for code reviews. Independently of Fagin, we developed active design reviews at about the same time to ameliorate the same problems for design reviews.

Active design reviews are designed to make reviews useful to the designers. They are driven by questions that the designers ask the reviewers, reversing the usual review process. The result is that the designers have a way to test whether or not their design meets the goals they have set for it. To get the reviewers to think hard about the design, active reviews try to get them to take an active role by requiring them to answer questions rather than to ask questions. Many of the questions force them to take the role of users of the design, sometimes making them think about how they would write a program to implement (parts of) the design. In an active review, no reviewer can be passive and silent.

We focus reviewers with different expertise on different sets of questions so as to use their time and knowledge most effectively. There is no large meeting at which designers make presentations. We conduct an initial meeting where we explain the process and then give reviewers their assignments, along with the design documentation that they need to complete their assignments.

Design reviews cannot succeed without proper design documentation. Information theory tells us that error correction requires redundancy. Active reviews use redundancy in two ways. First, we suggest that designers structure their design documentation so that it incorporates redundancy for the purpose of consistency checking. For example, module interface specifications may include assumptions about what functionality the users of a module require. The functions offered by the module's interface can then be checked against those assumptions. Incorporating such redundancy is not required for active design reviews but certainly makes it easier to construct the review questions.

Second, we select reviewers for their expertise in certain areas and include questions that take advantage of their knowledge in those areas. For example, the design of avionics software would include questions about devices controlled or monitored by the software, to be answered by experts in avionics device technology, and intended to insure that the designers have made correct assumptions about the characteristics, both present and future, of such devices. In so doing, we compare the knowledge in the reviewers' heads with the knowledge used to create the design.

I have used active design reviews in a variety of environments. With the proper set of questions, appropriate documentation, and appropriate reviewers, they never fail to uncover many false assumptions, inconsistencies, omissions, and other weaknesses in the design. The designers are almost always pleased with the results. The reviewers, who do not have to attend a long, often boring, meeting, like being able to go off to their desks and focus on their own areas of expertise, with no distractions, on their own schedule. One developer who conducted an active review under my guidance was ecstatic with the results. In response to the questions she used she had gotten more than 300 answers that pointed out potential problems with the design. She told me that she had never before been able to get anyone to review her designs so carefully.

Of course, active reviews have some difficulties as well. As with other review approaches, it is often difficult to find reviewers who have the expertise that you need and who will commit to the time that is required. Since the reviewers operate independently and on their own schedule, you must sometimes harass them to get them to complete their reviews on time. Some reviewers feel that there is a synergy that occurs in large review meetings that ferrets out problems that may be missed by individual reviewers carrying out individual assignments. Perhaps the most difficult aspect is creating design documentation that contains the redundancy that makes for the most effective reviews. Probably the second most difficult aspect is devising a set of questions that force the reviewer to be active. It is really easy to be lured into asking questions that allow the reviewer to be lazy. For example, "Is this assumption valid?" is too easy. In principle, much better is "Give 2 examples that demonstrate the validity of this assumption, or a counterexample." In practice, one must balance demands on the reviewers with expected returns, perhaps suggesting that they must give at least one example but two are preferable.

Active reviews are a radical departure from the standard review process for most designers, including architects. Since engineers and project managers are often conservative about changes to their development processes, they may be reluctant to try a new approach. However, active reviews are easy to explain and easy to try. The technology transfers easily and the process is easy to standardize; an organization that specializes in a particular application can reuse many questions from one design review to another. Structuring the design documentation so that it has reviewable content improves the quality of the design even before the review takes place. Finally, reversing the typical roles puts less stress on everyone involved (designers no longer have to get up in front of an audience to explain their designs, and reviewers no longer have to worry about asking stupid questions in front of an audience) and leads to greater productivity in the review.

A Glossary Would Have Helped

A colleague told me recently about an architecture review he attended for a distributed military command-and-control system, a major function of which was the tracking of ships at sea. "A major topic of interest was how the common operational picture handled tracks," he wrote. "But it was clear that the word *track* was hopelessly overloaded. The person making the presentation caused some of this confusion by using the word *track* to mean the following:

- The actual location of a target as determined by a single radar on a single mobile platform
- The actual location of a vessel as determined by fusing signals from multiple sensors on board a mobile platform
- The actual location of a vessel as determined by fusing tracks from different mobile platforms at a ground station
- The actual location of a vessel as determined by satellite observations
- The estimated location of a vessel that has recently moved out of sensor range
- Other, slightly different variations

The age, accuracy, and implicit history of each type of track mentioned is different. The person making the presentation was knowledgeable and easily changed context to answer questions as necessary. But the result was that people left the meeting with different impressions of the details of the system's capabilities and were somewhat confused as to how the common operational picture was to be displayed on each type of mobile platform and ground station."

A glossary was sorely needed, my colleague agreed. Even if everyone on your project has the identical vision for each of your specialized terms—which is highly unlikely—remember the wide audience of stakeholders for whom you're preparing your documentation. Taking the time to define your terms will reduce confusion and frustration later on, and the effort will more than likely pay for itself in saved time and rework.

—P.C.C.

10.5 Summary Checklist

- A complete architecture documentation package consists of a set of views, along with documentation of the information that applies to more than one view.
- The package can consist of one document, a few, or many.
- A view packet includes a primary presentation—usually graphical, including a key—and supporting documentation that explains the primary presentation.
- Supporting documentation in a view packet includes an element catalog, a context diagram, a variability guide, architecture background, other information, and relationship to other view packets.
- Documentation beyond views consists of a documentation roadmap, a view template, a system overview, mapping between views, a directory, a project glossary and acronym list, and rationale.
- Document the views, and documentation beyond views, using the templates in this chapter (tailored for your own use if necessary).
- Document the mapping between views by using a table showing how elements of one view correspond to elements of another.
- Document the rationale behind a design decision if it seems nonobvious, is the source of questions, is critical, or has widespread effect.
- Rationale for a design decision should include relevant constraints, rejected alternatives, ramifications of the decision, and evidence that the decision was the correct one.
- Review documentation for fitness of purpose, using the technique of active design reviews.

10.6 Discussion Questions

1. Discuss how you might use hypertext or a Web-based documentation suite to provide a custom package for each kind of architectural stakeholder.

2. Discuss the advantages and disadvantages of various packaging schemes: a single large document, a small number of separate documents, and a separate document for each kind of information. For a project you have in mind, which would you choose, and why? Make sure to consider configuration management concerns and stakeholder needs in your discussion. What other criteria would help you decide?

3. This chapter has prescribed—or at least allowed—certain kinds of information that might also exist in the overall project documentation: glossary of terms, list of acronyms, and system overview. Make a case for the architecture documentation package including its own version of these things, separate from the overall project set.

4. Imagine the sample documentation given in Appendix A was online. Mark all the places where hypertext links would make using the documentation easier.

10.7 For Further Reading

You can read more about active design reviews in [Clements+ 01] and [ParnasWeiss 85]. You can read more about global analysis in [Hofmeister+ 00].

Other Views and Beyond

The word architecture goes back through Latin to the Greek for "master builder." The ancients not only invented the word, they gave it its clearest and most comprehensive definition. According to Vitruvius—the Roman writer, whose *Ten Books on Architecture* is the only surviving ancient architectural treatise—architecture, is the union of "firmness, commodity, and delight"; it is, in other words, at once a structural, practical, and visual art. Without solidity, it is dangerous; without usefulness, it is merely large-scale sculpture; and without beauty…it is not more than utilitarian construction.

—Marvin Tachtenberg and Isabelle Hyman, *Architecture: From Prehistory to Post-Modernism/The Western Tradition* (Prentice-Hall, 1986, p. 41)

11.1 Overview

This book has presented guidance for assembling a package of effective, usable architecture documentation. We have offered a selection of viewtypes and styles that should fulfill the needs of most software architects and architectures and have shown how to document a wide range of architecture-centric information: from behavior to interfaces to rationale. The book stands on its own as a complete handbook for documentation.

But the book does not exist in a vacuum. Other writers, on their own or under the auspices of large organizations, have prescribed specific viewsets or other approaches for architecture. The IEEE has a standard for architecture documentation. Many people are writing about how to document an "enterprise architecture." It may not be clear whether the advice in this book is in concert or in conflict with these other sources. In some cases, it isn't clear whether there's a relationship at all.

Suppose, for example, that you're mandated to follow the precepts of the Rational Unified Process, with its five-view prescription. Or suppose that you think that the Siemens Four

Views approach is the way to go. Or perhaps you work for a part of the U.S. government, which mandates adherence to the C4ISR architectural framework. Or you want to make sure that your products are compliant with ANSI/IEEE-1471-2000, the recent standard on architecture documentation. Or it's your lot to write down your organization's enterprise architecture. Can you use the prescriptions in this book and still meet your goals?

This chapter takes a tour of some significant related work in the field, with an eye toward reconciling our advice with their advice. We cover

- Rational Unified Process/Kruchten 4+1
- UML
- Siemens Four Views
- C4ISR architecture framework
- ANSI/IEEE-1471-2000 for architecture documentation
- Data flow and control flow views
- RM-ODP

Additionally, some topics are related to documentation but are not part of it. We discuss a few of these in Section 11.9, where we consider

- Architecture description languages
- Commercial components
- Hypertext documentation
- Configuration management

11.2   Rational Unified Process/Kruchten 4+1

The Rational Unified Process (RUP) introduces a five-view approach to documenting software architectures, based on Kruchten's 4+1 approach.

- The use case view contains use cases and scenarios of architecturally significant behavior.
- The logical view contains the most important design classes.
- The implementation view captures the architectural decisions made for the implementation.
- The process view contains the description of the tasks—processes and threads—involved.
- The deployment view contains the description of the various physical nodes for the most typical platform configurations.

The RUP describes the *use case view* as representation of an architecturally significant subset of the use case model, which documents the system's intended functions and its environment. The use case view serves as a contract between the customer and the developers and represents an essential input to activities in analysis, design, and test.

Use cases are a vehicle for describing behavior, and behavior is a part of every view's supporting documentation. Consequently, you can document use cases as a behavior description of the system or parts of it. Table 11.1 shows the correspondence of terminology.

> **FOR MORE INFORMATION**
>
> See Chapter 8 for further discussion of behavior. See Chapter 10 for including behavior in supporting documentation.

Table 11.1: Rational Unified Process use case view

	Rational Unified Process Term	Our Term
Elements	Use case package	
	Actors	Actors
	Use cases	Use cases
Relations	Include	Include
	Extend	Extend
	Generalize	Generalize

Documenting a *logical view* of the RUP can be done by using the module or the C&C viewtype. A union of the module decomposition style, the module uses style, and the module generalization style allows you to represent the structural part of the logical view by using such elements as subsystems and classes, whereas a C&C viewtype allows you to represent the runtime aspects by using components and ports. Table 11.2 shows the correspondence of terminology.

> **FOR MORE INFORMATION**
>
> See Chapter 2 for further discussion of module styles and Chapter 3 for further discussion of the C&C viewtype.

Table 11.2: Rational Unified Process logical view

	Rational Unified Process Term	Our Term
Elements	Design packages	
	Design subsystems	Module
	Class	Module, Class
	Interface	Interface
	Capsule	Component
	Port	Port
	Protocol	Connector

Table 11.2: Rational Unified Process logical view (continued)

	Rational Unified Process Term	Our Term
Relations	Association	Uses
	Generalization	Generalization
	Owns	Decomposition

FOR MORE INFORMATION

See Section 6.3 for further information on combining views.

An implementation view can be represented by using a combination of the module decomposition style, the module uses style, and the module generalization style. The *implementation view* represents implementation elements, such as implementation subsystems and components. The RUP distinguishes between a design and an implementation model to separate general design aspects from implementation aspects introduced by the use of a specific programing language. To describe the relationships between elements of the design model and the implementation model, the mapping should be documented. Table 11.3 shows the correspondence of terminology.

Table 11.3: Rational Unified Process implementation view

	Rational Unified Process Term	Our Term
Elements	Implementation subsystems	Module
	Components	Module
Relations	Association	Uses
	Generalization	Generalization
	Owns	Decomposition

The RUP *process view* provides a basis for understanding the process organization of a system, illustrating the decomposition of a system into processes and threads and perhaps also showing the interactions among processes. The process view also includes the mapping of classes and subsystems onto processes and threads.

FOR MORE INFORMATION

The communicating-processes style is described in Section 4.6.

The communicating-processes style of the component-and-connector viewtype can be used to represent a process view. To accommodate the process view, define a style that uses the components as defined in the communicating-processes style—task, process, thread—and connectors that are based on the communication connector but are refined into more specific connectors, such as broadcast or remote procedure call. Table 11.4 shows the correspondence of terminology. To describe the relationships between processes and elements, such as subsystems and classes, the mapping among them should be documented.

Table 11.4: Rational Unified Process process view

	Rational Unified Process Term	Our Term
Components	Classes stereo-typed as process and/or threads	Concurrent units: task, process, thread
Connectors	Message/broadcast/RPC	Communication

A RUP *deployment view* describes one or more physical network—hardware—configurations on which the software is deployed and runs. This view also describes the allocation of processes and threads—from the RUP process view—to the physical nodes. The deployment style of the allocation viewtype is a good match for the RUP deployment view. Table 11.5 shows the correspondence in terminology.

FOR MORE INFORMATION
The deployment style is described in Section 5.3.

Table 11.5: Rational Unified Process deployment view

	Rational Unified Process Term	Our Term
Software components	Process/thread Deployment unit	Software element: process and/or thread from C&C viewtype
Environment components	Nodes/devices/connectors	Environmental element: processor, network
Relations	Communication channel	Communication
	Executes on	Allocated to

The RUP deployment view also allows you to assign deployment units to nodes. A deployment unit consists of a build—an executable—documents, and installation artifacts. It is a packaging of implementation elements for selling and/or downloading purposes. This is not part of architectural documentation and therefore is not mentioned in this book. Nevertheless, you can define a style of the module viewtype, showing implementation elements—subsystems/classes—and how they are packaged as deployment units.

The following list reconciles the prescribed Rational Unified Process views with our advice in this book:

To Achieve This RUP View	Use This Approach
Use case view	Adopt use cases to specify behavior, either associated with any of the views or as part of the documentation beyond views
Logical view	Use a module-based style that shows generalization, uses, and decomposition
Implementation view	Use a module-based style that contains implementation elements
Process view	Use the communicating-processes style of the C&C viewtype
Deployment view	Use the deployment style of the allocation viewtype

Furthermore, RUP does not preclude using additional views that may be useful, and so you are free to choose any others that can play a helpful role in your project.

Beyond its five views, RUP does not prescribe other kinds of documentation, such as interface specifications, rationale, or behavior of ensembles. It doesn't call for a view catalog, a mapping between views, view templates, or style guides. But it certainly does not rule these things out, either.

If you've chosen to follow RUP, you can certainly document the five suggested views, using viewtypes and styles in this book. But don't stop there. You are also free to consider additional views that may be important in your project's context, and you should do so. You should also augment the primary presentation of each view with the supporting documentation called for in Section 10.2, and you should complete the package by writing the documentation that applies beyond views, as described in Section 10.3. The result will be an RUP-compliant set of documentation having the necessary supporting information to complete the package.

11.3   UML

Up to now, we've shown how UML can be used to represent the concepts presented in this book. Here we present a summary that maps in the other direction.

Although UML was not developed for modeling software architectures, constructs have been added that are useful when documenting software architectures. This section gives a brief overview of diagrams defined within UML v1.4, the important elements and relations they contain, and how they relate to what we describe in this book.

11.3.1   Class and Object Diagrams

In the category of "static structure diagrams," UML offers two diagram types: the class diagram and the object diagram.

- A class diagram contains primarily classes and their variants, such as metaclass, parameterized class, utility, and so on. It can also contain structuring elements, such as model, subsystem, and package. UML defines generalization, association, and dependency as relations between classes, as well as containment and dependency among packages, subsystems, and models. Interfaces for classes and subsystems are also defined.

- An object diagram is an instance of a class diagram, showing a snapshot of the detailed state of a system at a point in time. UML defines that class diagrams can contain instances, and so it is possible to create object diagrams by using class diagrams.

UML class diagrams can be used in the module view. The following list reconciles UML class diagrams with our advice in this book.

UML Class Diagram Elements	Map to
Class diagram	A hybrid style that combines the decomposition, uses, and generalization styles of the module viewtype
Class and its variants	Specialized modules
Interface	Syntactic part of an interface: signature
Subsystem	A specialized module

Model	A complete view for a specific stakeholder
Package	Used to combine information about parts of a system-inclusive cartoon and supporting documentation, it maps to a view packet
Generalization and its variants	Generalization relation
Association and its variants	Uses and decomposition relations
Dependency and its variants	Depends-on relation
Instance	Requires the definition of a new style of the module viewtype, whereby an instance would be a specialized module

11.3.2 Component Diagrams

Component diagrams show the dependencies among software components, including the classifiers that specify them—for example, implementation classes—and the artifacts that implement them, such as source code files, binary code files, executable files, and scripts. Therefore, a component diagram can be seen as a hybrid style composed of the module viewtype and the implementation style of the allocation viewtype. The module viewtype part defines the components with their dependencies and the classifiers that define them, whereas the implementation style part defines the artifacts that implement the components. The following list reconciles UML component diagrams with our advice in this book.

UML Component Diagram Elements	Map to
Component diagram	A hybrid style that combines the module viewtype and the implementation style of the allocation viewtype
Component	Module
Classifier	Module

Artifact	Environmental element
Dependency (relationship between components)	Depends-on relation
Reside (relationship between classifier and component)	Is-part-of relation
Implement (relationship between component and artifact)	Allocated-to relation

11.3.3 Deployment Diagrams

Deployment diagrams show the configuration of runtime processing elements and the software components, processes, and objects that execute on them. Software component instances represent runtime manifestations of software code units. This definition maps well to the definition of the deployment style of the allocation viewtype, in which the software elements are either components or processes of the component-and-connector viewtype. The following list reconciles UML deployment diagrams with our advice in this book:

UML Deployment Diagram Elements	Map to
Deployment diagram	Deployment style of the allocation viewtype
Component	Component of the C&C viewtype
Process	Communicating-processes style of the C&C viewtype
Node	Environmental element (computational unit)
Communication	Environmental element (network)
Deploy (relationship between component and node)	Allocated-to relation
Become (migration from one node to another)	Migrates-to relation

11.3.4 Behavioral Diagrams

UML offers a wide variety of notations to model system behavior. Most of them are mentioned in Chapter 8 in this book. Table 11.6 summarizes those UML diagrams.

Table 11.6: UML behavioral diagrams

UML Diagram	Definition
Use case diagram	Shows actors and use cases together with their relationships. The use cases represent functionality of a system or parts of it, as manifested to external interactors with the system or the classifier.
Sequence diagram	Shows the explicit sequence of communications and is good for real-time specifications and for complex scenarios.
Collaboration diagram	Shows an interaction organized around the roles in the interaction and their relationships.
Statechart diagram	Represents the behavior of entities capable of dynamic behavior by specifying its response to the receipt of event instances.
Activity diagram	Shows workflow, in which the states represent the performance of actions or subactivities, and the transitions are triggered by the completion of the actions or subactivities.

11.4 Siemens Four Views

The Siemens approach uses four views to document an architecture. The four views and their associated design tasks are shown in Figure 11.1. The first task for each view is global analysis. The second and third groups of tasks are the central and final design tasks, which define the elements of the architecture view, the relationships among them, and important properties.

11.4.1 Global Analysis

In global analysis, you identify the factors that influence the architecture and analyze them to derive strategies for designing the architecture. This provides supporting documentation that captures the analysis of the factors that influence the architecture and the rationale for why the design decisions reflected in the view were made.

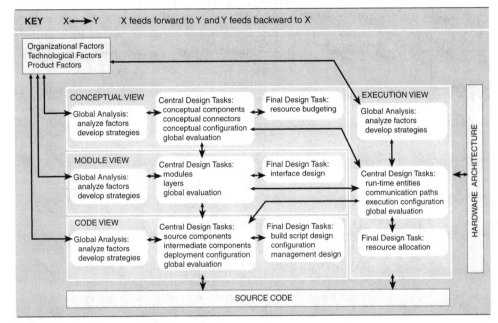

KEY   X◄──►Y   X feeds forward to Y and Y feeds backward to X

Figure 11.1
The Siemens Four Views approach to software architecture
(Adapted from Hofmeister, Nord, and Soni 2000, p. 20)

11.4.2   Conceptual Architecture View

The conceptual architecture view explains how the system's functionality is mapped to components and connectors. This view is closest to the application domain because it is the least constrained by the software and hardware platforms. Documenting the conceptual architecture view can be done by using the C&C viewtype. There is a close correspondence between the Siemens terminology and our terminology (see Table 11.7).

Table 11.7: Siemens Four Views conceptual architecture view

	Siemens Four Views	**Our Term**
Elements	CComponent	Component
	CPort	Port
	CConnector	Connector
	CRole	Role

Table 11.7: Siemens Four Views conceptual architecture view (continued)

	Siemens Four Views	Our Term
	Protocol	Protocol
Relations	Composition	Decomposition
	Cbinding	Binding
	Cconnection	Attachment
	Obeys, obeys congugate	Element property

11.4.3 Module Architecture View

The module architecture view explains how the components, connectors, ports, and roles are mapped to abstract modules and their interfaces. The system is decomposed into modules and subsystems. A module can also be assigned to a layer, which then constrains its dependencies on other modules.

Documenting the module architecture view can be done by using the module viewtype. There is a close correspondence between the Siemens terminology and our terminology. To describe the relationships between elements of the conceptual view and the module view, the mapping, as discussed in Section 6.3, should be documented. See Table 11.8.

Table 11.8: Siemens Four Views module architecture view

	Siemens Four Views	Our Term
Elements	Module	Module
	Interface	Interface
	Subsystem	Subsystem
	Layer	Layer
Relations	Contain	Aggregation
	Composition	Decomposition
	Use	Uses, allowed to use
	Require, provide	Element property
	Implement (module: conceptual element)	Cross-view mapping
	Assigned to (module: layer)	Property of a layer

11.4.4 Execution Architecture View

The execution architecture view explains how the system's functionality is mapped to runtime platform elements, such as processes and shared libraries. Platform elements consume platform resources that are assigned to a hardware resource.

Documenting the execution architecture view can be done by using the communicating-processes style of the C&C viewtype and the deployment style of the allocation viewtype. To describe an execution configuration in the execution architecture view, start with the components in the communicating-processes style—task, process, thread—and connectors, based on the communication connector. Add or refine existing component types for runtime entities: queue, shared memory, DLL, socket, file, and shared library. The communication connector is extended to include a *use-mechanism* relation to possible communication mechanisms, such as IPC, RPC, or DCOM. Use the deployment style as a guide to describe the execution configuration mapped to hardware devices. To describe the relationships between elements of the module view and the execution view, the mapping, as discussed in Section 6.3, should be documented. See Table 11.9.

Table 11.9: Siemens Four Views execution architecture view

	Siemens Four Views	Our Term
Elements	Runtime entity	Concurrent units: task, process, thread
	Communication path	Communication: data exchange, control
Relations	Use mechanism	
	Communicate over	Attachment relation
	Assigned to (module: runtime entity)	Cross-view mapping

11.4.5 Code Architecture View

The code architecture view explains how the software implementing the system is organized into source and deployment components. Documenting the code architecture view can be done by using the implementation style of the allocation viewtype. To describe the code architecture view, start with the packaging units, such as files and directories, in the implementation style to describe the source components and their allocation in the development environment. You will need to create new styles in the module and allocation viewtypes for describing the other elements for intermediate and deployment components, their relations, and how they are organized and packaged in the development environment. To describe the relationships between elements of the execution view and the executable elements in the code view, the mapping, as discussed in Section 6.3, should be documented.

11.4.6 Summary

If you wish to use views prescribed by the Siemens Four Views approach, you can do so as shown in the following list:

To Achieve This Siemens Four Views View	Use This Approach
Conceptual architecture	One or more styles in the C&C viewtype
Module architecture	One or more styles in the module viewtype
Execution architecture	Deployment style in the allocation viewtype; for processes, communicating-processes style in the C&C viewtype
Code architecture	Implementation style in the allocation viewtype

Like RUP, the Siemens Four Views approach does not preclude additional information, and so you are free to—and should—consider what other views may be helpful to your project. And, as with RUP, these views form the kernel of the architecture only; you should complete the package by adding the supporting documentation for each view and the documentation beyond views, as discussed in Chapter 10.

11.5   C4ISR Architecture Framework

The U.S. Department of Defense (DoD) has defined a framework for architecture development, presentation, and integration to be used across the military services and defense agencies. This framework defines a coordinated approach for the Command, Control, Computers, Communication, Intelligence, Surveillance, and Reconnaissance (C4ISR) military domains. The intent of the C4ISR Architecture Framework is to promote interoperable, integrated, and cost-effective computer-based systems within and across DoD organizations. This framework is becoming the required method for the description of information systems within the DoD and is also being adopted and mandated by several other U.S. government agencies.

The motivation for the development of this framework was the lack of a common approach for architecture development and use within the DoD. The architectures being developed by the various DoD organizations differ significantly in content and format, leading to the development of fielded products that are not interoperable. These differences also prohibit useful comparisons and contrasts when analyzing the various architectures. The C4ISR Architecture Framework is intended to provide a common lingua franca for the various DoD commands, services, and agencies to describe their diverse architectures. This is intended to help with cross-system analysis and fielded-system interoperability.

The framework differentiates between an architecture description and an architecture implementation. An architecture description is a representation of the parts, what those parts do, how they relate to one another, and under what rules and constraints. The C4ISR framework is concerned only with this representation, not the implementation in the field. This is the major difference between the C4ISR framework and the thrust of this book.

The C4ISR Architecture Framework has the following main components:

- Definition of common architectural views
- Guidance for developing the architecture
- Definition of common products
- Relevant reference resources

Our interest here is in the common views prescribed by the framework.

11.5.1 Common Architectural Views of the C4ISR Framework

The C4ISR Architecture Framework defines three views: operational, system, and technical. The C4ISR Framework does not map directly to our views. The C4ISR views can be summarized as follows:

- The *operational architecture* view is a description of the tasks and activities, operational elements, and information flows required to accomplish or to support operations. This view defines the types of information exchanged, the frequency of exchange, the tasks and activities supported by the information exchanges, and the nature of the information exchanges in enough detail to ascertain the relevant interoperability requirements.

* The *systems architecture* view is a description of systems and interconnections providing for and supporting the relevant requirements. This view associates physical resources and their performance attributes to the operational view and its requirements according to criteria defined in the technical architecture.

* The *technical architecture* view is a minimal set of rules governing the arrangements, interaction, and interdependence of system parts. This view articulates the criteria that describe compliant implementations of the various system capabilities.

To be consistent and integrated, an architecture description must provide explicit linkages among its views. This linkage is provided by the framework products.

11.5.2 Common Products

All the necessary C4ISR architecture representation products are defined by the framework, which contains detailed descriptions of the product types that must be used to describe operational, systems, and technical architecture views. In many cases, representation formats, product templates, and examples are also provided. The architecture products to be developed are classified into two categories.

* *Essential products* are the minimal set of products required to develop architectures that can be commonly understood and integrated within and across DoD organizational boundaries and between DoD and multinational elements. These products must be developed for all architectures.

* *Supporting products* provide data that will be needed for the particular purpose and objectives of a specific architectural effort. Appropriate products from the supporting product set will be developed on the basis of the purpose and objectives of the architecture.

Tables 11.10 and 11.11 summarize the essential and supporting products, respectively, defined by the C4ISR Architecture Framework. It must be said that C4ISR, for all its attention to architecture, in fact is directed almost exclusively to documenting *system* architecture. None of its three views

Table 11.10: C4ISR architecture framework essential products

Architecture Product	C4ISR Architecture View
Overview and Summary Information	All views
Integrated Dictionary	All views
High-Level Operational Concept Graphic	Operational
Operational Node Connectivity Description	Operational
Operational Information Exchange Matrix	Operational
System Interface Description	Systems
Technical Architecture Profile	Technical

Table 11.11: C4ISR architecture framework supporting products

Architecture Product	C4ISR Architecture View
Command Relationships Chart	Operational
Activity Model	Operational
Operational Activity Sequence and Timing Descriptions	Operational
Operational Activity Sequence and Timing Descriptions—Operational State Transition Description	Operational
Operational Activity Sequence and Timing Descriptions—Operational Event/ Trace Description	Operational
Logical Data Model	Operational
Systems Communications Description	Systems
Systems^2 Matrix	Systems
Systems Functionality Description	Systems
Operational Activity to System Function Traceability Matrix	Systems
System Information Exchange Matrix	Systems
System Performance Parameters Matrix	Systems
System Evolution Description	Systems
System Technology Forecast	Systems

Table 11.11: C4ISR architecture framework supporting products (continued)

Architecture Product	C4ISR Architecture View
System Activity Sequence and Timing Descriptions	Systems
Systems Activity Sequence and Timing Descriptions—Systems Rules Model	Systems
Systems Activity Sequence and Timing Descriptions—Systems State Transition Description	Systems
Systems Activity Sequence and Timing Descriptions—Systems Event/Trace Description	Systems
Physical Data Model	Systems
Standards Technology Forecast	Technical

and none of its essential or supporting products prescribe anything that remotely resembles *software* architecture. The operational architecture speaks in terms of user-visible operations. The system architecture addresses how those operations are carried out on physical resources, that is, hardware. And the technical architecture imposes rules and constraints, which in practice has come to mean the selection of a set of interface standards and nothing more. Nowhere is the software for the system described in terms of its structure or the behavior and interrelationships of the elements of that structure.

That said, however, if you're mandated to use C4ISR, you do have options at your disposal. The first is to recognize the difference between software and system architecture and to recognize that a software-intensive system needs documentation for both. Render unto C4ISR what is C4ISR's, and provide documentation for the software architecture, using the guidance of this book, separately. The second option is to work the documentation for the software architecture into the framework prescribed by C4ISR. This is plan B, for sure, but serves when management, having been told to adopt C4ISR, balks at learning that something separate is needed for the software aspects.

- Include system-level behavior documentation as part of the C4ISR operational architecture view, concentrating on use cases that depict information exchange. Include this documentation in the "operational activity sequence and timing descriptions" products.

- Include element-level behavior documentation as part of the C4ISR systems architecture view. Include this documentation in the "systems activity sequence and timing descriptions" products.

- Include views belonging to the allocation viewtype as part of the C4ISR system architecture view, where "physical resources" are documented.

- Include views belonging to the module and C&C viewtypes as part of the C4ISR technical architecture view, appealing to it as the repository of "rules governing the arrangements, interaction, and interdependence of system parts" and "the criteria that describe compliant implementations."

- For the information contained in the beyond views part of the documentation, C4ISR provides slots for overview and summary information and a dictionary. Use the former to hold the documentation roadmap, the view template, the system overview, and systemwide rationale. The latter can be home to the mapping between views, the element directory, and the glossary.

11.6 ANSI/IEEE-1471-2000

ANSI/IEEE-1471-2000, or simply 1471, is the IEEE Recommended Practice for Architectural Description of Software-Intensive Systems. This standard (IEEE 2000a) was developed by an IEEE working group and draws on experience from industry, academia, and other standards bodies. The recommendations of 1471 center on two key ideas: a conceptual framework for architectural description and a statement of what information must be found in any 1471-compliant architectural description.

The conceptual framework described in the standard ties together such concepts as system, architectural description, and view. Figure 11.2 summarizes a portion of this framework in UML.

In 1471, as in our work, views have a central role in documenting software architecture. In the standard, each view is "a representation of a whole system from the perspective of a related set of concerns." The architectural description of a system includes one or more views.

In this framework, a view conforms to a viewpoint. A viewpoint is "a pattern or template from which to develop individual views by establishing the purposes and audience for a view

Figure 11.2
Conceptual framework of
ANSI/IEEE-1471-2000.
Each box represents a concept, and each line represents an association
between two concepts.
Each association has two
roles—one in each direc-
tion—although both are not
always depicted. The role
from A to B is depicted
closest to B. Multiplicity is
optional in this diagram;
where identified, it follows
the UML convention,
whereby 1 means one and
1..* means one or more.
Stakeholders play a key
role; views conform to
viewpoints, which cover
stakeholder concerns.

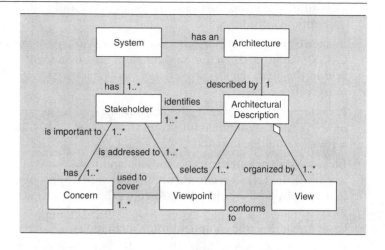

and the techniques for its creation and analysis." This is very
nearly the same as our idea of how a view corresponds to a
viewtype.

In 1471, the emphasis is on what drives the perspective of a
view or a viewpoint. Viewpoints are defined with specific stakeholder concerns in mind, and the definition of a viewpoint
includes a description of any associated analysis techniques.
These techniques are meant to produce results that help
address the specified stakeholder concerns. We certainly agree
with 1471 on this point. A fundamental principle about documentation appearing in the Prologue is that what one should
document about a system depends entirely on to what uses
one expects the documentation to be put. The documentation
roadmap prescribed in Chapter 10 is written precisely to facilitate stakeholder navigation and use.

However, our focus has been to document those viewtypes
that we've found in common use and that can be used to
address a large number of concerns. We've documented a
number of specific viewtypes and provided examples of their
use in producing views. Although 1471 does include a few
example viewpoints, each is described only briefly, and no
example views are provided. This simply reflects a difference
in the scope and goals of the two works. However, both works
do recognize, if not encourage, the definition of new viewtypes, or viewpoints, to meet specific needs.

Beyond its conceptual framework, 1471 defines what information should be found in any architectural description.
Table 11.12 summarizes the information required by the 1471
standard and how we address each in this book.

Table 11.12: 1471 information requirements and how we address them

General Requirement	How We Address This Requirement
Identification and overview information, including summary, context, glossary, references, and change history.	Several items in this category amount to good bookkeeping. Context is addressed in the context diagrams; the other items are prescribed in the standard organizations of Chapter 10.
Stakeholders and concerns. The standard lists minimum examples that must be addressed for both stakeholders and concerns.	The documentation roadmap called for in Section 10.3.1 captures information about stakeholders and their concerns—specifically, how they will use the documentation package.
Viewpoints. For each viewpoint, the following must be specified: • Stakeholders addressed by the viewpoint • Concerns addressed by the viewpoint • Language, modeling techniques, or analytical techniques to be used • Rationale for selection of the viewpoint *Any additional information,* such as completeness and correctness checks, evaluation criteria, heuristics, or guidelines may be included.	We define several commonly used viewtypes and styles of those viewtypes. Each defines the concepts—elements, relations, and properties—that should be used in documenting a system in accordance with the viewtype. Each also contains a section noting what it's for and not for, which should help users in deciding what concerns will be addressed by the viewtype. Chapter 9 provides additional guidance on how to decide which viewtypes to use, including information about stakeholders and concerns.
Views. Each view includes a representation of the system in accordance with the requirements of its viewpoint.	Chapter 10 discusses the information that should be documented for a view.
A record of all inconsistencies among views, preferably accompanied by an analysis of consistency among all views.	In Chapter 6, we discuss techniques for documenting relationships among views, which is then recorded in the "documentation beyond views" part of the package as detailed in Chapter 10.
Rationale for the architectural concepts selected, preferably accompanied by evidence of alternatives considered and rationale for the choices made.	Reserved spots for rationale are provided in each view, in the documentation beyond views, and in interface specifications.

11.7   Data Flow and Control Flow

For years, data flow and control flow were seen as the primary means to document a software system. Although modern software architecture principles have evolved into the more general study of structures and behavior, these two venerable aspects of software—data and control—rule the day in a few pockets of practice. How do they relate to what we would call a more holistic architecture documentation package?

11.7.1 Data Flow Views

Data flow views of a system are exemplified by data flow diagrams (DFDs), a concept made famous by the structured analysis methods of the 1970s. If your intent is to represent data flows as described earlier, you should choose a style in the C&C viewtype. This viewtype lets you define components for data processing and for data stores. A connector in a C&C view describes an interaction or a protocol between components but usually not the data that flows across the connector. Therefore, to represent data flow diagrams, define a C&C style in which components are procedures—processes—and/or data stores, and the connector is a "data exchange" connector with the additional property of names of data flows. Table 11.13 shows how to represent data flow diagrams in the C&C viewtype.

Table 11.13: Representing data flow diagrams by using the C&C viewtype

	Data Flow Diagram Term	Our Term
Components	Procedure	Component: functionality
	Data store	Component: data store
Connectors	Data exchange	Communication + data flow name

You may also want to describe data flow aspects of modules represented in a style of the module viewtype. To document data type dependencies, you can show which modules are producers or consumers of a specific data type. Representing data flow in a module viewtype is done by defining a style specializing the *depends-on* relation into a *sends-data-to* relation. In case it is of interest, data stores can be defined as a specialized type of module. Table 11.14 shows how to represent data flow diagrams in the module viewtype.

Table 11.14: Representing data flow diagrams by using the module viewtype

	Data Flow Diagram Term	Our Term
Element	Procedure	Module
	Data store	Specialized module as data store
Relation	Data flow	*Sends-data-to,* specialized from depends-on

The allocation viewtype also has the potential to document data flow aspects, especially if analyzing network or storage capacities is important. Such a diagram would represent how much information flows at a time over a network connection or how many megabytes are required for either persistent or temporary storage. Table 11.15 shows how to represent data flow diagrams in the allocation viewtype.

Table 11.15: Representing data flow diagrams by using the allocation viewtype

	Data Flow Diagram Term	Our Term
Software element	Procedure	Process
	Data store	Specialized module as data store
Environmental element	Processor	Physical unit: data store
	Data storage	Physical unit: processor
Relation	Data flow	*Sends-data-to*
	Communication channel	Communication

Finally, note that DFDs don't make the strong distinction among modules, components, and hardware platforms that more modern treatments of architecture do. So if your goal is to reproduce the classic data flow diagrams of structured-analysis fame, you may have to define a hybrid style that combines the module, C&C, and allocation styles. Data dictionaries, a strong part of DFD method, have their counterpart in the element catalogs described in Chapter 10. P-specs, which are essentially pseudocode representations of the elements, can be captured as behavioral information in our world.

If you are a diehard member of the DFD community, take comfort in the fact that you can achieve your goals with the methods of this book. But heed the advice given for the other documentation approaches in this chapter: Augment your favorite with other useful views; then complete the package by adding supporting documentation and beyond view documentation.

11.7.2   Control Flow Views

Whereas a data flow diagram portrays a system from the point of view of the data, a control flow graph, such as a flowchart, portrays the functionality that performs transformation on the data. In Chapter 8, we introduced several modeling languages, some of which have flowchartlike control symbols, such as decisions and loops. Therefore, if flowcharts are part of your system documentation and you are looking for a place to put them in a documentation package prescribed, you can regard them as a form of behavioral documentation and use them in conjunction with any viewtype. In some cases—for example, to support performance analysis or to build in an aid for later debugging—a control flow notation in the primary presentation of a view might be of interest.

In a C&C style, the use of a specific connector defines a control flow, or interaction, between the connected components. (See Table 11.16.) In a module viewtype, control flows would be represented as a uses relation specialized into a *transfers-control* relation. (See Table 11.17.) In a deployment viewtype, the change of control in the execution environment can be represented. Performance, security, and availability analyses that include the execution platform rely on understanding the flow of control within the system. (See Table 11.18.)

Thus, classic flowcharts, which detail the behavior of programs, can be used as a way to specify the behavior of elements, although many other, more suitable languages are available to do that. At coarser levels of granularity, however, it might make sense to show control flow among architectural elements as a view in its own right, but be clear on the expected use of such a view. Views based on other styles might do the same job and convey richer information as well.

> The flow chart is a most thoroughly oversold piece of program documentation.... The detailed blow-by-blow flow chart...is an absolute nuisance, suitable only for initiating beginners into algorithmic thinking.
>
> —(F. P. Brooks 1995, p. 167)

Table 11.16: Representing control flow diagrams by using the C&C viewtype

	Control Flow Diagram Term	Our Term
Components	Procedure	Component: process
Connectors	Control flow	Connector

Table 11.17: Representing control flow diagrams by using the module viewtype

	Control Flow Diagram Term	Our Term
Element	Procedure: process	Module
Relation	Control flow	*Transfers-control-to* specialized from uses

Table 11.18: Representing control flow diagrams by using the allocation viewtype

	Control Flow Diagram Term	Our Term
Software element	Procedure: process	Process
Environmental element		Physical unit
Relation	Control flow	Communication specialized to control flow

You're All Just Guessing!

The following humorous but sobering Socratic dialogue written by Michael Jackson (Addison-Wesley, 1995, pp. 42–47) reveals the confusion that happens when users of a documentation method—data flow diagrams in this case—are too loose with the definitions of terms used and the underlying semantics implied. Most of the miscommunication and unintended misdirection come from participants' lack of common understanding of the definitions of the important terms used. Each participant has a separate understanding of what the fundamental terms mean. Additionally, DFDs are bereft of any formal mechanisms that allow the designer to record unambiguous semantic information. Although a common and accepted data dictionary, as recommended by DFD advocates, would go a long way to alleviate many of the problems illustrated in this example, DFDs still do not have the semantic rigor to do more than present a simplistic view of a system.

This example might appear to be contrived, but these lessons generalize. We too have experienced situations in many different settings and with many different representation techniques and methods. The DFD notation is not the only one that suffers from these problems and misuses.

They were all ready to start the walkthrough. Fred had been working on part of the sales accounting system: the problem of matching customers' payments to their outstanding invoices. He had produced a data flow diagram, and was going to walk through it with Ann and Bill. Jane was there too, because she was new to the team and didn't know about data flow diagrams. This was a good opportunity for her to learn about them. Fred had invited her, and the project manager said it was a good idea.

"The diagram I'm going to show you," said Fred, "expands a process bubble in the diagram at the next level up. Here's the bubble to be expanded." He showed this viewgraph on the overhead projector:

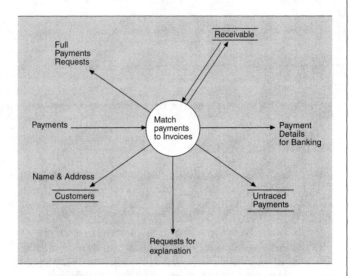

"The payments come in from customers—that's the arrow on the left. Basically, we have to send the payment details to the cashiers for banking—that's the arrow on the right—and put a payment record into the Receivables file on the top right. To do that, we must match the payments with invoices that we get from the Receivables file. If we can't match a payment we put it into the Untraced Payments file, and someone else deals with it. If the payment is not enough to cover the amount in the invoice we send the customer a request to pay in full—that's up at the top left. Oh, and we also send them requests to explain untraced payments. OK so far?"

"I suppose you need the Customer file so you can put names and addresses on the payment and explanation requests," said Ann.

"Right," said Fred. "Now here's the diagram I've done that expands the process bubble." He put another viewgraph on the projector. It was this:

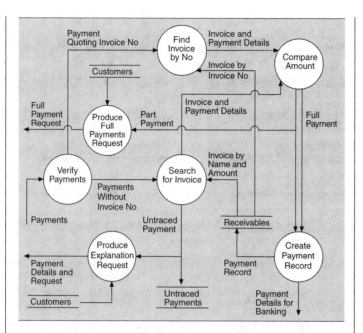

"Looks good," said Bill. "Let me see if I can walk through it. The Verify Payments process checks to see whether a payment has an invoice number. If it has, you find the invoice—that's the Find Invoice by No process at the top of the diagram—and send it with the payment to the Compare Amount process. If it hasn't, you have to search for the invoice by using the customer's name and the amount of the payment. If that doesn't work you have an untraced payment. Otherwise, you send the invoice and payment details to the Compare Amount process as before. Am I on the right lines?"

"Absolutely," said Fred. "Right on."

"The Compare Amount process checks the amount paid against the invoice, and whether it's a full or a part payment you send the details to the cashier for banking and put a payment record in the Receivables file. If it's a part payment you also produce a full payment request. Am I right, or am I right?"

"Terrific," said Fred. "You just forgot to say that untraced payments go to the Produce Explanation Request process so we can send a request to the customer."

"Sounds good to me," said Ann. "We could have an early lunch."

"Well, wait a minute," said Jane. "I haven't really understood what's going on. You said that Verify Payments sends each payment either to Find Invoice by No, or to Search for Invoice, depending on whether it has an invoice number or not. Where does it say that in the diagram?"

"Verify Payments has one input data flow and two out-puts," said Ann. "That's where it says it. It's just like the Search for Invoice process. That's got one input data flow of payments without invoice numbers, and two output flows, one for untraced payments, and one for payments with invoices."

"But the Create Payment Record process also has two output flows," said Jane, "one for payment records for the Receivables file, and one for payment details for the bank. But it sends each full or part payment to both of those, not just to one."

"Ann's a bit confused," said Bill. "A data flow diagram doesn't show whether a process writes to one or more of its output flows for each input message. That's at a lower level, probably in the process specification. It's a top-down technique."

"I'm not at all confused," said Ann. "It just depends on your conventions. And I know about top-down as well as you do."

"All right," said Jane. "So we're using Bill's convention. So how do you know that Verify Payments never writes on both its output data flows?"

"That's a funny question," said Fred. "It's obvious, because one flow is named Payment Quoting Invoice No and the other one is Payment Without Invoice No. You have to read the names. Names are very important in systems analysis."

"I am reading the names," said Jane, "and I don't understand them at all. For example, does 'Full Pay-ment' mean the exactly right amount has been paid, or does it include overpayments? And does 'Invoice and Payment Details' mean exactly one invoice and one payment? Don't customers sometimes send one pay-ment to cover more than one invoice? And they could send two checks to cover one invoice, I suppose, as well, couldn't they? And then, what's this Search for Invoice process doing? Suppose there are two invoices for the customer, both with the same amount as the payment? Or two invoices adding up to the amount of the payment? Does 'Search for Invoice' mean it's only searching for one invoice? Or suppose it finds just one invoice, but it's less than the payment? I don't see how you can work out from the diagram whether these are real possibilities, and, if so, what's supposed to happen when they turn up."

"Look, Bill's already said it's top-down," said Fred, "so you can't expect to answer all these detailed questions now. You'll have to come along to the next walkthrough when I'll have the next level of data flow diagrams for the more complicated processes here—probably for Search for Invoice and Compare Amount—and process specifications for the rest."

"But I don't think these are detailed questions," said Jane. "The problem is matching payments to invoices, and you're telling me that the diagram doesn't show whether the matching is one-to-one, one-to-many, many-to-one, or many-to-many. I'd have thought that was a fundamental question about a matching problem, not a detailed question. If the diagram doesn't show that, what does it show?"

"Well," said Bill, "it shows that the function of matching payments to invoices needs seven processes connected by the data flows you can see. That's what it shows."

"I don't understand," said Jane. "It seems to me that it just shows that Fred thinks that seven processes connected like that would be useful. But to find out what the function is, or what the processes are, we have to wait till the next level. So the diagram shows that Fred thinks seven processes would be good for the function, but we don't know what function and we don't know what processes. That can't be right, surely?"

"Hold on," said Fred. "We're going way off track here. The questions Jane is asking about the matching problem are all good questions, and the whole point of the data flow diagram is that it makes you think about the good questions—just like Jane is doing. She's got the idea pretty fast," he said, ingratiatingly. "That's what a walk-through's all about."

"Nice of you to say so," said Jane, "but I'm still lost. Suppose we do discuss and think about these questions, would we be able to show the answers in the diagram? From what everyone's been saying, we wouldn't be able to. We'd have to wait till the next level. But I don't see how you'd do it at the next level either. Until you get down to the process specifications you keep talking about. I suppose you could tell from them what it's all about, but if there are lots of levels you might have to wait a long time. The data flow diagrams in the levels above don't seem to be much use. They're just vague pictures suggesting what someone thinks might be the shape of a system to solve a problem, and no one's saying what the problem is."

"Jane, that's offensive," said Bill. "Everyone uses data flow diagrams here, and everyone knows that top-down is the right way to do things. There just isn't any other way. You have to start with the big picture and work your way down to the details."

"Perhaps," said Jane, "but the big picture isn't much use if it doesn't say anything you can understand. You're all just guessing what Fred's diagram means. It wouldn't mean anything at all to you if you didn't already have a pretty good idea of what the problem is and how to solve it."

They went to lunch after that. It was a rather uncomfortable lunch. After lunch Bill and Fred were walking together back to the office they shared. "I don't understand Jane," said Fred. "No," said Bill. "I don't think we should invite her to the next walkthrough, do you?"

—R. L.

11.8   RM-ODP

RM-ODP (Reference Model for Open Distributed Processing) is an ISO and ITU-T standard for documenting and designing a class of system sometimes referred to as "enterprise integration systems." These systems typically support the overall business processing needs of large corporations and include facilities for managing the business processes of an organization; handling its data storage, retrieval, and reporting needs; and enforcing its business policies. Such systems are typically realized as large, distributed, heterogeneous collections of programs, applications, and databases.

The RM-ODP standard specifies a set of five object-oriented "viewpoints" that are used to document such a system. Each of these viewpoints addresses a different set of concerns. The viewpoints are

- The *enterprise viewpoint* documents organizational requirements and structure, including domain objects, for example, bank tellers and accounts; communities, for example, a bank branch consisting of a bank manager and some tellers; and policies, for example, that money can be deposited only into an open account.

- The *information viewpoint* documents the information that is stored and manipulated by the system. This viewpoint is typically specified as a set of data "schemas" that prescribe the kinds of objects in the system and the relationships among them. For example, the information might specify the form and content of account and customer objects and indicate that each account must be associated with a customer via the "owns account" association.

- The *computational viewpoint* documents the behavior of objects and the interactions that occur among objects. This level of documentation identifies specific interfaces that the objects support. For example, a bank teller object might support deposit and withdrawal operations. Three types of interaction are allowed: operational: call-return, or client-server; stream-oriented: continuous streams of information flowing between producer and consumer objects; and signal oriented: low-level communication actions, such as "request" and "confirm."

- The *engineering viewpoint* documents the distribution-oriented aspects of a system, such as which object interactions are realized through distributed communications channels. This viewpoint is specified in terms of a prescribed vocabulary of concepts, such as clusters, which indicate which objects will be colocated on the same host; capsules or a set of clusters; and nodes, or physical computer systems.

- The *technology viewpoint* documents the implementation of the system in a form that aids system testing. This viewpoint is not well specified in RM-ODP.

In addition, RM-ODP identifies a set of common functions for managing a distributed processing system: checkpoint and recovery, process migration, transactions, groups and replication, and security.

Relating the RM-ODP viewpoints to the views and styles in this book, the informational viewpoint corresponds to a hybrid of our module viewtype styles. The computational viewpoint also is a module style, although at a more detailed level, as it defines the interfaces of each type of object. The engineering viewpoint corresponds most closely to our C&C views.

11.9 Where Architecture Documentation Ends

Early in this book, we examined the question of where architecture ends and nonarchitectural design begins. A related question is where architecture documentation ends and other documentation issues begin. Architects and architectures of all stripes exist. Data architectures, security architectures, enterprise architectures, reference architectures, installation architectures: The list is endless.

Some of the terms are clearly in scope. Reference architectures, for instance, appeared in our discussion of documenting variability, as the essence of a reference architecture is its ability to be tailored to the needs of any of a family of systems. Security architectures, although not addressed as such, are covered by making sure that a security specialist can find information of analytical use in one or more of the "normal" styles.

But some writers undoubtedly incorporate as architecture some aspects of system documentation that are outside the scope of this book. We completely agree with Boehm et al. (Boehm et al., p. 527) that architecture is not an island and should be related to other important system development documents; however, all the organizations, templates, and guidelines in this book were created to capture software and system architectures, which consist of the structure or structures of the system, which consist of software elements, the externally visible properties of those elements, and the relationships among them.

How does the guidance in this book relate to architectures that occupy outlying regions of the topic area? To the extent that these "architectures" depend on architectural structures as captured by styles and views, the principles in this book hold. But writing down system installation procedures, for example, is not architectural. Nevertheless, the principles for sound documentation extend well beyond the realm of "mainline" architectures. Involvement of stakeholders, letting the uses of documentation guide its contents, controlling repetition, using a standard organization, avoiding ambiguity: These and other principles form the foundation of a high-quality documentation task.

Many other topics in software engineering are related to documenting software architecture. Chief among them is the general topic of software architecture. Other topics that you want to be aware of but that are outside the scope of this book are architecture description languages, commercial components, hypertext documentation, and configuration management. In the remainder of this section, we give a glimpse at these topic areas and provide pointers for further study.

11.9.1 Architecture Description Languages

A large body of work is associated with the formal representation of software and system architectures. A number of researchers in industry and academia have proposed formal notations for representing and analyzing architectural designs.

Generically referred to as architecture description languages
(ADLs) or even architecture definition languages, these notations usually provide both a conceptual framework and a concrete syntax for characterizing software architectures. They
also typically provide tools for parsing, unparsing, displaying,
compiling, analyzing, or simulating architectural descriptions
written in their associated languages.

> **FOR MORE INFORMATION**
>
> ADLs are discussed in Section 4.7 and in Section 8.8.

While all these languages are concerned with architectural
design, each provides certain distinctive capabilities. Examples
of ADLs include

- **Acme** (Garlan, Monroe, and Wile 2000) supports the definition of new architectural styles.

- **Adage** (Coglianese and Szymanski 1993) supports the
  description of architectural frameworks for avionics navigation and guidance.

- **Aesop** (Garlan, Allen, and Ockerbloom 1994) supports the
  use of architectural styles.

- **Darwin** (Magee et al. 1995) supports the analysis of distributed message-passing systems.

- **MetaH** (Vestal 1998) provides guidance for designers of
  real-time avionics control software.

- **Rapide** (Luckham et al. 1995) allows architectural designs
  to be simulated, and has tools for analyzing the results of
  those simulations.

- **SADL** (Moriconi, Qian, and Riemenschneider 1995) provides a formal basis for architectural refinement.

- **UniCon** (Shaw et al. 1995) has a high-level compiler for architectural designs that support a mixture of heterogeneous component and connector types.

- **Wright** (Allen and Garlan 1997) supports the formal specification and analysis of interactions among architectural
  components.

No ADL provides the facilities to completely document a
software architecture, where "complete" is defined in the context of this book's prescriptions. But many ADLs provide
excellent means for discharging part of the architect's documentation obligation. Chapter 8, for instance, covered formal
notations for specifying behavior, and several ADLs could be
brought to bear in that regard. An ADL that provides a good
means to express rich structure could be used to help render
the views' primary presentations, with the added bonus that
analysis based on that ADL's capability would then be automatically placed on the fast track.

Besides their analytical powers, ADLs have the advantage of enforcing their formal models, making it more difficult to specify architectures that are internally inconsistent or ambiguous. Like all languages, however, this constraint can be helpful or painful, depending on how consistent that formal model is with your needs at the time.

11.9.2 Commercial Components

In recent years, software development using preexisting or purchased components has become commonplace. This trend has far-reaching effects, one of which is that systems are being composed of large-grained components over which the developer wields little control. The primary source of preexisting components is the commercial marketplace, and market dynamics add new dimensions of design complexity and risk to software development. These new dimensions create special documentation obligations that you should be aware of. Software projects composed of custom-built software components are dominated by optimization decisions in which the components are tweaked to meet the needs of the developer, whereas those composed primarily from preexisting software components are dominated by selection decisions, in which the developer's needs are tweaked to meet the available supply of components. Although software architecting is traditionally associated with top-down, custom design, nothing about documenting software architectures or our prescriptions about it precludes meeting the needs of either type of design method. As we prescribe throughout the book, documenting the rationale behind decisions is one of the most important aspects of architectural documentation.

Selection Decisions

Selection decisions arise when there is a bounded set of a priori design options. In this situation, the fundamental design problem is to select the option that best satisfies specific design qualities. When building from preexisting software components, you are not free to define the scope of components, their interfaces, and their interaction mechanisms, as these decisions have already been made by the component developer. This greatly restricted design freedom results in your need to focus on selection rather than on optimization. Component selection decisions are often strongly interdependent, with one selection decision constraining others. These interdependencies are, in themselves, a principal source of selection criteria and result in complex decision-making activ-

ity. You must document the criteria for component selection
and any interdependencies among the criteria. Working with
preexisting components requires a new way of designing; an
additional set of problems is introduced into the decision-
making process when the preexisting components come from
commercial vendors.

COTS-Related Selection Criteria

Today, and for the foreseeable future, the commercial marketplace is the primary source of software components; you cannot
ignore the effects of commerce when using COTS (commercial-
off-the-shelf) components. In particular, you must consider
three qualities of commercial software components.

1. Commercial software components are complex. Vendors
   package complexity to attract a market. However, components can become so complex that even experts do not
   know all their features. In practice, there are bound to be
   gaps in knowledge about component features and behavior, which poses a significant source of risk.

2. Commercial software components are idiosyncratic. Although components may implement standard features, it
   is innovation that attracts customers. Innovation results in
   knowledge that is component specific. However, it also results in integration difficulties owing to mismatches among
   innovative—and therefore nonstandard—component features.

3. Commercial software components are unstable. New features must be introduced to generate sales and to preserve
   product differentiation. Therefore, knowledge about components is not just vendor specific but also has a short
   lifespan. Moreover, design assumptions based on component features can be fragile and subject to untimely revision.

Documentation for systems built from commercial components must include information that helps mitigate the risk
associated with these three characteristics. As a guide, we suggest that you follow the prescription given by Wallnau,
Hissam, and Seacord [2002], in which they introduce *component ensemble* as a fundamental design abstraction and provide
a notation for capturing design decisions as the selection
activity progresses.

Key aspects of their prescription include annotating component interactions with constraints; design elements, with credentials or postulates. Credentials describe what is known about
an element and how it came to be known; postulates describe

what one should discover and how it might be discovered. What a designer chooses to credential or postulate is left open, but suggestions might include the version of the component, the credibility of the component supplier, other known risks associated with using the component, or some quality-related properties that must be measured before the component is selected. Additional constructs are provided to help record the progress of the decision-making activity in terms of which designs are feasible, which might be, which are not, and why.

We won't try to summarize the book here other than to say that working with commercial components requires a new way of thinking about design decisions; there's a whole book on the subject, and it is highly recommended if you are playing that game.

11.9.3 Hypertext Documentation

By now, you must have asked yourself at least once and maybe a hundred times, "How am I supposed to navigate through all these documents?" Fortunately, Web-based documentation is becoming the norm. Hyperlinking your documents can provide instant access to related documents, definitions, catalogues, and external references. Hyperlinking also relieves you of all the problems associated with keeping multiple copies of documents around: You make one copy and link to it wherever the information contained in it is needed. (Recall the second rule of sound documentation: Avoid unnecessary repetition.)

We have not dedicated a chapter to Web-based documentation, because we assume that you can easily find the places where hyperlinking will be the most use to you and other users of the documentation you create. However, don't underestimate the challenge of creating useful hypertext documentation. Usability and other issues are active areas of research. For more information on creating hypertext documentation, visit the Web site of the ACM special-interest group on hypertext, hypermedia, and the Web (ACM).

11.9.4 Configuration Management

And last, but not least, what book on documentation would be complete without stressing once again—recall the sixth rule of sound documentation, "Keep documentation current but not too current"—the importance of keeping your documentation complete and consistent? Nothing is worse than opening up a bunch of architecture documents and trying to figure out which of them represents the most recent version of the system. Documents should be dated and versioned. If someone is looking at several figures, it should be obvious at a glance which figures are from the same version of the system. You probably think of software configuration management systems more in terms of keeping track of the code associated with your project, but we recommend that you think of the documentation that you are creating as software too and treat it just as carefully as you do the code that is produced based on it.

11.10   A Final Word

One of us was recently asked to compose a short overview on the topic of software architecture. "The field is becoming a subject of such intense study," he wrote with a twinkle in his eye, "that, believe it or not, there is a whole book coming out that explains how software architectures should be *documented*."

Indeed. Another one explains how they should be reviewed and evaluated. Another explains how an architecture-centric development project should be managed. Another explains how to train to be an architect. We can only guess at what else is in the pipeline. It is a sign of the field's maturity that none of these books has to dwell on the criticality of architecture in system building; they all can assume that it's a known quantity within the community of practitioners. As a group, these books are filling in the gaps in knowledge and practice that will allow architecture to graduate from a guild craft to a legitimate engineering discipline.

Helping practitioners do their job more effectively is the goal of those books, and this one is no exception. We wanted to help an architect answer the question, What do I do now? Communicating the architecture is as important a task as creating it, for without effective communication, the architecture is nothing.

Architectures are too complex to be communicated all at once, just as a high-dimension object cannot be seen or grasped in its entirety in our 3-D world. As a way to divide and conquer complexity, views are by far the most effective means of architectural communication that we know. Views, like styles and patterns, establish a specialized and shared vocabulary, allow reuse of technical knowledge and practice from one system to the next, and facilitate analysis and prediction. Relating the views to one another and making the documentation accessible to its stakeholders completes the communication obligation to the present stakeholders. Capturing the rationale and why things are the way they are completes the communication obligation to the future.

That is the essence of documentation: recognizing and discharging the architect's obligations to the community of stakeholders, present and future, whose needs the architecture is intended to serve. We hope that we have provided guidance that will lead to high-quality products and that is also practical and flexible enough to be useful in the resource-constrained, never-enough-time environments in which all architects labor.

And we look forward to discovering what's on the horizon.

11.11   For Further Reading

To read about the Rational Unified Process (RUP), start with [Kruchten 98]. Philippe Kruchten's original paper proposing the 4+1 approach for architecture is still the best introduction to that concept [Kruchten 95]. As one might expect, Rational Software Corporation makes a wealth of information about RUP available on their Web site at www.rational.com/rup.

The Siemens Four Views approach is described in detail in [Hofmeister+ 00].

The C4ISR architecture framework is growing well beyond its original U.S. Department of Defense origins to become a widespread standard for federal agencies here and abroad. The DoD Web site at http://www.c3i.osd.mil/org/cio/i3/ is a jumping-off point for learning about C4ISR.

You can download ANSI/IEEE-1471-2000 from http://standards.ieee.org/catalog/olis/se.html for a price and registration. To simply read about it, a good introduction has been written by the people primarily responsible for creating it [Maier+ 01].

The seminal reference for RM-ODP is Janis Putman's "Architecting with RM-ODP" [Putman 00].

A good source of information about configuration management, is the Web site http://www.stsc.hill.af.mil/crosstalk/1999/mar/cmsites.asp which contains links to other CM-related sites and resources.

To read about building software from commercial components, a book by that very name just happens to exist [Wallanu+ 01] and does a good job of exploring that subject's complexities and how to document systems so built.

For more information on creating hypertext documentation, you can visit the Web site of the ACM special interest group on hypertext, hypermedia, and the Web at http://www.acm.org/sigweb/.

And finally, whither UML? As this book went to press, version 2.0 was in the works with a great deal of promise for addressing some of the shortcomings that have so far prevented it from becoming the hands-down choice for documentating architectures. You can follow the progress at http://www.omg.org/uml/.

Appendix A: Excerpts from a Software Architecture Documentation Package

These excerpts from a sample architecture documentation package are for a system called ECS, a system in use at the U.S. National Aeronautics and Space Administration (NASA). ECS ingests, stores, processes, and makes available a high volume of sensor data from a constellation of Earth-observing satellites.

Note these important caveats about this package:

- The documentation is not complete, emphasizing breadth over depth. Each part of the documentation package is illustrated with what could best be called a snippet.

- Where form or continued content should be clear, the use of [omitted] or [etc.] indicates information left out of the example but that would not be left out of an actual documentation package. This appendix is intended to be illustrative, not exhaustive.

- The documentation in this package is based on that for ECS but may not accurately document ECS software. Simplifications and fictions were introduced for pedagogical reasons.

- Comments about the documentation in the context of this book are given in footnotes.

- Finally, this example uses ten views, many more than most projects would find practical. The large number results from ECS's serving as the example for many of the views in this book.

Chapter 10 noted that either the documentation could all go in a single document, or each part could be assigned its own document. The ECS package takes a middle approach, creating a two-volume set. The boilerplate on the title page of each volume is for compliance with ANSI IEEE-1471-2000, the ANSI IEEE recommended practice for architectural description for software-intensive systems (see Section 11.6).

ECS Software Architecture Documentation

Volume I:
ECS Software Architecture Documentation Beyond Views

Date of issue: January 23, 2002

Status: Baselined; Version 2.0.14

Name of issuing organization: Software Contractors, Inc.

Change history: Available at http://www.ourinternalwebsite/ECS/documentation/architecture/vol1/change_history/

Summary: This document is Volume I of a two-volume set. This volume contains the ECS architectural information that applies to more than one view. Chapters include the documentation roadmap, the template for presenting architectural views, an ECS system overview, the mapping between views, an architectural element directory, and a discussion of design rationale. Architectural stakeholders new to ECS should begin by reading the documentation roadmap in Chapter 1 of this volume.

Volume I
ECS Software Architecture Documentation Beyond Views

CONTENTS

Chapter 1
ECS Architecture
Documentation Roadmap

1.1 Description of the ECS Software Architecture Documentation Package

This section describes the structure and contents of the entire ECS software architecture documentation package. The ECS architecture documentation package is arranged in two volumes. Volume I contains the information that applies to more than one view, including this roadmap of the entire package. The architectural views are collected in Volume II.

Volume I, ECS Software Architecture Documentation Beyond Views, contains the following chapters:

- Chapter 1, ECS Architecture Documentation Roadmap, lists and outlines the contents of the overall documentation package and explains how stakeholder concerns can be addressed by the individual parts. This is the first document that a new stakeholder should read.

- Chapter 2, ECS System Overview, gives a broad overview of the purpose and functionality of ECS. Architectural detail is purposely omitted from this overview; instead, the emphasis is on the system's background, its external interfaces, major constraints, and what functions the system performs. The purpose is to help someone new to the project understand what the architecture is trying to achieve.

- Chapter 3, View Template, explains the standard organization for the views given in Volume II. The purpose is to help a reader understand the information given in the views of Volume II.

- Chapter 4, Mapping Between Views, draws comparisons between separate views of the ECS architecture that are given in Volume II. The mapping points out places where the views overlap or have elements in common and resolves areas of apparent conflict between the views.

- Chapter 5, Directory, is a look-up index of all the elements, relations, and properties in the ECS architecture, listing where these items are defined and where they are used. The purpose of the directory is to help a stakeholder quickly locate the definition of an architectural entity.

- Chapter 6, Architecture Glossary and Acronym List, defines special terms and acronyms used elsewhere in the architecture documentation package. This list is intended to supplement the overall project glossary and acronym list.

- Chapter 7, Rationale, Background, and Design Constraints, explains the design rationale behind the ECS architecture, including the most relevant background information and imposed design constraints. Maintainers seeking to make changes, future architects, and lead designers can learn the motivation behind the major design decisions of ECS.

Volume II, ECS Software Architecture Views, contains the following chapters:[1]

- Chapter 1, Module Decomposition View: The module decomposition view shows how the system is decomposed into implementation units and, simultaneously, how the functionality of the system is allocated to those units. The elements of this view are modules. The relation is *is-part-of*.

  The decomposition view presents the functionality of a system in intellectually manageable pieces that are recursively refined to convey more and more details. Therefore, this style supports the learning process about a system. This view is a learning and navigation tool for newcomers in the project or other people who do not necessarily have the whole functional structure of the system memorized. The grouping of functionality shown in this view also builds a useful basis for defining configuration items within a configuration management framework.

  The decomposition view is the basis for creating work assignments, mapping parts of a software system onto the organizational units—teams—that will be given the responsibility for implementing and testing them. The module decomposition view also provides some support for analyzing effects of changes at the software implementation level. But because this view does not show all the dependencies among modules, you should not expect to do a complete impact analysis. Here, views that elaborate the dependency relationships more thoroughly, such as the module uses style described later, are required.

---

1. Each entry tells what the element and relation types are that are found in the view and then what the view can be used for. Both kinds of information can be extracted from the corresponding style catalog for the view, whether that catalog is in this book or another source. For instance, the style descriptions in this book include What It's For and What It's Not For sections.

- Chapter 2, Module Uses View: The uses view shows how modules are related to one another by the *uses* relation, a kind of *depends-on* relation. A module uses another module if the correctness of the first depends on the correctness of the second. The view is used to help integraters and testers field incrementally larger subsets of the system.

- Chapter 3, Module Generalization View: The generalization view shows how classes, a kind of module, are related to one another by inheritance, a kind of *generalization/specialization* relation.

  This view is used to show extension and evolution of architectures and individual elements. This view is the predominant means for expressing the inheritance-based object-oriented design of ECS. It shows where component and design reuse, or reuse with variation, occurs in the system. Like the decomposition view, the generalization view is also useful for analyzing the scope of a change.

- Chapter 4, Module Layered View: The layered view shows how the ECS software is structured as a set of seven abstract virtual machines. Lower layers provide abstract hardware, network, and data transport facilities. Intermediate layers provide common facilities and object services. The highest layers encapsulate the application-dependent aspects of the system. Elements of this view are layers, a kind of module. Layers are related by the *allowed-to-use* relation, where *use* has the meaning given in the uses view.

  Layers are used to provide portability and modifiability. Specifically, the implementation of any layer can be replaced without affecting other layers.

- Chapter 5, Component-and-Connector Pipe-and-Filter View: The pipe-and-filter view shows how data entering ECS flows through a series of order-preserving transformations before being assigned to the appropriate data warehousing facilities. The pipe-and-filter view of ECS is a conceptual view, meaning that in truth, the system is not structured as a series of pipes and filters in the formal sense. In fact, the shared-data view is a higher-fidelity picture of the sysem as it is built. However, the pipe-and-filter view conveys a valuable conceptual picture to project newcomers and users because it shows the transformations applied to the ingested data.

  Elements are pipes and filters, both a kind of component. The relations shown in this view are the *attachments* between pipes and filters.

- Chapter 6, Component-and-Connector Shared-Data View: The shared-data view shows how the system is structured as a number of data accessors that, at runtime, read and write data in the various ECS shared repositories. Elements are repositories, accessors, and the connectors between the two.

The shared-data view is used to help tune the system for performance to make sure that it can handle the volume of ingested data, as well as service data processing and production requests in a timely fashion.

- Chapter 7, Component-and-Connector Communicating-Processes View: The communicating-processes view represents the system as a set of concurrently executing units together with their interactions. A concurrent unit is an abstraction of more concrete software platform elements, such as tasks, processes, and threads. Any pair of concurrent units depicted in a process style has the potential to execute concurrently, either logically on a single processor or physically on multiple processors or distributed processors. Connectors enable data exchange between concurrent units and control of concurrent units, such as start, stop, synchronization, and so on.

  The communicating-processes view is used to perform concurrency-related analyses, including performance analysis and deadlock detection and prevention. It is also used as the basis for allocation of the software to hardware processors in the deployment view.

- Chapter 8, Allocation Deployment View: In the deployment view, processes and other software elements are allocated to execution platforms, physical units that store, transmit, or compute data. Physical units include processing nodes (CPUs), communication channels, and data stores.

  The relation depicted in the deployment view is a special form of *allocated to* that shows on which physical units the software elements reside. The allocation relation in ECS is static; that is, it does not change at runtime.

  The view is used as the basis for performance analysis by, among other things, analyzing the volume and frequency of communication among software units on different processing elements along the communication channels among those elements. The view is also used to support memory capacity analysis; reliability analysis, by examining the effects of a failed processor or communication channel; and security analysis, by examining the way each platform is connected and potentially vulnerable to external threats.

- Chapter 9, Allocation Implementation View: The implementation view shows how code units, or modules, are mapped, or allocated, to the ECS development and implementation environment. It is used to help plan the development environment and to manage the day-to-day artifact production and storage process, including configuration management.

- Chapter 10, Allocation Work Assignment View: The work assignment view shows how code units, or modules, are allocated to organizational work units—in this case, either internal government development teams or external contractors. It is used to help manage the teams and provides a basis for planning and measuring progress.

1.2   How Stakeholders Can Use the Documentation

This section lists the stakeholder roles of primary importance to ECS and how they might use the documentation package to address their concerns.

- *Someone new to the project:* Read the documentation roadmap for an understanding of the documentation package and the view template to understand how views are documented. Read the system overview and system-level design rationale. Examine the top-level view packets of the module decomposition view, the pipe-and-filter view, the deployment view, and the work assignment view.

- *Project manager:* To help with project planning, concentrate on the module decomposition view, which will help define work assignments and identify COTS products that will have to be qualified, procured, and integrated. Read the deployment view to understand the hardware environment that will have to be acquired and that will help identify testing environments that need to be set up. Read the work assignment view to begin to manage and coordinate the teams.

- *Performance engineer:* Read the communicating-processes view to understand the units of potential concurrency. Read the deployment view to understand how the software is to be allocated to hardware. Read the shared-data view to build performance models for ingesting data and producing data products on demand. Read the behavioral specifications in all the C&C views.

- *Security analyst:* Read the deployment view to understand the physical environment in which the system operates.

- *Maintainer:* Read the system-level rationale in Volume I. Read the decomposition view to understand the units of implementation that exist and the area of responsibility of each. Read the generalization view to see how the units relate to one another in terms of generalization and specialization. Especially read the rationale in each view and in each interface specification. Read the top-level view packet of the deployment view to understand where each software unit is allocated. Read the implementation view to understand how the code units are allocated to the development environment.

- *Customer/Acquirer:* Read the system overview. Read the top-level view packets of the decomposition, deployment, and pipe-and-filter views to gain a broad understanding of how the system is structured to carry out its mission and to gain an appreciation for the work that must be done to build it.

- *Users:* Users will not generally be voracious consumers of architecture documentation, but they can read the behavioral specifications in the C&C views to gain an understanding of how various parts of the system behave. Reading the pipe-and-filter view will give users an intuition about how the system functions.

- *Developer:* Read the decomposition view to understand the basic units of software in the system, the uses view to see how the current subset being developed is structured, the implementation view to see where the software resides in the development environment, the layered view to see which software developers are allowed to use, and the work assignment view to understand the other organizational units with which developers must coordinate. Read the interface specifications of other units to find out how to use them. Then, using the mapping between views, read the relevant parts of the other views that reveal how their units are deployed onto hardware or manifested as runtime components.

Chapter 2
ECS System Overview

2.1 Background[2]

Mission to Planet Earth (MTPE) is a long-term, multi- and interdisciplinary NASA research mission to study the processes leading to global climate change and to develop a predictive capability for the Earth system on time scales of decades to centuries. To accomplish these objectives, researchers require a readily accessible collection of diverse observations of Earth over an extended period of time, with the capability to create and add new data products to this collection, based on improved understanding. MTPE aims at not only a study of the disciplinary sciences of the atmosphere, oceans, cryosphere, biosphere, and solid Earth but also the interdisciplinary interactions among these often disparate realms of study. This is necessary for development of a predictive capability for modeling the Earth system as the scientific basis for global environmental policy.

MTPE consists of three major components:

1. The Earth Observing System (EOS) will collect Earth science data, with emphasis on long-term, sustained data sets from carefully calibrated instruments on satellites in low Earth orbit. The EOS includes NASA instruments on satellites to be launched by NASA, the European Space Agency (ESA), and the Japanese National Space Development Agency (NASDA).

2. The EOS Data and Information System (EOSDIS) will provide the Earth science community with easy, affordable, and reliable access to EOS and other Earth science data.

3. An integrated scientific research program will investigate processes in the Earth system and use this information to improve predictive models.

The EOSDIS will provide a broader community of users with a unique resource for enhancing their understanding of

---

2. As noted in Chapter 10, the system overview is not intended to divulge much about the system's architecture but rather to ground a new reader in the system's background. If such an overview exists in the overall project documentation, as it well may, the architect's obligation for this information is satisfied by referring the reader to that overview.

global change issues and for acquiring data for use in other applications.

The EOSDIS Core System (ECS) is the major component of the EOSDIS and the subject of this document. The ECS will control the EOS spacecraft and instruments, process data from the EOS instruments, and manage and distribute EOS data products and other selected data sets and updated NASA/SPSO Product List Tables. Interoperating with other data systems maintained by government agencies and the research community, the ECS will provide comprehensive services for accessing Earth science data.

The ECS is part of a much larger data collection and research enterprise. The ECS development process provides flexibility to accommodate changes in user needs and to incorporate new data system technologies while also satisfying cost and schedule constraints.

2.2   EOS Mission Science Data Flow

To understand the ECS, it helps to understand how data moves throughout the entire system of which ECS is a part. In general, NASA satellites will transmit their data through the Tracking and Data Relay Satellites (TDRS), which will forward the data to the receiving station at White Sands, New Mexico. From there, the data will be transmitted via dedicated circuits to the new Fairmont Complex in West Virginia, where the data will be processed to recover the raw instrument data. International Partner satellites downlink directly to the International Partner Ground Systems (IPGS) via their ground receiving stations. Data from NASA instruments on the International Partner platforms will be transmitted to Fairmont via commercial networks. Landsat 7 downlinks data directly to the EDC and to the IPGS.

The data from each instrument will be sent from Fairmont (part of EDOS) to Distributed Active Archive Center (DAAC). These seven data centers will house the ECS computing facilities and operational staff needed to produce EOS Standard Products and to manage and store EOSDIS data as well as the associated metadata and browse data required for effective use of the data holdings. The DAACs will exchange data via dedicated EOSDIS networks to support processing at one DAAC, which requires data from another DAAC. DAACs will provide the facilities, management, and operations support for the production, archiving, and distribution of EOS Standard Products. At the DAACs, users can expect a level of service that would be difficult to maintain in a single data center attempting to serve the extraordinarily wide range of disciplines encompassed by the EOS program. It is important that a user interacting with any given DAAC will be able to access data from all the DAACs. The DAACs also house systems for processing and/or storing non-EOS Earth science data.

Flight Operations, including Spacecraft and Instruments, will be conducted from the EOS Operations Center (EOC). Non-U.S. Instruments on U.S. Platforms will be operated and monitored through International Partner (IP) Instrument Control Centers (ICC).

Most science users will access EOS data products via shared networks. Open access to the data by all members of the science community distinguishes the EOS from previous research satellite projects, on which selected investigators have had proprietary data rights for a number of years after data acquisition.

Scientific Computing Facilities (SCFs), located at EOS investigators' home institutions, are used to develop and to maintain algorithms for both Standard and Special Products, calibrate the EOS instruments, validate data and algorithms, generate Special Products, provide data and services to other investigators, and analyze EOS and other data in pursuit of the MTPE science objectives. The SCFs may range from single workstations to large supercomputer data centers. Whereas the SCFs will be developed and acquired directly by the EOS investigators, the ECS will provide software toolkits to the SCFs and other users to facilitate data access, transformation and visualization, and algorithm development. Some SCFs will play an operational role in quality control of the EOS Standard Products; these SCFs will be linked to the DAACs via guaranteed service quality communications lines to support reliable exchange of large volumes of data.

Comprehensive understanding of Earth system processes requires data from a diverse range of sensors. Field campaign and other *in situ* data will be contributed by NOAA and by the scientific users. Remote-sensing data from the EOS instruments will be supplemented by measurements from operational sensors, most notably on satellites operated by NOAA. Some data centers will interoperate with the EOSDIS, allowing the DAACs and their users to search data inventories, much as if the data resided at one of the DAACs. Other data centers will not necessarily interoperate with the EOSDIS but may provide data for the EOS science investigations.

2.3 Broad Requirements for ECS

ECS must satisfy the following broad requirements:

- Ingest, process, archive, and distribute data from 24 sensors on ten spacecraft, numbers destined to grow steadily over time
- Compute about 250 standard data products, which are pre-defined analyses that transform raw data into information packets about the physical world
- Archive the data and these data products in eight data centers—warehouses—across the United States
- Enable heterogeneous access and analysis operations at these data centers and forty-some distributed scientific computing facilities
- Provide capacity for testing and incorporating new processing algorithms and new data product definitions, as well as support data/information searches
- Manage large geospatial databases
- Meet the performance and reliability requirements to allow it to keep up with the never-ending flood of incoming data and never-ending stream of scientific analysis to be performed on it

About 1.5 terabytes of raw data per day flow into the system: data about vegetation, lightning, surface images, atmospheric soundings, trace gas quantities, atmospheric dynamics and chemistry, ice topography, sea surface winds, ocean color, volcanic activity, evaporation amounts, and altimetry. The data is processed, analyzed, and refined using complex algorithms provided by the science community. The system daily produces and distributes about 2 terabytes of data that get warehoused and made available to the scientific community in several formats. The overall mission is to understand Earth processes and potential global climate changes and to provide information for planning and adaptation.

In addition to meeting day-to-day objectives, a goal of the ECS program is to provide a highly adaptable system that is responsive to the evolving needs of the Earth science community. Over the system lifetime—at least two decades beyond the launch of the first EOS spacecraft—evolution will come from at least three separate sources:

1. Scientific needs will change as Earth system science matures and new applications of the data emerge.
2. Information system technologies must be refreshed as maintaining older technologies becomes more difficult and new technologies emerge in their place.

3. Changes in the information infrastructure, such as high bandwidth networking, will lead to migration of functions to take full advantage of these capabilities.

Thus, the ECS will support the "vision" of an evolving and comprehensive information system to promote effective use of data for research in support of the MTPE goals. To support these goals, the ECS will

- Accommodate growth in all its functions, as well as the addition of new functions.
- Be expandable with respect to storage and processing capacity for instrument data products and algorithms.
- Be extended by unique capabilities developed by the individual data centers, tailored to the needs of their user communities.
- Be designed to promote cost-effective development of such extensions.
- Interoperate with data systems of other agencies associated with the U.S. Global Change Research Program to form the Global Change Data and Information System (GCDIS) and with International Partner data systems. Interoperating with investigator data systems, the ECS will provide input data for their higher-level data processing, receive products and their associated metadata for distribution and long-term management, and provide users with access to data and services provided at the investigators' facilities.

ECS development is being accomplished in cooperation with the user community, with a shared commitment to the vision of an information system that promotes effective use of data across the entire Earth science community.

Before EOSDIS, satellite data was stored and formatted in ways specific to each satellite; accessing this data—let alone using it for analysis—was almost impossible for scientists not directly affiliated with that satellite's science project. An important feature of EOSDIS is to provide a common way to store and hence process data and a public mechanism to introduce new data formats and processing algorithms, thus making the information widely available to the scientific community at large.

2.4 Deploying the System

The same version of the software runs on each of four distributed sites in Maryland, Virginia, Colorado, and South Dakota. It is deployed on about 20 UNIX servers from multiple vendors at each site.

Authority for various aspects of the system is decentralized. Data centers maintain control of their local facilities and interface with data users. Scientific teams maintain control over their science software and data products. The ECS project management team is responsible for maintaining and planning the evolution of the system.

The first operational version of ECS was delivered in early 1999. The system has been fielded incrementally, its growing capabilities coordinated with the launch of new spacecraft that will "feed" it. The intended operational life of the system is roughly through 2013.

Chapter 3
ECS Software Architecture
View Template[3]

Each ECS view is presented as a number of related view packets. A view packet is a small, relatively self-contained bundle of information about the system or a particular part of the system, rendered in the language—element and relation types—of the view to which it belongs. Two view packets are related to each other as either parent/child—because one shows a refinement of the information in the other—or as siblings—because both are children of another view packet.

This chapter describes the seven-part standard organization that the documentation for view packets—in Volume II of the ECS software architecture documentation package—obeys:

1. A primary presentation that shows the elements and their relationships that populate the view packet. The primary presentation contains the information important to convey about the system, in the vocabulary of that view, first. It includes the primary elements and relations of the view packet but under some circumstances might not include all of them. For example, the primary presentation may show the elements and relations that come into play during normal operation, relegating error handling or exception processing to the supporting documentation.

    The primary presentation is usually graphical. If so, the presentation will include a key that explains the meaning of every symbol used. The first part of the key identifies the notation: If a defined notation is being used, the key will name it and cite the document that defines it or defines the version of it being used. If the notation is informal, the key will say so and proceed to define the symbology and the meaning, if any, of colors, position, or other information-carrying aspects of the diagram.

2. Element catalog detailing at least those elements depicted in the primary presentation and others that were omitted from the primary presentation. Specific parts of the catalog include

---

3. The material for this part of the documentation package comes from the view template in Section 10.1 of this book.

a. *Elements and their properties.* This section names each element in the view packet and lists the properties of that element. For example, elements in a module decomposition view have the property of "responsibility," an explanation of each module's role in the system, and elements in a communicating-process view have timing parameters, among other things, as properties.

b. *Relations and their properties.* Each view has a specific type of relation that it depicts among the elements in that view. However, if the primary presentation does not show all the relations or if there are exceptions to what is depicted in the primary presentation, this section will record that information.

c. *Element interface.* An interface is a boundary across which elements interact or communicate with each other. This section is where element interfaces are documented.

d. *Element behavior.* Some elements have complex interactions with their environment and for purposes of understanding or analysis, the element's behavior is documented. For ECS, behavior of elements is specified in component-and-connector views in Volume II, Chapters 5, 6, and 7.

3. Context diagram showing how the system depicted in the view packet relates to its environment.

4. Variability guide showing how to exercise any variation points that are a part of the architecture shown in this view packet.

5. Architecture background explaining why the design reflected in the view packet came to be. The goal of this section is to explain why the design is as it is and to provide a convincing argument that it is sound. Architecture background includes

a. *Rationale.* This explains why the design decisions reflected in the view packet were made and gives a list of rejected alternatives and why they were rejected. This will prevent future architects from pursuing dead ends in the face of required changes.

b. *Analysis results.* This documents the results of analyses that have been conducted, such as the results of performance or security analyses, or a list of what would have to change in the face of a particular kind of system modification.

   c. *Assumptions.* This documents any assumptions the architect made when crafting the design. Assumptions are generally about either environment or need.

      Environmental assumptions document what the architect assumes is available in the environment that can be used by the system being designed. They also include assumptions about invariants in the environment. For example, a navigation system architect might make assumptions about the stability of Earth's geographic and/or magnetic poles. Finally, assumptions about the environment may be about the development environment: tool suites available or the skill levels of the implementation teams, for example.

      Assumptions about need state why the design provided is sufficient for what's needed. For example, if a navigation system's software interface provides location information in a single geographic frame of reference, the architect is assuming that is sufficient, and that alternative frames of reference are not useful.

6. Other information. This section includes nonarchitectural and organization-specific information.[4]

7. Related view packets. This section will name other view packets that are related to the one being described in a parent/child or sibling capacity.

---

4. This section will not be filled in for the ECS example package. As discussed in Section 10.2, "other information" will usually include management or configuration control information, change histories, bibliographic references or lists of useful companion documents, mapping to requirements, and the like.

Chapter 4
Mapping Between Views

This chapter establishes the relationship between corresponding elements and structures that appear in different views in Volume II. Not all pairwise view combinations have a mapping in this section, and not every element is mapped. The emphasis is on mappings that provide useful insights.

The following table summarizes the mappings in this chapter. The table cells tell which section contains a mapping between the corresponding views on the cell's row and column header.

	Module Decomposition	Module Generalization	Module Uses	Module Layered	C&C Pipe-and-Filter	C&C Shared-Data	C&C Communicating-Processes	Allocation Deployment	Allocation Implementation	Allocation Work Assignment
Module Decomposition		4.1	4.4			4.2	4.3		4.4	4.4
Module Generalization	4.1									
Module Uses	4.4								4.4	4.4
Module Layered										
C&C Pipe-and-Filter										
C&C Shared-Data	4.2									
C&C Communicating-Processes	4.3									
Allocation Deployment										
Allocation Implementation	4.4		4.4							4.4
Allocation Work Assignment	4.4		4.4						4.4	

4.1 Mapping Between Module Decomposition View and Module Generalization View

Generalization View Element	Decomposition View Element	Relation
IngestData class	Ingest subsystem	The subsystem contains the named classes and all their child classes. The interface of the Ingest subsystem is provided completely by the union of the interfaces of all the named classes and their children.
DataTypeL0Data		
DataTypeNMCData		
DataTypeAlgorithm		

4.2 Mapping Between Module Decomposition View and C&C Shared-Data View

Shared-Data View Element	Decomposition View Element	Relation
DictServ	Data Management subsystem	The named shared-data elements are part of the given subsystem.
V0GW		
AsterGW		
MTool		
RPC	Communications and Systems Management Segment	
InstallData		
[etc.]	[etc.]	[etc.]

4.3 Mapping Between Module Decomposition View and C&C Communicating-Processes View

Communicating-Processes View Element	Decomposition View Element	Relation
EcInAuto	Ingest subsystem	The named processes are part of the given subsystem.
EcInPolling		
EcInGUI		
EcInReqMgr		
EcInEmailGWServer		
EcInGran		
Sybase Server		
RPC		
Notification		
SQL		
[etc.]	[etc.]	[etc.]

4.4 Mapping Between Module Decomposition View, Module Uses View, Allocation Implementation View, and Allocation Work Assignment View

The segments and subsystems named in the two allocation views and the module uses view are exactly the same elements as those named in the module decomposition view.

[Other mappings omitted.][5]

---

5. It not necessary or desirable to include mappings between every pair of views. A minimum goal is to establish at least one strong module/C&C mapping and a mapping from allocation views to the views whose elements they allocate.

Chapter 5
Directory

The directory is an index of all the elements, relations, and properties that appear in any of the views. This index is intended to help a reader find all places where a particular kind of element, relation, or property is used.[6]

Item	Type	Volume II Section Where Used
ACRIM SCF	External entity; context of module decomposition view	1.2
ADSRV CSCI	Element of module uses view	2.1
Allocated to	Relation of allocation deployment view	8.1
	Relation of allocation implementation view	9.1
Allowed to use	Relation of module layered view	4.1
AMSR-E SCF	External entity; context of module decomposition view	1.2
Analysis	Subsystem; element of module decomposition view	1.14
	Element of allocation implementation view	9.1
	Element of allocation work assignment view	10.1
ASTER Gateway	Data accessor; element of C&C shared-data view	6.1
Assigned to	Relation of allocation work assignment view	10.1
ASTER GDS	External entity; context of module decomposition view	1.2
	External entity; context of C&C shared-data view	6.1
Attachment	Relation of C&C pipe-and-filter view	5.1
	Relation of C&C shared-data view	6.1
	Relation of C&C communicating-processes view	7.1
Build Frequency	Property of allocation implementation view	9.1

6. Note how useful hypertext links would be here.

Item	Type	Volume II Section Where Used
Client	Subsystem; element of module decomposition view	1.2, 1.3
	Element of C&C communicating-processes view	7.4
	Element of allocation implementation view	9.1
	Element of allocation work assignment view	10.1
Command Management	Subsystem; element of module decomposition view	1.14
	Element of allocation implementation view	9.1
	Element of allocation work assignment view	10.1
Commanding	Subsystem; element of module decomposition view	1.14
	Element of allocation implementation view	9.1
	Element of allocation work assignment view	10.1
Common Facilities	Layer; element of module layered view	4.1
Communications	Subsystem; element of module decomposition view	1.10, 1.12
	Element of C&C communicating-processes view	7.8
	Element of allocation implementation view	9.1
	Element of allocation work assignment view	10.1
Communications Speed	Property of allocation deployment view	8.1
Communications and System Management Segment (CSMS)	Segment; element of module decomposition view	1.1, 1.10
	Element of module uses view	2.2
	Element of allocation implementation view	9.1
	Element of allocation work assignment view	10.1
Contact	Property of allocation implementation view	9.1
Contents	Property of module layered view	4.1
Contractor or Internal Team	Property of allocation work assignment view	10.1

[etc.]

Chapter 6
Architecture Glossary and Acronym List[7]

asynchronous   A format used in digital communication between computers with no timing requirements for transmission and with the start of each character individually signaled by the transmitting device.

attitude data   Data representing spacecraft orientation and on-board pointing information: (1) sensor data to determine the pointing of the spacecraft axis, calibration and alignment data, Euler angles or quaternions, rates and biases, and associated parameters; (2) data generated on-board in quaternion or Euler angle form; (3) refined and routine production data related to the accuracy or knowledge of the attitude.

Communications Subsystem (CSS)   The ECS subsystem for transferring ECS data between sites and within a single site, providing connections between ECS users and ECS service providers and providing requested services to support the System Management Subsystem operations. The CSS is composed of one CSCI, the Distributed Computing Configuration Item (DCCI), and one HWCI (a Sun workstation with an external disk.)

Computer Software Configuration Item (CSCI)   An element in the module decomposition view. A CSCI is a subelement of a subsystem, implemented with COTS and custom-developed software to satisy a particular subset of subsystem-level software requirements.

Distributed Active Archive Center (DAAC)   A facility that manages one or more data products and, possibly, the production of one or more products; archives are "active" in that their data holdings are always available.

data granule   A file or file group containing science data and referenced as a single entity.

data product   A class of similar data granules, usually produced by the same source.

---

7. As noted in Chapter 10 of the book, some projects maintain a single overall glossary and acronym list, which would include the terms and acronyms used throughout the architecture documentation and in other documentation. In that case, the architect's obligation for this part is discharged simply by pointing the reader to the overall project glossary acronym list.

Interoperability Subsystem (IOS)   Allows ECS servers and non-ECS users to insert and subsequently search for Earth science–related services, advertisement providers, and data. The IOS consists of the Advertising Service CSCI and the Interface Hardware CI. The Interface Hardware CI is shared with the Data Management subsystem

Level of data   Categorization of ECS data into levels, depending on the amount of processing that has been performed.

Level 0 data is the raw, instrument telemetry data extracted from the spacecraft telemetry and has been time ordered, with duplicate and corrupted packets discarded. Level 0 gives the truest form of data produced by the instrument.

Levels 1a and 1b data is radiometrically (1a) calibrated and geometrically (1b) located to a reference surface. For each instrument, we maintain either the level 1a or the level 1b data. Older versions of level 1 data are discarded 6 months after reprocessing to a new version.

Level 2 data consists of geophysical data sets created by applying scientific algorithms developed by the instrument or science team investigators. Level 2 data sets retain the "full" resolution of the instrument or sensor: swath format for imaging sensors. Older versions of level 2 data sets are discarded 6 months after reprocessing.

Level 3 data consists of geophysical data sets averaged in space or time, using algorithms developed by the instrument or science team investigators. In most cases, level 3 data constitutes the "final" product for an investigation and is maintained in the archives for the extent of the mission or investigation. Older versions of level 3 data sets are discarded 6 months after reprocessing.

Level 4 data sets are value-added data sets, created through application of a model to the satellite data. Currently, ESE archives only a few standard level 4 data products—primarily Data Assimilation Office products—and they are maintained for the extent of the mission or investigation:

message passing   The peer-to-peer asynchronous communications service notifying processes of specific event triggers. This service is provided by the CSS within the ECS.

Mission to Planet Earth (MTPE)   A NASA-initiated concept that uses space-, ground-, and aircraft-based measurement systems to provide the scientific basis for understanding the climate system and its variations. The science objectives address the fundamental physical, chemical, and biological phenomenon that govern and integrate the Earth system.

network ingest request   An Ingest Request to automatically transfer data into the SDPS from an external data provider. The Network Ingest Request contains the following information: (a) external data provider, (b) date/time prior to which the data remains available, (c) requested ingest priority, (d) list of Data Type Identifiers, (e) for each Data Type Identifier, a list of file identifiers, (f) the corresponding file volumes.

on-board attitude data   The attitude data generated by the spacecraft or its instruments.

science software   A program used to generate data products.

Science Computing Facility (SCF)   A facility that develops science software.

Science Data Processing Segment (SDPS)   An ECS segment that provides the capabilities for science data processing and data product or data searching, ordering, archiving, and distribution.

Science Investigator-led Processing System (SIPS)   A facility, external to ECS, that manages production of data products; products are stored in ECS.

scientist   An individual with direct usage or support of the data collected and generated by, or the instruments contained within the EOSDIS. Included are principal investigators, coinvestigators, research facility team leaders and team members, interdisciplinary investigators, instrument investigators, non-EOS-affiliated science users, and other users of a diverse nature.

[etc.][8]

---

8. The ECS project glossary is about 90 pages long and contains about 700 terms. A separate acronym list contains some 1,500 entries.

Chapter 7
Rationale, Background, and Design Constraints

The following records those contextual and requirements aspects of ECS that were the primary motivators behind the major architectural decisions. There were, of course, a large number of specific requirements that had to be satisfied, but these are the major ones that had profound architectural influence.

- *Business context:* ECS is expected to have a long operational life (1999 to around 2012), meaning that it needs to be easy to change in a variety of ways. It will be installed and distributed across four data centers in South Dakota, Maryland, Virginia, and Colorado. It is designed to serve a broad community of stakeholders: the data centers' staffs, instrument-specific science teams, interdisciplinary science users, other agencies and data user groups, and even the general public. Decentralized authority is the rule; data centers maintain control of their own facilities and interface with data users, and instrument teams maintain control over their science software and data products. ECS represents an unprecedented problem size for NASA and must support about 1,300 product types. It must archive large amounts of data, adding about 1 terabyte per day (today), about 3 picobytes by 12/03, and about 9 picobytes by 2011. It must manage large geospatial databases adding about 140 megabytes per day, or about 293 gigabytes by 12/03. And it must distribute large amounts of data in several formats: almost 2 terabytes per day. ECS must execute complex science algorithms provided by the science community. It must interface with about 35 external systems. ECS is a large system with heavy dependence on COTS. The architecture includes almost 50 COTS products, many integrated with custom code.

- *Key data management features:* In order to support the widely varying data needs, ECS relies on a common metadata model. Core attributes are standardized for all data types, to permit queries across data types. Each data type may define additional data type–specific attributes. Access to both core and data type–specific attributes are provided through system interfaces; for example, the same interface can be used for searching and/or access. New data types can be dynamically added to the system. Data types can have unique services, such as subsetting and transformation. Data type versioning supports management of evolutionary changes to data. Data type updates allow new attributes and attribute values to be added on-the-fly. Access control is based on data quality.

- *Key data ingest features:* ECS needs to support concurrent ingest from multiple data sources, including external processing systems. It must accommodate diverse interface requirements and allow tailoring of data checking, conversion, and preprocessing. ECS must perform data source authentication, data transmission checking, and metadata validation.

- *Key data processing features:* ECS platforms and infrastructure support the integration and execution of standards-based software algorithms developed by Earth science teams. Automated scheduling of algorithm executions are based on either data arrival or user requests. Multiple algorithms may be chained. Production rules determine which data is used for input. Example rules include spatial/temporal selection, optional inputs, and alternative inputs. Product lineage information is collected, archived, and available to users. Production by external systems is also supported. Standard interfaces are provided, for example, for distributing input data to external systems or other ECS sites.

- *Key user interface features:* The primary user interface is a Web-based client, EOS Data Gateway (EDG). This permits searches against common and data type–specific metadata attributes; provides integrated, online access to browse data prior to ordering a full product; provides interfaces to support external search and order systems; and supports data navigation–based interfaces, that is, "select and get," as well as search and order interfaces.

[etc.]

ECS Software Architecture Documentation

Volume II:
ECS Software Architecture Views

Date of issue: January 29, 2002

Status: Baselined; Version 2.0.21

Name of issuing organization: Software Contractors, Inc.

Change history: Available at http://www.ourinternalwebsite/
ECS/documentation/architecture/vol2/change_history/

Summary: This document contains architectural views for ECS. Ten views are included: Decomposition, Uses, Generalization, Layered, Pipe and Filter, Shared Data, Communicating Processes, Deployment, Implementation, and Work Assignment. For more information about the purpose and contents of each view, see the ECS Architecture Documentation Roadmap in Chapter 1 of Volume I.

Volume II
ECS Software Architecture Views

CONTENTS

Chapter 1
Module Decomposition View

The decomposition view consists of 14 view packets. View packet 1 shows the decomposition of the entire ECS system into a group of three *segments,* each of which is further decomposed into a number of *subsystems.* Subsequent view packets (2–14) show the further decomposition of each of the subsystems.

1.1 Module Decomposition View Packet 1: The ECS System

1.1.1 Primary Presentation[9]

System	Segment
ECS	Science Data Processing Segment (SDPS)
	Communications and System Management Segment (CSMS)
	Flight Operations Segment (FOS)

1.1.2 Element Catalog

1.1.2.1 Elements and Their Properties

Properties of ECS modules are

- Name, given in the following table
- Responsibility, given in the following table
- Visibility; all elements are visible across the entire system
- Implementation information: See the implementation view in Volume II, Chapter 9

---

9. This is an example of a textual primary presentation. Text, such as a table or an outline, is sometimes superior to graphical presentations, which can easily become cluttered and difficult to lay out when the number of elements is large or when more than one level of decomposition is shown. A tabular primary presentation also can be combined with the element catalog in many cases, although that option is not exercised in this example.

Element Name	Element Responsibility
SDPS	The Science Data Processing Segment (SDPS) receives, processes, archives, and manages all data from EOS and other NASA Probe flight missions. It provides support to the user community in accessing the data and products resulting from research activities that use this data. SDPS also promotes, through advertisement services, the effective use and exchange of data within the user community. Finally, the SDPS plays a central role in providing the science community with the proper infrastructure for development, experimental use, and quality checking of new Earth science algorithms. SDPS is a distributed system, and its components are located at eight Distributed Active Archive Centers (DAACs).
CSMS	The Communications and System Management Segment (CSMS) focuses on the system components involved with the interconnection of user and service providers and with system management of the ECS components. The CSMS is composed of three major subsystems; here, they are introduced simply to explain the system configuration. They are the Communications Subsystem (CSS), the Internet-working Subsystem (ISS), and System Management Subsystem (MSS). The MSS, which includes several decentralized local system management capabilities at the DAAC sites and the mission operation center, provides system management services for the EOS ground system resources. The services provided by the MSS, even though they rely on the CSS-provided services, are largely allocable to the application domain.
FOS	The Flight Operations Segment (FOS) manages and controls the EOS spacecraft and instruments. The FOS is responsible for mission planning, scheduling, control, monitoring, and analysis in support of mission operations for U.S. EOS spacecraft and instruments. The FOS also provides investigator-site ECS software (the Instrument Support Terminal (IST) toolkit) to connect a Principal Investigator (PI) or Team Leader (TL) facility to the FOS in remote support of instrumental control and monitoring. PI/TL facilities are outside the FOS but connected to it by way of the EOSDIS Science Network (ESN). The FOS focuses on the command and control of the flight segment of EOS and the interaction it has with the ground operations of the ECS.

1.1.2.2 Relations and Their Properties

The relation type in this view is *is-part-of*. There are no exceptions or additions to the relations shown in the primary presentation.

1.1.2.3 Element Interfaces

Element interfaces for segments are given in subsequent decompositions.

1.1.2.4 Element Behavior

Not applicable.

1.1.3 Context Diagram

[omitted]

1.1.4 Variability Guide

None.

1.1.5 Architecture Background

1.1.5.1 Design Rationale

- *Rationale for three segments:* In the system design phase, broadly scoped decisions were made about the overall architecture of the ECS. Three major activities of the system were established and influenced by the system specification. These activities were Flight Operations, Science Data Processing, and Communications and Systems Management; each of these activities was allocated as the responsibility of a segment. During this activity, the ECS was organized into subsystems under each segment, based primarily on the analysis of ECS requirements. After taking into account the science and evolutionary requirements of the ECS, it should be noted that not all segment-designated requirements were allocated to the implied segment; rather, requirements were allocated to the design subsystems that logically would implement the designated functional and performance requirements.

[etc.]

1.1.5.2 Results of Analysis

- *Change analysis:* In June 2001, a change analysis was performed on the ECS architecture, using the Architecture Trade-off Analysis Method (ATAM). ATAM is a scenario-based method. Several scenarios dealt with likely changes and were applied to the module decomposition view. Results of the analysis can be found in the ATAM final report,

available at http://www.ourinternalwebsite/ECS/documen-
tation/architecture/atam_final_report.

[etc.]

1.1.5.3   Assumptions

- Future network upgrades will provide performance and
  bandwidth equal or superior to current capabilities. Given
  that, changes in system communication and management
  functions are unlikely to have any detrimental impact on
  the amount or type of science data processing that can be
  performed by ECS.
- Future needs for science data processing will require more,
  not less, capacity for computation, data storage, and communication.
- Communications and system management functions are
  independent of specific data processing algorithms used
  and data products produced by ECS.
- Communications and system management functions are
  independent of specific flight operation functions, such as
  planning and command transmission.

  [etc.]

1.1.6   Other Information

[omitted]

1.1.7   Related View Packets

- Parent: None.
- Children
  - Module Decomposition View Packet 2: The Science Data
    Processing Segment (Volume II, Section 1.2, page 418)
  - Module Decomposition View Packet 10: The Communi-
    cations and System Management Segment (CSMS), (Vol-
    ume II, Section 1.10, page 422)
  - Module Decomposition View Packet 14: Flight Opera-
    tions Segment (FOS), (Volume II, Section 1.14, page
    424)
- Siblings: None in this view. View packets in other views that
  express the same scope as this one—namely, the whole sys-
  tem—include

- Module Layered View Packet 1: The ECS System, (Volume II, Section 4.1, page 435)
- C&C Pipe-and-Filter View Packet 1: The ECS System, (Volume II, Section 5.1, page 439)
- Allocation Deployment View Packet 1: The ECS System, (Volume II, Section 8.1, page 457)
- Allocation Implementation View Packet 1: The ECS System, (Volume II, Section 9.1, page 461)
- Allocation Work Assignment View Packet 1: The ECS System, (Volume II, Section 10.1, page 464)

1.2 Module Decomposition View Packet 2: The Science Data Processing Segment

1.2.1 Primary Presentation

Segment	Subsystem
Science Data Processing Segment (SDPS)	Client
	Interoperability
	Ingest
	Data Management
	Data Processing
	Data Server
	Planning

1.2.2 Element Catalog

1.2.2.1 Elements and Their Properties

Properties of SDPS modules are

- Name, given in the following table
- Responsibility, given in the following table
- Visibility; all elements are visible across the entire system
- Implementation information: See the implementation view in Volume II, Chapter 9.

Element Name	Element Responsibility
Client	The SDPS Client subsystem provides a collection of components through which users access the services and data available in ECS and other systems interoperable with ECS. The Client subsystem also includes the services needed to interface an application, such as a science algorithm, with ECS for data access or to make use of ECS provided toolkits.
Interoperability	In general, support for the communication between SDPS clients and services is provided by CSMS, as described elsewhere. Any additional functions SDPS may require to support the interoperation of its components form part of the SDPS Interoperability subsystem and involve primarily the advertising service, which advertises service offerings.
Ingest	A provider site within EOSDIS will normally need to ingest a wide variety of data types to support the services it wishes to offer. This data may be delivered through a wide variety of interfaces— network file transfer, machine-to-machine transfer, media, hard copy, and so on—with a wide variety of management approaches to these interfaces. This interface heterogeneity and the need to support extendability and new data/interfaces as algorithms and provider functionality changes is handled within the Ingest subsystem.
Data Management	The Data Management subsystem is responsible for supporting the location, search, and access of data and service objects made available in the SDPS. The components of the subsystem decouple the location, search, and access functions from the components performing the data server and client interface functions, in order to accommodate the anticipated variety of users' search and access needs and to provide a growth path as capabilities evolve.
Data Processing	The Data Processing subsystem is responsible for managing, queuing, and executing processes on the processing resources at a provider site. Requests for processing are submitted from the Planning subsystem, which in turn have been triggered by data arrival or user request (Data Server) or through Planning itself, such as reprocessing.
Data Server	This subsystem has the responsibility for storing Earth science and related data in a persistent fashion, providing search and retrieval access to this data, and supporting the administration of the data and the supporting hardware devices and software products. As part of its retrieval function, the subsystem also provides for the distribution of data on physical media.

Element Name	Element Responsibility
Planning	The Planning subsystem supports the operations staff in developing a production plan based on a locally defined strategy, reserving the resources to permit the plan to be achieved and the implementation of the plan as data and processing requests are received. It also allows the site operations staff to negotiate on a common basis with other provider sites and EOSDIS management, via MSS, if any change to their production plan causes conflict with other provider sites' plans, such as where dependencies between processing algorithms cannot be fulfilled.

1.2.2.2   Relations and Their Properties

The relation type of concern in this view is *is-part-of*. Every subsystem *is part of* exactly one segment, namely, the Science Data Processing Segment, as shown in the primary presentation.

1.2.2.3   Element Interfaces

[omitted][10]

1.2.2.4   Element Behavior

Not applicable.

1.2.3   Context Diagram

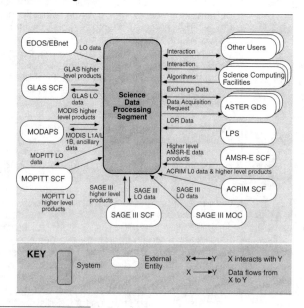

---

10. For examples of interface specifications, see Chapter 7.

1.2.4 Variability Guide

None.

1.2.5 Architecture Background

[omitted]

1.2.6 Other Information

[omitted]

1.2.7 Related View Packets

- Parent: Module Decomposition View Packet 1: The ECS System (Volume II, Section 1.1, page 414)
- Children
  - Module Decomposition View Packet 3: The Client Subsystem (Volume II, Section 1.3, page 422)
  - Module Decomposition View Packet 4: The Interoperability Subsystem (Volume II, Section 1.4, page 422)
  - Module Decomposition View Packet 5: The Ingest Subsystem (Volume II, Section 1.5, page 422)
  - Module Decomposition View Packet 6: The Data Management Subsystem (Volume II, Section 1.6, page 422)
  - Module Decomposition View Packet 7: The Data Processing Subsystem (Volume II, Section 1.7, page 422)
  - Module Decomposition View Packet 8: The Data Server Subsystem (Volume II, Section 1.8, page 422)
  - Module Decomposition View Packet 9: The Planning Subsystem (Volume II, Section 1.9, page 422)
- Siblings
  - Module Decomposition View Packet 10: The Communications and System Management Segment (CSMS) (Volume II, Section 1.10, page 422)
  - Module Decomposition View Packet 14: Flight Operations Segment (FOS) (Volume II, Section 1.14, page 424)

[The following view packets are omitted from the example. Each of them would refer to Module Decomposition View Packet 2: The Science Data Processing Segment as their parent view packet and to one another as their sibling view packets. Finally, each could be further decomposed into finer-grained modules; in fact, for a system the size of ECS, this would be highly likely.]

1.3 Module Decomposition View Packet 3: The Client Subsystem

1.4 Module Decomposition View Packet 4: The Interoperability Subsystem

1.5 Module Decomposition View Packet 5: The Ingest Subsystem

1.6 Module Decomposition View Packet 6: The Data Management Subsystem

1.7 Module Decomposition View Packet 7: The Data Processing Subsystem

1.8 Module Decomposition View Packet 8: The Data Server Subsystem

1.9 Module Decomposition View Packet 9: The Planning Subsystem

1.10 Module Decomposition View Packet 10: The Communications and System Management Segment (CSMS)

1.10.1 Primary Presentation

Segment	Subsystem
Communications and System Management Segment (CSMS)	System Management
	Communications
	Internetworking

1.10.2 Element Catalog

1.10.2.1 Elements and Their Properties

Properties of CSMS modules are

- Name, given in the following table
- Responsibility, given in the following table

- Visibility; all elements are visible across the entire system
- Implementation information: For this information, see the implementation view in Volume II, Chapter 9.

Element Name	Element Responsibility
System Management	The System Management subsystem is made of two classes: the manager and the managed objects. The manager uses management applications—typically, fault, performance, accounting, configuration, and security management; communications services—agents that manage the communications traffic between the manager and the services; and an information model that defines the information flow between the manager and the managed objects. The manager also uses several applications to monitor and to configure system resources, or managed objects, as required.
Communications	The Communications subsystem consists of the session, presentation, and application layers from an open system interconnection-reference model perspective. The Communications subsystem provides support for peer-to-peer, advanced distributed, messaging, management, and event-handling communications facilities. The Communications subsystem is functionally dependent on the services provided by the Internetworking subsystem.
Internetworking	The Internetworking subsystem consists of the physical, data link, network, and transport layers, according to the open systems interconnection-reference model specified by ISO 7498:1994, Open System Interconnection. The Internetworking subsystem supports alternative transports between communicating end stations; alternative networking methods between end systems and intermediate systems; and alternative circuit, packet, or cell-based LAN and WAN distribution services.

[The remainder of this view packet is omitted from the example.]

1.11   Module Decomposition View Packet 11: The System Management Subsystem

[omitted]

1.12   Module Decomposition View Packet 12: The Communications Subsystem

[omitted]

1.13 Module Decomposition View Packet 13: The Internetworking Subsystem

[omitted]

1.14 Module Decomposition View Packet 14: Flight Operations Segment (FOS)

1.14.1 Primary Presentation

Segment	Subsystem
Flight Operations Segment (FOS)	Planning and Scheduling
	Data Management
	Command Management
	Commanding
	Resource Management
	Telemetry
	User Interface
	Analysis

1.14.2 Element Catalog

1.14.2.1 Elements and Their Properties

Properties of FOS modules are

- Name, given in the following table
- Responsibility, given in the following table
- Visibility: all elements are visible across the entire system
- Implementation information; See the implementation view in Volume II, Chapter 9.

Element Name	Responsibility
Planning and Scheduling	The Planning and Scheduling subsystem integrates plans and schedules for spacecraft, instrument, and ground operations and coordinates DARs for U.S. instruments and multi-instrument observations, if any. Planning and Scheduling provides the operational staff with a common set of capabilities to perform what-if analyses and to visualize plans and schedules.

Element Name	Responsibility
Data Management	The Data Management subsystem is responsible for maintaining and updating the Project Database (PDB) and the FOS history log.
Command Management	The Command Management subsystem manages the preplanned command data for the spacecraft and instruments. Based on inputs received from Planning and Scheduling, Command Management collects and validates the commands, software memory loads, table loads, and instrument memory loads necessary to implement the instrument and spacecraft scheduled activities.
Commanding	The Commanding subsystem is responsible for transferring command data—real-time commands or command loads—to EDOS for uplink to the spacecraft during each real-time contact. Command data can be received in real time by the operational staff or as preplanned command groups generated by the Command Management subsystem. The Commanding subsystem is also responsible for verifying command execution on-board the spacecraft.
Resource Management	The Resource Management subsystem provides the capability to manage and monitor the configuration of the EOC: configuring EOC resources for multimission support, facilitating failure recovery during real-time contacts, and managing the real-time interface with the NCC.
Telemetry	The Telemetry subsystem receives and processes housekeeping telemetry in CCSDS packets from EDOS. After the packet decommutation, the telemetry data is converted to engineering units and checked against boundary limits.
User Interface	The User Interface subsystem provides character-based and graphical display interfaces for FOS operators interacting with all the previously described FOS subsystems.
Analysis	The Analysis subsystem is responsible for managing the on-board systems and for the overall mission monitoring. Its functions include performance analysis and trend analysis. It also cooperates with the Telemetry subsystem to support fault detection and isolation.

[The remainder of this view packet is omitted from the example. Subsequent view packets that further decompose this segment's eight subsystems—Planning and Scheduling, Data Management, Command Management, Commanding, Resource Management, Telemetry, User Interface, and Analysis—are also omitted.]

Chapter 2
Module Uses View

2.1 Module Uses View Packet 1: The Science Data Processing Segment (SDPS)

2.1.1 Primary Presentation

SDPS Element	Uses This Element
Science Data Processing Segment	

	Ingest Subsystem		
		INGST CSCI	ADSRV CSCI in the Interoperability Subsystem
			STMGT CSCI in the Data Server Subsystem
			SDSRV CSCI in the Data Server Subsystem
			DCCI CSCI in the Communications Subsystem
	[etc.]	other CSCIs within the Ingest Subsystem	

	Data Server Subsystem		
		DDIST CSCI	MCI CSCI in the System Management Subsystem
			DCCI CSCI in the Communications Subsystem
			STMGT CSCI in the Data Server Subsystem
			INGST CSCI in the Ingest Subsystem
	[etc.]	other CSCIs within the Data Server Subsystem	

[etc.]	other subsystems within the Science Data Processing Segment

2.1.2 Element Catalog

2.1.2.1 Elements and Their Properties

Properties of ECS modules are

- Name, given in the following table
- Responsibility, given in the following table

- Visibility: all elements are visible outside their parent
- Implementation information: see Volume II, Chapter 9.

The elements in this view are CSCIs, which are subelements of subsystems as defined in the module decomposition view of Chapter 1.[11]

Element Name	Responsibility
INGST CSCI	The INGST CSCI supports a variety of interfaces to external systems. The application-level protocol set up for data transfer is potentially different for each of the external interfaces. As a result, a separate ingest software application is required to facilitate data transfer for each interface. To minimize the software development effort and make it easier to accommodate interfaces to new external systems, data ingest from external systems is categorized, based on common characteristics and ingest processes.
ADSRV CSCI	The Advertising Service (ADSRV) CSCI manages Earth Science related advertisements. The advertisement information is stored persistently in a relational Database Management System (DBMS). The Advertising Service data is replicated within each DAAC using Sybase COTS software.
SDSRV CSCI	The Science Data Server (SDSRV) CSCI manages and provides user access to collections of non-document (non-hard copy) Earth science data; extracts and modifies data by request; accepts browse, search, and retrieval requests from users; and catalogs data insert requests from other SDPS or CSMS CSCIs, CSCs, and processes. The SDSRV CSCI manages Earth science data as logical collections of related data, via interfaces independent of data formats and hardware configurations inherent in underlying storage technologies. The SDSRV manages interactive sessions with service requesters and informs the service requester of the availability of data and services via the IOS.
DCCI CSCI	The DCCI CSCI consists mainly of COTS software and hardware providing servers, gateways, and software library services to other SDPS and CSMS CSCIs.

11. The excerpt of the module decomposition view in Chapter 1 did not delve to the level of CSCIs. A complete decomposition view would have, documenting their responsibilities there. That would make the element catalog here redundant. In a real documentation package, it would probably consist of pointers or hyperlinks to the information in Chapter 1.

Element Name	Responsibility
DDIST CSCI	The Data Distribution (DDIST) CSCI monitors and controls processing for distribution requests. Data Distribution processing consists of directing the STMGT CSCI to place data for distribution in working storage and creating packing lists, and directing the STMGT CSCI to copy data on to hard media or push data as required via FTP, and sending notifications for pulls completed via FTP. Data handled electronically is either pushed via FTP to a user specified location or placed in a directory to be pulled. If data is to be pulled, once the data is ready, the DDIST CSCI sends an electronic message to the user providing the required information for the user to pull the data. If data is to be distributed via hard media, a complete packing list is generated as well as an inventory list for each hard media generated. The DDIST CSCI has a GUI interface with the administration/operations staff (Admin. /Ops). The GUI provides error conditions and status to operations staff and enables the operations staff to set parameters and control operations including suspending, canceling, and resuming requests, changing the priorities of requests, changing the media type, performing multiple selects, and setting threshold sizes. The DDIST CSCI provides limited automatic error response by suspending requests when most errors are encountered. The hard media types supported are 8mm tape, D3 tape, CD-ROM, and Digital Linear Tape (DLT).
MCI CSCI	The Management Software CSCI (MCI) provides distributed system management support capabilities in the fault, configuration, accountability, performance, and security service areas.
STMGT CSCI	The Storage Management (STMGT) CSCI stores/archives, manages, and retrieves nondocument Earth science data and provides a user-friendly graphical user interface (GUI) for operations. The STMGT CSCI manages all physical storage resources for all the DSS CSCIs and processes including tape robotic archive, RAID disk cache, online storage, and peripheral devices used for ingesting data from and distributing data to hard media such as various hard media sizes or drive types.
[etc.]	[etc.]

2.1.2.2 Relations and Their Properties

The relation type in this view is *uses*. An element uses another element if the correctness of the first depends on a correct implementation of the second being present. It is not enough for an element to invoke another element; if the behavior of the invoked element does not affect the correctness of the invoking element, it is not used. Similarly, an element may use another element that it does not invoke, if it relies on that element to take an action or to perform a function autonomously.

There are no exceptions or additional *uses* relations among the elements in this view packet beyond those shown in the primary presentation.

2.1.2.3 Element Interfaces

Interfaces for the elements shown in this view are specified under the corresponding elements in the module decomposition view (Volume II, Chapter 1).

2.1.2.4 Element Behavior

Not applicable.

2.1.3 Context Diagram

The context for this view packet is established by the context diagram shown on page 420 as part of the module decomposition view.

2.1.4 Variability Guide

None.

2.1.5 Architecture Background

[omitted]

2.1.6 Other Information

[omitted]

2.1.7 Related View Packets

- Parent: None in this view. View packets in other views whose scope is the entire system could be considered beyond views parents. They include
  - Module Decomposition View Packet 1: The ECS System (Volume II, Section 1.1, page 414)

- Module Layered View Packet 1: The ECS System (Volume II, Section 4.1, page 435)
- C&C Pipe-and-Filter View Packet 1: The ECS System (Volume II, Section 5.1, page 439)
- Allocation Deployment View Packet 1: The ECS System (Volume II, Section 8.1, page 457)
- Allocation Implementation View Packet 1: The ECS System (Volume II, Section 9.1, page 461)
- Allocation Work Assignment View Packet 1: The ECS System (Volume II, Section 10.1, page 464)
- Children: None.[12]
- Siblings
  - Module Uses View Packet 2: The Communications and System Management Segment (CSMS), (Volume II, Section 2.2, page 430)
  - Module Uses View Packet 3: The Flight Operations Segment (FOS), (Volume II, Section 2.3, page 430)

2.2 Module Uses View Packet 2: The Communications and System Management Segment (CSMS)

[omitted]

2.3 Module Uses View Packet 3: The Flight Operations Segment (FOS)

[omitted]

---

12. There may well be finer-grained *uses* relations shown for a large system such as this one, in which case those view packets would be children of this one.

Chapter 3
Module Generalization View

3.1 Module Generalization View Packet 1: The Science Data Processing Segment (SDPS)

3.1.1 Primary Presentation

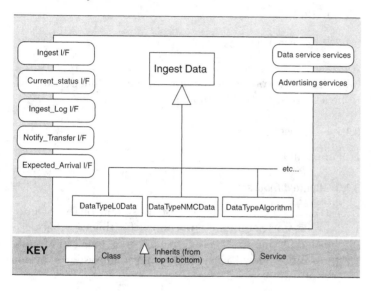

3.1.2 Element Catalog

3.1.2.1 Elements and Their Properties

Properties of SDPS modules are

- Name, given in the following table
- Responsibility, given in the following table
- Visibility: all elements are visible across the system
- Implementation information: see Volume II, Chapter 9.

Element Name	Responsibility
IngestData	This class handles the data ingested into the EOSDIS site. This is the abstract superclass from which all ingest instances inherit the basic ingest-related characteristics.

Element Name	Responsibility
DataTypeL0Data	Ingester for raw instrument data (L0).
DataTypeNMCData	Ingester for National Meteorological Center (NMC) data.
DataTypeAlgorithm	Ingester for science algorithm–based data.

3.1.2.2 Relations and Their Properties

The relation types of concern to this view are *implementation* and *interface inheritance*. All relations are shown in the primary presentation.

3.1.2.3 Element Interfaces

Interfaces for the elements shown in this view are specified under the corresponding elements in the module decomposition view (Volume II, Chapter 1).

3.1.2.4 Element Behavior

Not applicable.

3.1.3 Context Diagram

IngestData is a part of the Ingest subsystem of the Science Data Processing Segment. The context for this view packet is established by that for the Ingest subsystem, given in Module Decomposition View Packet 5: The Ingest Subsystem (Volume II, Section 1.5, page 422).

3.1.4 Variability Guide

None.

3.1.5 Architecture Background

3.1.5.1 Design Rationale

- *Handling the variety of data sources.* The Ingest subsystem is responsible for the reception and storage of several types of sensor data. A specific Ingest subsystem needs to ingest a wide variety of data types that can be delivered via a wide variety of interfaces. Given the many sources for ingested data, it will not be possible to mandate a single interface approach. These diversities and the need to support extensibility and new data/interfaces lead to a design in which the ingest functionality is generalized in a top-level class with which the users of ingest functionality interface.

IngestData is the top-level ingest type class. The users of ingest functionality interface with that class. Currently, DataTypeL0Data, DataTypeNMCData, and DataTypeAlgorithm are the subclasses for the specific data/interface that must be ingested.

The diversity is exhibited in the following characteristics: volume, format, structure, metadata, periodicity, interface protocol/media, and action to be taken on ingestion in EOSDIS. This diversity means that the specific ingest subclasses will inherit some basic characteristics of IngestData, such as logging of data arrival, but considerable specialization for each subclass will be needed. It would be desirable to try and limit the diversity, and therefore the specialization, but this would significantly reduce the flexibility and extensibility to support changes and new interfaces, which would significantly reduce the flexibility of EOSDIS to support future science investigations.

Because of the way the Ingest subsystem handles the variety of data, other ECS Science Data Processing subsystems can be designed and built to use a systemwide common data type, thus simplifying their design and obviating the need for them to require generalization/specialization.

[etc.]

3.1.5.2   Results of analysis

None.

3.1.5.3   Assumptions

[omitted]

3.1.6   Other Information

[omitted]

3.1.7   Related View Packets[13]

* Parent: None in this view. Module Decomposition View Packet 5: The Ingest Subsystem (Volume II, Section 1.5, page 422) is a beyond views parent.

---

13. IngestData is a class that is a part of the Ingest subsystem. Were there an overall "System" class that every other class inherits from, that view packet would be a parent of this one. Were there lower-level specializations of, for example, DataTypeL0Data, those would be shown in children view packets.

- Children: None.
- Siblings: None in this view. View packets in the Module Decomposition View (Volume II, Chapter 1) that deal with subsystems of the Science Data Processing Segment are beyond views siblings.

Chapter 4
Module Layered View

4.1   Module Layered View Packet 1: The ECS System

4.1.1   Primary Presentation

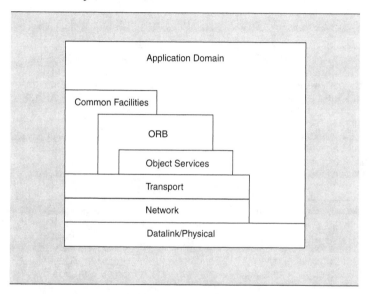

4.1.2   Element Catalog

4.1.2.1   Elements and Their Properties

Properties of ECS layers, given in the following table, are

- Name
- Responsibilities
- Contents

Element Name	Responsibilities	Contents
Common Facilities	Common Facilities are defined as those interfaces and uniform sequencing semantics that are shared across applications. Common Facilities consist of generic facilities as defined by the OMG, ECS domain specific facilities, and other industry standards. Common Facilities includes legacy service categories such as File Access (ftp), Electronic Mail, and Remote Services (rlogin, rcp, rcmd...).	Object Linking Service, Embedded Objects Service, Object Interchange Service, Clipboard Service, Cataloging and Browsing Service, Object Rendering Service, Document Interchange Service, Help Facilities Service, Printing and Spooling Service, Application Agents Service, File Access Service, Electronic Mail Service, Virtual Terminal Service, Bulletin Board/Information Search and Retrieval Service, and Management Data Access Service.
ORB	An Object Request Broker (ORB) provides the communication backbone for transparently making requests to and receiving responses from objects locally or remotely without client awareness of the mechanisms used to communicate with, activate, or store the objects. The ORB is the core set of object services that enables distributed processing of objects.	Interface definition language (IDL) compiler, an interface repository, an implementation repository, a static invocation interface, and a dynamic invocation interface.
Object Service	Object services provide low-level building-block capabilities. Since these services are (or are expected to be) mostly COTS, they represent potential building blocks for all ECS applications. An ORB does not provide interoperability by itself. Semantic support is provided by Object Services in the form of additional interfaces, protocols, and policies. The services are general purpose and necessary to construct any distributed application. Object Services augment the functionality of the ORB and are a collection of services (interfaces and objects) that support basic functions for using and implementing objects. Operations provided by Object Services serve as building blocks for OMG Common Facilities and Application Objects.	Event Service, Naming Service, LifeCycle Service, Security Service, Persistence Service, Association Service, Trading Service, Query Service, Property Service, Concurrency Service, Externalization Service, Transaction Service, Threads Service, Time Service, Change Management Service, Replication Service, Data Interchange Service, Archive Service, Backup/Restore Service, Startup/ Shutdown Service, Installation and Activation Service, and Operational Control Service.

Element Name	Responsibilities	Contents
Transport	The transport layer provides transparent transfer of data between higher level entities and relieves them from any concern with how reliable and cost-effective transfer of data is achieved. Cost/performance optimization is achieved within constraints imposed by the overall demands of all concurrent higher-level sessions, and the overall quality and capacity of the network-service available to the Transport layer. Primary services provided by the transport services for connection-mode communication include transport connection establishment, transport connection release, data transfer, expedited data transfer, and suspend. Connectionless-mode communication provides all of the above except that data transfer omits segmentation and PDU reassembly.	TCP transport service, UDP transport service, ISO Transport Protocol 4 service, and XTP transport service.
Network	The network layer provides the functional and procedural means to exchange network data units between transport entities over network connections, both for connection-mode and connectionless-mode communications. It relieves upper layers from concern of all routing and relay operations associated with network connection. The basic function of the network layer is to provide the transparent transfer of data between transport entities. This layer contains all functions to provide upper layers with a firm network/transport layer boundary, independent of underlying communications media in all things other than QoS. In this way, the network layer masks the differences in the characteristics of different transmission and subnetwork technologies into a consistent service.	IP services, ICMP Protocol service, ARP protocol service, OSPF protocol service, BGP protocol service, and RIP protocol service.
[etc.]	[etc.]	[etc.]

4.1.2.2 Relations and Their Properties

The relation in the layered view is *allowed-to-use*. Software in a layer is *allowed to use* other software in the same layer. Software in a layer is *allowed to use* software in any other layer immediately below, as shown in the primary presentation.

4.1.2.3 Element Interfaces

[omitted]

4.1.2.4 Element Behavior

Not applicable.

4.1.3 Context Diagram

The context for this view packet is established by the context diagram in Volume II, Section 1.1.3 in the highest-level view packet of the module decomposition view.

4.1.4 Variability Guide

None.

4.1.5 Architecture Background

[omitted]

4.1.6 Other Information

[omitted]

4.1.7 Related View Packets

- Parent: None.
- Children: None.
- Siblings: None in this view. View packets in other views that express the same scope as this one—namely, the whole system—include
  - Module Decomposition View Packet 1: The ECS System (Volume II, Section 1.1, page 414)
  - C&C Pipe-and-Filter View Packet 1: The ECS System (Volume II, Section 5.1, page 439)
  - Allocation Deployment View Packet 1: The ECS System (Volume II, Section 8.1, page 457)
  - Allocation Implementation View Packet 1: The ECS System (Volume II, Section 9.1, page 461)
  - Allocation Work Assignment View Packet 1: The ECS System (Volume II, Section 10.1, page 464)

Chapter 5
C&C Pipe-and-Filter View

5.1   C&C Pipe-and-Filter View Packet 1: The ECS System

5.1.1   Primary Presentation

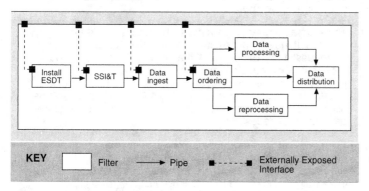

5.1.2   Element Catalog

5.1.2.1   Elements and Their Properties

Properties of ECS filter components, given in the following table, are

- Name
- Type
- Description

Element Name	Type	Description
Install ESDT	Proc	All data interactions within the ECS are performed against Earth Science Data Types (ESDTs). An ESDT is the logical object that describes both the inventory holdings for particular data and the services (insert, acquire, and so on) that can be applied to that data. Before a user (including DAAC operations) can perform any data services against a data set in the ECS, the ESDT for that data type must be installed. Installation includes defining the collection level and granule level metadata in the inventory (Science Data Server), advertising the data type and its services, defining metadata attribute valids in the Data Dictionary, and defining subscribable data events.

Element Name	Type	Description
SSI&T	Proc	Science Software Integration & Test (SSI&T) is the process by which Instrument Team developed algorithms get qualified for use in the ECS production environment. Much of this process is algorithm specific and/or manual or semiautomatic. These aspects are not dealt with in this document. However, the reception of the original algorithm package (Delivered Algorithm Package—DAP) and the qualified algorithm package (Science Software Archive Package—SSAP) are automated tasks.
Data Ingest	Proc	Once the ESDT is defined, and any production algorithms have been integrated, then the ECS is ready to accept data and generate higher-level products.
Data Ordering	Proc	There are a number of ways in which data can be requested in the ECS. If the product exists in the archive, then a user can simply request it for distribution. If the product doesn't exist, but the algorithms for producing the product have been integrated, then the user can request production. Alternatively if the product exists, but has been generated with a set of runtime algorithms different from those desired, then the user can request that the product be reprocessed.
Data Processing	Proc	Many products are produced automatically upon the availability of the necessary input data. But in addition to this "standard" production, the ECS also has the capability to produce products on demand in response to a user request.
Data Reprocessing	Proc	An important feature of the ECS is the ability to reprocess data when either the original production data or algorithm were faulty, or if another user needs different execution parameters.
Data Distribution	Proc	Once data is generated or ingested into the ECS, it is made available to other users. The distribution system provides for a flexible data delivery system that can provide data either automatically based on preestablished event triggers, or by direct request.

5.1.2.2   Relations and Their Properties

The only relation in the pipe-and-filter view is *attachment*, between pipes and filters. It is as shown in the primary presentation.

5.1.2.3   Element Interfaces

[omitted]

5.1.2.4   Element Behavior

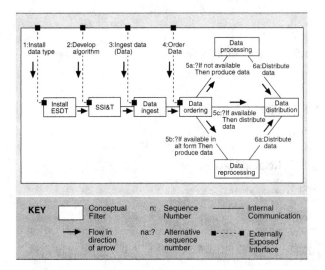

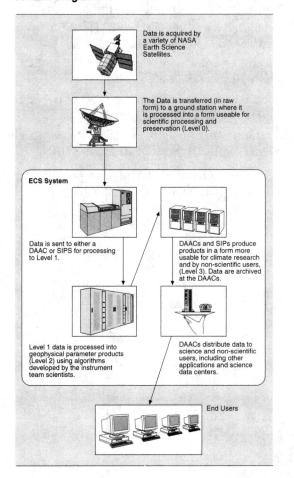

5.1.3   Context Diagram

5.1.4 Variability Guide

None.

5.1.5 Architecture Background

[omitted]

5.1.6 Other Information

[omitted]

5.1.7 Related View Packets

- Parent: None.
- Children: None.
- Siblings: None in this view. View packets in other views that express the same scope as this one—namely, the whole system—include
  - Module Decomposition View Packet 1: The ECS System (Volume II, Section 1.1, page 414)
  - Module Layered View Packet 1: The ECS System (Volume II, Section 4.1, page 435)
  - Allocation Deployment View Packet 1: The ECS System (Volume II, Section 8.1, page 457)
  - Allocation Implementation View Packet 1: The ECS System (Volume II, Section 9.1, page 461)
  - Allocation Work Assignment View Packet 1: The ECS System (Volume II, Section 10.1, page 464)

An implementation refinement of the pipe-and-filter view is the C&C Shared-Data View (Volume II, Chapter 6).

Chapter 6
C&C Shared-Data View

6.1 C&C Shared-Data View Packet 1: The Data Management Subsystem

6.1.1 Primary Presentation

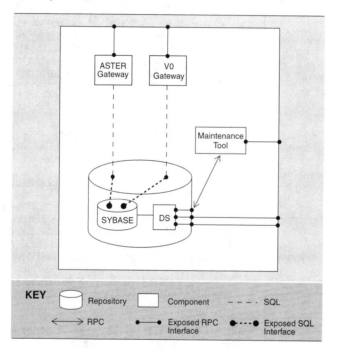

6.1.2 Element Catalog

6.1.2.1 Elements and Their Properties[14]

Properties of Data Management Subsystem elements are

- Name, given in the following table
- Whether the element is a data repository, a data accessor, a synchronization operation, a message, or a query
- A description of the element

---

14. Often, the shared-data view also includes element properties dealing with data distribution, the kind of data stored or transmitted, and performance or capacity properties.

Element Name	Type	Description
DictServ (DS)	Data repository	Data Dictionary/Server: The primary server interface to collection and collection-related information for the DMS and other subsystems. It allows DDICT client processes the capability to perform data searches, insertions, updates, or deletions to the collection information held in the DDICT database. The Data Dictionary offers two basic interfaces. DDICT Data Search: The Data Dictionary Server allows a user to specify search requests on the Data Dictionary database, using a GIParameter List. DDICT Data Insert and Delete: Provides a client process with the capability to insert and delete data within the Data Dictionary database. The Data Dictionary Service supports • Single requests at a time • Synchronous request processing • Asynchronous request processing
VOGW (VO Gateway)	Data accessor	V0 Gateway: provides access to data and services between the SDSRV CSCI and the V0 IMS. V0 GTWAY services include inventory searches, requests for browse data, product requests, and price estimate requests.
AsterGW (ASTER Gateway)	Data accessor	ASTER Gateway: provides access to data and services between the ECS Science Data Server and the ASTER GDS. Services include inventory searches, requests for browse data, product requests, and price estimate requests.
MTool (Maintenance Tool)	Data accessor	Data Maintenance Tool: provides a graphical user interface (GUI) to insert, update, or delete schema information held in the DDICT database, allowing DAAC operations staff to maintain the data stored in the Data Dictionary database. The Data Dictionary Maintenance Tool also provides the following capabilities:

Element Name	Type	Description
		• Import and export of valids: Allows DAAC operations staff to import and export data collection attribute valids to and from the GDS, ECS, and V0 IMS for catalog interoperability.
		• Data collection attribute and keyword mapping: Allows DAAC operations staff to map data collection attributes and keyword valids from ECS to V0 IMS and between the ASTER GDS and ECS. The V0 GTWAY CSCI processes (EcDmEcsToV0Gateway and EcDmV0ToEcsGateway) that translate requests from ECS to V0 IMS and the ASTGW CSCI processes (EcDmEcsToAsterGateway and EcDmAsterToEcsGateway) that translate requests between ECS and the ASTER GDS use this information.
RPC	Synchronization operation	Remote procedure call via CORBA interfaces. See Communications and Systems Management Segment.
Sybase	Data repository	Sybase SQL server.
SQL	Query	SQL query.

6.1.2.2   Relations and Their Properties

The relation of this C&C view is *attachment*, dictating how components and connectors are attached to each other. The relations are as shown in the primary presentation; there are no additional ones.

6.1.2.3   Element Interfaces

Interfaces for the elements shown in this view are specified under the corresponding element in the module decomposition view (Volume II, Chapter 1). To identify those elements, consult Volume I, Chapter 4.

6.1.2.4   Element Behavior

[omitted]

6.1.3 Context Diagram

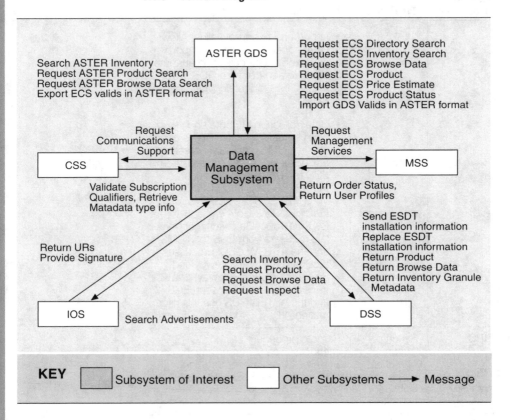

6.1.4 Variability Guide

None.

6.1.5 Architecture Background

6.1.5.1 Design Rationale

- *Technology issues.* The Data Management Subsystem contains hardware resources for the persistent storage of data dictionary and schema data across one or more DBMS servers and will be sized to meet the demands on a site-by-site basis. The primary technologies used within this subsystem are DBMS servers, host-attached spinning disk, possible use of channel-attached RAID disk, and a variety of communications capabilities. Pools of local X-terminals and display workstations support administration, help desk, and data repository maintenance activities. At sites where client request rates are low and the data collections and schema repository maintenance activities. At sites where client request rates are low and the data collections and schema relatively few in number and in scale, the option exists to share server and data repository resources with the Data Server subsystem's Data Repositories. This possibility will be explored as the physical database analysis matures in the future.

- *Interface design.* Here is an informal view of how the interface to this subsystem is intended to work. It may provide some insight into the more rigorous interface specifications presented elsewhere. The subsystem consists of three services:

  - A distributed search service, called the Distributed Information Manager (DIM)

  - A service called the Local Information Manager (LIM), that acts as the gateway between the data management services used by a site and the distributed search services

  - A Data Dictionary Service, which provides data names and explanations of the data and access operations in a distributed fashion

  Both DIM and LIM accept queries and data access requests for execution but do not process the queries. Rather, they act as search agents on behalf of the users by identifying the sources of this data, transforming the search and access operations into requests that are acceptable to these sources. Users interface with their agent DIM or LIM to determine the status of a search or to obtain the search results. They are decoupled from the actual sources, as well as from the methods their DIM and LIM agents use to perform the searches and obtain optimal results.

  Users formulate their queries by using query user interface programs that are part of the client subsystem. The query user interfaces will interact with the Data Dictionary Service—often transparently to the user—to present the user with choices—for example, of the data names applicable in a particular context—and interpret user input. Any intelligence available in the Data Dictionary about this data can be used by the query interfaces to formulate the search: to improve its accuracy, for example. The Data Dictionary service is accessible to the components that process queries—DIM and LIM—and the components that formulate queries, user query interface programs. As a result, a query interface can make references to data dictionary concepts that DIM and LIM can interpret. For example, a sciences user may enter search parameter names taken from a particular context, such as Atmospheric Dynamics. The query program will insert a reference to *Atmospheric Dynamics* into the query. DIM and LIM can then interpret the parameter names in the proper context.

- *Two levels of query processing.* The SDPS Data Management architecture uses two levels of query processing: the distribution level, which is serviced by the DIM, and the site level, which is serviced by the LIM. The two levels are motivated by the following considerations.

  - *Different concerns.* A LIM provides an interface to a site. The inner workings of the site are hidden by its LIM, and each site can implement its own, specialized version of a LIM. DAACs and SCFs thus have the ability to decide how to best organize their data internally. On the other hand, the network needs only one type of DIM implementation, regardless of the number of LIMs. As a result, DAACs and SCFs need not be concerned about tailoring a DIM design to their requirements and implementing and maintaining DIM software.

  - *Distributed query processing.* Distributed query processing poses a number of difficult issues, which SDPS plans to address in an evolutionary manner. Over time, the DIM design will be changed to provide better optimization of distributed searches or enhanced capabilities for merging search results. With a separated DIM, none of these changes will force DAACs and SCFs to change their LIMs. Nor will DAACs and SCFs have to address the issues of distributed searching in a wide area network when they implement the LIM software.

  - *Data administration concerns.* Separation of DIM and LIM also simplifies data administration. The responsibility of each site is clearly defined and confined to the LIM as its interface into the data and information network. It is not necessary to coordinate the definition of a single, integrated schema across all sites. Instead, each site defines its schema only and has freedom in deciding what information to make accessible through it.

  - *New LIM services for new clients.* One of the objectives of SDPS is that it provide DIM and LIM implementations for ECS. However, other organizations may want to join the network by developing their own LIM services. Separating the DIM functions from the LIM will make their task easier. In addition, organizations, such as commercial software vendors or universities, may become interested in developing new DIM versions, perhaps with special features that provide improved search capabilities, such as those tailored to specific science disciplines. A DIM that is separate from LIM components and their site-unique aspects will facilitate their work.

[etc.]

6.1.5.2 Results of Analysis

None.

6.1.5.3 Assumptions

- The provider sites within ECS can interoperate at three levels: tightly coupled, loosely coupled, or minimally coupled. The main impact on which level of interoperation is chosen rests with the type of schema integration versus federation that is supported at the Distributed Information Management level of the data management architecture. ECS assumes a loose coupling, which provides the most provider site autonomy. This leads to a federated schema with a global core schema. An important issue arises concerning the process to establish and maintain this global core. Although the initial global core schema will be established as part of the ECS data modeling activity, ECS assumes that a group will be chartered to define procedures for ensuring that it is used and maintained.

[etc.]

6.1.6 Other information

[omitted]

6.1.7 Related View Packets

- Parent: None in this view. View packets in other views showing the Science Data Processing Segment (SDPS) are beyond views parents.
- Children: None
- Siblings: None.[15]

---

15. Thus, the shared-data style is limited to the Data Management subsystem in ECS. This is an example of a system exhibiting different styles in different places.

Chapter 7
C&C Communicating-Processes View

7.1 C&C Communicating-Processes View Packet 1: Ingest Subsystem

The Ingest subsystem deals with the initial reception of all data received at an EOSDIS facility and triggers subsequent archiving and processing of the data. It makes data ingest schedules available for access by users and programs and reports deviations from the schedules as exceptions so they can be handled through intervention by operations or science users.

7.1.1 Primary Presentation

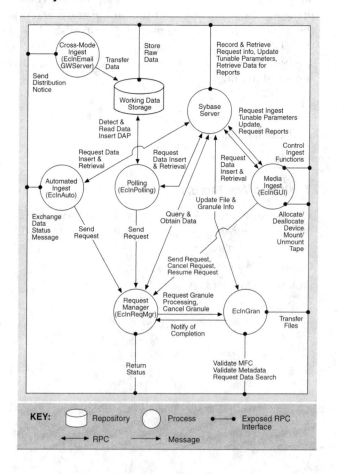

7.1.2   Element Catalog

7.1.2.1   Elements and Their Properties

Properties of Ingest subsystem communicating-processes components and connectors, given in the following table, are

* Name
* Type
* Description

Element Name	Type	Description
EcInAuto	Process	Auto Ingest: Provides fundamental capabilities for data ingest into the SDPS, on receipt of a data availability notice (DAN). This process can be tailored for a specific interface. RPCs are used to request ingest services to schedule data transfer from the source. EcInAuto also • Manages single requests at a time • Invokes an RPC to the EcInReqMgr to begin request processing • Checks DAN information • Sends and receives data status messages
EcInPolling	Process	Polling Ingest • Creates the appropriate polling request • Detects new files of interest at tunable periods of time in either external or local disk locations by checking an agreed on network location for available data • Creates a unique identifier for the request • Submits requests • Reports the status of the ongoing requests
EcInGUI	Process	Ingest GUI: provides Maintenance and Operations (M&O) personnel with the capability, via GUI Interface, to • Perform physical media ingest: to ingest data from hard media • Monitor the ingest history log, to monitor the status of ongoing ingest requests, to cancel ingest requests and granules, and to resume suspended ingest requests and granules • Modify ingest configuration parameters

Element Name	Type	Description
EcInReqMgr	Process	Request Manager • Manages the ingest request traffic and the processing of the ingest requests • Provides the capability to process multiple ingest requests concurrently by placing the request in a queue In the event of a failure, the EcInReqMgr process restores ongoing requests from the Ingest database.
EcIn Email GWServer	Process	Ingest E-mail Gateway Server • Receives e-mail distribution notification messages • Stores e-mail messages into files • Detects new files of interest at a regular time interval, which can be configured, on a local disk • Creates a polling request and puts it on a local disk location
EcInGran	Process	Granule Server provides services to perform the required data preprocessing and the subsequent data insertion into the appropriate Data Server. The preprocessing of data consists of • Converting the data, if needed • Extracting the metadata into the standard SDPS metadata format, if needed • Performing required metadata existence and parameter range checks • Updating the metadata with ingest-specific metadata, such as start and stop date/time for ingest EcInGran coordinates the ingest granule processing, including • Performing data preprocessing • Sending an insertion request to the appropriate Data Server • Updating the granule state • Transferring data files into Ingest • Building file lists • Grouping files with a valid ESDT
Sybase Server	Process	Stores and provides access to the INS internal data. In particular, the database stores the Ingest operations databases: Ingest History Logs and the Ingest request checkpoint state and template information.
RPC	Synch call	Exchanges data status, detects and reads data, sends updates, deletions, and other instructions.

Element Name	Type	Description
Notification	Event	Notifies of activity completion and data distribution. The two approaches to initiating event communication are called the *push* model and the *pull* model. The push model allows a supplier of events to initiate the transfer of the event data to consumers. The pull model allows a consumer of events to request the event data from a supplier. In the push model, the supplier is taking the initiative.
SQL	DB Query/ Resp	Database query/response mechanism.
[etc.]	[etc.]	[etc.]

7.1.2.2   Relations and Their Properties

Attachment, showing how the components and connectors are attached to each other. The primary presentation shows all attachments.

7.1.2.3   Interfaces

Interfaces for the elements shown in this view are specified under the corresponding element in the module decomposition view (Volume II, Chapter 1). To identify those elements, consult Volume I, Chapter 4.

7.1.2.4   Element Behavior

[omitted]

7.1.3 Context Diagram

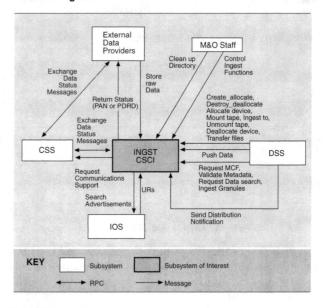

7.1.4 Variability Guide

None.

7.1.5 Architecture Background

7.1.5.1 Design Rationale

- The subsystem supports the ingest of data into ECS repositories on a routine and ad hoc basis. Given the variety of possible data formats and structures, each external interface and each ad hoc ingest task may have unique aspects. Therefore, the Ingest subsystem is organized into a collection of software components—ingest management software, translation tools, media-handling software—from which those required in a specific situation can be readily configured. The resultant configuration is called an *ingest client,* which can either operate on a continuous basis to serve a routine external interface or exist only for the duration of a specific ad hoc ingest task.

- Ingest subsystem software services are designed to support fault tolerance, graceful degradation, and effective recovery, such as automatic switchover to backup resources when primary resources fail; flexibility to handle various types of quality assurance for products, on-site as well as off-site; and retaining production history to allow reprocessing in case of data loss.

[etc.]

7.1.5.2 Results of Analysis

None.

7.1.5.3 Assumptions

- A DAAC will often preprocess ingested ancillary data, correlative data, documents, and so on into another format for the purposes of processing. This will result in data represented in both the original native format and the preprocessed format.

- Only preprocessed data will be archived unless there is no means by which the native data could be reacquired.

[etc.]

7.1.6 Other Information

[omitted]

7.1.7 Related View Packets

- Parent: None in this view. View packets in other views showing the Science Data Processing Segment (SDPS) are beyond views parents.
- Children: None
- Siblings
  - C&C Communicating-Processes View Packet 2: Data Server Subsystem (Volume II, Section 7.2, page 456)
  - C&C Communicating-Processes View Packet 3: Data Management Subsystem (Volume II, Section 7.3, page 456)
  - C&C Communicating-Processes View Packet 4: Client Subsystem (Volume II, Section 7.4, page 456)
  - C&C Communicating-Processes View Packet 5: Interoperability Subsystem (Volume II, Section 7.5, page 456)
  - C&C Communicating-Processes View Packet 6: Planning Subsystem (Volume II, Section 7.6, page 456)
  - C&C Communicating-Processes View Packet 7: Data Processing Subsystem (Volume II, Section 7.7, page 456)
  - C&C Communicating-Processes View Packet 8: Communications Subsystem (Volume II, Section 7.8, page 456)
  - C&C Communicating-Processes View Packet 9: System Management Subsystem (Volume II, Section 7.9, page 456)
  - C&C Communicating-Processes View Packet 10: Internetworking Subsystem (Volume II, Section 7.10, page 456)

7.2 C&C Communicating-Processes View Packet 2: Data Server Subsystem

[omitted]

7.3 C&C Communicating-Processes View Packet 3: Data Management Subsystem

[omitted]

7.4 C&C Communicating-Processes View Packet 4: Client Subsystem

[omitted]

7.5 C&C Communicating-Processes View Packet 5: Interoperability Subsystem

[omitted]

7.6 C&C Communicating-Processes View Packet 6: Planning Subsystem

[omitted]

7.7 C&C Communicating-Processes View Packet 7: Data Processing Subsystem

[omitted]

7.8 C&C Communicating-Processes View Packet 8: Communications Subsystem

[omitted]

7.9 C&C Communicating-Processes View Packet 9: System Management Subsystem

[omitted]

7.10 C&C Communicating-Processes View Packet 10: Internetworking Subsystem

[omitted]

Chapter 8
Allocation Deployment View

8.1 Allocation Deployment View Packet 1: The ECS System

8.1.1 Primary Presentation

The figure on page 458 shows the ECS subsystems and the various environmental elements on which they execute. The table in 8.1.2.1 describes this in more detail. Additionally, the figure contains external items which help place the ECS subsystems and environmental elements in context. These are the EOSDIS Backbone Network (EBnet) and the external system connection (other DAACs and non-ECS institutional systems).

8.1.2 Element Catalog

8.1.2.1 Elements and Their Properties

The elements in this diagram are ECS subsystems, host computers, routers, switches, and networks. The ECS subsystems are those defined in the ECS Module Decomposition View (Volume II, Section 1.1), while the other elements are environmental elements defined in this view. The elements are described in the table below; the ECS subsystems are above the double line, while the environmental elements are below the double line.

The Processor Speed column defines the required minimum speed for each subsystem and the provided processor speed for the host computer environmental elements. The speeds are in units of million-instructions-per-second (MIPS). The Communication Speed column defines the network connection speed required by the various subsystems and network speed provided by the various environmental elements. The units are in megabits per second (MBPS).

Element Name	Processing Speed (MIPS)	Communication Speed (MBPS)
Planning Subsystem	10	1,000
Data Processing Subsystem	100	10,000
Ingest Subsystem	25	1,000

Element Name	Processing Speed (MIPS)	Communication Speed (MBPS)
Data Server (DS), Data Management (DM), Local System Management (LSM) Subsystems	10	1,000
System Management Subsystem (MSS)	10	1,000
Communications Subsystem (CSS)	10	1,000
High Performance Parallel Switch (HiPPI)	N/A	10,000
Production Network	N/A	1,000
User Network	N/A	10
HiPPI Network	N/A	10,000
Fiber Distributed Data Switch (FDDI)	N/A	1,000
Data Server (DS) Host	25	10,000
Miscellaneous server computer	20	1,000
Ingest Server computer	50	1,000
Science Processor	200	10,000

8.1.2.2   Relations and Their Properties

The primary presentation shows how ECS subsystems are *allocated to* host computers. The ovals in the diagram contain ECS subsystem names. Each oval crosses one or more network lines. A subsystem may execute on any host machine connected to a line crossing the subsystem. This is in part to provide flexibility in data processing to support various data sources and various user needs.

8.1.2.3   Element Interfaces

Not applicable.

8.1.2.4   Element Behavior

Not applicable.

8.1.3   Context Diagram

See Section 1.1.3.

8.1.4 Variability Guide

None.

8.1.5 Architecture Background

[omitted]

8.1.6 Other Information

[omitted]

8.1.7 Related View Packets

- Parent: None.
- Children: None.
- Siblings: None in this view. View packets in other views that express the same scope as this one—namely, the whole system—include
  - Module Decomposition View Packet 1: The ECS System (Volume II, Section 1.1, page 414)
  - Module Layered View Packet 1: The ECS System (Volume II, Section 4.1, page 435)
  - C&C Pipe-and-Filter View Packet 1: The ECS System (Volume II, Section 5.1, page 439)
  - Allocation Implementation View Packet 1: The ECS System (Volume II, Section 9.1, page 461)
  - Allocation Work Assignment View Packet 1: The ECS System (Volume II, Section 10.1, page 464)

Chapter 9
Allocation Implementation View

9.1 Allocation Implementation View Packet 1: The ECS System

9.1.1 Primary Presentation and Properties[16]

ECS Element (Module)		Properties			
Segment	Subsystem	Where Stored	Files	Build Frequency	Contact
Science Data Processing Segment (SDPS)	Client				
	Interoperability				
	Ingest				
	Data Management				
	Data Processing				
	Data Server				
	Planning				
Communications and System Management Segment (CSMS)	System Management				
	Communications				
	Internetworking				
Flight Operations Segment (FOS)	Planning and Scheduling				
	Data Management				
	Command Management				
	Commanding				
	Resource Management				
	Telemetry				
	User Interface				
	Analysis				

---

16. Here is a slight deviation from the standard template. Because the primary presentation is tabular, it was combined with the element catalog to prevent having to list the software elements twice. For this example, the properties are not filled in.

9.1.2 Element Catalog

9.1.2.1 Elements and Their Properties

As shown in the primary presentation, properties include the server location where the subsystem is stored during development, the files that it consists of, the build cycle—nightly, weekly, and so on—that it subscribes to, and contact information for the team member responsible for providing the latest version or accepting bug reports.

9.1.2.2 Relations and Their Properties

The relation type of this view is *is-allocated-to*, and the relations are as shown in the primary presentation. Software elements are allocated to locations in the development environments' file structures.

9.1.2.3 Element Interfaces

[omitted]

9.1.2.4 Element Behavior

Not applicable.

9.1.3 Context Diagram

None.

9.1.4 Variability Guide

None.

9.1.5 Architecture Background

[omitted]

9.1.6 Other Information

[omitted]

9.1.7 Related View Packets

- Parent: None.
- Children: None.
- Siblings: None in this view. View packets that express the same scope as this one—namely, the whole system—include
  - Module Decomposition View Packet 1: The ECS System (Volume II, Section 1.1, page 414)

- Module Layered View Packet 1: The ECS System (Volume II, Section 4.1, page 435)
- C&C Pipe-and-Filter View Packet 1: The ECS System (Volume II, Section 5.1, page 439)
- Allocation Deployment View Packet 1: The ECS System (Volume II, Section 8.1, page 457)
- Allocation Work Assignment View Packet 1: The ECS System (Volume II, Section 10.1, page 464)

Chapter 10
Allocation Work Assignment View

The work assignment view consists of a single view packet that assigns each available work unit to one or more ECS subsystems.

10.1 Allocation Work Assignment View Packet 1: The ECS System

10.1.1 Primary Presentation

ECS Element (Module)		Organizational Unit
Segment	**Subsystem**	
Science Data Processing Segment (SDPS)	Client	Science team
	Interoperability	Prime contractor team 1
	Ingest	Prime contractor team 2
	Data Management	Data team
	Data Processing	Data team
	Data Server	Data team
	Planning	Orbital vehicle team
Communications and System Management Segment (CSMS)	System Management	Infrastructure team
	Communications	
	Internetworking	
Flight Operations Segment (FOS)	Planning and Scheduling	Orbital vehicle team
	Data Management	Database team
	Command Management	Orbital vehicle team
	Commanding	Orbital vehicle team
	Resource Management	Prime contractor team 3
	Telemetry	Orbital vehicle team
	User Interface	User interface team
	Analysis	Orbital vehicle team

10.1.2   Element Catalog

10.1.2.1   Elements and Their Properties

In the following table, elements are working groups named in the primary presentation.

Element	Properties		
	Contractor or Internal Team	Point of Contact (phone, e-mail)	Skill Set
Data team	Internal	K. Kelliher, x6532 k_kelliher@ oursite.gov	Ability to work closely with Science team to understand the types and structure of data ingested, processed, and produced by ECS. Extensive experience in scientific computing, numerical algorithms, and multidimensional reference frames.
Database team	Contractor 3	C. Solberg, 301-555-3342 cs@contractor2. com	Experience with large relational database systems, including performance issues associated with choice of schema, query optimization schemes, and backup operations.
Infrastructure team	Contractor 2	L. Woods, 202-555-7580 l_woods@ oursite.gov	Experience with contracting for and acquiring commercial off-the-shelf software, especially in the area of communications and system management, and maintaining and evolving COTS-intensive systems, paying special attention to cross-product version compatibility.
Orbital vehicle team	Internal	D. Sirius, x6644 sirius@ oursite.gov	Extensive experience with Earth orbital satellites, including onboard sensors, telemetry and command languages, orbital dynamics, and satellite–ground segment communication.
Prime contractor teams (all)	Contractor 1	R. Fetchick, 703-555-3471 brodnax@prime contractor.com	Experience with object-oriented development models and the ability to coordinate multiple development activities.
Science team	Internal	S. Hadow, x4211 shadow@ oursite.gov	Experience with science data processing and algorithm implementation. Access to science user community and ability to translate scientists' needs into implementable requirements and designs.
[etc.]	[etc.]	[etc.]	[etc.]

10.1.2.2   Relations and Their Properties

The only relation type in this view is *is-assigned-to*. The relations are as shown in the primary presentation.

10.1.2.3 Element Interfaces

Not applicable.

10.1.2.4 Element Behavior

Not applicable.

10.1.3 Context Diagram

See Module Decomposition View Packet 1: The ECS System (Volume II, Section 1.1, page 414) for a relevant context diagram.

10.1.4 Variability Guide

None.

10.1.5 Architecture Background

* *Procuring COTS.* Those subsystems whose implementation is planned to be satisfied largely by purchasing commercial off-the-shelf software have been assigned to a single contractor in the hopes of achieving cost savings by localizing the tasks of product qualification, managing product evolution, and making sure that procured components are version compatible with one another. COTS is expected to dominate the Communications and System Management Segment (CSMS), and so it will fall to the infrastructure team to manage the acquisition and integration of those commercial products.

[etc.]

10.1.6 Other Information

[omitted]

10.1.7 Related View Packets

* Parent: None.
* Children: None.
* Siblings: None in this view. View packets that express the same scope as this one—namely, the whole system—include
  - Module Decomposition View Packet 1: The ECS System (Volume II, Section 1.1, page 414)
  - Module Layered View Packet 1: The ECS System (Volume II, Section 4.1, page 435)

- C&C Pipe-and-Filter View Packet 1: The ECS System (Volume II, Section 5.1, page 439)
- Allocation Deployment View Packet 1: The ECS System (Volume II, Section 8.1, page 457)
- Allocation Implementation View Packet 1: The ECS System (Volume II, Section 9.1, page 461)

Glossary

Actors the other elements, users, or systems with which an element interacts.

Architectural cartoon the graphical portion of a view's primary presentation, without supporting documentation.

Architectural style a specialization of element and relation types, together with a set of constraints on how they can be used.

Architecture description language (ADL) a language (graphical, textual, or both) for describing a software system in terms of its architectural elements and the relationships among them.

ATAM (Architecture Tradeoff Analysis Method) an architecture evaluation method published by the Software Engineering Institute.

Bridging element one that can appear in the view packets of two separate views. The element is common to both view packets and is used to provide the continuity of understanding from one view to the other. A bridging element appears in both view packets and has supporting documentation, usually a mapping between views, that makes the correspondence clear, perhaps by showing the combined picture.

Combined view a view that contains elements and relationships that come from two or more other views.

Components the principal computational elements and data stores that execute in a system.

Connector a runtime pathway of interaction between two or more components.

Context diagram a representation of what's in and what's out of the system under consideration and the external entities with which the system interacts.

Decomposition refinement a refinement in which a single element is elaborated to reveal its internal structure, and then each member of that internal structure is recursively refined.

Descriptive completeness descriptively complete view packets show all elements and relations within the view they document.

Dynamism refers to the decisions that will be made or reconsidered by the system itself during execution.

Element the architectural building block that is native to a viewtype/style. The description of elements tells what role they play in an architecture and furnishes guidelines for effective documentation of the elements in views.

Hybrid style the combination of two or more existing styles. It introduces the same documentation obligations as any of the styles introduced earlier in this book. In addition, the mapping between the styles that constitute the hybrid style must also be documented. Hybrid styles, when applied to a particular system, produce views.

Implementation inheritance the definition of a new implementation based on one or more previously defined implementations. The new implementation is usually a modification of the ancestors' behavior.

Implementation refinement a refinement in which many or all the elements and relations are replaced by new, typically more implementation-specific, elements and relations.

Interface a boundary across which two independent entities meet and interact or communicate with each other.

Interface inheritance the definition of a new interface based on one or more previously defined interfaces. The new interface is usually a subset of the ancestors' interface(s).

Interface specification a statement of what an architect chooses to make known about an element in order for other entities to interact or communicate with it.

Layer a collection of code that forms a virtual machine and that interacts with other layers only according to predefined roles.

Module an implementation unit of software that provides a coherent unit of functionality.

Overlay a combination of the primary presentations of two or more views. It is intended for short-term use. An overlay has the same documentation requirements as a primary presentation of a normal view; for example, a key must be provided. But an overlay introduces no additional documentation obligations beyond those of a primary presentation and a definition of the mapping among the constituent views.

Property additional information about elements and relations. When an architect documents a view, the properties will be given values.

Refinement the process of gradually disclosing information across a series of descriptions.

Relation a definition of how elements cooperate to accomplish the work of a system. The definition names the relations among elements and provides rules on how elements can and cannot be related.

Software architecture the structure or structures of a system, which comprise elements, their externally visible properties, and the relationships among them.

Software product line a set of software-intensive systems sharing a common, managed set of features that satisfy the specific needs of a particular market segment or mission and that are developed from a common set of reusable core assets in a prescribed way.

Stakeholder someone who has a vested interest in an architecture.

Stereotype a type of modeling element in UML that extends the semantics of the metamodel. Stereotypes must be based on certain existing types or classes in the metamodel. Stereotypes may extend the semantics but not the structure of preexisting types and classes. Certain stereotypes are predefined in UML; others may be user defined.

Style guide the description of an architectural style that specifies the vocabulary of design (sets of element and relationship types) and the rules (sets of topological and semantic constraints) for how that vocabulary can be used.

System a collection of entities (elements, components, modules, and so forth) that are organized for a common purpose.

Tier a mechanism for system partitioning. Usually applied to client-server-based systems, where the various parts (tiers) of the system (user interface, database, business application logic, and so forth) execute on different platforms.

Topology a definition of constraints on how elements and relations can be associated in a particular viewtype/style.

Unified Modeling Language (UML) a graphical language for visualizing, specifying, constructing, and documenting the artifacts of a software-intensive system.

Variability refers to the decisions that will be made by a member of the development team prior to system deployment.

Variation point a place in the architecture where a specific decision has been narrowed to several options but the option for a particular system has been left open. The options within a variation point are a list of alternatives. Each alternative has, in turn, a list of elements that are affected if that option is chosen.

View a representation of a set of system elements and the relationships among them.

View packet the smallest cohesive bundle of documentation that you would give to a stakeholder, such as a development team or a subcontractor.

Viewtype the element types and relation types used to describe the architecture of a software system from a particular perspective.

Virtual machine an abstract computing device; typically a program that acts as an interface between other software and actual hardware (or another virtual machine).

References

ACM. http://www.acm.org/sigweb/.

Allen, R. J., and D. Garlan. 1997. "A Formal Basis for Architectural Connection," *ACM Transactions on Software Engineering and Methodology* 6(3): 213–249.

Alur, D., J. Crupi, and D. Malks. 2001. *Core J2EE Patterns: Best Practices and Design Strategies.* Prentice-Hall.

Bachmann, F., L. Bass, G. Chastek, P. Donohoe, and F. Peruzzi. 2000. *The Architecture Based Design Method.* Carnegie Mellon University, Software Engineering Institute Technical Report CMU/SEI-2000-TR-001.

Bachmann, F., and L. Bass. 2001. "Managing Variability in Software Architectures." Symposium on Software Reusability. Toronto. May 18–20.

Bass, L., P., Clements, and R. Kazman. 1998. *Software Architecture in Practice.* Addison-Wesley.

Binns, P., and S. Vestal. 1993. "Formal Real-Time Architecture Specification and Analysis." *Proceedings of 10th IEEE Workshop on Real-Time Operating Systems and Software,* May.

Booch, G., I. Jacobson, and J. Rumbaugh. 1999. *The Unified Modeling Language User Guide.* Addison-Wesley.

Bosch, J. 2000. *Design and Use of Software Architectures: Adopting and Evolving a Product Line Approach.* Addison-Wesley.

Britton, Kathryn Heninger, Parker, R. Alan, and Parnas, David L. "A Procedure for Designing Abstract Interfaces for Device Interface Modules," in Hoffman, D., and Weiss, D. *Software Fundamentals: Collected Papers by David L. Parnas,* Addison-Wesley, 2001.

Brooks, F. P., Jr. 1995. *The Mythical Man-Month: Essays on Software Engineering, Anniversary Edition.* Addison-Wesley.

Buhr, R. J. A., and R. S. Casselman. 1996. *Use Case Maps for Object-Oriented Systems.* Prentice-Hall.

Buschmann, F., R. Meunier, H. Rohnert, P. Sommerlad, and M. Stal. 1996. *Pattern-Oriented Software Architecture, Volume 1: A System of Patterns.* Wiley.

Cheng, S. W. and D. Garlan. 2001. "Mapping Architectural Concepts to UML-RT." *Proceedings of the Parallel and Distributed Processing Techniques and Applications Conference,* Las Vegas, Nevada, June 25–28.

Clements, P., D. Parnas, and D. Weiss. 1985. "The Modular Structure of Complex Systems." *IEEE Transactions in Software Engineering,* SE-11(3): 259–266. Also published in Hoffman and Weiss 2001.

Clements, P., R. Kazman, and M. Klein. 2002. *Evaluating Software Architectures: Methods and Case Studies.* Addison-Wesley.

CM. http://www.cmtoday.com/yp/configuration_management. html.

Coglianese, L., and R. Szymanski. 1993. "DSSA-ADAGE: An Environment for Architecture-Based Avionics Development." *Proceedings of Advisory Group for Aeronautical Research and Development 1993 (AGARD'93).*

Conway, M. 1968. "How Do Committees Invent?" *Datamation* (April): 28–31.

Dashofy, E. M., A. van der Hoek, and R. N. Taylor. 2001. "A Highly-Extensible, XML-Based Architecture Description Language." In *Proceedings of the 2001 Working IEEE/IFIP Conference on Software Architecture (WICSA'01),* Amsterdam.

DeRemer, F., and H. H. Kron. 1976. "Programming-in-the-Large versus Programming-in-the-Small." *IEEE Transactions on Software Engineering,* SE-2(2): 80–86.

Dijkstra, E. W. 1968. "The Structure of the 'T.H.E.' Multiprogramming System." *Communications of the ACM* 18(8): 453–457.

Duke, R., G. Rose, and G. Smith. 1995. "Object A: A Specification Language Advocated for the Description of Standards," Computer Standards and Interfaces, vol. 17, no. 511-533.

Ellsberger, J., D. Hogrefe, and A. Sarma. 1997. *SDL Formal Object-Oriented Language for Communicating Systems.* Prentice-Hall.

Feiler, P., B. Lewis, and S. Vestal. 2000. "Improving Predictability in Embedded Real-Time Systems." Life Cycle Software Engineering Conference, Redstone Arsenal, AL, August. Also available as Software Engineering Institute technical report CMU/SEI-00-SR-011.

Gamma, E., R. Helm, R. Johnson, and J. Vlissides. 1995. *Design Patterns: Elements of Reusable Object-Oriented Software.* Addison-Wesley.

Garlan, D., and A. Kompanek. 2000. "Reconciling the Needs of Architectural Description with Object-Modeling Notations." *Proceedings of the Third International Conference on the Unified Modeling Language,* pages 498–512.

Garlan, D., and M. Shaw. 1993. "An Introduction to Software Architecture." In V. Ambriola and G. Tortora, eds. *Advances in Software Engineering and Knowledge Engineering,* Vol. 2. World Scientific.

Garlan, D., and D. Perry. 1995. "Introduction to the Special Issue on Software Architecture." *IEEE Transactions on Software Engineering* 21(4): 269–274.

Garlan, D., R. Allen, and J. Ockerbloom. 1994. "Exploiting Style in Architectural Design Environments." In *Proceedings of SIGSOFT'94: The Second ACM SIGSOFT Symposium on the Foundations of Software Engineering,* pages 179–185.

———. 1995. "Architectural Mismatch: Why Reuse Is So Hard." *IEEE Software* 12(6): 17–26.

Garlan, D., A. J. Kompanek, and S. Cheng. 2000. "Reconciling the Needs of Architectural Description with Object-Modeling Notations." In S. Kent and S. Bran, eds., *Science of Computer Programming, Special UML Edition,* Elsevier Press.

Garlan, D., R. Monroe, and D. Wile. 2000. "ACME: Architectural Description of Component-Based Systems." In G. Leavens and M. Sitaraman, eds. *Foundations of Component-Based Systems,* Cambridge University Press, pages 47–68.

Harel, D. 1987. "Statecharts: A Visual Formalism for Complex Systems." *Science of Computer Programming* 8:231–274.

Harel, D., and M. Politi. 1998. *Modeling Reactive Systems with Statecharts: The Statemate Approach.* McGraw-Hill.

Herzum, P., and O. Sims. 2000. *Business Component Factory: A Comprehensive Overview of Component-Based Development for the Enterprise.* Wiley.

Hoare, C. A. R. 1985. *Communicating Sequential Processes.* Prentice-Hall.

Hoare, C. A. R. 1987. "An Overview of Some Formal Methods for Program Design." *IEEE Computer* (September): 85–91.

Hoffman, D. M., and D. M. Weiss, eds. 2001. *Software Fundamentals: Collected Papers by David L. Parnas.* Addison-Wesley.

Hofmeister, C., R. L. Nord, and D. Soni. 1999. "Describing Software Architecture with UML." In *Software Architecture,* edited by Patrick Donohoe, pages 145–159. Kluwer Academic Publishers.

Hofmeister, C., R. Nord, and D. Soni. 2000. *Applied Software Architecture,* Addison-Wesley.

Honeywell Laboratories. 2000. *MetaH User's Guide*. Minneapolis. Available at http://www.htc.honeywell.com/metah/uguide.pdf.

IEEE. 2000a. *IEEE Product No.: SH94869-TBR: Recommended Practice for Architectural Description of Software-Intensive Systems*. IEEE Standard No. 1471-2000. Available at http://shop.ieee.org/store/.

IEEE. 2000b. *IEEE Standard No.: 1516.1-2000: Standard for Modeling and Simulation (M&S) High Level Architecutre (HLA)—Federate Interface Specification*. IEEE Product No.: SS94883-TBR. Available at http://shop.ieee.org/store/.

ISO/JTC1/SC21 N 8228. 1993. Revised text of DIS 7498-1, *Information Technology—Open Systems Interconnection—Basic Reference Model*, Second Edition. Nov.

Jackson, M. 1995. *Software Requirements and Specifications: A Lexicon of Practice, Principles, and Prejudices*. Addison-Wesley.

Jacobson, I. 1992. *Object-Oriented Software Engineering: A Use Case Driven Approach*. Addison-Wesley.

Jacobson, I., G. Booch, and J. Rumbaugh. 1999. *The Unified Software Development Process*. Addison-Wesley.

Jacobson, I., M. Griss, and P. Jonsson. 1997. *Software Reuse: Architecture, Process, and Organization for Business Success*. Addison-Wesley.

Jazayeri, M., A. Ran, and F. van der Linden. 2000. *Software Architecture for Product Families: Principles and Practice*. Addison-Wesley.

Kazman, R., and M. Klein. 1999. *Attribute-Based Architectural Styles*. Software Engineering Institute Technical Report CMU/SEI-99-SR-022.

Kiczales, G., J. Lamping, A. Mendhekar, C. Maeda, C. Lopes, J.-M. Loingtier, and J. Irwin. 1997. "Aspect-Oriented Programming." *Proceedings of the European Conference on Object-Oriented Programming (ECOOP)*. Published as *Lecture Notes in Computer Science*, Number 1241. Springer Verlag, pages 220–242.

Knuth, D. E., and R. W. Moore. 1975. "An Analysis of Alpha-Beta Pruning." *Artificial Intelligence* 6: 293–326.

Kobryn, C. 1998. "Modeling Enterprise Software Architectures Using UML." *1998 Proceedings International Enterprise Distributed Object Computing Workshop*, IEEE, San Diego, November.

Kruchten, P. 1995. "The 4+1 View Model of Architecture." *IEEE Software* 12(6): 42–50.

———. 2001. *The Rational Unified Process: An Introduction*, Second Edition. Addison-Wesley.

Leon, A. 2000. *A Guide to Software Configuration Management*. Artech House Publishers.

Lewis, B. 1999. "Software Portability Gains Realized with MetaH, an Avionics Architecture Description Language." *18th Digital Avionics Systems Conference*, St. Louis, MO, October 24–29.

Liskov, B. "Data Abstraction and Hierarchy." 1987. OOPSLA'87: Conference on Object Oriented Programming, Systems, Languages and Applications. Orlando. Also available as *SigPlan Notices* 23(5): 17–34.

Luckham, D.C., and J. Vera. 1995. "An Event-Based Architecture Definition Language." *Transactions on Software Engineering* 21(9): 717–734.

Luckham, D.C., L.M. Augustin, D. Bryan, J. J. Kenney, W. Mann, and J. Vera. 1995. "Specification and Analysis of System Architecture Using Rapide." *IEEE Transactions on Software Engineering, Special Issue on Software Architecture* 21(4): 336–355.

Magee, J., N. Dulay, S. Eisenbach, and J. Kramer. 1995. "Specifying Distributed Software Architectures." *Proceedings of the Fifth European Software Engineering Conference, ESEC'95*, LNCS 989, Springer-Verlag, pages 137–153.

Mahoney, B., and J. S. Dong. 2000. "Timed Communicating Object Z," IEEE Trans Engineering, vol. 26(2), February. Pp 150–177.

Malveau, R., and T. Mowbray. 2001. *Software Architect Bootcamp*. Prentice-Hall.

Maier, M. W., D. Emery, and R. Hilliard. 2001. "Software Architecture: Introducing IEEE Standard 1471." *IEEE Computer* 34(4): 107–109.

Medvidovic, N., and S. Rosenblum. 1999. "Assessing the Suitability of a Standard Design Method for Modeling Software Architectures." *Proceedings of the TC2 1st Working IFIP Conference on Software Architecture (WICSA1)*.

Medvidovic, N., P. Oreizy, J. E. Robbins, and R. N. Taylor. 1996. "Using Object-Oriented Typing to Support Architectural Design in the C2 Style." *Proceedings of ACM SIGSOFT'96: 4th Symposium on the Foundations of Software Engineering (FSE4)*.

Medvidovic, N. and R. N. Taylor. 1997. "A Framework for Classifying and Comparing Architecture Description Languages." *Proceedings of the 6th European Software Engineering Conference together with with FSE4*, 60–76.

Monroe, R. T., A. Kompanek, R. Melton, and D. Garlan. 1997 "Architectural Style, Design Patterns, and Objects." *IEEE Software* 14(1):43–52.

Moriconi, M., X. Qian, and R. A. Riemenschneider. 1995. "Correct Architecture Refinement." *IEEE Transactions on Software Engineering* 21(4): 356–372.

Nii, H. P. "Blackboard Systems." 1986. *AI Magazine* 7(3): 38–53 and 7(4): 82–107.

Nygaard, K., and O.-J. Dahl. "The Development of the SIM-ULA Language." In R. Wexelblat, ed. *History of Programming Languages.* Academic Press, pages 439–493.

Object Management Group. 1999. "Analysis and Design Platform Task Force." White Paper on the Profile mechanism Version 1.0. OMG Document ad/99-04-97, April.

————. 1999. *UML Profile for CORBA. RFP.* OMG Document ad/99-03-11, March 26.

————. 1993. *Object Request Broker Architecture; Version 0.0.* TC Document 93.7.2, July 18.

————. 1999. *UML Profile for Performance, Scheduling and Time.* OMG Document ad/99-93-13, March 26.

————. *UML Semantics.* OMG ad/97-08-04. Available at http://www.omg.org/docs/ad/97-08-04.pdf.

————. *IDL.* http://www.omg.org/gettingstarted/omg_idl.htm.

————. *UML Notation Guide.* OMG ad/97-08-05. Available at http://www.omg.org/docs/ad/97-08-05.pdf.

————. *UML Specification v. 1.4.* OMG document ad/01-02-13. Available at http://www.omg.org/docs/ad/01-02-13.pdf.

The Open Group. 2000. *Architecture Description Markup Language (ADML) Version 1.* Available at http://www.opengroup.org/publications/catalog/i901.htm.

Parnas, D. L. 1971. "Information Distribution Aspects of Design Methodology." *Proceedings of the 1971 IFIP Congress.* North Holland Publishing, pages 339–334.

————. 1972. "On the Criteria to Be Used in Decomposing Systems into Modules." *Communications of the ACM* 15(12): 1053–1058. Also published in Hoffman and Weiss 2001.

————. 1974. "On a 'Buzzword': Hierarchical Structure." *Proceedings of the IFIP Congress '74,* pages 336–339. Also published in Hoffman and Weiss 2001.

————. 2001. "Designing Software for Ease of Extension and Contraction." *IEEE Transactions on Software Engineering* SE-5 (2): 128–137. Also published in Hoffman and Weiss.

Parnas, D. L., and P. C. Clements. 1986. "A Rational Design Process: How and Why to Fake It." *IEEE Transactions on Software Engineering* SE-12(2): 251–257. Also published in Hoffman and Weiss 2001.

Parnas, D. L., and D. M. Weiss. 1985. "Active Design Reviews: Principles and Practices." *Proceedings of the Eighth International Conference on Software Engineering,* pages 215–222. Also published in Hoffman and Weiss 2001.

Parnas, David L., and Wuerges, H., "Response to Undesired Events in Software Systems," in Hoffman, D,. and Weiss,

D. *Software Fundamentals: Collected Papers by David L. Parnas*, Addison-Wesley, 2001.

Perrochon, L., and W. Mann. 1999. "Inferred Designs." *IEEE Software* 16(5) 46–51.

Paulish, D. J. 2002. *Architecture-Centric Software Project Management: A Practical Guide*. Addison-Wesley.

Perry, D.E., and A. L. Wolf. 1992. "Foundations for the Study of Software Architecture." *Software Engineering Notes* 17(2): 40–52.

Prieto-Diaz, R., and J. M. Neighbors. 1986. "Module Interconnection Languages." *Journal of Systems and Software* 6(4): 307–334.

Putman, J. 2000. *Architecting with RM-ODP*. Prentice-Hall.

Rational Software Corporation and IBM. *OCL Specification*. OMG document ad/97-8-08. Available online at http://www.omg.org/docs/ad.

Robbins, R. E., N. Medvidovic, D. F. Redmiles, and D. S. Rosenblum. "Integrating Architecture Description Languages with a Standard Design Method." 1998. In *Proceedings of the 20th International Conference on Software Engineering (ICSE'98)*, pages 209–18.

Rosenberg, D., and K. Scott. 1999. *Use Case Driven Object Modeling with UML: A Practical Approach*. Addison-Wesley.

Rumbaugh, J., I. Jacobson, and G. Booch. 1999. *The Unified Modeling Language Reference Manual*. Addison-Wesley.

Schmidt, D., M. Stal, H. Rohnert, and F. Buschmann. 2000. *Pattern-Oriented Software Architecture, Volume 2: Patterns for Concurrent and Networked Objects*. Wiley.

SEI ATA. http://www.sei.cmu.edu/ata/ata_init.html.

SEI ATAM. http://www.sei.cmu.edu/architecture/sw_architecture.html.

SEI SAAM. http://www.sei.cmu.edu/architecture/sw_architecture.html.

Selic, B. 1999. "UML-RT: A Profile for Modeling Complex Real-Time Architectures." Draft, ObjecTime Limited, Dec.

Selic, B., G. Gullekson, and P. T. Ward. 1994. *Real-Time Object-Oriented Modeling*. Wiley.

Selic, B., and J. Rumbaugh. 1998. "Using UML for Modeling Complex Real-Time Systems." White Paper. Available at http://www.objectime.com/otl/technical/.

Shaw, M. 1995. "Making Choices: A Comparison of Styles for Software Architecture." *IEEE Software, Special Issue on Software Architecture* 12(6): 27–41.

———. 1996a. "Truth vs Knowledge: The Difference Between What a Component Does and What We Know It Does." *Proceedings of the 8th International Workshop on Software Specification and Design*, pages 181–185.

————. 1996b. "Procedure Calls Are the Assembly language of Software Interconnection: Connectors Deserve First-Class Status." In D. A. Lamb, ed. *Studies of Software Design, Proceedings of a 1993 Workshop:* published as *Lecture Notes in Computer Science* No. 1078. Springer-Verlag, pages 17–32.

Shaw, M., and P. Clements. 1997. "A Field Guide to Boxology: Preliminary Classification of Architectural Styles for Software Systems." *Proceedings of First International Computer Software and Applications Conference (COMPSAC97).* IEEE Computer Society Press, pages 6–13. Also available at http://www2.cs.cmu.edu/afs/cs.cmu.edu/project/vit/www/paper_abstracts/Boxology.html.

Shaw, M., and Garlan, D. 1996. *Software Architecture: Perspectives on an Emerging Discipline.* Prentice-Hall.

Shaw, M., R. DeLine, D. V. Klein, T. L. Ross, D. M. Young, and G. Zelesnik. 1995. "Abstractions for Software Architecture and Tools to Support Them." *IEEE Transactions on Software Engineering, Special Issue on Software Architecture* 21(4): 314–335.

Smith, C. U. 1990. *Performance Engineering of Software Systems.* Addison-Wesley.

Smith, C., and L. Williams. 2002. *Performance Solutions: A Practical Guide for Creating Responsive, Scalable Software.* Addison-Wesley.

Snyder, A. 1986. "Encapsulation and Inheritance in Object-Oriented Programming Languages." In Norman K. Meyrowitz, ed. *Proceedings of the Conference on Object-Oriented Programming Systems, Languages, and Applications (OOPSLA'86),* pages 38–45. Available as SIGPLAN Notices 21(11), November.

Soni, D., R. L. Nord, and C. Hofmeister. 1995. "Software Architecture in Industrial Applications." *Proceedings of the 17th International Conference on Software Engineering,* pages 196–207.

Sowmya, A., and S. Ramesh. 1998. "Extending Statecharts with Temporal Logic." *Transactions on Software Engineering* 24(3): 216–231.

Spitznagel, B., and D. Garlan. 1998. "Architecture-Based Performance Analysis." *Proceedings of the 1998 Conference on Software Engineering and Knowledge Engineering,* San Francisco, June, pages 146–151.

Spivey, J. M. 1992. *Understanding Z: A Specification Language and Its Formal Semantics.* 2d ed. Cambridge Tracts in Theoretical Computer Science.

Stafford, J. A., and A. L. Wolf. 2000 "Annotating Components to Support Component-Based Static Analyses of Software

Systems." *Proceedings of Grace Hopper Conference 2000*, Hyannis, MA: September. Also available as University of Colorado Technical Report No. CU-CS-896-99.

———. 2001. "Software Architecture," in G. T. Heineman and W. T. Council, eds. *Component-Based Software Engineering: Putting the Pieces Together.* Addison-Wesley.

Stroustrup, B. 1997. *The C++ Programming Language, Third Edition.* Addison-Wesley.

Sun Microsystems. 2000. *JavaPhone™ API Specification, Version 1.0.* March 22, available at http://web2.java.sun.com/products/javaphone/.

Szyperski, C. 1998. *Component Software: Beyond Object-Oriented Programming.* Addison-Wesley.

Vestal, S. 1998. *MetaH Programmer's Manual Version 1.27.* Honeywell.

Wallnau, K., S. Hissam, and R. Seacord. 2002. *Building Systems from Commercial Components.* Addision-Wesley.

W3C. *SOAP.* http://www.w3.org/TR/soap12-part0/.

———. *XML.* http://www.w3.org/XML/.

Youngs, R., D. Redmond-Pyle, P. Spaas, and E. Kahan. 1999. "A Standard for Architecture Description." *IBM Systems Journal* 38(1): pp 32–50.

Index

Carnegie Mellon
Software Engineering Institute

SEI^{SM} Classroom Training

Based on decades of experience and supported by four widely acclaimed practitioner books in the SEI Addison-Wesley Series, the SEI offers the Software Architecture Curriculum and the Software Product Lines Curriculum.

Software Architecture Curriculum

Collection of six courses, three certificate programs, and a field exercise that equip software professionals with state-of-the-art practices so they can efficiently design software-intensive systems that meet their intended business and quality goals.

Courses:

Software Architecture: Principles and Practices

Documenting Software Architectures

Software Architecture Design and Analysis

Software Product Lines

Architecture Tradeoff Analysis Method (ATAM) Evaluator Training

ATAM Facilitator Training

ATAM Coaching and Observation

Certificate Programs:

Software Architecture Professional Certificate Program

ATAM Evaluator Certificate Program

ATAM Lead Evaluator Certificate Program

Software Product Lines Curriculum

Collection of five courses and three certificate programs that equip software professionals with state-of-the-art practices so they can efficiently use proven product lien practices to achieve their strategic reuse and other business goals.

Courses:

Software Product Lines

Adopting Software Product Lines

Product Line Technical Probe Training

Developing Software Product Lines

Product Line Technical Probe Facilitator Training

Certificate Programs:

Software Product Lines Professional Certificate

Product Line Technical Probe Team Member Certificate

Product Line Technical Probe Leader Certificate

For current course information visit: *www.sei.cmu.edu/products/courses/*
To register for courses call: 412.268.7388
or email: *courseregistration@sei.cmu.edu*

In addition to the curricula and certificate programs, the SEI has developed software architecture and product line methods and approaches to assist organizations in achieving their technical and business objectives.

To learn more, visit: *www.sei.cmu.edu/programs/pls/*

Software Engineering Institute
4500 Fifth Avenue
Pittsburgh, PA 15213

412.268.5800   www.sei.cmu.edu

^{SM} SEI is a service mark of Carnegie Mellon University

The SEI Series in Software Engineering

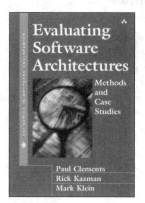

Evaluating Software Architectures
Methods and Case Studies
Paul Clements, Rick Kazman, and Mark Klein

This book is a comprehensive, step-by-step guide to software architecture evaluation, describing specific methods that can quickly and inexpensively mitigate enormous risk in software projects. The methods are illustrated both by case studies and by sample artifacts put into play during an evaluation: viewgraphs, scenarios, final reports—everything you need to evaluate an architecture in your own organization.

0-201-70482-X • Hardcover • 368 Pages • © 2002

Software Product Lines
Practices and Patterns
Paul Clements and Linda Northrop

Building product lines from common assets can yield remarkable improvements in productivity, time to market, product quality, and customer satisfaction. This book provides a framework of specific practices, with detailed case studies, to guide the implementation of product lines in your own organization.

0-201-70332-7 • Hardcover • 608 Pages • © 2002

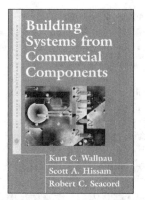

Building Systems from Commercial Components
Kurt C. Wallnau, Scott A. Hissam, and Robert C. Seacord

Commercial components are increasingly seen as an effective means to save time and money in building large software systems. However, integrating pre-existing components, with pre-existing specifications, is a delicate and difficult task. This book describes specific engineering practices needed to accomplish that task successfully, illustrating the techniques described with case studies and examples.

0-201-70064-6 • Hardcover • 432 pages • © 2002

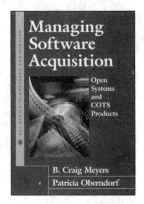

Managing Software Acquisition
Open Systems and COTS Products
B. Craig Meyers and Patricia Oberndorf

The acquisition of open systems and commercial off-the-shelf (COTS) products is an increasingly vital part of large-scale software development, offering significant savings in time and money. This book presents fundamental principles and best practices for successful acquisition and utilization of open systems and COTS products.

0-201-70454-4 • Hardcover • 400 pages • © 2001

Software Architecture in Practice
Len Bass, Paul Clements, and Rick Kazman

This book introduces the concepts and practice of software architecture, not only covering essential technical topics for specifying and validating a system, but also emphasizing the importance of the business context in which large systems are designed. Enhancing both technical and organizational discussions, key points are illuminated by substantial case studies.

0-201-19930-0 • Hardcover • 480 pages • © 1998

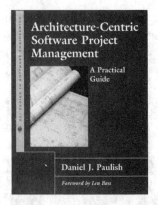

Architecture-Centric Software Project Management
A Practical Guide
Daniel J. Paulish

Written for project managers and software architects, this book demonstrates how to draw on software architecture to design schedules, generate estimates, make scope decisions, and manage the team for a successful outcome. With case studies and examples based on practical experience, each cornerstone of effective project management is addressed—planning, organizing, implementing, and measuring.

0-201-73409-5 • Paperback • 320 pages • ©2002

The SEI Series in Software Engineering

ISBN 0-201-73500-8

ISBN 0-321-11886-3

ISBN 0-201-73723-X

ISBN 0-201-54664-7

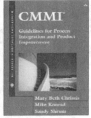
ISBN 0-321-15496-7

ISBN 0-201-70372-6

ISBN 0-201-70482-X

ISBN 0-201-70332-7

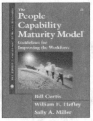
ISBN 0-201-60445-0

ISBN 0-201-60444-2

ISBN 0-201-25592-8

ISBN 0-201-54597-7

ISBN 0-201-54809-7

ISBN 0-201-18095-2

ISBN 0-201-54610-8

ISBN 0-201-47719-X

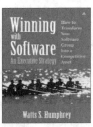
ISBN 0-201-77639-1

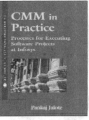
ISBN 0-201-61626-2

ISBN 0-201-70454-4

ISBN 0-201-73409-5

ISBN 0-201-85480-5

ISBN 0-321-11884-7

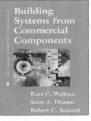
ISBN 0-201-70064-6

ISBN 0-201-17782-X

ISBN 0-201-52577-1

Please see our Web site at http://www.awprofessional.com for more information on these titles.